LEGAL ETHICS AND PROFESSIONAL RESPONSIBILITY

D1709626

TITLES IN THE DELMAR PARALEGAL SERIES

Ransford C. Pyle, *Foundations of Law for Paralegals: Cases, Commentary, and Ethics,* 1992.

Peggy N. Kerley, Paul A. Sukys, Joanne Banker Hames, *Civil Litigation for the Paralegal,* 1992.

Jonathan Lynton, Donna Masinter, Terri Mick Lyndall, *Law Office Management for Paralegals,* 1992.

Daniel Hall, *Criminal Law and Procedure,* 1992.

Daniel Hall, *Survey of Criminal Law,* 1993.

Jonathan Lynton, Terri Mick Lyndall, *Legal Ethics and Professional Responsibility,* 1994.

Michael Kearns, *The Law of Real Property,* 1994.

Angela Schneeman, *The Law of Corporations, Partnerships, and Sole Proprietorships,* 1993.

William Buckley, *Torts and Personal Injury Law,* 1993.

Gordon W. Brown, *Administration of Wills, Trusts, and Estates,* 1993.

Richard Stim, *Intellectual Property: Patents, Copyrights, and Trademarks,* 1994.

Ransford C. Pyle, *Family Law,* 1994.

Daniel Hall, *Administrative Law,* 1994.

Jonathan Lynton, *Ballentine's Thesaurus for Legal Research & Writing,* 1994.

Jack Handler, *Ballentine's Law Dictionary: Legal Assistant Edition,* 1994.

Angela Schneeman, *Paralegals in American Law,* 1994.

Susan Covins, *Federal Taxation,* 1994.

LEGAL ETHICS AND PROFESSIONAL RESPONSIBILITY

Jonathan S. Lynton

Terri Mick Lyndall

Lawyers Cooperative Publishing

Delmar
Publishers Inc

Delmar Publishers' Online Services

To access Delmar on the World Wide Web, point your browser to:

http://www.delmar.com/delmar.html

To access through Gopher: gopher://gopher.delmar.com

(Delmar Online is part of "thomson.com", an Internet site with information on
more than 30 publishers of the International Thomson Publishing organization.)

For information on our products and services:

email: info@delmar.com

or call 800-347-7707

Cover design by The Drawing Board
Cover photo courtesy of Washington, DC Convention and Visitors Association

Delmar staff:
Administrative Editor: Jay Whitney
Developmental Editor: Christopher Anzalone
Project Editors: Judith Boyd Nelson/Andrea Edwards Myers
Production Supervisor: Larry Main
Production Coordinator: James Zayicek
Art and Design Coordinator: Karen Kunz Kemp

For information, address Delmar Publishers Inc.
3 Columbia Circle, Box 15-015,
Albany, NY 12212-5015

Copyright 1994 by Delmar Publishers Inc., AND
LAWYERS COOPERATIVE PUBLISHING
A DIVISION OF THOMSON LEGAL PUBLISHING INC.

Printed in the United States of America

5 6 7 8 9 10 XXX 00

Library of Congress Cataloging-in-Publication Data

Lynton, Jonathan S.
    Legal ethics and professional responsibility / Jonathan S. Lynton,
Terri Mick Lyndall ; illustrations by Jay Church.
        p.   cm.
    Includes index.
    ISBN 0-8273-5504-1 (textbook)
    1. Legal ethics—United States.   2. Legal assistants—United States.   I. Lyndall,
Terri Mick.   II. Title.
    KF306.L96   1993
    174'.3'0973—dc20   92-36136
                                                                            CIP

CONTENTS

DELMAR PUBLISHERS INC.

 AND

LAWYERS COOPERATIVE PUBLISHING

ARE PLEASED TO ANNOUNCE THEIR PARTNERSHIP
TO CO-PUBLISH COLLEGE TEXTBOOKS FOR
PARALEGAL EDUCATION.

DELMAR, WITH OFFICES AT ALBANY, NEW YORK, IS A PROFESSIONAL EDUCATION PUBLISHER. DELMAR PUBLISHES QUALITY EDUCATIONAL TEXT-BOOKS TO PREPARE AND SUPPORT INDIVIDUALS FOR LIFE SKILLS AND SPECIFIC OCCUPATIONS.

LAWYERS COOPERATIVE PUBLISHING (LCP), WITH OFFICES AT ROCHESTER, NEW YORK, HAS BEEN THE LEADING PUBLISHER OF ANALYTICAL LEGAL INFORMATION FOR OVER 100 YEARS. IT IS THE PUBLISHER OF SUCH RE-KNOWNED LEGAL ENCYCLOPEDIAS AS **AMERICAN LAW REPORTS, AMERICAN JURISPRUDENCE, UNITED STATES CODE SERVICE, LAWYERS EDITION,** AS WELL AS OTHER MATERIAL, AND FEDERAL- AND STATE-SPECIFIC PUBLICATIONS. THESE PUBLICATIONS HAVE BEEN DE-SIGNED TO WORK TOGETHER IN THE DAY-TO-DAY PRACTICE OF LAW AS AN INTEGRATED SYSTEM IN WHAT IS CALLED THE "TOTAL CLIENT-SERVICE LI-BRARY®" (TCSL®). EACH LCP PUBLICATION IS COMPLETE WITHIN ITSELF AS TO SUBJECT COVERAGE, YET ALL HAVE COMMON FEATURES AND EXTEN-SIVE CROSS-REFERENCING TO PROVIDE LINKAGE FOR HIGHLY EFFICIENT LEGAL RESEARCH INTO VIRTUALLY ANY MATTER AN ATTORNEY MIGHT BE CALLED UPON TO HANDLE.

INFORMATION IN ALL PUBLICATIONS IS CAREFULLY AND CONSTANTLY MON-ITORED TO KEEP PACE WITH AND REFLECT EVENTS IN THE LAW AND IN SOCIETY. UPDATING AND SUPPLEMENTAL INFORMATION IS TIMELY AND PROVIDED CONVENIENTLY.

FOR FURTHER REFERENCE, SEE:

AMERICAN JURISPRUDENCE 2D: AN ENCYCLOPEDIC TEXT COVERAGE OF THE COMPLETE BODY OF STATE AND FEDERAL LAW.

AM JUR LEGAL FORMS 2D: A COMPILATION OF BUSINESS AND LEGAL FORMS DEALING WITH A VARIETY OF SUBJECT MATTERS.

AM JUR PLEADING AND PRACTICE FORMS, REV: MODEL PRACTICE FORMS FOR EVERY STAGE OF A LEGAL PROCEEDING.

AM JUR PROOF OF FACTS: A SERIES OF ARTICLES THAT GUIDE THE READER IN DETERMINING WHICH FACTS ARE ESSENTIAL TO A CASE AND HOW TO PROVE THEM.

AM JUR TRIALS: A SERIES OF ARTICLES DISCUSSING EVERY ASPECT OF PARTICULAR SETTLEMENTS AND TRIALS WRITTEN BY 180 CONSULTING SPECIALISTS.

UNITED STATES CODE SERVICE: A COMPLETE AND AUTHORITATIVE ANNOTATED FEDERAL CODE THAT FOLLOWS THE EXACT LANGUAGE OF THE STATUTES AT LARGE AND DIRECTS YOU TO THE COURT AND AGENCY DECISIONS CONSTRUING EACH PROVISION.

ALR AND ALR FEDERAL: SERIES OF ANNOTATIONS PROVIDING IN-DEPTH ANALYSES OF ALL THE CASE LAW ON PARTICULAR LEGAL ISSUES.

U.S. SUPREME COURT REPORTS, L ED 2D: EVERY REPORTED U.S. SUPREME COURT DECISION PLUS IN-DEPTH DISCUSSIONS OF LEADING ISSUES.

FEDERAL PROCEDURE, L ED: A COMPREHENSIVE, A–Z TREATISE ON FEDERAL PROCEDURE—CIVIL, CRIMINAL, AND ADMINISTRATIVE.

FEDERAL PROCEDURAL FORMS, L ED: STEP-BY-STEP GUIDANCE FOR DRAFTING FORMS FOR FEDERAL COURT OR FEDERAL AGENCY PROCEEDINGS.

FEDERAL RULES SERVICE, 2D AND 3D: REPORTS DECISIONS FROM ALL LEVELS OF THE FEDERAL SYSTEM INTERPRETING THE FEDERAL RULES OF CIVIL PROCEDURE AND THE FEDERAL RULES OF APPELLATE PROCEDURE.

FEDERAL RULES DIGEST, 3D: ORGANIZES HEADNOTES FOR THE DECISIONS REPORTED IN FEDERAL RULES SERVICE ACCORDING TO THE NUMBERING SYSTEMS OF THE FEDERAL RULES OF CIVIL PROCEDURE AND THE FEDERAL RULES OF APPELLATE PROCEDURE.

FEDERAL RULES OF EVIDENCE SERVICE: REPORTS DECISIONS FROM ALL LEVELS OF THE FEDERAL SYSTEM INTERPRETING THE FEDERAL RULES OF EVIDENCE.

FEDERAL RULES OF EVIDENCE NEWS

FEDERAL PROCEDURE RULES SERVICE

FEDERAL TRIAL HANDBOOK, 2D

FORM DRAFTING CHECKLISTS: AM JUR PRACTICE GUIDE

GOVERNMENT CONTRACTS: PROCEDURES AND FORMS

HOW TO GO DIRECTLY INTO YOUR OWN COMPUTERIZED SOLO PRACTICE WITHOUT MISSING A MEAL (OR A BYTE)

JONES ON EVIDENCE, CIVIL AND CRIMINAL, 7TH

LITIGATION CHECKISTS: AM JUR PRACTICE GUIDE

MEDICAL LIBRARY, LAWYERS EDITION

MEDICAL MALPRACTICE — ALR CASES AND ANNOTATIONS

MODERN APPELLATE PRACTICE: FEDERAL AND STATE CIVIL APPEALS

MODERN CONSTITUTIONAL LAW

NEGOTIATION AND SETTLEMENT

PATTERN DEPOSITION CHECKLISTS, 2D

QUALITY OF LIFE DAMAGES: CRITICAL ISSUES AND PROOFS

SHEPARD'S CITATIONS FOR ALR

SUCCESSFUL TECHNIQUES FOR CIVIL TRIALS, 2D

STORIES ET CETERA — A COUNTRY LAWYER LOOKS AT LIFE AND THE LAW

SUMMARY OF AMERICAN LAW

THE TRIAL LAWYER'S BOOK: PREPARING AND WINNING CASES

TRIAL PRACTICE CHECKLISTS

2000 CLASSIC LEGAL QUOTATIONS

WILLISTON ON CONTRACTS, 3D AND 4TH

FEDERAL RULES OF EVIDENCE DIGEST: ORGANIZES HEADNOTES FOR THE DECISIONS REPORTED IN FEDERAL RULES OF EVIDENCE SERVICE ACCORDING TO THE NUMBERING SYSTEM OF THE FEDERAL RULES OF EVIDENCE.

ADMINISTRATIVE LAW: PRACTICE AND PROCEDURE

AGE DISCRIMINATION: CRITICAL ISSUES AND PROOFS

ALR CRITICAL ISSUES: DRUNK DRIVING PROSECU-
TIONS

ALR CRITICAL ISSUES: FREEDOM OF INFORMATION
ACTS

ALR CRITICAL ISSUES: TRADEMARKS

ALR CRITICAL ISSUES: WRONGFUL DEATH

AMERICANS WITH DISABILITIES: PRACTICE AND COM-
PLIANCE MANUAL

ATTORNEYS' FEES

BALLENTINE'S LAW DICTIONARY

CONSTITUTIONAL LAW DESKBOOK

CONSUMER AND BORROWER PROTECTION: AM JUR
PRACTICE GUIDE

CONSUMER CREDIT: ALR ANNOTATIONS

DAMAGES: ALR ANNOTATIONS

EMPLOYEE DISMISSAL: CRITICAL ISSUES AND
PROOFS

ENVIRONMENTAL LAW: ALR ANNOTATIONS

EXPERT WITNESS CHECKLISTS

EXPERT WITNESSES IN CIVIL TRIALS

FORFEITURES: ALR ANNOTATIONS

FEDERAL LOCAL COURT RULES

FEDERAL LOCAL COURT FORMS

FEDERAL CRIMINAL LAW AND PROCEDURE: ALR AN-
NOTATIONS

FEDERAL EVIDENCE

FEDERAL LITIGATION DESK SET: FORMS AND ANAL-
YSIS

TABLE OF CASES

PREFACE

Legal Ethics and Professional Responsibility is an introduction to the issues and rules that govern the legal profession, oriented to the paralegal or legal assistant. It is critically important for all those working in the legal system to understand and appreciate the rules by which the legal profession operates, for it is only through an understanding of those issues and guidelines that paralegals can be successful at their work. Regardless of the area of the law in which one works, regardless of whether one represents huge corporations or a single individual, regardless of whether one works in a large firm, in a small firm, for the government, or independently, legal work requires understanding and application of the principles that constitute legal ethics.

This textbook was designed to help the paralegal student or practicing paralegal gain an appreciation for the importance of ethics to the law, understand the major issues in ethics and the rules governing those issues, and apply that developing ethical sensitivity and knowledge to a variety of hypothetical (and not-so-hypothetical) situations. The practicing paralegal can also use this book as a reference manual, because it offers a thorough discussion of all the ethical issues relevant to paralegals, complemented by the relevant sections of the ABA Model Code, the ABA Model Rules, and the ABA Model Guidelines for the Utilization of Legal Assistants, as well as the Codes from the two national organizations for legal assistants and paralegals, the National Association of Legal Assistants (NALA) and the National Federation of Paralegal Associates (NFPA).

Legal Ethics and Professional Responsibility is divided into three major sections. The first section, Introduction to Legal Ethics and Professional Responsibility, is an introduction to ethics in the legal profession. The first chapter describes the reasons ethics is important for the legal professional and the sources that combine to define ethics for the paralegal.

The second section, Substantive Issues in Paralegal Ethics, describes the seven major areas of ethics that are relevant for the paralegal. These chapters present the substance of legal ethics; each chapter helps you identify the kinds of situations and problems that might give rise to an ethical issue in that area and helps you understand the ethical standards relating to that issue. This knowledge will prepare the paralegal to deal professionally and effectively with the ethical issues that will arise in the workplace.

The following ethical issues, each of which is discussed in a separate chapter, represent the most important and relevant areas for paralegals:

Confidentiality
Conflict of interest
Unauthorized practice of law
Advertising and solicitation
Zealous representation
Client funds and other money matters
Competence.

Each issue is introduced by a general discussion and a hypothetical case to orient the reader to the kinds of problems that arise in the particular area. These are followed by an analysis of the rules and regulations relevant to that area; all relevant rules, including those from ABA, NALA, and NFPA, are discussed. One extremely helpful feature is the inclusion of relevant rules in the text with the discussion; this makes it easy to find the relevant rule. All the chapters discuss the relevance of the issues to legal assistants and give direction on handling conflicts and problems. Each chapter ends with questions that review the material and present problems for thought and discussion. By understanding these major ethical issues, the paralegal will be well prepared to handle problems in a professional and ethical way.

The final section of the book contains two chapters. Chapter 10 looks at the major specializations in which paralegals work and analyzes ethical issues unique to each specialty. Chapter 11 pulls all the preceding information together and creates a profile of an ethical paralegal.

Rather than merely explaining the ethical rules that guide legal professionals, this book uses features that bring the issues to life, enabling the reader to actively experience the process of analyzing situations and making ethical choices. Each chapter begins with the "Law, Literature, and Ethics" feature, where a selection from a literary work that relates to the contents of the chapter introduces the material. In these enjoyable and relevant pieces, the reader will gain a perspective on legal issues from various sources, from Melvin Belli to Scott Turow to Chester Himes. These pieces reinforce the idea that ethical issues concern people, because literary pieces can frequently get to the heart of an issue in ways that a textbook cannot. We are confident that you will really enjoy these pieces and that they will help you think in a deeper and broader way about the issues involved.

Perhaps the most exciting feature of the book, which really makes the material come alive in a fun yet realistic way, are the hypothetical cases. Each chapter contains many cases to help readers increase their appreciation of ethical dilemmas and sharpen their ability to handle situations ethically. These cases allow you to apply your knowledge of ethical guidelines to the kinds of questions that will arise in your work.

Each chapter also features at least one "Guest Editorial," in which a distinguished writer tackles an issue relevant to the material in that chapter. Additionally, each chapter reproduces excerpts from actual cases, showing how the courts have handled various issues relative to ethics. The cases were chosen because they are especially relevant to paralegals, frequently feature nonlawyer assistants, and show how a court might analyze an ethical issue. Finally, many chapters have illustrations that provide humorous visual commentaries on the state of legal ethics.

All these features combine to make this book much more than a mere restatement of ethical rules, where the reader passively, and sometimes reluctantly, learns the letter of the rules. *Legal Ethics and Professional Responsibility* is, rather, an introduction to an ethical way of thinking and acting based on the reader's becoming an active participant in the process of learning about legal ethics—and it is through the literary pieces, hypothetical cases, guest editorials, and actual cases that this active involvement is achieved. So if you think that the study of ethics is not relevant to the legal profession, or if you believe that the study of ethics is dull, boring, unstimulating, or unchallenging, take a peek inside. Read how Charles Manson wants to represent himself in court, or how Melvin Belli zealously represents his clients. Consider whether a client should sign a confidentiality agreement with his attorney or whether attorneys should be able to solicit business. Read how paralegals staff a program that provides legal assistance for prison inmates or how governmental ethics differs from private sector ethics. Solve The Case of Claudette's Conflicts, The Case of the Sleeptalking Assistant, or The Case of the Mellow Yellows. You will learn not only that legal ethics is perhaps the most relevant area of knowledge for a paralegal, because ethical issues arise with each case and with each client, but also that this area is challenging, stimulating, and enlightening.

ACKNOWLEDGMENTS

Many thanks to Delmar editor Jay Whitney, who has continued his tradition of support, dynamic leadership, and tolerance, and to his excellent support staff, especially Glenna Stanfield. Thanks also to Brooke Graves of Graves Editorial Service for her outstanding copyediting and great sense of humor. It is a pleasure to work with professionals who are committed to quality and who can put up with the insanity of author idiosyncrasies while continuing to smile and provide assistance at every turn.

Many thanks to all of the contributors to the "Law, Literature and Ethics" features and the "Guest Editorial" features, as well as to the organizations that granted permission for their use. Extra appreciation goes to those who wrote pieces especially for this book: Tom Collins, Dennis Grady, Philip Lewin, Susan Chin, and Dianne Soroko.

Much thanks and appreciation to Jay Church, whose pen and wit have given illustrative life to many of the ethical conflicts discussed in the book.

We appreciate the advice and support of William P. Smith, General Counsel, State Bar of Georgia.

Many thanks to Lori "Sid" Taylor, who performed valiant typing service at all hours of the day and night; and to Jeff Davis of the Georgia Bar and attorney Carol Willingham for their research and assistance.

Thanks to Jerry Percifield, Hugh Maxwell, Mariah Ramsey, and Alison Sherrill for their friendship and support.

Terri Lyndall extends her deep gratitude and appreciation to Dr. Michael Hamm and Dr. Daniel Stroup of Centre College, whose patience and guidance mean more than they will ever know.

We also thank those reviewers who read early stages of the manuscript and provided excellent feedback and guidance:

Margaret Stopp
University of West Florida
Pensacola, Florida

Chanda Miller
Des Moines Area Community College
Des Moines, Iowa

Christopher Sadler
Denver Paralegal Institute
Denver, Colorado

Patricia Griffith
Pellissippi Technical Community College
Knoxville, Tennessee

Katherine A. Currier
Elms College
Chicopee, Massachusetts

Susan Gardiner
Southwestern Paralegal Institute
Houston, Texas

Susan Brewer
J. Sargent Reynolds Community College
Richmond, Virginia

Martin Weinstein
Schenectady Community College
Schenectady, New York

Finally, and most importantly, we thank our families for their continual support: Joan S. Lynton, Bill Klein, Julian Lynton, Joan L. Lynton, Vicki Sendele, Kim Lim Sang, Nicky Lynton, Aaron Lynton, Gabie Mick, John Mick, Michael Lyndall, Stuart Lyndall, and Morgan Lyndall.

Jonathan S. Lynton
Terri Mick Lyndall

INTRODUCTION

We welcome you to the study of legal ethics and professional responsibility. We are confident that this book will provide you with an informative and entertaining vehicle to help you appreciate and understand this area of the law. Legal ethics outlines the rules and regulations by which the law operates. It is therefore a highly important area, because every case, every client, and every activity you perform must be understood in the context of those rules and guidelines.

In addition to outlining your duties and responsibilities as a paralegal, legal ethics should be pursued because it will increase the satisfaction you get out of your work, as well as your professional reputation as a legal assistant. By acting ethically, you will increase your value to your firm, help your firm avoid negative consequences (such as malpractice suits), and develop a reputation for excellence through ethics that will enhance your career.

This book has many features that will entertain, amuse, and challenge you, as well as give you a thorough understanding of legal ethics as they apply to paralegals. We encourage you to give thought and attention to the literary excerpts in each chapter, the guest editorials, the hypothetical cases, and the illustrations. We are confident that these features will make the material come to life in a relevant and enjoyable way; they will help you understand and appreciate ethics because they encourage you to apply your understanding of ethics to real-life situations.

There is no denying the importance of legal ethics to the legal professional. No matter what the specialty or environment in which you work, you will be faced with ethical questions on a daily basis. In your quest to be a professional, no area is as important as ethics, and no other area says as much about who you are and what you represent. If you develop a sensitivity to ethics and a commitment to pursuing your work and career in an ethical way, you will have taken a significant step toward developing your professional—as well as personal—identity.

Our challenge was to write a book that not only covered the relevant material, but also encouraged readers to become passionate about ethics. We hope and we believe that we have stimulated that passion in you.

DEDICATION

The Zen master took all the young moths out into the evening. As they flew through the twilight, they saw a bright light. They flew closer.

"What is that?" all the young moths cried.

The old master paused for a moment before he answered, contemplating the flickering light. "That is fire," he said.

"Fire, fire, what is that?" They all crowded close behind the old master. The master gestured. "You have to fly close to the fire to understand it. But it is dangerous to fly too close to the fire."

There was silence, and then the biggest and strongest of the young moths came forward. "I will find out about the fire," he said. He flew out, circling right behind the fire, and came back. "It's warm," he said, "like the sun."

The moths looked at the fire. "That's not it," the master said, "that's not the meaning of fire."

Then the swiftest flier of all the young moths came forward. "I will go," he said. He flew out, so close to the fire that all the young moths gasped. "It's hot," he said, "very hot."

"That's not it at all," the master said, "not at all. You must come close to the fire to understand it."

There was a hush, and then the youngest of the moths came forward. "I will try it," he said. And with that, out he flew, straight as an arrow, right into the fire. In a flash he was gone.

The old master pointed. "He knows the meaning of fire."

Traditional Zen story, told by Alexander

This book is for my parents, Joan S. Lynton and Julian E. Lynton,
who not only encouraged me to fly into the fire,
but helped me fly out of it as well.

LAW, LITERATURE, AND ETHICS

From To Kill a Mockingbird
By Harper Lee

"You can just take that back, boy!"

This order, given by me to Cecil Jacobs, was the beginning of a rather thin time for Jem and me. My fists were clenched and I was ready to let fly. Atticus had promised me he would wear me out if he ever heard of me fighting any more; I was far too old and too big for such childish things, and the sooner I learned to hold it in, the better off everybody would be. I soon forgot.

Cecil Jacobs made me forget. He had announced in the schoolyard the day before that Scout Finch's daddy defended niggers. I denied it, but told Jem.

"What'd he mean sayin' that?" I asked.

"Nothing," Jem said. "Ask Atticus, he'll tell you."

"Do you defend niggers, Atticus?" I asked him that evening.

"Of course I do. Don't say nigger, Scout. That's common."

"'S what everybody at school says."

"From now on it'll be everybody less one—"

"Well, if you don't want me to grow up talkin' that way, why do you send me to school?"

My father looked at me mildly, amusement in his eyes. Despite our compromise, my campaign to avoid school had continued in one form or another since my first day's dose of it: the beginning of last September had brought on sinking spells, dizziness, and mild gastric complaints. I went so far as to pay a nickel for the privilege of rubbing my head against the head of Miss Rachel's cook's son, who was afflicted with a tremendous ringworm. It didn't take.

But I was worrying another bone. "Do all lawyers defend n—Negroes, Atticus?"

"Of course they do, Scout."

"Then why did Cecil say you defended niggers? He made it sound like you were runnin' a still."

Atticus sighed. "I'm simply defending a Negro—his name's Tom Robinson. He lives in that little settlement beyond the town dump. He's a member of Calpurnia's church, and Cal knows his family well. She says they're clean-living folks. Scout, you aren't old enough to understand some things yet, but there's been some high talk around town to the effect that I shouldn't do much about defending this man. It's a peculiar case—it won't come to trial until summer session. John Taylor was kind enough to give us a postponement . . ."

"If you shouldn't be defendin' him, then why are you doin' it?"

"For a number of reasons," said Atticus. "The main one is, if I didn't I couldn't hold up my head in town, I couldn't represent this county in the legislature, I couldn't even tell you or Jem not to do something again."

"You mean if you didn't defend that man Jem and me wouldn't have to mind you anymore?"

"That's about right."

"Why?"

"Because I could never ask you to mind me again. Scout, simply by the nature of the work, every lawyer gets at least one case in his lifetime that affects him personally. This one's mine, I guess. You might hear some ugly talk about it at school, but do one thing for me if you will: you just hold your head high and keep those fists down. No matter what anybody says to you, don't you let 'em get your goat. Try fighting with your head for a change . . . it's a good one, even if it does resist learning."

"Atticus, are we going to win it?"

"No, honey."

"Then why—"

"Simply because we were licked a hundred years before we started is no reason for us not to try to win," Atticus said.

1

"You sound like Cousin Ike Finch," I said. Cousin Ike Finch was Maycomb County's sole surviving Confederate veteran. He wore a General Hood type beard of which he was inordinately vain. At least once a year Atticus, Jem, and I called on him, and I would have to kiss him. It was horrible. Jem and I would listen respectfully to Atticus and Cousin Ike rehash the war. "Tell you, Atticus," Cousin Ike would say, "the Missouri Compromise was what licked us, but if I had to go through it agin, I'd walk every step of the way there an' every step back jist like I did before an' furthermore we'd whip 'em this time . . . now in 1864, when Stonewall Jackson came around by—I beg your pardon, young folks. Ol' Blue Light was in heaven then, God rest his saintly brow . . . ."

"Come here, Scout," said Atticus. I crawled into his lap and tucked my head under his chin. He put his arms around me and rocked me gently. "It's different this time," he said. "This time we aren't fighting the Yankees, we're fighting our friends. But remember this, no matter how bitter things get, they're still our friends and this is still our home."

With this in mind, I faced Cecil Jacobs in the schoolyard next day: "You gonna take that back, boy?"

"You gotta make me first!" he yelled. "My folks said your daddy was a disgrace an' that nigger oughta hang from the water-tank!"

I drew a bead on him, remembered what Atticus had said, then dropped my fists and walked away, "Scout's a cow-ward!" ringing in my ears. It was the first time I ever walked away from a fight.

■ Excerpt from *To Kill a Mockingbird* by Harper Lee. Copyright © 1960 by Harper Lee. Copyright © renewed 1988 by Harper Lee. Reprinted by permission of HarperCollins Publishers Inc.

Legal Ethics and Professional Responsibility

LAW, LITERATURE, AND ETHICS

From **Blind Ambition**
By John Dean

The tests started that first day at the White House. After a brief examination of my meager quarters, I had sat down at my desk. I didn't have anything to do, but then my secretary brought me a sealed envelope with a small red tag. I asked her what it was. She had not opened it; it was stamped "CONFIDENTIAL," and the red tag meant "priority." Someone had been planning work for the new counsel. The cover memorandum was a printed form, with striking blue and red instructions filled in:

ACTION MEMORANDUM
FROM THE STAFF SECRETARY
LOG NO.: P523
Date: Friday, July 24, 1970   Time: 6:30 P.M.
Due Date: Wednesday, August 5, 1970
    Time: 2:00 P.M.
SUBJECT: Request that you rebut the recent
    attack on the Vice-President.

An attached "confidential memorandum" said that a new muckraking magazine called *Scanlan's Monthly* had published a bogus memo linking Vice-President Agnew with a top-secret plan to cancel the 1972 election and to repeal the entire Bill of Rights. Agnew had publicly denounced the memo as "completely false" and "ridiculous," and the editors of *Scanlan's* had replied: "The Vice President's denial is as clumsy as it is fraudulent. The document came directly from Mr. Agnew's office and he knows it." My instructions were clear: "It was noted that this is a vicious attack and possibly a suit should be filed or a federal investigation ordered to follow up on it."

"Noted" by whom? Since the memorandum was signed by John Brown, a member of Haldeman's staff, I called him to find out. The "noter" was the President, I was told; he had scrawled my orders in the margin of his daily news summary. No one had to explain why the President's name was not used. He

was always to be kept one step removed, insulated, to preserve his "deniability."

So this is my baptism, I thought. I was astounded that the President would be so angrily concerned about a funny article in a fledgling magazine. It did not square with my picture of his being absorbed in diplomacy, wars and high matters of state. Was it possible that we had a secret plan to cancel the election and the Bill of Rights? I was embarrassed by the thought. Now I cannot look back on this episode without laughing, but then I was not at all loose about it. It was the President of the United States talking. Maybe he was right.

On the due date, I wrote my first memorandum to the President, explaining the hazards of a lawsuit and the wisdom of waiting to see what an FBI investigation produced. I thought the affair had been put to rest. Not so. Back came another action memorandum from the staff secretary. The President agreed with my conclusions, but he wasn't yet content. "It was requested," said the memorandum, "that as part of this inquiry you should have the Internal Revenue Service conduct a field investigation on the tax front."

This was the "old Nixon" at work, heavy-handed, after somebody. I began to fret. How could anything be at once so troubling and so absurd? The President was asking me to do something I thought was dangerous, unnecessary and wrong. I did nothing for several days, but the deadline was hard upon me. I couldn't simply respond, "Dean opposes this request because it is wrong and possibly illegal." I had to find some practical reason for doing the right thing or I would be gone. I called Bud Krogh several times, but he was out. Then I thought of my recent acquaintance, Murray Chotiner, and arranged to meet him.

"I need some counsel, Murray."

"You're the lawyer. You're the one who is supposed to give counsel around here," he said with a chuckle.

"I'm still trying to find the water fountains in this place," I said. "Murray, seriously, I need some advice. The President wants me to turn the IRS loose on a shit-ass magazine called *Scanlan's Monthly* because it printed a bogus memo from the Vice-President's office about canceling the 'seventy-two election and repealing the Bill of Rights."

Murray laughed. "Hell, Agnew's got a great idea. I hope he has a good plan worked out. It would save us a lot of trouble if we dispensed with the 'seventy-two campaign." Murray wasn't taking my visit as seriously as I was. We joked about Agnew for a few minutes before I could get him to focus on my problem, and he had the answer. "If the President wants you to turn the IRS loose, then you turn the IRS loose. It's that simple, John."

"I really don't think it's necessary, Murray. The President's already got Mitchell investigating it. The FBI, I guess."

"I'll tell you this, if Richard Nixon thinks it's necessary you'd better think it's necessary. If you don't, he'll find someone who does."

I was not convinced and said so, but nicely. "Okay, but let me ask you this, Murray. You're a lawyer. Isn't it illegal and therefore crazy to use IRS to attack someone the President doesn't like?"

"Not so," he snorted. He stopped and retrieved the calm he rarely lost. "John, the President is the head of the executive branch of this damn government. If he wants his tax collectors to check into the affairs of anyone, it's his prerogative. I don't see anything illegal about it. It's the way the game is played. Do you think for a second that Lyndon Johnson was above using the IRS to harass those guys who were giving him a hard time on the war? No sir. Nor was Lyndon above using IRS against some good Republicans like Richard Nixon. I'll tell you he damn near ruined a few."

Murray was testy, or maybe defensive—I couldn't decide. It was clear that he didn't want to discuss the matter further. I thanked him and left. If I was going to play ball in Richard Nixon's league, I would have to get over my squeamishness.

■ Copyright © 1976 by John W. Dean. Reprinted by permission of Simon & Schuster, Inc.

CHAPTER 1
Introduction to Legal Ethics

CHAPTER OVERVIEW

In this chapter you will learn about the role ethics plays in the practice of the law and why and how the legal profession regulates the activities and behaviors of lawyers and legal assistants.

1.1   LAW AND ETHICS: STRANGE BEDFELLOWS?

[The Lawyer] has become keen and shrewd; he has learned how to flatter his master in word and indulge him in deed; but his soul is small and unrighteous. His condition, which has been that of a slave from his youth onward, has deprived him of growth and unrighteousness and independence; dangers and fear, which were too much for his truth and honesty, came upon him in early years, when the tenderness of youth was unequal to them, and he has been driven into crooked ways; from the first he has practiced deception and retaliation, and has become stunted and warped.

Plato, "Theaetetus"

Q: What's black and brown and looks great on a lawyer?

A: A doberman.

Anonymous

When first registering for this class, you may have wondered what exactly ethics is and what, if anything, it has to do with the law, let alone paralegals. You might also have been a little confused or skeptical at the notion of legal ethics, for many people see legal professionals as distinctly unethical, devoid of moral sensibilities, and motivated solely by greed or power. Naturally, in the law as in any profession, you will find examples of behavior ranging from the ethically commendable to the morally reprehensible, but the overall practice of the law is intimately connected to the ethical principles that guide it. You will find that the practice of law is driven by ethical considerations, and that you cannot work in the legal system if you are unaware of the professional responsibilities of lawyers and legal assistants. More than ruminating on interesting philosophical speculations, legal ethics provides the context in which the law is practiced: legal ethics really defines the rules by which lawyers practice the law. Ethics also provides the standards of conduct for nonlawyer personnel working in the legal profession.

These rules do not merely delineate the appropriate behaviors for legal professionals; they also ensure that the legal system upholds basic principles of fairness and justice. Without these rules, the American legal system would not function the way it does today. Consider the notion of confidentiality between attorney and client. It is extremely unlikely that a client would tell an attorney the truth about his alleged criminal conduct if the client believed that these facts would be subject to disclosure. Thus, the principle that legal professionals must keep clients' secrets and confidences private assists the legal team by enabling them to use all of those facts to present the best possible case for the client. This ethical mandate is a good illustration of how legal ethics helps protect individual rights but also enables the legal professional to fully and zealously represent his or her client.

So if you think that legal professionals and ethics make strange bedfellows, it is time to reassess your thinking. In a society where the law works effectively, legal practice exists only in relation to the rules that

"Oh, no, not him . . . Professional courtesy, y'know."

guide the profession. There is no such thing as practicing law without concern for the ethical guidelines that define the parameters of the profession.

1.2 ETHICS, LEGAL ETHICS, AND PROFESSIONAL RESPONSIBILITY

Ethics is concerned with human conduct and motives; it attempts to delineate the right from the wrong, the permissible from the impermissible, and thereby to guide human thought and action. As applied to the practice of the law, legal ethics, sometimes known as professional responsibility, is much more specific and codified than a general conception of ethics. Ethical standards in the law guide the behavior of both lawyers and nonlawyer employees, attempting to assure the public that those working in the law are doing so in an honorable and effective way. Legal ethics really outlines the duties of the members of the legal profession and describes appropriate conduct for those working in the legal profession.

Black's Law Dictionary (5th ed. 1979) defines *legal ethics* as

> usages and customs among members of the legal profession, involving their moral and professional duties toward one another, toward clients, and toward courts. That branch of moral science which treats of the duties which a member of the legal profession owes to the public, to the court, to his professional brethren, and to his clients.

In their introduction to *Ethics and the Legal Profession* (1986), Michael Davis and Frederick Elliston emphasize that professional ethics has both a theoretical and applied side when they define *ethics* as "the philosophical study of moral problems that arise within a profession . . . [and] the articulation of a set of ethical principles that enable one to conceptualize and address these problems in a systematic and comprehensive fashion."

Although these definitions are necessarily imprecise, they do point the way toward an understanding that the law is a process that is somehow connected to a sense of morality, honesty, and fairness, and that this sense of morality must not only contain theoretical ideas, but also must be able to apply to the variety of situations arising in legal practice that present ethical dilemmas. Certainly no single definition of ethical behavior can possibly cover all the situations that legal professionals will encounter in the course of their work. However, the pragmatic definition of ethics can best be set forth as the rules by which attorneys and other legal professionals "play" the "game" of law. If you think of ethics as the game rules for practicing law, then you will understand its real importance, because every client, and every cause of action, is embedded in an ethical context. Not every client or case concerns only a single specific legal area, such as breach of contract— but every situation a lawyer or legal assistant faces, whether the legal issue is in contract or tort or immigration law, must be handled ethically. Legal ethics defines the rules by which the law is practiced, and it is therefore the common denominator among all of the activities a legal professional performs and all of the clients and interests a legal professional represents.

The recognition of the importance of ethics to success in the legal profession and to the reputation of the profession in society is reflected in the educational requirements concerning ethics, as well as the codes developed by the governing bodies of the legal profession. A course in legal ethics, sometimes called professional responsibility, is mandatory in all American Bar Association (ABA) accredited law school curricula. Many states also require passing of the Multistate Professional Responsibility Examination (MPRE) as a prerequisite to admission to the state bar; however, some states waive the MPRE for those students who received a grade of B or above in their law school ethics class. For paralegal students attending an ABA-approved program, or a program in compliance with ABA guidelines, an ethics course is a mandatory part of the curriculum. At present, there are about 500 programs of various kinds in paralegal studies; 150 of them have been approved by the ABA, which is a voluntary process. Each program must, of course, also comply with the relevant state and agency accreditation requirements that apply to any educational program.

Admission to the bar also requires that each candidate be scrutinized as to moral character and fitness to practice law. Part of the process of becoming admitted to the bar involves being evaluated by a Board to Determine Fitness of Bar Applicants, commonly called the Fitness Board. In judging fitness to practice law, Fitness Boards consider candor in the application process, the fiscal responsibility of the applicant, the applicant's past compliance with court orders, the applicant's criminal activity, any drug or chemical use, and mental and emotional stability. To make these determinations, Fitness Boards investigate the information given on the lengthy application, conduct interviews or review records, and check fingerprints. When there are unresolved concerns about an applicant, the board will bring in the applicant for an informal interview, which may be followed by a formal hearing.

The importance the legal profession places on ethics is also illustrated by the fact that the major governing bodies of attorneys and legal assistants have created standards for ethical conduct. The American Bar Association (ABA), National Federation of Paralegal Associations (NFPA), and National Association of Legal Assistants (NALA) have all created rules of ethical conduct that are to be followed by their members. These rules, in large part, form the basis for the definition of ethical behavior for legal assistants and lawyers; they are discussed fully in the second section of this book.

Lawyers and legal assistants can fulfill their professional responsibility by adhering to the standards and principles articulated in the rules that comprise legal ethics. Yet this professional responsibility goes beyond adherence to ethical rules and guidelines to include an awareness that the ethical practice of law relates to more than the legal profession. An ethical legal practice contributes to the development of a free and just society, because it preserves and upholds the principles upon which the entire society is based. The Preamble to the ABA's Model Code of Professional Responsibility emphasizes this point:

> The continued existence of a free and democratic society depends upon recognition of the concept that justice is based on the rule of law grounded in respect for the dignity of the individual and his capacity through reason for enlightened self-government. Law so grounded makes justice possible, for only through such law does the dignity of the individual attain respect and protection. Without it, individual rights become subject to unrestrained power, respect for law is destroyed, and rational self-government is impossible.
>
> Lawyers, as guardians of the law, play a vital role in the preservation of society. The fulfillment of this role requires an understanding by lawyers of their relationship with and function in our legal system. A consequent obligation of lawyers is to maintain the highest standards of ethical conduct.
>
> In fulfilling his professional responsibilities, a lawyer necessarily assumes various roles that require the performance of many difficult tasks. Not every situation which he may encounter can be foreseen, but fundamental ethical principles are always present to guide him. Within the framework of these principles, a lawyer must with courage and foresight be able and ready to shape the body of the law to the ever-changing relationships of society.
>
> The Model Code of Professional Responsibility points the way to the aspiring and provides standards by which to judge the transgressor. Each lawyer must find within his own conscience the touchstone against which to test the extent to which his action should rise above minimum standards. But in the last analysis it is the desire for the respect and confidence of members of his profession and of the society

which he serves that should provide to the lawyer the incentive for the highest degree of ethical conduct. The possible loss of that respect and confidence is the ultimate sanction. So long as its practitioners are guided by these principles, the law will continue to be a noble profession. This is its greatness and strength, which permit no compromise.

It is this fundamental connectedness to society and the quest for justice which imposes responsibility on the legal profession. In many ways, the strength and vigor of a society is directly related to the fairness and humanity of its justice system. The law is an integral part of the human quest to create and maintain a positive, productive, free, and just society; those who choose to work in the legal system, therefore, have a tremendous personal and professional responsibility to uphold the highest ethical standards. In the words of Lon Fuller and John Randall, co-chairs of the Joint Conference on Professional Responsibility:

> A profession to be worthy of the name must inculcate in its members a strong sense of the special obligations that attach to their calling. One who undertakes the practice of a profession cannot rest content with the faithful discharge of duties assigned to him by others. His work must provide direction within a larger frame. All that he does must evidence a dedication, not merely to a specific assignment, but to the enduring ideals of his vocation. Only such a dedication will enable him to reconcile fidelity to those he serves with equal fidelity to an office that must at all times rise above the involvements of immediate interest.

What is it specifically about the nature of legal work and the legal profession that gives rise to this need for principles of professional responsibility? First, it is the reality that the law concerns issues important to both the individuals involved and society at large, and that the law has the authority to impose serious consequences on those who violate it. Ask anyone who has been involved with the law, from receiving a speeding ticket to being convicted of first-degree murder, and you will learn that involvement with the law is a weighty, anxiety-producing experience that can affect a person for his or her entire life. The law, in its essence, concerns serious issues with life-changing consequences.

Second, the legal process inherently contains the potential for abuse of power or position by those practicing in the legal system. Perhaps it is the closeness of lawyers to the legal system that provides the impetus for unethical behavior, because lawyers know how the system works and may believe that they have the ability to beat it. Perhaps it is the position of power characteristic of the lawyer, a position that may beget a desire for increasing power and influence. Perhaps it is greed that causes lawyers to use their positions of power and influence corruptly. In 1905, in a speech delivered to the Harvard Ethical Society (May 4, 1905), Supreme Court Justice Louis Brandeis observed:

> It is true at the present time that the lawyer does not hold as high a position with the people as he held seventy-five or indeed fifty years ago;

but the reason is not lack of opportunity. It is this: Instead of holding a position of independence, between the wealthy and the people, prepared to curb the excesses of either, able lawyers have, to a large extent, allowed themselves to become adjuncts of great corporations and have neglected the obligation to use their powers for the protection of the people.

His words perhaps ring as true now as they did when he first said them.

Regardless of the reason, lawyers have been known to do some very unethical things. There are instances too numerous to detail of basic lawyer dishonesty, involving, for example, improprieties with funds or use of the legal system to gain power or prestige. Regardless of the reason or particular manifestation, it is clear that lawyers do abuse their positions; intimidate, overreach, or defraud their clients; and use their knowledge or position for personal gain. Many would also say the seduction of power, fame, or money has also inhibited the legal profession from fulfilling its potential as a protector of those most in need of legal service, as too many lawyers, one might argue, use their knowledge for material acquisition rather than public need.

It is the combination of powerful work, significant consequences, and potential for abuse that necessitates the requirement of professional responsibility for legal professionals. This responsibility has both a theoretical and practical dimension. Legal professionals must gain more than a mere understanding of ethical principles; they must also gain the resolve and the ability to apply those principles to situations arising in the course of legal work. Professional responsibility, therefore, requires the articulation of a set of principles that also guide behavior, and the determination and ability to apply those principles effectively.

Just as there are many examples of legal professionals who have not developed a sense of ethical responsibility, so are there many examples of persons in the legal system whose work displays the highest sense of morality, ethics, and duty; whose work is driven by a fundamental sense of responsibility to both self and society. For example, many attorneys are motivated not by a desire for power, influence, and monetary gain, but rather a deep conviction that a lawyer has an obligation to help cure some of society's ills. Attorneys who work for public defenders' offices, legal aid, legal clinics, or law foundations devoted to a particular cause usually receive salaries significantly less than their colleagues in private practice. These individuals are as skilled and work as many hours as do their counterparts; they are different primarily in their application of their abilities and their elevation of their moral interests over their material needs. Unfortunately, many people do not realize this. It is not uncommon to hear a criminal defendant turn down a judge's offer of a public defender because she wants a "real lawyer." A public defender, of course, is as real as any lawyer; what differs is only the working environment in which those attorneys use their skills.

One example of legal work reflecting the highest ethical standards has resulted in the freeing of two men who were given life sentences for murder. Jim McClosky, a Protestant lay minister from Princeton, New Jersey, is the founder of and sole investigator for Centurion Ministries. His organization provides free detective services for those who were improperly convicted because of police or prosecutorial corruption, incompetent legal defense, or human error, and McClosky takes a case only if he is absolutely convinced of the person's innocence. The latest recipients of his efforts, Clarence Chance and Benny Powell, were freed from prison on March 25, 1992, after having served 17 years each for a crime they did not commit. In their case, the evidence showed that the police had framed the two, pressured witnesses into lying, and withheld relevant evidence. Although McClosky is not a lawyer, he surely understands the ethical responsibility that characterizes the best part of the legal profession, and his work is truly the kind that fulfills the highest moral imperatives of the profession.

A high sense of professional responsibility is also required of those who work in the legal system because of the nature of the attorney-client relationship. The relationship between an attorney and a client is special. Lawyers and their assistants learn private things about their clients, and they are in a position of knowledge with respect to clients and their situations. Imagine for a moment the position of trust and power a legal team occupies when advising a wealthy client about her will. That client is sharing her innermost thoughts and wishes and is dependent on the attorney to advise her of the legal consequences of her wishes. Additionally, it is surely human to wish that a client, who might be leaving $2 million to the American Cancer Society, would leave just a little of it—perhaps only a hundred thousand—to you!

To describe the degree of trust and importance that the lawyer-client relationship demands, the law has developed the notion of fiduciary relationships. Think of this as a duty of absolute loyalty that affixes to all legal representation.

> The fiduciary obligations which are the premise of trust may be simply stated. The attorney is under a duty to represent the client with undivided loyalty, to preserve the client's confidences, and to disclose any material matters bearing upon the representation of these obligations. Although the phrasing of this definition of fiduciary obligations is varied and often dependent upon the context of particular circumstances, this rule exists in virtually every jurisdiction in the United States.

Rice v. Perl, 320 N.W.2d 407 (Minn. 1982).

Lawyers and legal assistants both have a fiduciary relationship with their clients, and it is from an understanding of the responsibilities and obligations of being in a fiduciary relationship that ethical representation must proceed. Additionally, the fiduciary relationship may arise during preliminary consultation, before an actual lawyer-client relationship has been established. For example, if a potential client comes to an attorney for a preliminary interview and the attorney decides not to accept the case, the

"Are you ready to have a fiduciary relationship?"

attorney may still have an obligation of fairness, good faith, and competence toward that individual. It is therefore very important to understand the requirements that this kind of relationship imposes on the parties.

By thinking of a fiduciary relationship as similar to the relationship of a small child and a parent, you can understand the reasons for denoting this relationship as a special one. Just as a young child is completely dependent on a parent and is not competent to question the parent's actions, the client has the same dependent relationship with the attorney and/or paralegal. The law looks unfavorably upon the legal professional who takes undue advantage of a client, and provides the client with a possible cause of action called *breach of fiduciary duty.* This cause of action gives relief to those whose lack of information and position of dependency left them vulnerable to unscrupulous professionals who use their positions of power and trust to take advantage of others.

The following hypothetical case is the first of many cases you will find throughout this book. These cases present factual situations containing ethical issues and dilemmas, and it is your task to analyze each situation and decide on the appropriate course of action. Not only will these cases give you a fun and interesting way to learn and apply the principles of legal ethics, but they will help you anticipate the kinds of situations that might arise in the real world of the law.

THE CASE OF CAMTECH'S COLLAPSE

Peter Henderson is a corporate paralegal specializing in security transactions. His background as a stockbroker, combined with his outstanding legal skills, have made him a well-respected corporate paralegal.

Peter frequently has lunch with officers of the Wildwood Corporation, his firm's client. John Richards, Wildwood's vice president, is especially close to Henderson, and the two trade advice on stock purchases. On Henderson's advice over crab cakes and chablis, Richards purchases for himself $100,000 worth of stock of a fledgling company called Camtech. Henderson believes that Camtech will be first to develop an emerging camcorder technology and expresses to Richards that he believes the new company would be a good buy.

Unfortunately for Richards, Camtech's stock plummets when an entrepreneur from Cranston, Rhode Island, develops a process that instantaneously makes Camtech's technology obsolete. Richards's stock is now worth less than $1,000. Frustrated and angry, Richards threatens Henderson that he will sue him for breach of fiduciary duty for recommending the stock and for not preventing him from investing in the stock.

Is Richards correct? Has Henderson done anything to breach his fiduciary duty to Richards?

1.3 THE REGULATION OF LAWYERS AND LEGAL ASSISTANTS

A number of sources combine to regulate the legal profession. Although each source has its own unique position, they all interact to provide a comprehensive approach to any ethical issues that might arise.

State Courts and State Bar Associations

The legal profession has historically been regulated by the states, which have the ability to license attorneys because legal work protects the public interest. This authority is given to the state's highest appellate court, which can retain or delegate the authority to another entity. When the court delegates this authority to a bar association, bar membership is mandatory for all attorneys licensed in the state. This is called an *integrated bar,* and most bar associations are integrated. Examples of states with integrated bars are Florida, Georgia, Maine, Michigan, and Texas. In other jurisdictions, bar membership is not obligatory, and the highest appellate court in the state maintains absolute authority over the attorneys it licenses. These are called *nonintegrated bars;* states that do not have mandatory bar membership include New Hampshire, New Jersey, Pennsylvania, and Tennessee. California presents a unique situation; although it has an integrated bar, authority over attorneys is given to the State Bar Court of the State Bar of California, rather than the bar itself.

Whether it be the mandatory bar association or the highest appellate court in the state, the entity with the ultimate authority over lawyers in the jurisdiction has many duties. These duties include investigating applicants for bar membership, administering the bar examination, providing ethical opinions, and disciplining attorneys under its jurisdiction. In addition, both integrated and nonintegrated bars have many committees to help to investigate and solve many of the problems unique to the legal profession, such as revising and compiling various codes and developing continuing legal education requirements. The results of these committees' work are often used by legislatures in the state to amend, revise, or adopt specific statutes. For example, in Georgia, the state bar is working with the General Assembly to revise the Georgia ethical rules to be more in line with the Federal Rules of Evidence.

Each state has its own rules of legal ethics, developed by either the state bar or the state's highest court (except California). Generally, a state uses one of the American Bar Association's sets of rules as a blueprint for its own specific rules. In addition to developing and enforcing ethical codes, state bar associations also confront ethical issues by writing and publishing ethical opinions in state bar journals. These opinions are generally not binding, but they serve as guides to bar members as to how they might respond when confronted with a similar situation. Additionally, the highest appellate court is responsible for disciplining attorneys for ethical violations, even though the bar association may be an integrated one. Thus, if an attorney is charged with an ethical violation, the state's highest appellate court will render a decision on the attorney's guilt or innocence and order appropriate sanctions.

American Bar Association

The American Bar Association (ABA) is the largest single national organization for lawyers. Membership in the ABA is voluntary; however, approximately half of the attorneys in the nation are members. The ABA is over a century old and actively participates in the development of law. The ABA may issue opinion statements on particular legal issues and has a certification process for the approval of law schools. Although the ABA does not certify paralegal education programs, schools that wish to participate may seek ABA approval.

The ABA has developed two sets of ethical rules. The first was the Model Code of Professional Responsibility, initially published in 1969. Shortly after its publication, the Model Code was adopted by the ABA and, in some form, by all the states. However, the Code had many limitations and weaknesses; its provisions were both difficult to understand and difficult to apply. To come up with a more effective code for ethical conduct, a special commission, known as the Kutak Commission after its chairman, began work on what was to become the Model Rules of Professional Conduct. The Model Rules were adopted by the ABA House of Delegates in 1982.

The Code is divided into three major sections. First, the Code has nine *Canons,* which are general statements of ethical conduct. These Canons are followed by *Ethical Considerations,* designated as ECs, which are aspirational in nature. ECs provide guidance on how the Canons apply to situations commonly faced by attorneys. Third, the ECs are followed by the

Disciplinary Rules, which are designated as DRs. Disciplinary Rules outline the minimum level of ethical behavior to which lawyers must conform. Prosecutions for ethical violations are the result of not complying with the provisions of the DRs.

The newer Model Rules are more straightforward than the Code. Instead of having general statements, aspirational statements, and disciplinary rules, the Model Rules are direct statements about ethical and unethical conduct. To assist in the interpretation of the Rules, each is rule is followed by *Comments* that provide practical guidance and examples. Many legal professionals find the Rules more pragmatic and easier to apply and understand than the Code. Most jurisdictions have enacted ethical rules modeled on the ABA Model Rules, although California has its own ethics code, which is not modeled on either the Model Code or Model Rules. It is nonetheless important for every legal professional to understand both sets of rules, because they each are used in various jurisdictions, and because the Rules used the Code as their basis.

Besides the Code and the Rules governing ethical conduct for attorneys, the ABA also enacted the Model Guidelines for the Utilization of Legal Assistants in 1991. These Guidelines were intended not only to be utilized by individual states in developing their own guidelines, but also to educate and encourage attorneys to use legal assistants effectively. These guidelines are not rules of law but suggested approaches for working with paralegals.

National Association of Legal Assistants

The National Association of Legal Assistants (NALA) is a voluntary organization of professionals who are practicing legal assistants. NALA works with local, state, and national bar associations in setting standards for legal assistants. It also provides its own continuing legal education seminars and workshops.

The Code of Ethics and Professional Responsibility of the National Association of Legal Assistants, Inc., is set up similar to the ABA Code. The NALA Code has 12 Canons that establish the parameters of conduct for legal assistants. Although the NALA Code does not have ethical considerations and disciplinary rules, in nature it is similar to the ABA Code. The topical subjects dealt with in the NALA Code are as follows:

1. Canons 1 through 6 deal with the unauthorized practice of law.
2. Canon 7 deals with the protection of client confidences.
3. Canon 8 deals with the obligation of a legal assistant to avoid conduct that might appear unethical or cause the attorney to be or appear unethical.
4. Canons 9 through 11 are aspirational in nature and encourage legal assistants to maintain the integrity and a high degree of competence throughout the legal profession, to make legal services available to the

public, and to do all things to ensure that the legal assistant's conduct conforms with all responsibilities conferred by statute or the court.

5. Canon 12 states that the legal assistant is governed by the ABA Code of Professional Responsibility.

Perhaps the most significant issue that the NALA has confronted concerns the issue of certification of paralegals. At this time, there is no national consensus on the desirability of a certification program for paralegals. Proponents of certification argue that certification provides better control over the profession; if certification existed, mandatory educational requirements, standards for competency, and the ability to discipline would combine to create a more qualified, educated, and responsible legal assistant. Additionally, paralegal and bar associations could discipline paralegals for ethical violations and could use loss of certification as an impetus for ethical behavior. Proponents of certification argue that this would put more teeth into attempts to regulate paralegals.

Critics of certification are concerned that the process of certification would confuse the distinction between lawyers and nonlawyers. In their view, this would invite unauthorized practice violations and confuse the public, who might not understand the different duties and responsibilities of a certified paralegal and a licensed lawyer.

The NALA is the leading proponent of certification, and it has developed and implemented a program for certifying legal assistants. The program consists of completing a comprehensive examination and taking continuing legal education courses. The body giving this test is the Certifying Board for Legal Assistants, which is comprised of legal assistants, educators, and attorneys. Once this test has been successfully completed, and the other requirements of the organization satisfied, the legal assistant can use the initials "CLA" to designate that he or she is a certified legal assistant.

National Federation of Paralegal Associations

The other major national organization for paralegals is the National Federation of Paralegal Associations, Inc. (NFPA). NFPA is an organization comprised of individual state organizations; an individual legal assistant would therefore be an indirect member of the NFPA through his or her local paralegal organization.

NFPA's Affirmation of Responsibility divides its standards of ethical conduct into six areas, with the principle stated first and a discussion of the principle following the general statement. NFPA's Affirmation seems to be more oriented to the development and expansion of the paralegal profession than does the NALA Code. Another interesting difference is that NALA consistently uses the term *legal assistant,* whereas NFPA's Affirmation favors use of the term *paralegal*.[1] The six sections of the NFPA Affirmation are as follows:

1. A paralegal shall take initiative in the expansion of the paralegal's role in the legal profession within the parameters of the unauthorized practice of law statutes.
2. A paralegal shall maintain the highest level of ethical conduct.
3. A paralegal shall maintain a high level of competence and shall contribute to the integrity of the paralegal profession.
4. A paralegal shall preserve client confidences and privileged communications.
5. A paralegal shall serve the public interests by contributing to the availability and delivery of quality legal services.
6. A paralegal shall promote the development of the paralegal profession.

State Statutes

Over and above the ethical codes adopted by the state bar, other statutes exist that may apply to attorneys or paralegals. These statutes are not necessarily applicable only to legal professionals, because they relate to the prohibited behavior, not the identity or occupation of the violator. These statutes exist to prevent activities such as the unauthorized practice of law, solicitation, or conversion. Besides bar sanctions, which emanate from the ethical rules of each state, an attorney or paralegal may be subject to criminal punishment for violating a prohibition, such as that concerning the unauthorized practice of law, or civil liability for committing malpractice. If the attorney's unethical conduct is a violation of a criminal statute in the jurisdiction, such as when an attorney steals a client's money, the attorney can suffer criminal prosecution and punishment as well as sanctions from the bar. Further, an attorney who violates an ethical principle may be liable to the client in a civil suit such as a legal malpractice action. Finally, attorneys may be disciplined by the bench. Judges have the authority to declare an attorney in contempt of court for certain conduct. A contempt of court charge can result in a fine, imprisonment, or even bar sanctions.

1.4 ATTORNEY DISCIPLINE

When an attorney is convicted of violating a disciplinary rule, the attorney is ordinarily punished in some respect. The type of punishment given is usually discretionary and based on the severity of the violation. Punishments or sanctions range from a private reprimand to disbarment or even criminal prosecution.

The least severe punishment is a *reprimand*, sometimes called a *reproval*, which may be private or public. A private reprimand is a "parent/child" discussion privately with the offending lawyer. The judge or bar personnel usually give private reprimands. This mild sanction is analogous to a slap on

"I think I would rather have been disbarred."

the wrist and is usually reserved for only the most minor ethical violations, although no ethical violation should be viewed as minor.

The public reprimand is a more embarrassing sanction. Like the private reprimand, the public reprimand is usually given by a judge or bar official. However, these discussions of why the attorney's conduct was unethical and why the conduct should be corrected are held publicly, usually in open court before other members of the bar. This action may also be part of the court's public record or may be published in the bar journal.

The sanction of *license suspension* means that the attorney is permitted to continue practicing law, but cannot practice for a specific period of time. This sanction can cover a wide range of time periods, from one week to several years. Not being able to practice means not being able to represent clients in court or perform other activities that would constitute practicing law. If the attorney practices during the period of suspension, he or she is engaging in the unauthorized practice of law and may be disciplined or prosecuted for that activity either by the bar or by the state.

One of the most severe sanctions is *disbarment.* Unlike suspension, which provides that an attorney cannot practice for a certain period of time, disbarment means that an attorney loses his or her membership in the bar and cannot practice in that jurisdiction. However, disbarment is not necessarily permanent. In many jurisdictions, a disbarred lawyer may reapply for admission after a period of time. In the event of application for readmission, the courts will consider various factors, including the attorney's fitness to practice law, the reason for the disbarment, the attorney's conduct while disbarred, the public interest, and so forth.

In most cases, if an attorney has been disbarred in one jurisdiction, he or she will not be admitted to practice in another jurisdiction. If the attorney who is disbarred from practice in one jurisdiction is also concurrently licensed to practice in another, the disbarment in one jurisdiction may act as a disbarment in the other jurisdiction.

THE CASE OF THE DISBARRED CPA

Anthony Amos ran a successful practice as both an accountant and an attorney. He was recently disbarred because of misappropriation of client funds, but he continues his accounting practice.

Anthony calls in his experienced legal assistant, Marilyn, to explain the new office procedures in light of his disbarment. First, Marilyn is instructed to write a notice to existing clients stating that from now on the firm's legal work will be handled by the law firm of Jandrlich and Padilla, but that Amos will continue to function as a CPA. "The rigors of a dual career have finally caused me to focus on one area, and that will be my accounting practice," the letter says. In truth, Amos will be advising Padilla and Jandrlich on the referred cases for a 25 percent referral fee. Amos also tells Marilyn to put an ad in the newspaper advertising herself as an advisor for wills. "I'll help you with anything you don't know," Amos assures Marilyn.

What should Marilyn do? What ethical dilemmas does she face?

THE RETURN OF THE DISBARRED ATTORNEY

Attorney Williams has been disbarred from the practice of law. Even though Williams realizes that her career as an attorney is over, she is still desirous of working in the legal profession; she has a good mind and a good heart, but she made some mistakes along the way.

Williams is now seeking a position as a legal assistant. Williams reasons that even though she has been forbidden from practicing law as a lawyer, she still has skills and abilities that could make her a productive member of a legal team. Also, being a paralegal would require that she be supervised by an attorney, who would ultimately be responsible for her work.

You are the paralegal/office administrator for your law firm and are responsible for hiring new paralegals. You are leaning strongly toward hiring Williams for your open paralegal position and, following standard procedure, have forwarded the paperwork with your recommendation to the managing partner for approval. The managing partner responds by recognizing that this is an unusual case and wondering if there are any ethical issues that should be addressed before making an offer.

What ethical issues do you see inherent in this situation?

1.5 PARALEGAL DISCIPLINE

Like an attorney, a paralegal can suffer sanctions for failure to do something as well as for the negligent performance of a duty. *Misfeasance,* similar to a "sin of commission," occurs when someone handles something inappropriately. An example of misfeasance would be the cause of action a client would have against an attorney who sued the wrong defendant on the day the statute of limitations for the suit expired. *Nonfeasance,* on the other hand, is the failure to do something, similar to a "sin of omission." For example, if an attorney failed to assert an affirmative defense of satisfaction, in a contract dispute in which the defendant client had already satisfied his obligations under the contract, the attorney would be guilty of nonfeasance.

Some jurisdictions have local paralegal associations which, like bar associations, can prosecute paralegals for unethical conduct. If a jurisdiction licenses legal assistants, a violation of ethical standards can result in the loss of a paralegal's license. A paralegal might also lose certification by a national or local organization. A somewhat less severe but practical result of unethical conduct is the loss of a paralegal's reputation, which can result in an inability to find employment. You will find that the legal community in most cities is a relatively tight network, and if you have engaged in unethical conduct, it is likely that others will learn of your experience. Like the attorney, the paralegal is also subject to criminal prosecution if her unethical conduct violates a criminal statute in the jurisdiction. Criminal conviction can result in a fine, imprisonment, or both.

Finally, paralegals can potentially be parties to a legal malpractice action if their conduct is deemed unethical or negligent. The threat of malpractice actions is a significant force in ensuring ethical conduct by attorneys and paralegals. Malpractice actions, or even the threat of malpractice actions, represent a very real deterrent to unethical behavior because of their potential to cause a loss of respect or employment, not to mention the financial liability that usually accompanies a malpractice suit.

Paralegals, like attorneys, are subject to a number of different disciplinary methods which are intended to assure the public that those practicing in the law are held to high ethical standards. Remember, however, that the purpose of articulated ethical standards is to complement and particularize the ethical impulse arising from within a person and that person's ethical sensibility. Ethical rules and guidelines cannot make an individual an ethical person; as Dr. Philip Lewin argues in his guest editorial in the final chapter of this book, ethical behavior must emanate from the very fibers of your being. Although you will be faced with many ethical choices in the course of your work as a legal professional, remember that being ethical is not a choice: it is a way of being. From this way of being, you will then be able to make ethical choices, although, as we have already warned you, it is sometimes very difficult to determine which choice is correct.

In the *Ruark* case, the Colorado appellate court found that a legal assistant might be liable for violating a prisoner's constitutional rights by denying him access to the law library and legal materials.

Theodore RUARK, Plaintiff-Appellant,
v.
Henry SOLANO and Colorado
928 F.2d 947 (Colo. Ct. App. 1991)

Plaintiff Theodore Ruark appeals the district court's dismissal of his pro se complaint under 42 U.S.C. [§] 1983. Plaintiff complains that he was confined as a prisoner in the Diagnostic Unit of the Colorado Department of Corrections (CDOC) in violation of the due process clause of the fourteenth amendment. He further complains about various aspects of the conditions of his confinement, including thirteenth amendment and equal protection violations. Plaintiff also alleges he was totally denied access to a law library or alternative legal resources for his entire month of confinement in the Diagnostic Unit. He sues Henry Solano, who was director of the CDOC during the relevant period, and Annette Porter, a CDOC legal assistant, for damages of $100,000 each.

Plaintiff's complaint was referred to a magistrate. The magistrate concluded: (1) the conditions of plaintiff's confinement did not rise to the level of constitutional violations; (2) because plaintiff filed a complaint, he must have had some knowledge of the law and suffered no prejudice from lack of access to legal resources; and (3) defendant Solano was not properly named as a defendant. The magistrate therefore recommended dismissal of the complaint. The district court adopted the magistrate's findings and dismissed the complaint. We affirm in part and reverse in part. . . .

[The court then explained why the plaintiff's § 1983 claim and arguments alleging violations of the Eighth, Thirteenth, and Fourteenth amendments did not state a cause of action.]

However, plaintiff's claim of denial of access to legal materials was improperly dismissed. The rule governing prisoners' access to courts was stated by the Supreme Court in *Bounds v. Smith,* 430 U.S. 817, 827, 97 S. Ct. 1491, 1497, 52 L. Ed. 2d 72 (1977): "We hold . . . that the fundamental constitutional right of access to the courts requires prison authorities to assist inmates in the preparation and filing of meaningful legal papers by providing prisoners with adequate law libraries or adequate assistance from persons trained in the law."

Unlike the magistrate and district court, we do not find the plaintiff's allegations insufficient under this standard. The magistrate concluded that "[e]xcept in the most general terms, plaintiff does not allege why he needs to access a law library, nor has he alleged that he has suffered any harm from not being able to use one." In support of this conclusion, the magistrate cited *Love v. Summit County,* 776 F.2d 908, 915 (10th Cir. 1985), *cert. denied,* 479 U.S. 814, 107 S. Ct. 66, 93 L. Ed. 2d 25 (1986) and *Harrell v. Keohane,* 621 F.2d 1059, 1061 (10th Cir. 1980) for the rule that in the absence of allegations of injurious consequences, [a] plaintiff presents no actionable claim.

These two cases are distinguishable from the instant case. In both the cited cases, the court held that plaintiffs show no prejudice from lack of access to law libraries when they have adequate access to alternative legal resources. Here, there is no showing of access to alternative legal resources. Plaintiff complains he was totally denied access to any legal resources in the Diagnostic Unit. A prisoner's constitutional right to access to legal resources is not conditioned on a showing of need.

Even reading plaintiff's complaint liberally, however, we find no allegations to support a claim against defendant Solano. Plaintiff has not alleged defendant Solano was personally responsible for the denial of access to legal resources. Moreover, "there is no concept of strict supervisor liability under section 1983." Plaintiff's vague and wholly unsupported allegations of a conspiracy between defendants Solano and Porter are inadequate to implicate Solano individually in a deprivation of plaintiff's constitutional rights in violation of section 1983. Nor is Solano a proper defendant in his official capacity. As a representative of the state, Solano is not a "person" within the meaning of section 1983. The complaint against defendant Solano was properly dismissed.

Plaintiff's allegations of denial of access to legal resources can be construed to state a claim against defendant Porter, however. Plaintiff complains his requests for access to resources went unanswered by Porter. Although she is not a proper party in her official capacity, plaintiff's allegations fairly can be read to complain of Porter's violation of his fourteenth amendment rights while acting under color of state law. The district court's dismissal of Count I of the section 1983 claim regarding access to legal resources against defendant Porter was inappropriate at this stage of the proceedings. We therefore AFFIRM the district court's dismissal of the complaint against defendant Solano and REVERSE as to Count I against defendant Porter. The mandate shall issue forthwith.

CASE QUESTIONS

1. How did Porter deny Ruark his constitutional rights?
2. What are the possible ramifications of Porter's actions?

1.6 ATTORNEY MALPRACTICE

Perhaps the greatest external motivation for an attorney to behave ethically and responsibly is the threat of legal malpractice. *Malpractice* is the civil action clients may bring against their attorneys for not properly handling a legal matter. Successful malpractice actions define the circumstances and behaviors where lawyers have not fulfilled their professional responsibilities.

Legal malpractice actions arise when clients believe that the attorney representing them did not handle the case or situation appropriately or competently. For example, if an attorney failed to file a lawsuit prior to the running of the statute of limitations, this would constitute legal malpractice. Also, if a real estate attorney failed to designate in a title opinion that a particular lien existed against the property in question, malpractice would again have occurred. Malpractice acts as a kind of quality control for lawyer behavior and can be characterized as a breach of contract or a tortious breach of duty of care.

Generally, four elements must be proven to establish a claim of legal malpractice. These elements are:

1.   Proof of a lawyer-client relationship
2.   Acts that show breach of contract or negligence
3.   Causation
4.   Ability to succeed on the merits but for the lawyer's conduct.

Proof of the attorney-client relationship is especially important in situations where a potential client discusses a case with an attorney and there is no clear evidence that the attorney accepted the case. This problem can be avoided by making it a practice to confirm or deny representation in a letter. Further, if the purpose of the letter is to decline representation, the letter should tell the client to contact another lawyer and identify any potential perils, such as failing to file within the statute of limitations or failing to answer a complaint.

Malpractice can exist in contract law or in tort law; the plaintiff must show that the attorney breached contractual obligations to the client and/or that the attorney's conduct fell below the standard of care required of the attorney. An attorney is generally held to the standard of care exercised by other professionals in the area.

The client must also show causation, which demands proof that the client's injuries were caused by the actions of the attorney. For example, a malpractice action would probably lie for the client whose attorney failed to timely file responses to discovery, if this failure caused the client's action to be dismissed. An action would not lie if the client retained the attorney after the answer to the complaint was due and the client was found in default for failure to timely respond. In the first example, the attorney's action was the cause of the dismissal; in the second, the client's action was the cause. A cause of action for malpractice would also not necessarily lie if a particular litigation strategy turned out to be ineffective. A chosen strategy might not work out, but that does not automatically mean that the lawyer committed malpractice, because a lawyer can promise only reasonable efforts, not a guaranteed result, especially in litigation.

Finally, the plaintiff client must prove that the lawyer's conduct was the reason the claim was not successful on the merits. Thus, if the claim was for a breach of contract and the evidence showed overwhelmingly that the plaintiff client breached the terms of the contract, it is unlikely that a legal malpractice suit against the attorney would be successful. This is known as proving the "case within a case"; in other words, in a malpractice action, the client must show that he or she would have been successful in his or her original suit. Clients cannot win on malpractice if they cannot show that they would have been successful in the original action.

When these elements are proven according to the civil standard of preponderance of the evidence, then the attorney will be liable for malpractice. The attorney will not have lived up to the professional duty to the client; his or her acts or omissions fell below the standard of care to which attorneys are held, and the attorney will have committed malpractice.

In addition to direct liability for malpractice, attorneys may also be vicariously liable for the acts or omissions of their employees, including legal assistants, investigators, or secretaries. They are thus responsible for the ethical conduct of persons who assist them in practicing law. This requirement is hinted at in the Model Code and fully developed in the newer Model Rules. Rule 5.3 of the Model Rules makes attorneys responsible for the ethical conduct of their assistants; the comment to the rule says that the attorney should give assistants "appropriate instruction and supervision concerning the ethical aspects of their employment." If an assistant does commit an ethical breach, such as revealing confidential information, it is the lawyer who may be liable, on the basis that the training or supervision of the assistant was negligent. Therefore, attorneys who use paralegals must delegate work properly, respecting the restrictions on the unauthorized practice of law; supervise the work of assistants and law clerks; review the work of assistants adequately; and assure that others know the status of nonlawyer individuals working on the case. After all, the attorney carries ultimate responsibility for the work that goes out under his or her name.

 ## THE CASE OF MIKE'S LEGAL JABS

Distraught at having been found guilty of rape when he insisted that he had consensual sex with Desiree Washington, Mike Tyson wonders if he can win a malpractice action against the legal team that defended him. Mike hires you to advise him as to whether any of the following actions by the defense team might constitute malpractice:

1. Having Tyson testify

2. Losing a motion to call an eyewitness, who contradicted Washington's testimony by saying that she saw Tyson and Washington kissing before going to his room, because the judge considered the witness's testimony irrelevant

3. Not calling another celebrity as a witness to testify that, on the circuit, it is well known that if you go back to the single male superstar's room after midnight, you are going to have sex

4. Not filing an appeal on the eyewitness exclusion prior to the appeals deadline because the computerized tickler system malfunctioned.

Do any of these situations implicate malpractice liability?

Most legal assistants and paralegals are directly supervised by an attorney who is ultimately responsible for their ethical violations. However, a growing trend, which is strongest in California, involves paralegals working without direct attorney supervision. These paralegals are coming to be known as *legal technicians,* and it may be that their situation is appropriate for regulation and licensure, because they are not supervised by attorneys. California has, thus far, rejected the licensing of legal technicians, but some other states, such as Oregon and Minnesota, have developed formalized licensing statutes in their legislatures. This idea also implicates the unauthorized practice of law and is discussed further in chapter 5.

The *Goldberg* case demonstrates how an attorney may be held liable for his employees' negligence, on the theory that it is the attorney's duty to supervise their work.

ATTORNEY GRIEVANCE COMMISSION OF MARYLAND
v.
Ronald S. GOLDBERG

Misc. (Subtitle BV) No. 11
441 A.2d 338 (Md. 1982)
Court of Appeals of Maryland
Feb. 23, 1982.

SMITH, Judge.

Bar Counsel, acting pursuant to the provisions of Maryland Rule BV9, filed a petition with us on behalf of the Attorney Grievance Commission seeking disciplinary action against Ronald S. Goldberg, a member of the Maryland bar. The petition alleged sixteen instances of professional misconduct which essentially involved neglect. Pursuant to Rule BV9 b, we referred the matter for hearing to a judge of the Circuit Court for Montgomery Court. He made the following findings of fact after hearings that consumed three days:

"There is little, if any, dispute by the Respondent, Ronald S. Goldberg, that in each of the sixteen incidences he was retained as an attorney to perform legal services on behalf of a client. This Court will not go through each complaint separately because the real issue is not what occurred but what caused the failure of representation with respect to each of the complaints.

"The Respondent, Ronald S. Goldberg, has been in the practice of law since his admission to the Bar of this Court on October 20, 1961. At the time that he entered into an attorney-client relationship with the subjects of these complaints, Mr. Goldberg was operating a legal clinic. Sometime in 1978, upon the recommendation of one of his clients, he hired Sandra H. Ofterdinger . . . as a secretary. Subsequent to her hiring, Mrs. Ofterdinger was given increasing responsibilities, resulting in her position in the nature of an office manager. She had the responsibility to see that the pleadings were prepared from Mr. Goldberg's dictation, the cases properly filed, dates appropriately calendared, the keeping of the financial books and records, and authority to sign checks for disbursements from the office account and client's trust account.

"There came a time while in the employment of Mr. Goldberg that Mrs. Ofterdinger failed to prepare the necessary pleadings, documents or papers required to be done. As she got increasingly behind she would remove the files and not calendar them, preventing the lack of progress on those files from coming to the attention of Mr. Goldberg. In order to cover her inactivity on these files, Mrs. Ofterdinger then started going through all of the office mail, removing any letters that had reference to the work that had not been done. She also removed any phone messages and intercepted calls to Mr. Goldberg. She made excuses or misrepresentations as to why the work had not been done in some instances and falsely represented that the work had been done in others. Checks received from clients were not deposited in the appropriate account, and from the exhibits it would appear that unauthorized checks were drawn by Mrs. Ofterdinger for improper purposes. She further intercepted the letters from the Attorney Grievance Commission.

"From testimony presented, there is no evidence that Respondent, Ronald S. Goldberg, was aware of any of the activities of Mrs. Ofterdinger until the time of her termination. None of the misrepresentations to clients were authorized by Mr. Goldberg. As soon as he became actually aware of what had

occurred, Mr. Goldberg attempted to locate all of the removed or hidden files, contact the clients, and rectify the situation where possible. One might question whether an attorney can give effective representation to all of his clients with the volume that Mr. Goldberg has undertaken. There is, however, no indication that volume or improper delegation was a contributing factor in any of the incidents that are the subject of this complaint.

"For the aforegoing reasons, this Court finds that there was no knowing violation of the Code of Professional Responsibility by Respondent, Ronald S. Goldberg."

Testimony adduced before Judge Cave included the fact that there were instances in which deeds were not recorded and pleadings were not timely filed; that disbursement was not promptly made on sums collected for the account of clients; that the gross income of Goldberg was in excess of $12,000 per month from legal fees; that his escrow account showed negative balances from time to time; that Goldberg never examined monthly bank statements; that at the time Mrs. Ofterdinger came to work for Goldberg she was on probation in the District of Columbia as a result of embezzling funds from a title company there; that in an earlier incident she had misappropriated funds from yet another title company, which did not bring criminal charges because of its desire to avoid publicity; that when Goldberg ultimately terminated the services of Mrs. Ofterdinger as a result of his investigations, following a fellow employee's complaints to him, undeposited checks totalling more than $11,000.00 were located; and that among the items found in that investigation were unopened communications from the Attorney Grievance Commission of Maryland.

Given this testimony, we make one further observation before proceeding with our review of the Commission's petition which is now before us. When we note the prior background of Mrs. Ofterdinger, we do not mean to imply that she should not necessarily have been hired by Goldberg. We do suggest, however, that had Goldberg been aware of her background he might have supervised her duties in a different manner.

Bar Counsel filed exceptions to the findings of fact and conclusions of law of the trial judge. He contended relative to certain of the complaints that there was clear and convincing evidence to support a conclusion that Goldberg had violated Disciplinary Rules 6-101(A)(3), 7-101(A)(1), (2), and (3), and 9-102(B)(3), and (4) . . . .

At the very least there was clear and convincing evidence to support a conclusion that Goldberg violated DR 8-101(A)(3) relative to neglect of a legal matter entrusted to him. The trial judge was very clearly in error in not finding a violation of that disciplinary rule. An attorney may not escape responsibility to his clients by blithely saying that any shortcomings are solely the fault of his employee. He has a duty to supervise the conduct of his office. A very telling aspect here is that although at one time the escrow account showed an overdraft of nearly $40,000.00 (possibly brought about by Mrs. Ofterdinger's apparent tardiness in depositing a check), Goldberg was unaware of this because he never at any time took the simple precaution of running his eye over the bank statements at the end of the month . . . .

We are advised there have been no previous complaints against Goldberg. We are further advised that Goldberg has overhauled his office and, among other things, has brought in his wife to oversee operations in an effort to avoid any recurrence of incidents similar to those now before the Court. Additionally, we are now advised that he otherwise has been regarded as a competent attorney.

We understand the difficulties of a busy solo practitioner, which is what Goldberg was during most of this time. We also understand that one cannot watch every single thing which takes place in his office. It would appear, however, that Goldberg just did not adequately supervise his employee. He is fortunate, under the circumstances, that there appears to have been no actual loss to his clients by virtue of the negative balance in his escrow account.

Nonetheless, the public must be protected. Lawyers must be impressed with the fact that at all times they have a responsibility to their clients. This responsibility necessarily includes adequate supervision of their employees.

Goldberg asserts that no sanctions should be imposed because the problem here stemmed from the activities of his employee. Bar Counsel on the other hand suggests a reprimand. We are of the view that we cannot discharge our responsibility to protect the public by merely giving a reprimand.

We concluded, therefore, that the proper sanction to be imposed here, taking into account the nature and number of incidents here involved and Goldberg's prior unblemished record, is a suspension of thirty days. Accordingly, Ronald S. Goldberg shall stand suspended from the practice of law in this State for the period of thirty days accounting from thirty days after the filing of this opinion. He shall stand suspended beyond that date unless and until all costs incurred in connection with this proceeding are paid in full.

IT IS SO ORDERED, RESPONDENT SHALL PAY ALL COSTS AS TAXES BY THE CLERK OF THIS COURT, INCLUDING THE COSTS OF TRANSCRIPTS, PURSUANT TO MARYLAND RULE BV15c FOR WHICH SUM JUDGMENT IS ENTERED IN FAVOR OF THE ATTORNEY GRIEVANCE COMMISSION AGAINST RONALD S. GOLDBERG.

DAVIDSON, J., would have reprimanded.

1.7 PARALEGAL MALPRACTICE

The *Goldberg* case follows the general rule that, as an agent of the attorney, the legal assistant will not have individual liability for negligence and that the attorney will be vicariously liable for the negligence of his or her employees. Although paralegals are usually not named parties in a malpractice suit, there always exists the potential for paralegal liability. Just as nurses are becoming more and more the subject of medical malpractice suits, so will legal assistants see an increase in suits filed against them. This could be especially harmful if the firm in which the legal assistant is employed either does not carry legal malpractice insurance or does not carry insurance covering paralegals. Practically, even though an attorney is ultimately responsible for the work of a paralegal, if the paralegal is independently wealthy or even has a home, a lawyer named in a malpractice suit could move to have the paralegal joined as a party. The rationale for such actions would be that the legal assistant failed to discharge his or her duties properly. For example, many paralegals have the job of calendar control in a firm. If the suit resulted from nonappearance or default because of calendaring error, and most attorneys in the area relied on legal assistants to advise them of such dates, a jury may very well find that the lawyer was not liable for negligence, but that the paralegal was. Certainly this is an evolving area of the law, but as paralegals become more recognized and accepted as professionals, it is not unlikely that such an action might occur.

Even outside the realm of classical legal malpractice actions, paralegals are subject to suit because of their unique duties. For example, many legal assistants are notaries public. This official duty subjects legal assistants to potential civil and criminal liability. By not fulfilling the obligations of witnessing signatures, paralegals can subject themselves to possible civil suit. In the case of *Johnson v. State,* 238 N.E.2d 651 (Ind. 1968), the court affirmed the criminal conviction of a notary public for falsely attesting an affidavit. Besides being responsible for having affidavits and other legal documents properly signed and notarized, paralegals often are responsible for contacting witnesses and doing the initial investigative work on a case. Suggesting details to a potential witness or misconstruing facts significant to a particular case could also subject a paralegal to civil as well as criminal liability. For example, if a paralegal is interviewing a witness to an automobile accident and suggests to the witness that the witness's statement could sound better for the client if the witness said the light was red, the paralegal could face criminal charges for obstructing justice or tampering with evidence. Also, by engaging in conduct that could constitute practicing law without a license, legal assistants subject themselves to civil as well as criminal suit.

For a paralegal, being accused or convicted of malpractice, although unusual, is the harshest disciplinary action that might occur. If you are not sure whether your conduct is proper, ask your supervising attorney or a respected colleague in the profession for advice and assistance. It is always better to get an objective viewpoint when you are confronted with a complex situation that might implicate something as serious as malpractice issues.

In the *Torres* case, the Illinois Appellate Court found that a nonlawyer may be liable to a plaintiff for damages arising out of the unauthorized practice of law.

Teodoro TORRES, Mariano de Jesus Rivera, Leyda Rivera, Plaintiffs-Appellants,

v.

Lorenzo FIOL, Jr., Defendant-Appellee

No. 81-2099
Appellate Court of Illinois,
First District, Fifth Division.
Oct. 29, 1982.
110 Ill. App. 3d 9, 441 N.E.2d 1301, 85 Ill. Dec. 706 (1982)

LORENZ, Justice:

Plaintiffs appeal from a dismissal of that portion of their amended complaint seeking damages against defendant, Lorenzo Fiol, Jr., a non-attorney, for his alleged practice of law involving a business transaction. On appeal plaintiffs contend that the trial court erred in concluding that in this State an action for compensatory damages is not cognizable for the negligent practice of law by a non-attorney.

The 2-count amended complaint recited that plaintiffs owned a certain parcel of real estate and managed a grocery and liquor store situated thereon. In 1979 they agreed to lease the store to Octavio Serrano, who assumed the contractual obligations to the mortgage holder. Plaintiffs alleged that they contacted defendant, who held himself out to the public for the purpose of rendering legal services, to prepare the necessary documents for the transaction. Plaintiffs claimed that defendant rendered a legal opinion and advice on the transaction and also prepared the documents for the transaction, although they averred he performed the latter in an improper and careless manner.

The parties then filed memorandums of law following defendant's motion to dismiss the complaint. The trial court held that no private cause of action for damages for the unauthorized practice of law is recognized in Illinois.

In *Rathke* [a previous case], a real estate buyer sought damages against several realtors for their unauthorized practice of law when one or more allegedly inserted a provision into a printed sales contract. The appellate court opinion recited that plaintiff had not alleged that defendants were negligent or that they had represented themselves as attorneys. Rather, plaintiff's claim was predicated upon section 1 of "An act to revise the law in relation to attorneys and counselors" dealing with the unauthorized practice of law, and plaintiff apparently asserted that a mere violation of this statute gave rise to a cause of action for damages. The court held that this statute did not permit a claim for damages.

The statute in question provides a contempt sanction against a person for the unauthorized practice of law. In addition, the statute recites:

> "The provisions of this Act *shall be in addition to other remedies permitted by law* and shall not be construed to deprive courts of this State of their inherent right to punish for contempt or to restrain the unauthorized practice of law." Ill. Rev. Stat. 1979, ch. 13, par. 1 (emphasis added).

The underscored language of the statute plainly evidences a legislative intent not to circumscribe other theories of recovery against a non-attorney who is retained to perform legal duties and who then mishandles the matter. We therefore conclude that the statute and *Rathke,* which interpreted that provision, do not preclude this action.

While not extensive, there appear several reported decisions allowing for the recovery against a non-attorney for the unauthorized and negligent practice of law. In *Biakanja v. Irving* (1958), 49 Cal.2d 647, 320 P.2d 16, a non-attorney was charged with improperly preparing a will. The court commented that "such conduct should be discouraged and not protected by immunity from civil liability, as would be the case if plaintiff, the only person who suffered a loss, were denied a right of action." (320 P.2d 16, 19.) Our supreme court in *Pelham v. Griesheimer,* 92 Ill.2d 13, 64 Ill. Dec. 544, 440 N.E.2d 96 (1982) rejected *Biakanja* insofar as it allowed a third party to seek recovery against an attorney for alleged malpractice. However, *Pelham* is not related to the issue presented in this case.

Similar to the *Biakanja* case is *Latson v. Eaton* (Okl.1959), 341 P.2d 247, where a non-attorney was held liable for the preparation of legal documents. Further, in *Mattieligh v. Poe* (1960), 57 Wash.2d 203, 356 P.2d 328, the court remarked that the undertaking involving the practice of law by a real estate broker, who was not an attorney, may render him liable if the work is negligently performed.

Because of the above authorities and the lack of contrary precedent in this State, we conclude that plaintiffs are not prevented from proceeding against defendant upon a negligence theory for his alleged improper activity. The judgement of the circuit court is reversed, and the cause is remanded.

Reversed and remanded.

SULLIVAN, P.J., and MEJDA, J., concur.

1.8 ETHICAL QUESTIONS—NOT JUST ONCE IN A BLUE MOON

Now that we have an understanding of ethics and its importance to the legal profession, we need to examine how it arises in the actual context of practicing law. With all of the ethereal definitions and philosophical discussions, it is easy to convince yourself that ethical problems arise only very infrequently. However, in the real world ethical questions arise on an almost daily basis. Just as a client will not come into the office and say, "I have a breach of fiduciary duty problem," the client will not come into the office and say, "I have a legal problem that might present a conflict of interest issue for you." It is up to you to gain an understanding of the ethical dimensions of your work and to sensitize yourself to problems and issues that cause ethical considerations to arise. Understanding the ethical dimension of your work is one of the key aspects of being a successful legal professional.

Situations presenting ethical issues and dilemmas arise every single day in legal work. By thinking about the problems they present, you can begin to realize how ethical issues arise and what questions you must ask yourself before you proceed. Your study of ethics in this book, therefore, will focus not merely on the rules and concepts but also, and perhaps more significantly, on the application of those ideas in cases and fact situations. Because ethics is not a pure science, you should not expect to merely learn the "answers," for, as you will discover, the answers are often elusive and, in the long run, are less important than gaining sensitivity to the ethical dimensions of the situations you are faced with and becoming able to analyze the situation from the ethical context. In order for you to gain this sensitivity and analytical ability, the text is interspersed with cases and problems to cause you to think about and grapple with the ethical issues presented. In some cases, there is an "answer," in that the courts have already confronted a certain issue; other times, there really is no right answer, because the situation presented is truly a difficult one, with no clear answer. Although you might find this elusiveness frustrating at times, it is also the reason that ethics is such an interesting and challenging area, lending itself to robust disagreements about what a person should do.

This chapter has been concerned with introducing you to the idea of ethics as it affects the legal profession and the conduct of attorneys and legal assistants. In a sense, ethical rules and regulations provide the "road map" to help a person become a good lawyer or a good legal assistant. In her guest editorial, Attorney Emily Brantley shares a tragic life experience that helped shape her opinion as to what it takes to be an ethical professional in the legal system.

WHAT IT MEANS TO BE A GOOD LAWYER

By Emily Brantley

I quickly decided, in my early years of life, exactly what I wanted to do when I became an adult. While my playmates spoke of being movie stars, astronauts, or famous athletes, I talked about being a good lawyer. I thought Mr. Griffin was the most intelligent and honest man I had ever known, besides my dad. Because my father suffered from poor health at an early age, I tried not to disturb him with my problems. Instead, I sought solutions from Mr. Griffin. I thought he had all the answers to life's secrets. He always knew the right things to say and had a way of making me feel better.

Lawyers ranked high on my childhood list of heroes. I think I kept that notion in place until February 1989, the spring semester of my second year in law school. It was during this particular period of my life that my entire world was introduced to me—one not as pretty and kind as my old one. Included in this ugliness was my new perception of lawyers.

I was not able to go directly into law school after college graduation. I was employed part-time during my four years of college, but my earnings did not cover all my costs. Scholarships helped, but I was also forced to obtain several loans. My substantial debt forced a temporary postponement of law school.

When I began my first year at Georgia State College of Law, I maintained a full-time job in the corporate security and inventory control department of a large department store. From my first day in class, I knew law was my calling. I would be a good lawyer: trusted, respected, and loved. My parents would be proud of me, and more importantly, I would be proud of myself.

Nothing could have made this period of my life sweeter. I was happily married, and my husband and I learned that we were going to have a baby. I remember daydreaming about how my child would grow up to be proud of its mother because she was an achiever, a good person, and a lawyer. Then February 28, 1989, arrived. This day should have been the happiest day of my life, for this was the day my baby was due. Instead, this day quickly became not only the worst day of my life, but the beginning of a long nightmare.

I awoke around midnight to discover that our baby was on its way. I excitedly called my doctor and began gathering my things for the hospital. Then something went terribly wrong. I began to hemorrhage severely. We immediately jumped into the car and rushed to the hospital.

Eleven minutes after I entered the hospital, and forty-one minutes after I began to bleed, I gave birth to our daughter. She was not breathing and had no heartbeat. The doctors worked with her, pumping oxygen into her small body and doing cardiopulmonary resuscitation. After twenty-two minutes, the doctors pronounced her dead, called the chaplain, and went out to break the news to my husband. While my husband was hearing the devastating news, our baby gasped for breath and began to breathe. She was rushed to the emergency unit of the neonatology section, where she remained for the following three months. We named her Alexandria, Allie for short.

Allie's first few weeks of life were not pleasant, for she had numerous problems, including heart failure and kidney failure, and she could breathe only with the aid of a ventilator. But she beat most of the odds and was able to function without the help of any machines by the third week of her life. Still, her prognosis was not bright; my husband and I were told that Allie would never know her parents and would never see, hear, cry, suck a bottle, or eat. The portion of her brain that controls these bodily functions was completely destroyed because she had been deprived of oxygen for such a long period of time. Allie would remain in a comatose state all of her life.

The day Allie was released from the hospital, she was admitted to the hospital unit of Georgia Retardation Center in Dunwoody, Georgia. It was the collective opinion of those who knew and cared for Allie that she would not live to see her first birthday. Miraculously, Allie learned to suck a bottle and eat baby food like any other healthy baby. Her body movements are very limited, but she receives physical therapy every day and is steadily improving. She can hear and has developed a great love for music. She can also cry and recently has begun to make baby sounds. There have been no signs that Allie can see, but we never give up hope and continue our prayers.

Allie, with her many accomplishments, is still severely handicapped and can never live with us. She has her own special home, however, where many wonderful people love her, and where we visit daily.

Even now, two years after Allie's birth, I cannot adequately describe the deep pain and the struggle this experience has been for me. Initially, it took all my strength to make it through each day. My husband and I never looked at tomorrow, for it was too painful. It was at this time, when I was at my lowest and had to remind myself each day of reasons to continue living, that I received nine telephone calls that forever changed my opinion of lawyers and challenged me to form the basis of what I now believe makes a good lawyer.

The first telephone call came from a lawyer who wanted to discuss representing me in a malpractice action against my gynecologist and the hospital. I do not remember anything I said because I was horrified. When I finally hung up the telephone, I was physically ill. Although I had a reasonable chance of prevailing in a medical malpractice suit, I could hardly believe a lawyer would use my pain to his advantage. From the voice on the other end of the telephone line, I detected no sympathy or understanding of my pain; I heard only sounds of greed.

Eight more calls followed that first call. I was surprised at how quickly the legal community learned of my misfortune, and I am still horrified that nine lawyers approached me unsolicited. My shock, disappointment, and anger that these lawyers could be so insensitive and unprofessional are engraved in my memory. The same thought rolled through my head as I politely spoke with each of them: "They do not care what happened to my family. They called because they want to gain from my misfortune." I tried to justify those nine telephone calls, but I could not formulate a reason that would explain the behavior of these lawyers.

My family and friends encouraged me to return to school right away, believing this would force me not to think about Allie so much. I knew that I could not drop

any further behind in my classes, with exams just a few weeks away. The thought of returning to law school sickened me. I no longer wanted to be a lawyer. I had finally learned what being a lawyer was all about. I was angry at myself for being so wrong about my career choice, and I felt I had lived an ostrich life with my head in the sand.

Although I did return to school, I still have many unanswered questions about Allie and about being a lawyer. I have spent endless days asking why this had to happen. Recently, I realized that I probably will never know why Allie's plight was put upon us and her. But after a long search for truth and understanding, I have crystallized my concept of a good lawyer into four main attributes that represent my current stand.

The first attribute is communication. For a relationship to work smoothly and benefit both parties, open, continuous, and honest communication must exist. It cannot be over-stressed in the lawyer-client relationship. A good lawyer must establish the ground rules for the legal arena, since she is the guardian of the rules. She must fully explain every rule and its purpose. Understanding the rules makes the lawyer-client relationship easier for the client and the lawyer. A client should always know exactly where he stands in his legal action, with each step of the procedure carefully explained by the lawyer. This gives the client a sense of control and reminds the lawyer who has that control. The suit belongs to the client; the lawyer is the instrument who puts life into this action. The decisions on how, when, how long, and for how much should be made by the client.

The second attribute of a good lawyer is awareness. A good lawyer does not wear tinted glasses or blinders to narrow her view. She looks at the total picture and is aware of all the surrounding circumstances in selecting the most appropriate representation for her client. Too often, otherwise intelligent, capable lawyers give inadequate advice to their clients because they omit one important element: old-fashioned common sense. Common sense and life experience should not be left outside the office door when a lawyer speaks to a client.

Common sense is the foundation upon which our legal system was built. We bring a jury, twelve representatives of life, into our technical world and ask them to interject common sense gained from life's experiences. Some lawyers assume a client expects them to use legal-sounding words or to expound complex legal theories, but a client really needs someone who can relate his legal problems to common, everyday experiences.

Again and again in law school, professors proclaim that in the world of law, one must think with one's head and not with one's heart. Certainly, following one's heart can be dangerous if it is the solo path, but a good lawyer should combine awareness of both her heart and her mind.

The third attribute is respect—for the goal of the client. The client must always participate in defining the goal, while the lawyer defines the means to achieve the goal. This is the area that disappointed me most in my experience with lawyers. Those with whom I spoke appeared more interested in discussing damages than in learning my goals. They were disrespectful of my needs, and I pictured conversations with cash registers rather than lawyers.

Had I chosen to pursue a malpractice suit, my goal would not have been money. When I tried to explain this, the lawyers with whom I spoke seemed not to care; they made no effort to determine my goal. This personal experience led me to feel that respect for a client's goal is a trait that must be found in every good lawyer.

The last attribute is empathy. Empathy requires a lawyer to identify with the various reasons for the client's suit. Some clients want disputes settled, others want revenge, and some just want to make life a little better. Many clients would prefer to take home a smaller settlement than to go through a long trial. Many people do not want confrontation. A good lawyer must be able to identify what is important to her client and to act accordingly. A client and a lawyer may have different concepts of winning. Thus, a lawyer who is not empathetic to the needs of her client may win a substantial award and still have a dissatisfied client. When a client is dissatisfied with the judgment or the results of his legal service, the lawyer has a shallow victory.

These four attributes—communication, awareness, respect, and empathy—are not intended to represent all the elements of a good lawyer, for there are many others. These attributes simply form a foundation from which I can build. Through my attempts to understand the events that led to my personal pain, I have realized something very important to me. I watch my beautiful little girl struggle to do the things that most of us take for granted; she becomes tired after eating because it take so much effort. I want to see something good arise from Allie's misfortune and to know that her suffering in not in vain.

I am realizing that my search is over, for the good I seek is not something that can be found, but a treasure that must be created. I can make that good happen by living a richer life, by appreciating all that life has to offer, and by being a good lawyer.

■ Emily Brantley is an attorney with Long, Weinberg, Ansley & Wheeler in Atlanta, Georgia. This essay was reprinted with permission from the *Georgia State University Law Review.*

1.9 CONCLUSION

This chapter has introduced you to legal ethics by explaining the connection between ethics and legal practice and by showing how ethical considerations work to regulate the legal profession. This chapter should have given you an understanding of the range and variety of situations in which ethical questions arise, and we hope it has motivated you to follow the highest ethical principles as you define your own professional identity as a paralegal.

REVIEW QUESTIONS

1. Why does the law have rules and guidelines concerning ethical conduct?
2. What are the sources of ethical rules for lawyers and paralegals?
3. What types of disciplinary measures can be taken against lawyers and legal assistants who violate ethical rules?
4. Why is it important for those working in the legal profession to understand and abide by ethical guidelines?

NOTES

[1] This book uses the terms *paralegal* and *legal assistant* interchangeably, because the terms are used interchangeably by legal professionals practicing law.

Chapter 2 Feature: Not Just Legal Ethics

LAW, LITERATURE, AND ETHICS

From **A Rage in Harlem**
By Chester Himes

A tall, slim colored man with a cop's scowl rushed into the kitchen. He had a pistol in his right hand and a gold-plated badge in his left.

"I'm a United States marshal. I'm shooting the first one who moves."

He looked as if he meant it.

The kitchen had filled with smoke and stunk like black gunpowder. Gas was pouring from the stove. The scorched cardboard tubes that had been cooking in the oven were scattered over the floor.

"It's the law!" Imabelle screamed.

"I heard him!" Jackson yelled.

"Let's beat it!" Jodie shouted.

He tripped the marshal into the table and made for the door. Hank got there before him and Jodie went out on Jodie's back. The marshal sprawled across the table top.

"Run, Daddy!" Imabelle said.

"Don't wait for me," Jackson replied.

He was on hands and knees, trying as hard as he could to get to his feet. But Imabelle was running so hard she stumbled over him and knocked him down again as she made for the door.

Before the marshal could straighten up all three of them had escaped.

"Don't you move!" he shouted at Jackson.

"I ain't moving, Marshal."

When the marshal finally got his feet underneath him he yanked Jackson erect and snapped a pair of handcuffs about his wrists.

"Trying to make a fool out of me! You'll get ten years for this."

Jackson turned a battleship gray.

"I ain't done nothing, Marshal. I swear to God."

Jackson had attended a Negro college in the South, but whenever he was excited or scared he began talking in his native dialect.

"Sit down and shut up," the marshal ordered.

He shut off the gas and began picking up the cardboard tubes for evidence. He opened one, took out a brand-new hundred-dollar bill and held it up toward the light.

"Raised from a ten. The markings are still on it."

Jackson had started to sit down but he stopped suddenly and began to plead.

"It wasn't me what done that, Marshal. I swear to God. It was them two fellows who got away. All I done was come into the kitchen to get a drink of water."

"Don't lie to me, Jackson. I know you. I've got the goods on you, man. I've been watching you three counterfeiters for days."

Tears welled up in Jackson's eyes, he was so scared.

"Listen, Marshal, I swear to God I didn't have nothing to do with that. I don't even know how to do it. The little man called Hank who got away is the counterfeiter. He's the only one who's got the paper."

"Don't worry about them, Jackson. I'll get them too. But I've already got you, and I'm taking you down to the Federal Building. So I'm warning you, anything you say to me will be used against you in court."

Jackson slid from the chair and got down on his knees.

"Leave me go just this once, Marshal." The tears began streaming down his face. "Just this once, Marshal. I've never been arrested before. I'm a church man, I ain't dishonest. I confess, I put up the money for Hank to raise, but it was him who was breaking the law, not me. I ain't done nothing wouldn't nobody do if they had a chance to make a pile of money."

"Get up, Jackson, and take your punishment like a man," the marshal said. "You're just as guilty as the others. If you hadn't put up the tens, Hank couldn't have changed them into hundreds."

Jackson saw himself serving ten years in prison. Ten years away from Imabelle. Jackson had only had Imabelle for eleven months, but he couldn't live without her. He was going to marry her as soon as she got her divorce from that man down South she was still married to. If he went to prison for ten years, by then she'd have another man and would have forgotten all about him. He'd come out of prison an old man, thirty-eight years old, dried up. No one would give him a job. No woman would want him. He'd be a bum, hungry, skinny, begging on the streets of Harlem, sleeping in doorways, drinking canned heat to keep warm. Mama Jackson hadn't raised a son for that, struggled to send him through the college for Negroes, just to have him become a convict. He just couldn't let the marshal take him in.

He clutched the marshal about the legs.

"Have mercy on a poor sinner, man. I know I did wrong, but I'm not a criminal. I just got talked into it. My woman wanted a new winter coat, we want to get a place of our own, maybe buy a car. I just yielded to temptation. You're a colored man like me, you ought to understand that. Where are we poor colored people goin' to get any money from?"

The marshal yanked Jackson to his feet.

"God damn it, get yourself together, man. Go take a drink of water. You act as if you think I'm Jesus Christ."

Jackson went to the sink and drank a glass of water. He was crying like a baby.

"You could have a little mercy," he said. "Just a little of the milk of human mercy. I've done lost all my money in this deal already. Ain't that punishment enough? Do I have to go to jail too?"

"Jackson, you're not the first man I've arrested for a crime. Suppose I'd let off everybody. Where would I be then? Out of a job. Broke and hungry. Soon I'd be on the other side of the law, a criminal myself."

Jackson looked at the marshal's hard brown face and mean, dirty eyes. He knew there was no mercy in the man. As soon as colored folks got on the side of the law, they lost all Christian charity, he was thinking.

"Marshal, I'll pay you two hundred dollars if you let me off," he offered.

The marshal looked at Jackson's wet face.

"Jackson, I shouldn't do this. But I can see that you're an honest man, just led astray by a woman. And being as you're a colored man like myself, I'm going to let you off this time. You give me the two hundred bucks, and you're a free man."

The only way Jackson could get two hundred dollars this side of the grave was to steal it from his boss. Mr. Clay always kept two or three thousand dollars in his safe. There was nothing Jackson hated worse than having to steal from Mr. Clay. Jackson had never stolen any money in his life. He was an honest man. But there was no other way out of this hole.

"I ain't got it here. I got it at the funeral parlor where I work."

"Well, that being the case, I'll drive you there in my car, Jackson. But you'll have to give me your word of honor you won't try to escape."

"I ain't no criminal," Jackson protested. "I won't try to escape, I swear to God. I'll just go inside and get the money and bring it out to you."

The marshal unlocked Jackson's handcuffs and motioned him ahead. They went down the four flights of stairs and came out on Eighth Avenue, where the apartment house fronted.

The marshal gestured toward a battered black Ford.

"You can see that I'm a poor man myself, Jackson."

"Yes sir, but you ain't as poor as me, because I've not only got nothing but I've got minus nothing."

"Too late to cry now, Jackson."

They climbed into the car, drove south on 134th Street, east to the corner of Lenox Avenue, and parked in front of the *H. Exodus Clay Funeral Parlor.*

Jackson got out and went silently up the red rubber treads of the high stone steps; entered through the curtained glass doors of the old stone house, and peered into the dimly lit chapel where three bodies were on display in the open caskets.

Smitty, the other chauffeur and handyman, was silently embracing a woman on one of the red, velvet-covered benches similar to the ones on which the caskets stood. He hadn't heard Jackson enter.

Jackson tiptoed past them silently and went down the hall to the broom closet. He got a dust mop and cloth and tiptoed back to the office at the front.

At that time of the afternoon, when they didn't have a funeral, Mr. Clay took a nap on the couch in his office. Marcus, the embalmer, was left in charge. But Marcus always slipped out to Small's bar, over on 135th Street and Seventh Avenue.

Silently Jackson opened the door of Mr. Clay's office, tiptoed inside, stood the dust mop against the wall and began dusting the small black safe that sat in the corner beside an old-fashioned roll-top desk. The door of the safe was closed but not locked.

Mr. Clay lay on his side, facing the wall. He looked like a refugee from a museum, in the dim light from the floor lamp that burned continuously in the front window.

He was a small, elderly man with skin like parchment, faded brown eyes, and long gray bushy hair. His standard dress was a tail coat, double-breasted dove-gray vest, striped trousers, wing collar, black Ascot tie adorned with a gray pearl stickpin, and rimless nose-glasses attached to a long black ribbon pinned to his vest.

"That you, Marcus?" he asked suddenly without turning over.

Jackson started. "No sir, it's me, Jackson."

"What are you doing in here, Jackson?"

"I'm just dusting, Mr. Clay," Jackson said, as he eased open the door of the safe.

"I thought you took the afternoon off."

"Yes sir. But I recalled that Mr. Williams' family will be coming tonight to view Mr. Williams' remains, and I knew you'd want everything spic and span when they got here."

"Don't overdo it, Jackson," Mr. Clay said sleepily. "I ain't intending to give you a raise."

Jackson forced himself to laugh.

"Aw, you're just joking, Mr. Clay. Anyway, my woman ain't home. She's gone visiting."

While he was speaking, Jackson opened the inner safe door.

"Thought that was the trouble," Mr. Clay mumbled.

In the money drawer was a stack of twenty-dollar bills, pinned together in bundles of hundreds.

"Ha ha, you're just joking, Mr. Clay," Jackson said as he took out five bundles and stuck them into his side pants-pocket.

He rattled the handle of the dust mop while closing the safe's two doors.

"Lord, you just have to forgive me in this emergency," he said silently, then spoke in a loud voice, "Got to clean the steps now."

Mr. Clay didn't answer.

Jackson tiptoed back to the broom closet, put away the cloth and mop, tiptoed silently back toward the front door. Smitty and the woman were still enjoying life.

Jackson let himself out silently and went down the stairs to the marshal's car. He palmed two of the hundred-dollar bundles and slipped them through the open window to the marshal.

The marshal held them down between his legs while he counted them. Then he nodded and stuck them into his inside coat-pocket.

"Let this be a lesson to you, Jackson," he said. "Crime doesn't pay."

■ Reprinted by permission of Roslyn Targ Literary Agency, Inc. Copyright © 1957, 1985 by Chester Himes.

OUTLINE

CHAPTER OVERVIEW

In this chapter you will learn about ethical issues that arise in the course of work, which are not limited in their relevance or applicability to the legal profession. The legal profession has specific rules and guidelines that define legal ethics. This chapter goes beyond those specific provisions and considers ethical issues that are relevant to all working individuals.

UNETHICAL URSULA IN THE BIG CITY

Unethical Ursula, a paralegal at Bigger & Biggest law firm, has just signed off on Paralegal Paula's computer. Paula had already left for the day and had not authorized this use by Ursula, but Ursula wanted to see Paula's files on the Green Acres case, as her boyfriend was considering a further investment in that property and she wanted to help him with some inside information. As Ursula returns to her desk, she lights a cigarette, carefully blowing the smoke out of the window, as the office is supposed to be a smoke-free environment. After enjoying a few puffs, Ursula throws away her collection of the week's newspapers in her trash, despite her firm's policy of recycling newspapers in the designated bins.

Unethical Ulysses, a senior partner in the firm, comes by Ursula's office. "Have you got those notes?" he asks, and she turns over to him the information she has secretly collected on the firm's attorneys and the accuracy of their billable hours. She then accompanies Ulysses out of the office to their favorite in-town hotel for a night of passion. (Mrs. Ulysses, of course, had been told her husband was out of town on business.) But Unethical Ursula was not going to be taken for a fool—she put her tape recorder on "record," just in case she ever needed it.

2.1 NOT JUST LEGAL ETHICS: AN INTRODUCTION

Because of the depth and complexity of the field of legal ethics, it is tempting to forget that the law exists in the context of society, and that in addition to legal ethics, which concerns problems and situations specific to the legal profession, legal professionals will inevitably be confronted with ethical issues of a more general nature. General ethical considerations and legal ethics exist side by side and are equally applicable to all who work in the legal process. When Clarence Thomas was going through his confirmation hearings, he was not alleged to have violated any legal ethics; he was not questioned about a conflict of interest, misuse of client funds, or a breach of confidentiality, for example. Rather, he was alleged to have sexually harassed Anita Hill; sexual harassment, unlike specific legal ethics, is an ethical issue that appears in many different venues but is also relevant to legal practice. Therefore, legal professionals must be sensitive to issues in specific legal ethics as well as in more general areas of ethics.

This chapter will help you identify and understand general ethical issues that might arise in the course of doing your work. By combining an understanding of and sensitivity to these general ethical concerns with a knowledge of specific legal ethics, legal assistants can truly pursue their work in an ethical, professional, responsible way.

2.2 THE RESPONSIBLE ORGANIZATION: ENSURING ETHICAL CONDUCT

The ethical behavior of individuals within an organization is frequently a byproduct of the importance that the leadership of the organization has put on ethics. Writing in *Managers and the Legal Environment: Strategies for the 21st Century* (1991), Constance Bagley observes that

> Ethical behavior is reinforced when top management exemplifies the company's values and takes a leadership role in programs to promote ethics; when the company creates an atmosphere of openness and trust in which employees feel comfortable in reporting violations; and when activities to enhance and reward ethics are part of every operating level of the company.

The leadership of an organization sets the tone for the organization's understanding of ethics and application of ethics to their work.

In law firms, this ethical leadership must come from the partners and senior partners. Frequently, ethical leadership in a law firm will fall to an ethics committee. A firm's ethics committee would normally be comprised of the managing partner and representatives from the various sections of the firm, such as the head of the corporate, tax, or litigation sections. The members will vary depending on the specialties of the firm. Further, some firms even have representatives from the legal assistants and the legal secretaries on the ethics committee, but this is the exception rather than the rule.

This idea of ethics emanating from the top has found its way into the specific legal ethics guides. ABA Model Rules 5.1 and 5.3 define the responsibility of supervising attorneys to make their employees conform to ethical standards. Although a lawyer bears the ultimate responsibility for a legal secretary or paralegal who violates an ethical requirement, such as the preservation of client secrets and confidences, the ethical rules governing attorneys' conduct require that they help ensure that those legal personnel assisting them comply with such standards. Because of this supervisory

"I just don't understand why these young lawyers don't have a better sense of ethics."

liability, many attorneys require that all documents relating to any files for which they are responsible first be reviewed by the attorney personally. This may even include such simple things as letters to the clerk of the court asking the court to file the documents and return a stamped, filed copy. If, during the course of your work as a paralegal, you begin to feel that attorneys are being overly vigilant and cautious, just remember that they are responsible not only for their own breaches of ethics but also for breaches by other members of the legal team. By attempting to ensure that you never violate any ethical standard, you can relieve a significant amount of pressure on your supervising attorney, as well as establish yourself as an ethical paralegal.

CASE STUDY: ETHICS AT THE IRS

The Internal Revenue Service (IRS) has pursued an ethics awareness and education program, in part in response to allegations of past improprieties on the part of IRS managers for conflict of interest and involvement with a scheme that enabled some criminal tax evaders to avoid prosecution. The agency hired the Josephson Institute to prepare and evaluate a company-wide ethics survey and to develop and implement an ethics awareness program for every IRS employee. The survey asked IRS employees about issues such as lying to taxpayers, unfair treatment of taxpayers with grievances, and using the government letterhead to gain personal advantage. The Josephson Institute estimated that its ethics program at the IRS would require about 410 staff years (the equivalent of a full year's work by 410 workers). This kind of ethics awareness program is intended not only to develop an awareness of ethical issues by all employees, but also to demonstrate to employees that the senior management is taking the lead in creating an ethical workforce. This kind of commitment from an agency or company's leadership communicates to the workforce that ethics is a priority of the highest order.

2.3 ENVIRONMENTAL ETHICS

Environmental ethics concerns ethical issues that result from the relationship of the law office to the environment, as well as the internal policies that create the environment of the office.

The recycling of materials, especially paper, is one of the most common and important ways in which a law firm can positively contribute to environmental awareness. Many law firms today are voluntarily adopting procedures to encourage recycling of all renewable resources, and there are movements in many state bars to adopt mandatory regulations for recycling. Of all resources, paper is the most important for a law firm because of the vast quantity of paper used in the practice of law. Estimates suggest that an average lawyer generates over 7,000 sheets of paper a year, and the vast quantity of paper used by the legal profession makes the law a natural target for progressive environmental regulation. Rules mandating the use of recycled paper for documents filed in state courts, for example, will proliferate as the law attempts to be increasingly conscious of the environmental impact of the profession.

Law offices should also be environmentally conscious when it comes to supporting causes that are oriented to improving our environment. This support may be through direct financial contributions or contribution of services, such as committee participation or pro bono work. Law firms should also be sure to purchase recycled materials, such as paper, and to use products that are not harmful to the environment, such as appropriate cleaning materials.

Law offices can also contribute positively to the larger environment by creating an office environment that is responsive to issues in environmental ethics. Perhaps the most common phenomenon today is the creation of a smoke-free workplace, where no smoking is allowed. If a firm changes and becomes smoke-free, it will frequently offer employees help in stopping smoking, and may provide an outdoor space where smoking is permitted. The creation of a no-smoking policy itself presents ethical issues, insofar as it clearly limits the rights of the smokers. Protests by smokers have proliferated at the Veterans Administration, emanating out of a VA hospital policy of not allowing smoking inside its hospital buildings. Smokers are required to smoke outside, and veterans, who may be severely disabled, believe that their service to the country affords them the privilege of having an inside space to relax and smoke. From the hospital's perspective, smoke-free hospitals are becoming the norm because of health reasons; from the perspective of the veteran patients, they are only seeking rights that are accorded prisoners, who are given designated indoor smoking areas in prison. Veterans hope that the federal Veterans Dignity in Health Care Act, which designates one indoor smoking area per facility, will aid their plight; hospitals, however, will likely be regulated by the Joint Commission on Accreditation of Health Care Organizations' requirement that all health care facilities be smoke-free. Even when it comes to the ethics of smoking, there truly are two sides to the story.

In addition to referring to ecological awareness, environmental ethics also refers to the ethics of the law firm or organization itself, seen as an environment. This idea complements the idea of the ethical organization receiving leadership from the top, as previously discussed. If a law firm does not practice ethics in its policies, procedures, and decision making, it is unlikely that the firm will create an environment that fosters ethical conduct. If, for example, a law firm allowed racial or sexual discrimination in its promotion practices among associates or paralegals, the environment created would not be an ethical one. In response, associates who leave the firm might well take clients with them to their new positions, or paralegals might not be concerned about revealing confidential information gained from their unethical past employers. Ethics must therefore be an integral part of the law firm's environment.

2.4 SEXUAL HARASSMENT

Although the confirmation hearings of Supreme Court Justice Clarence Thomas brought the issue of sexual harassment to the forefront of American consciousness, sexual harassment is not a new problem in the workplace. Rather, sexual harassment has been a continuing problem that has only recently gotten the attention it deserves.

Although there is no single definition of *sexual harassment,* the Equal Employment Opportunity Commission's (EEOC) guidelines for sexual harassment are frequently the basis for a firm's sexual harassment policy. Those guidelines state:

> Harassment on the basis of sex is a violation of Sec. 703 of Title VII. Unwelcome sexual advances, requests for sexual favors, and other verbal or physical conduct of a sexual nature constitute sexual harassment when (1) submission to such conduct is made either explicitly or implicitly a term or condition of an individual's employment, (2) submission to or rejection of such conduct by an individual is used as the basis of employment decisions affecting such individual, or (3) such conduct has the purpose or effect of unreasonably interfering with the individual's work performance or creating an intimidating, hostile or offensive working environment.

29 C.F.R. § 1064.11(a)(1989).

Under the law, sexual harassment is a form of discrimination in the workplace, which makes it a violation of Title VII of the Civil Rights Act of 1964. Civil rights legislation was originally directed at discrimination on the basis of race, religion, sex, or national origin, and sexual harassment is a form of discrimination on the basis of sex.

The courts have long recognized quid pro quo harassment, where an employee (almost always a woman) suffers an adverse, job-related action because of her refusal to submit to sexual advances. Additionally, the creation of a hostile working environment is considered a form of sexual harassment. In *Meritor Savings Bank v. Vinson,* 477 U.S. 57, 106 S. Ct. 2399 (1986), the Supreme Court held that sexual harassment does not require retaliatory action against the employee; rather, the creation of a hostile work environment suffices to create sexual harassment. Two years after *Meritor,* an attorney for the Securities and Exchange Commission (SEC) alleged that female attorneys and staff were exchanging sex for promotions, and that her poor performance ratings and possible termination were the result of her rebuffing of sexual overtures. She also alleged that the sexually permissive environment made it impossible for her to work as a professional or relate effectively to her co-workers and managers. The Federal District Court for the District of Columbia found, in *Broderick v. Ruder,*

485 F. Supp. 1269 (D.D.C. 1988), that these facts did constitute a hostile working environment for the purpose of a claim of sexual harassment under Title VII.

Although the exact meaning of "hostile or offensive working environment" is unclear, and despite the relative novelty of sexual harassment as a legal concern, society's interest in the prevention of sexual harassment has created a strong mandate to curb that form of unethical behavior. Legal professionals should be aware that the highest standards of behavior will be expected of them, and that people can easily misperceive even the most innocent of comments. For example, even a comment from a male paralegal or attorney that he likes the outfit of a female attorney, although sincere and genuine, may be perceived as harassment. The safest policy is to realize that any form of sexual talk or conduct in the workplace is inappropriate. What you may intend or perceive to be innocent may be perceived as rude, intimidating, or sexual by another person, whose values, attitudes, or experiences may vary from your own. Professionals can best deal with the varying standards and sensitivities of other professionals by refraining from any form of sexual talk or conduct. It is far better to be seen as overly polite than to be put in the position of being accused of improper behavior that might constitute sexual harassment. Because the avoidance of any impropriety, not to mention a severe impropriety such as sexual harassment, is critical to the maintenance of a firm's professional image, many companies have written policies prohibiting sexual harassment and delineating the procedures for bringing a claim of sexual harassment.

Many state bar associations have considered or taken measures to deal with sexual harassment by developing new ethical rules that relate specifically to the ethics of sexual relations between attorney and client. Various states are considering new rules to prohibit attorneys from engaging in sexual relations with clients if the affair results from "duress, intimidation or undue influence," or from engaging in affairs when they know or should know that the client's agreement to the sexual relation "is impaired by the client's emotional or financial dependency or some other reason." Many bar presidents agree that the adoption of a specific rule concerning sexual relations between lawyer and client will best protect the public interest.

THE CASE OF THE JUVENILE "JOKE"

Attorney Anita files a motion in the Sanders case which, if successful, will guarantee success for her client in the upcoming case. Upon receipt of the motion, Attorney Clarence, who is representing the adverse party in the case, sends Attorney Anita a note in which he writes, "Should you succeed on your motion, we will send somebody over to perform plastic surgery on some of your more outstanding features."

Attorney Anita is shocked and intimidated by this language. Attorney Clarence thought Anita would "get a kick" out of the note.

What do you think: Is this a joke, or does it constitute sexual harassment?

2.5 ROMANCE IN THE WORKPLACE

As more and more females have entered the workforce, the question of office romance has become not only more apparent, but also more convoluted. When the practice of law was a primarily male phenomenon, most firms and agencies had a policy absolutely forbidding office romances. This policy reflected their belief that most of the females in the firms were legal secretaries who could be easily coerced into having a relationship with an attorney or who might use the workplace to "catch" a lawyer for a husband. In today's legal world, however, this paradigm no longer fits, as many more women are lawyers, partners, and judges, working in positions of equality with their male counterparts.

Even though office romances are neither illegal nor, in many cases, prohibited by office policy, the best and safest policy is to avoid such entanglements. Further, if they do occur, it would probably be wisest for one of the parties to go elsewhere for employment. Although it may be tempting to think that you can separate your personal life from your professional life, the reality is that it is very difficult to separate work and personal issues.

2.6 ETHICS AND CULTURAL DIVERSITY

Like the changes that occurred in the workplace when females began entering the workforce in great numbers, other changes also occurred when more and more minorities began to enter the workforce. Each of us comes from a different cultural background, and it is important to accept the idea that American culture is a diverse one, with different perspectives, opinions, experiences, and beliefs. From this acceptance of American cultural diversity should spring a fundamental acceptance of people and their differences. This is especially important for those practicing in the legal field, for in the practice of the law you will come into contact with people from all cultures and all walks of life. They may work in your office, be your clients, be the judge, be jurors on a case, or be witnesses. It is vitally important, therefore, for the legal professional to be able to communicate and interact with all types of people, and this multicultural interaction requires a sensibility that truly accepts each person as a fully human individual. By learning to respect others, keeping your private and professional life separate, and retaining a professional and neutral appearance and demeanor, you can respect your own personal heritage as well as the cultural heritage of those with whom you come into contact, while also fulfilling your obligations as a legal professional.

As in many areas, the application of acceptance of cultural diversity is harder—sometimes much harder—than the theory. American cultural history has been one of domination and exploitation, and transcending this divisive history takes hard, continuous work. In her guest editorial, Professor Patricia J. Williams describes, in personal and eloquent terms, how very difficult this acceptance of cultural diversity can be and how vitally important it is to go beyond cultural stereotyping in the quest to create a truly multicultural society.

GUEST EDITORIAL

OVERCOMING CULTURAL STEREOTYPING:
Each Day Is a New Labor

By Patricia J. Williams*

Not long ago, a white acquaintance of mine described her boyfriend as "having a bit of the Jewish in him." She meant that he was stingy with money. I said, "Don't talk like that! I know you didn't mean it, but there are harmful implications in thinking like that." She responded with profuse apologies, phone calls, tears, then anger. She said repeatedly that she had no wish to offend me or anyone: that it was just a cultural reality, there was no offense in it, she had heard Jewish people say the same thing, it was just the way things were, nothing personal. There was an odd moment at which I thought we were in agreement, when she said she was sorry and it was "just a cultural reality": I thought she was referring to racism's being so deeply imbedded in culture that it was unconscious—but what she meant was that stinginess was a Jewish "thing."

As we argued, words like "overly sensitive," "academic privilege," and "touchy" began to creep into her description of me. She accused me of building walls, of being unrealistic, of not being able to loosen up and just be with people. She didn't use the word "righteous," but I know that's what she meant. I tried to reassure her that I didn't mean to put her on the defensive, that I had not meant to attack or upset her, and that I deeply valued her friendship. But I could not back down. I felt our friendship being broken apart. She would be consoled with nothing less than a retraction of my opinion, an admission that I was wrong. She didn't want me to understand merely that she meant no harm, but wanted me to confess that there was no harm. Around this time, my sister sent me an article about the difficulties of blacks and whites in discussing racial issues in social settings. It included the warning of Shelby Steele, a black professor of English at San Jose State University ("If you are honest and frank, you may come to be seen as belligerent, arrogant, a troublemaker"), and the advice of Harvard professor Alvin Poussaint ("Defuse the situation; devise a way of getting out of it quickly. Develop some humorous responses . . . and take charge by steering the conversation in another direction").

Not long after that, I went shopping for a sweatshirt in the emptiness of nearly closing time at Au Coton, a clothing store near my home. The three young salespeople told me that a waffle-weave sweater would make me look "really fly." I said I was too old to be fly. One of them persisted: "Well, all the really fly people are wearing waffle weave." As I continued to shop, I could hear them laughing among themselves. When I came closer to the counter, I heard that they were joking about Jews. They mentioned "princesses" and imitated "Jewish" accents— New Yorkers imitating other New Yorkers. To an outsider like me, it sounded as if they were imitating themselves.

"Speak of the devil," said one of them as four other young people came into the store. I don't know why the salespeople had decided that the newcomers were Jews—again, it was as if they were pointing fingers at themselves. They all wore waffle-weave tops; denim jackets with the collars turned up; their hair in little moussed spikes and lacquered ringlets; colorful kerchiefs knotted at their throats.

"Tell that girl to get a job," murmured one of the salesgirls. There was both playfulness and scorn in her voice. Her friends tittered. The designated Jews wandered around the store, held clothes on hangers up to their chins, generally looked as youthfully fly as could be. One of the salesgirls said, "Can I help you guys?" Her voice was high-pitched and eager. Then she turned her head and winked at her friends.

I didn't say anything. I wanted to say something and, since I'm usually outspoken about these things, I was surprised when no words came out. It is embarrassing but worthwhile nonetheless, I think, to run through all the mundane, even quite petty, components of the self-consciousness that resulted in my silence. Such silence is too common, too institutionalized, and too destructive not to examine it in the most nuanced way possible.

My self-consciousness was a powerful paralyzer. I was self-conscious about being so much older than they. I was afraid of sounding so maternally querulous that they would dismiss my words. I was self-conscious too about shopping in a store with posters that said "As advertised in *Seventeen Magazine*." As old as I was, I felt very young again, in a sticky, tongue-tied awful adolescent way. In some odd way

that is extremely hard to admit in print, I wanted their approval. I was on the edge of their group, the odd person out (as I always was as a teenager, that time in one's life when attitudes about everything social— including race—are most powerfully reinforced). I didn't want to be part of them, but I didn't want to be the object of their derision either. The whole room was filled with adolescent vanity, social pressure, and a yearning to belong. The room was ablaze with the crossfire of self-assertive groupings. The four who wandered in, preening and posing and posturing, pretending self-confidence. The three who worked there, lounging and diffident, pretending they owned the place. For those brief, childish, powerful moments, I wasn't sure I could survive being on the wrong side.

I was also caught short because they were so *open* about their antisemitism. They smiled at me and commented on the clothing I was looking at; they smiled and commented on the clothing being looked at by the others. Their antisemitism was smiling, open, casually jocular, and only slightly conspiratorial or secretive. They were such nice young people—how could they possibly mean any harm? This little piece of cognitive dissonance was aided and abetted by my blackness, the fact that I am black: I grew up in a neighborhood where blacks were the designated Jews. I can think of few instances in which I have ever directly heard the heart, the uncensored, undramatic day-to-day core of it—heard it as people think it and heard it from the position of an "insider." And it was irresistible, forbidden, almost thrilling to be on the inside. I was "privileged" to hear what these people thought, ear-marked as someone who would not reveal them; I was designated safe. I was also designated as someone who didn't matter.

What they had constructed around me was the architecture of trust. As strange as it sounds, I realized that breaking the bond of my silence was like breaking the bond of *our* silence. At the same time, I realized that their faith in me was oppressively insulting. I became an antisemite by the stunning audacity of their assumption that I would remain silent. If I was "safe," I was also "easy" in my desire for the illusion of inclusion, in my capitulation to the vanity of mattering enough even to be included. It did not occur to me that I was simply being ignored. I could have been Jewish, as much as the four random souls who wandered into the store; but by their designation of me as "not Jewish" they made property of me, as they made wilderness of the others. I became colonized as their others were made enemies.

I left a small piece of myself on the outside, beyond the rim of their circle, with those others on the other side of the store; as they made fun of the others, they also made light of me; I was watching myself be made fun of. In this way I transformed myself into the third person; I undermined the security of my most precious property, I. I gave much power to the wilderness of strangers, some few of whom I would feel as reflections of my lost property by being able to snare them in the strong beartraps of my own familiarizing labels.

I have thought a lot about this incident. Part of my reaction was premised on the peculiarities of my own history. Although I was quite young, I remember the Woolworth sit-ins; I remember my father walking trepidatiously into stores in Savannah, Georgia, shortly after desegregation, cautiously disbelieving of his right to be there, disproportionately grateful for the allowance just to be. Very much my father's daughter, I am always grateful when storekeepers are polite to me; I don't expect courtesy, I value it in a way that resembles love and trust and shelter. I value it in a way that is frequently misleading, for it is neither love nor trust nor shelter.

I know that this valuing is a form of fear. I am afraid of being alien and suspect, of being thrown out at any moment; I am relieved when I am not. At the same time, I am enraged by the possibility of this subsurface drama-waiting-to-happen. My rage feels dangerous, full of physical violence, like something that will get me arrested. And also at the same time I am embarrassed by all these feelings, ashamed to reveal in them the truth of my insignificance. All this impermissible danger floats around in me, boiling, exhausting. I can't kill and I can't teach everyone. I can't pretend it doesn't bother me; it eats me alive. So I protect myself. I don't venture into the market very often. I don't deal with other people if I can help it. I don't risk exposing myself to the rage that will get me arrested. The dilemma—and the distance between the "i" on this side of the store and the me that is

"them" on the other side of the store—is marked by an emptiness in myself. Frequently such emptiness is reiterated by a hole in language, a gap in the law, or a chasm of fear.

I think the hard work of a nonracist sensibility is the boundary crossing, from safe circle into wilderness: the testing of boundary, the consecration of sacrilege. It is the willingness to spoil a good party and break an encompassing circle, to travel from the safe to the unsafe. The transgression is dizzyingly intense, a reminder of what it is to be alive. It is a sinful pleasure, this willing transgression of a line, which takes one into new awareness, a secret, lonely, and tabooed world—to survive the transgression is terrifying and addictive. To know that everything has changed and yet that nothing has changed; and in leaping the chasm of this impossible division of self, a discovery of the self surviving, still well, still strong, and, as a curious consequence, renewed.

But as I said earlier, the perspective we need to acquire is one beyond those three boxes that have been set up. It is a perspective that exists on all three levels and eighty-five more besides—simultaneously. It is this perspective, the ambivalent, multivalent way of seeing, that is at the core of what is called critical theory, feminist theory, and much of the minority critique of the law. It has to do with a fluid positioning that sees back and forth across boundary, which acknowledges that I can be black and good and black and bad, and that I can also be black and white, male and female, yin and yang, love and hate.

Nothing is simple. Each day is a new labor.

Ursula Le Guin, in her novel *The Lathe of Heaven,* writes that making love is like baking bread: each time it must be done with care and from the beginning.

Each day is a new labor.

■ Patricia J. Williams is Associate Professor of Law at the University of Wisconsin and the author of *The Alchemy of Race and Rights: Diary of a Law Professor* (Harvard University Press, 1991), from which this essay was taken.

2.7 PERSONAL USE OF PRIVATE EQUIPMENT

When an employer provides supplies, equipment, or space to an employee, the expectation is that those things will be used solely in furtherance of the work of the employer. Ethical dilemmas arise when employees want to do their own work on company time or with company equipment or supplies. The best and safest rule, in the absence of clear and specific permission from the appropriate authority, is never to use the company's supplies or equipment and never to do personal work on the job. Although you may argue that it is common practice to do both, ethics is connected to the idea of *correct*—not necessarily popular—behavior. Further, it is hardly worth the risk of being reprimanded, written up, or terminated for posting a letter on your firm's postage machine or taking a roll of tape home with you to wrap Christmas presents. Remember that this concerns unauthorized use; if you have a particular situation that necessitates the use of your work computer, for example, obtaining permission for the activity would make it ethical.

2.8 WHISTLEBLOWING

Becoming aware of ethical improprieties at work can frequently put the employee in a difficult position. Even if the employee has witnessed a clear violation, that employee also knows that blowing the whistle may cause him or her to be perceived as a troublemaker and cost him or her a job. It is understandable, therefore, that employees are reluctant to get involved in these types of situations.

The law has been active in creating and enforcing legislation that protects those who report unethical or illegal activity by management. More than 20 federal laws, including the Civil Service Reform Act, the False Claims Act, and the Whistleblower Protection Act of 1989, have been

passed to prevent retaliation against employees who report illegal or unethical activities. Additionally, state and local jurisdictions have also passed laws to protect whistleblowers.

Even though the law and the courts have protected whistleblowers, the reality is that it can be very difficult to "just say no" when your supervisor or your organization asks you to do something. The possible repercussions of being ostracized, plateaued, or fired are great indeed. Perhaps the most challenging aspect of ethics is dealing with the unethical behavior of others when your job—your means of survival—is threatened; it is sometimes hard to make the choice to sacrifice those realities to the higher ethical ideal.

2.9 COMPUTERS: ETHICS AND SECURITY

The marriage of law offices and technology, which has witnessed law firms' use of the most sophisticated technology, including networking, telecommunications, optical scanning, and CD-ROM technology, has also created new ethical concerns. Once information is electronically communicated and stored, the possibilities of ethical or security violations increase significantly, because there are many means of accessing and modifying the information, from both on-site and remote locations.

The legal system is a natural venue for computer technology because the law is essentially information-based, and computer information systems are vital to the practice of law. An individual law office might have personal computers, mini- or mainframe computers, telecommunication networks, electronic mail, and document or storage retrieval systems. Law firms also frequently have access to legal databases such as LEXIS or WESTLAW, and modern law offices might also have electronic mail among lawyers, where people can communicate without being on-line at the same time. The future will also witness the further development of electronic courthouses, where it might be possible to file documents or argue routine motions by a combination of electronic mail, computer conferencing, and database technology. As an integral part of the practice of law, technology brings its own set of ethical and security issues to the legal profession. Legal professionals must not only develop the ability to use this technology productively, they must also become sensitized to the ethical and security issues created by use of computer technology.

Technology Requires Standards and Procedures

One important aspect of effective technology management is the orientation toward standardized systems (hardware and software) and procedures. This systematic approach is required for several reasons. First, standardization helps create consistency in use of the system. Second, it guards against errors and miscommunications. Third, a systematic approach makes the computer technology easier to use, maintain, and support.

Many firms have an introduction to computer systems as part of the general orientation of a new worker. There may also be a network administrator, office manager, or technical services manager who helps users with accessing the equipment. If you are unsure of proper protocol when it comes to computer technology, ask! Do not assume, because a wrong assumption could lead to the corruption of data, the loss of documents, or other undesirable results.

Because of the potential for abuse of electronic media, firms frequently have procedures that separate the duties relating to the computer systems. This limits the ability of an individual to use a computer system for personal ends. Firms might limit access to the computer room, but even if access is allowed, the firm can maintain an audit trail, which enables the auditors to see who has used the equipment. So do not be surprised or offended if you do not have full access to the entire system, because the securities and controls require this action.

When using computer systems, you must follow your organization's policies and procedures to maximize your ability to use those systems effectively. Additionally, the issues of security and ethics can be addressed only if all users are committed to following established procedures. Legal assistants and attorneys, who are tremendous users of technology, from networks to PCs to electronic mail to faxes to electronic conferencing, must respect established procedures when it comes to using technology; only by following appropriate computer protocol can the law firm get optimal use out of its investment in technical systems.

Technology Impacts Privacy and Confidentiality

One of the cornerstones of ethical legal practice is the concern for protection of the client's individual interests, through the doctrines of privacy and confidentiality. Later you will learn about these as substantive issues, but for now it is important to realize that modern electronic technology creates new security and ethical issues regarding maintenance of client privacy and confidentiality. The possibility of improper use of your system arises both from those who use it in the office and from those who can access it from outside the office. Therefore, security systems must be concerned with both internal and external abuse.

Perhaps the greatest danger is that others may access your computer files and use or modify whatever information they find. Sometimes this theft of information is intentional; sometimes it is accidental. In either case, however, the results can be extremely harmful, as the integrity of your work and the confidence of your client may erode after such a breach of confidentiality. Many paralegals, for example, might unthinkingly leave their computers on while making a quick trip to the restroom, believing that the trip will be short and that it would be a waste of time to turn off the computer, only to turn it back on in a few minutes. Leaving an unattended computer, rather than being a matter of ease or convenience, might well be catastrophic. All of the information stored on the computer's files becomes easy, instantaneous prey for anyone who happens by; it is like leaving an open vault. People have no idea how valuable the information stored in the computer is, or how easily the information can be lost or modified. Lest you think that no one would be interested in or able to invade sophisticated computer technology, be aware that the mentality of a "hacker" is to solve the puzzle for its own sake. Remember the chaos caused when some young hackers broke into the computer system of the Sloan Kettering Cancer Center, which was part of Telenet, a large computer network. The invaders changed the master program so that those entering the system automatically revealed their passwords. For doctors or lawyers, for whom privacy and confidentiality are an essential part of their practice, this illegal entry into computer systems can be devastating.

Over and above the practices within the law firms, law firms must also be aware of the vendors who service them, and any of their activities that affect privacy and confidentiality. If a firm uses a vendor to dispose of paper, for example, the firm should inquire into the vendor's disposal procedures, to ensure that the papers will really be destroyed; make sure the vendor is bonded; and perhaps have the vendor sign a confidentiality or nondisclosure agreement with the firm. Likewise, the firm may prefer that all documents be shredded. In response to the need for efficient, ethical vendors for the legal profession, the National Association for Legal Vendors (NALV) was formed to provide publishing, technology, and product information for members of the legal industry. The members of this growing organization are committed to ethical servicing of law practices; they also assist in planning exhibits and informing members about relevant developments in the industry.

Many unethical uses of the computer can be avoided by monitoring access to the system and by restricting access to computers through the use of passwords and other security devices. Effective monitoring of the system will enable those who use its reports to assess productivity, plan for system usage, and analyze violations or unauthorized use.

Technology Uses Electronic Media

The fact that electronic media possess particularities and idiosyncrasies, that they are imperfect and fallible, and that they require maintenance is lost on most people. The fact is, however, that electronic media are susceptible to certain dangers and realities that, if not anticipated, might have extremely negative consequences for the law firm. Computer technology can be affected by electrical surges and spikes, the weather, environmental conditions where the equipment is located, static electricity, mistakes by users, and computer viruses. An awareness of the particular characteristics of electronic technology will lead a law firm to adopt procedures to safeguard against dangerous consequences. For instance, imagine the consequences if a legal assistant, who worked on the development of an expert witness database for two years, made only one copy of the file in addition to the copy on her hard drive—and then her hard drive is corrupted by an electrical surge and her only copy on disk contains a read error. Years of work may be irretrievably lost.

In response to these dangers, law firms and technical administrators in firms should provide surge protection, acceptable environmental conditions, an effective system of usage procedures, checks and balances, and an approach to data safekeeping or a disaster recovery plan. To ensure the integrity of electronic information, firms may store full or incremental backup information in different locations in the firm, and may also have off-site storage. There exist data security firms, whose sole business is to provide the appropriate environment to store and retrieve data safely. They charge a monthly fee to come to your site, transport the information in special containers on special trucks, and maintain the information in optimal environmental conditions. Whenever the firm needs information that is being stored off-site, the data security firm delivers it to the customer, either on a rotation schedule or on an emergency basis.

On the individual level, it is essential for all computer users to make it a habit to create backups of all files. Users should perform incremental backups as they work, to avoid the risk of an accident perhaps corrupting the entire file. They should also perform full, frequent backups of all programs and data, to be used in case of emergencies. Following these practices will greatly reduce the likelihood that the idiosyncrasies of electronic media may destroy data and information vital to your representing clients effectively and ethically.

Computer viruses also threaten the integrity of a computer system. Most virus problems in law firms start with the innocent act of a user loading a piece of software, which they got from a friend or from a bulletin board, into a work computer. This could be a violation of the copyright laws, assuming the software is not in the public domain, but it is also an easy way to pick up a virus and corrupt the data in the law firm. Ethics, practicality, and legality all dictate that users should never load any software into their computers on their own without prior approval, and that individual additions to the computer system should be approved in writing by the administrator in charge of information systems.

CASE STUDY: LAWYER TELECOMPUTER NETWORKING

Lawyer Telecomputer Networking (LTN) is a subscription-based service that enables lawyers and law firms to tie their telecommunications systems into the LTN, thereby empowering their offices with the benefits of a powerful mainframe computer. The basic services of an LTN include electronic mail, bulletin boards, and group conferencing, all of which enable lawyers to communicate quickly and effectively with clients, other lawyers, community-based networks, and even the ABA, through its ABA/net. LTN is effective for document transfer and communication with courts that subscribe to LTN; it also provides attorneys and paralegals with interactive software to assist in legal analysis. Referral services and advertising for lawyers may be carried on an LTN as well.

Although LTN services have many advantages, including increasing the access to legal services for many people, they also present ethical issues that must be addressed. One issue is the possible unauthorized practice of law out-of-state, as the LTN would enable lawyers to reach people nationwide. Because the communication is electronic and hard to monitor, state bars may well find this type of activity difficult to regulate. Two additional problems also emerge. First, nonlawyer (such as legal assistant) access to the LTN implicates unauthorized practice issues, as the user does not see or physically interact with the sender. Second, states have different rules for the free exchange of legal advice and different rules if counsel is sought only once or multiple times.

Communicating electronically rather than personally also increases the possibility of error or miscommunication. If a lawyer, for example, responded to a client by stating "will let you know if a legal claim exists," should the client assume that no claim exists, and therefore forgo the opportunity to seek other legal advice? If an individual posts a message asking for legal advice, giving a name, state, and brief facts, and an attorney gives a general response and suggests seeing a lawyer in the individual's state, have they established a lawyer-client relationship? Or is further communication needed? Relative to advertising, does the inclusion of an attorney in a listing that reaches many states comply with advertising regulations in each of the affected states? Should there be different rules concerning bulletin boards for lawyers, as opposed to bulletin boards that include nonlawyers as well?

"This virus is so bad I've lost my memory!"

All of these questions speak to the essential reality that, as the law embraces more and more technology, new ethical issues and dilemmas will certainly accompany that development. If the law is to embrace high technology services such as LTNs, it is clear that legal practitioners must also address the new ethical issues that arise with their use, as M. Thomas Collins points out in his guest editorial.

GUEST EDITORIAL

A COMMENT ON ETHICS, SOFTWARE AND THE LEGAL PROFESSIONAL

by M. Thomas Collins, Chairman,
National Association of Legal Vendors (1992)

It's too simple to say that unethical behavior, while not illegal, skirts the edges of the law. There is a blurred line between unethical and the illegal. When is it a question of illegal behavior and when is it instead a question of unethical behavior? The "unethical tag" is often hung on those illegal acts that go unprosecuted. The aggrieved parties may be unaware of the injurious act against them. The act may fall in the category of the almost unprovable. It may be so petty that prosecution looms as too mighty a response. On the other hand, many a career has shattered and crumbled because of an uncovered wrong deed, or because the almost unprovable was proved, or because the insignificant was not so immaterial in the eyes of the injured.

You cannot count on a successful career in the legal community unless your ethical conduct is above reproach; and if misconduct is found to be illegal, you will not remain a welcomed member of the legal community. The risk to most of us is not that we will intentionally and willfully set out to injure other parties through unethical or illegal acts; the risk is that we will fail to see our actions through the eyes of others until it's too late.

Make no mistake, when you make or accept an unauthorized copy of most software, you have injured another party. Virtually all software is protected by license or contract and most is protected by copyright or patent laws. It is frightening to me that a young aspiring professional could regard this issue so lightly as to jeopardize his career. Or, that a law firm that has worked for years to build a reputation could have it at risk because of a casual disregard for the property rights and laws involved.

What you need to know is that almost all software is traceable to the licensee of record. If, as a licensee, you permit someone to make an unauthorized copy, there is a clear electronic trail of that event that will live as long as that unauthorized software exists. If you have an unauthorized copy of software in your possession, the fact that it is a pirated copy is determinable and its source is traceable.

This is not a victimless act, but is one where the evidence of wrongdoing remains long after the memory of the deed fades away. Don't do this to yourself, and don't let your future firm do it to itself.

■ M. Thomas ("Tom") Collins is the 1992 Chairman of the National Association of Legal Vendors and is the President of Juris, Inc.

2.10 NOT JUST LEGAL ETHICS: A SUMMARY

Despite the completeness and complexity of specific legal ethics, ethics for the legal practitioner does not comprise only legal ethics. To be sure, legal ethics determine the choices and actions that a lawyer or paralegal will take in a particular circumstance. But every legal professional is also guided in thought and action by a sense of ethics and morality that applies to the law as it does to other fields or professions. So when it comes to applying ethics to the legal profession, remember that it is not just legal ethics which deserves our concern and attention. Rather, an ethical legal professional is bounded by both legal ethics, the rules which guide the particular profession, and general ethics, which applies to all who work with and service other people. By conceptualizing ethics in this broader, more complete way, the legal professional can truly fulfill the responsibility of providing ethical legal work.

REVIEW QUESTIONS

1. How can an organization communicate to its employees that ethical behavior is a high priority?
2. How can law firms develop an ecological awareness?
3. What is sexual harassment, and what kinds of actions constitute sexual harassment?
4. What ethical issues are implicated by the use of technology in law offices?

QUESTION FOR THOUGHT AND DISCUSSION

1. Consider each of the topics discussed in this chapter and explain how they are related to legal ethics.

Substantive Issues in Paralegal Ethics

LAW, LITERATURE, AND ETHICS

From **The Firm**
By John Grisham

Mitch ducked low in the rear seat and watched the traffic. The driver moved with a slow confidence and seven minutes later stopped in front of the station. Mitch threw two fives over the seat and darted into the terminal. He bought a one-way ticket on the four-thirty bus to Atlanta. It was four thirty-one, according to the clock on the wall. The clerk pointed through the swinging doors. "Bus No. 454," she said, "Leaving in a moment."

The driver slammed the baggage door, took his ticket and followed Mitch onto the bus. The first three rows were filled with elderly blacks. A dozen more passengers were scattered toward the rear. Mitch walked slowly down the aisle, gazing at each face and seeing no one. He took a window seat on the fourth row from the rear. He slipped on a pair of sun-glasses and glanced behind him. No one. Dammit! Was it the wrong bus? He stared out the dark windows as the bus moved quickly into traffic. they would stop in Knoxville. Maybe his contact would be there.

When they were on the interstate and the driver reached his cruising speed, a man in blue jeans and madras shirt suddenly appeared and slid into the seat next to Mitch. It was Tarrance. Mitch breathed easier.

"Where have you been?" he asked.

"In the rest room. Did you lose them?" Tarrance spoke in a low voice while surveying the backs of the heads of the passengers. No one was listening. No one could hear.

"I never see them, Tarrance. So I cannot say if I lost them. But I think they would have to be supermen to keep my trail this time."

"Did you see our man in the terminal?"

"Yes. By the pay phone with the red Falcons cap. Black dude."

"That's him. He would've signaled if they were following."

"He gave me the go-ahead."

Tarrance wore silver reflective sunglasses under a green Michigan State baseball cap. Mitch could smell the fresh Juicy Fruit.

"Sort of out of uniform, aren't you?" Mitch said with no smile. "Did Voyles give you permission to dress like that?"

"I forgot to ask him. I'll mention it in the morning."

"Sunday morning?" Mitch asked.

"Of course. He'll wanna know all about our little bus ride. I briefed him for an hour before I left town."

"Well, first things first. What about my car?"

"We'll pick it up in a few minutes and babysit it for you. It'll be in Knoxville when you need it. Don't worry."

"You don't think they'll find us?"

"No way. No one followed you out of Memphis, and we detected nothing in Nashville. You're as clean as a whistle."

"Pardon my concern. But after that fiasco in the shoe store, I know you boys are not above stupidity."

"It was a mistake, all right. We—"

"A big mistake. One that could get me on the hit list."

"You covered it well. It won't happen again."

"Promise me, Tarrance. Promise me no one will ever again approach me in public."

Tarrance looked down the aisle and nodded.

"No, Tarrance. I need to hear it from your mouth. Promise me."

"Okay, okay. It won't happen again. I promise."

"Thanks. Now maybe I can eat at a restaurant without fear of being grabbed."

"You've made your point."

An old black man with a cane inched toward them, smiled and walked past. The rest-room door slammed. The Greyhound rode the left lane and blew past the lawful drivers.

Tarrance flipped through a magazine. Mitch gazed into the countryside. The man with the cane finished his business and wobbled to his seat on the front row.

"So what brings you hear?" Tarrance asked, flipping pages.

"I don't like airplanes. I always take the bus."

"I see. Where would you like to start?"

"Voyles said you had a game plan."

"I do, I just need a quarterback."

"Good ones are very expensive."

"We've got the money."

"It'll cost a helluva lot more that you think. The way I figure it, I'll be throwing away a forty-year legal career at, say, an average of half a million a year."

"That's twenty million bucks."

"I know. But we can negotiate."

"That's good to hear. You're assuming that you'll work, or practice, as you say, for forty years. That's a very precarious assumption. Just for fun, let's assume that within five years we bust up the firm and indict you along with all of your buddies. And that we obtain convictions, and you go off to prison for a few years. They won't keep you long because you're a white-collar type, and of course you've heard how nice the federal pens are. But at any rate, you'll lose your license, your house, your little BMW. Probably your wife. When you get out, you can open up a private investigation service like your old friend Lomax. It's easy work, unless you sniff the wrong underwear."

"Like I said. It's negotiable."

"All right. Let's negotiate. How much do you want?"

"For what?"

Tarrance closed the magazine, placed it under his seat and opened a thick paperback. He pretended to read. Mitch spoke from the corner of his mouth with his eyes on the median.

"That's a very good question," Tarrance said softly, just above the distant grind of the diesel engine. "What do we want from you? Good question. First, you have to give up your career as a lawyer. You'll have to divulge secrets and records that belong to your clients. That, of course, is enough to get you disbarred, but that won't seem important. You and I must agree that you will hand us the firm on a silver platter. Once we agree, if we agree, the rest will fall in place. Second, and most important, you will give up enough documentation to indict every member of the firm and most of the top Morolto people. The records are in the little building there on Front Street."

"How do you know this?"

Tarrance smiled. "Because we spend billions of dollars fighting organized crime. Because we've tracked the Moroltos for twenty years. Because we have sources within the family. Because Hodge and Kozinski were talking when they were murdered. Don't sell us short, Mitch."

"And you think I can get the information out?"

"Yes, Counselor. You can build a case from the inside that will collapse the firm and break up one of the largest crime families in the country. You gotta lay out the firm for us. Whose office is where? Names of all secretaries, clerks, paralegals. Who works on what files? Who's got which clients? The chain of command. Who's on the fifth floor? What's up there? Where are the records kept? Is there a central storage area? How much is computerized? How much is on microfilm? And, most important, you gotta bring the stuff out and hand it to us. Once we have probable cause, we can go in with a small army and get everything. But that's an awfully big step. We gotta have a very tight and solid case before we go crashing in with search warrants."

"Is that all you want?"

"No. You'll have to testify against all of your buddies at their trials. Could take years."

Mitch breathed deeply and closed his eyes. The bus slowed behind a caravan of mobile home split in two. Dusk was approaching, and, one at a time, the cars in the west-bound lane brightened with headlights. Testifying at trial! This, he had not though of. With millions to spend for the best criminal lawyers, the trials could drag on forever.

Tarrance actually began reading the paperback, a Louis L'Amour. He adjusted the reading light above them, as if he was indeed a real passenger on a real journey. After thirty miles of no talk, no negotiation, Mitch removed his sun-glasses and looked at Tarrance.

"What happens to me?"

"You'll have a lot of money, for what that's worth. If you have any sense of morality, you can face yourself each day. You can live anywhere in the country, with a new identity, of course. We'll find you a job, fix your nose, do anything you want, really."

Mitch tried to keep his eyes on the road, but it was impossible. He glared at Tarrance. "Morality? Don't ever mention that word to me again, Tarrance. I'm an innocent victim, and you know it."

Tarrance grunted with a smart-ass grin.

They rode in silence for a few miles.

"What about my wife?"

"Yeah, you can keep her."

"Very funny."

"Sorry. She'll get everything she wants. How much does she know?"

"Everything." He though of the girl on the beach. "Well, almost everything."

"We'll get her a fat government job with the Social Security Administration anywhere you want. It won't be that bad, Mitch."

"It'll be wonderful. Until an unknown point in the future when one of your people opens his or her mouth and lets something slip to the wrong person, and you'll read about me or my wife in the paper. The Mob never forgets, Tarrance. They're worse than elephants. And they keep secrets better than your side. You guys have lost people, so don't deny it."

"I won't deny it. And I'll admit to you that they can be ingenious when they decide to kill."

"Thanks. So where do I go?"

"It's up to you. Right now we have about two thousand witnesses living all over the country under new names with new homes and new jobs. The odds are overwhelmingly in your favor."

"So I play the odds?"

"Yes. You either take the money and run, or you play big-shot lawyer and bet that we never infiltrate."

"That's a hell of a choice, Tarrance."

"It is. I'm glad it's yours."

■ From *The Firm* by John Grisham. Copyright © 1991 by John Grisham. Used by permission of Doubleday, a division of Bantam Doubleday Dell Publishing Group, Inc.

CHAPTER 3
Confidentiality

CHAPTER OVERVIEW

In this chapter you will learn about confidentiality in the context of the legal environment. Of all the ethical considerations applicable to legal assistants, the duty to maintain confidentiality is of paramount importance. Without confidentiality, it is unlikely that the legal system would be able to function effectively. This chapter helps you identify the ethical dimensions of confidentiality and learn how to recognize and solve problems that you may encounter in your work as a paralegal.

THE CASE OF THE SLEEPTALKING ASSISTANT

John Haddox is a criminal defense attorney who has a reputation for being the best in the state. He handles only the most complex and heinous cases. John's paralegal, Ann Gabby, is John's right-hand person. Ann investigates the cases, sits in during client interviews, and goes to trials with John. John tells everyone that he would not have won as many cases as he has if he did not let Ann play such a critical role.

About a year ago, Dan Stroup was indicted for the murder of 17 girls who died as a result of extended torture. Dan, a serial killer, was indicted when someone saw him through a window whipping a teenage girl. The police were called to investigate and found evidence of other victims in the apartment where Stroup was staying. Stroup, a successful and influential senator, had a pristine reputation; however, the murders occurred only in Washington, D.C., and in Stroup's home state. Other evidence found in the apartment made the case seem open-and-shut.

Stroup retains John Haddox to represent him. As she has done in all other cases, Ann sits in on all of John's conferences with Stroup. At first, Stroup is leery of Ann's presence, but John assures Stroup that Ann is completely trustworthy, has assisted him on numerous other cases, and is bound by the duty of confidentiality. During one of their interviews, Stroup confesses to all of the crimes in the presence of both John and Ann. He believes he has a mental disorder and needs help, but he wants John and Ann to help him obtain a not guilty verdict so that he can go for the proper treatment.

Ann Gabby is married to Frank Stuart, the district attorney who will be prosecuting the Stroup case. Frank has often told Ann that she talks in her sleep and has advised her to see a physician about the problem. Ann knows she talks in her sleep, but believes that it is stress-related and that she can control it. At this time, Ann is under a great deal of pressure, because the Stroup trial is scheduled to begin next week.

What kinds of ethical issues does Ann face, and what should she do?

THE CASE OF CAROL'S CAR PHONE

Carol Willis, an attorney specializing in trademark and patent work, is so overwhelmed with work that she has had a car phone installed so that she can conduct business while traveling from one appointment to the next. One day, while going back to the office from a pretrial conference on a patent infringement suit in federal court, Carol's car phone rings. She answers it using the microphone installed on the driver's side of her car. The call is from the president of Carol's biggest client, Beau Belle, a large cosmetics company. The head chemist at Beau Belle has just discovered a skin cleanser that actually washes away wrinkles, and Beau Belle wants to apply for a patent immediately. Carol is at a stop light, so she asks for the formula so that when she gets back to the office, she can start on the paperwork for the patent application.

In the next lane sits the president of La Rouge, Beau Belle's major competitor, whose phone is on the same frequency as Carol's. He hears the entire conversation with Beau Belle. He immediately copies down the formula and prepares to rush to his attorney so that he can begin the paperwork for the patent.

What problems do you see in this situation? What should Carol have done?

3.1 CONFIDENTIALITY: AN INTRODUCTION

The issue of confidentiality arises in the context of communications between legal professionals and their clients. To provide an environment in which clients fully reveal all relevant information (to assure them of the most effective representation possible), communications between lawyer and client are confidential. Because paralegals and secretaries are agents of the lawyer, communications from clients to these individuals are also protected; together they form a "privileged network." Many believe that this tenet of ethics is so fundamental and important that, without the protections of the right of confidentiality, the legal system would not and could not work effectively.

Why is the concept of confidentiality so fundamental and important to the legal profession? A basic tenet of the attorney-client relationship is the principle that an attorney will keep confidential information private. Without assurances that information will be kept private, it is very likely that a client will either go without legal representation or will not divulge all of the facts pertaining to the case. Unless an attorney knows all of the facts involved in a particular situation, even embarrassing facts, the attorney will not be able to represent that client to the best of his or her ability. Keeping clients' secrets and confidences not only preserves the integrity of the profession but assures clients that they will receive good representation.

In general, all communications between an attorney, his or her agents, and the client are absolutely confidential, but there are certain exceptions. The first exception, when the client waives the right to confidentiality, springs from the fact that the privilege belongs to the client, who therefore has the power to relinquish it if it is an informed relinquishment. The second exception, when the client tells the attorney that he or she will commit a crime in the future, is based on the concept of an attorney as an officer of the court. The lawyer has an obligation as an officer of the court to inform the proper authorities of a future crime (under the Rules, the crime must be one that is likely to result in imminent death or substantial bodily harm to the victim); however, if a crime has already been committed, that communication is privileged. The third exception is for the collection of legal fees.

The attorney may use information gained during the course of representing the client to aid in collecting an outstanding legal fee. The fourth exception arises when an attorney is accused of wrongdoing, such as when a former client has filed a malpractice claim against him, or when there is a bar complaint; in that case, the lawyer may use information gained during representation of the client to defend himself and his actions.

3.2 CONFIDENTIALITY AND THE ATTORNEY-CLIENT PRIVILEGE

An ethical consideration that complements the idea of confidentiality is the attorney-client privilege. The following statement is the classic articulation of the elements of the attorney-client privilege by the renowned legal scholar Wigmore:

> (1) Where legal advice of any kind is sought (2) from a professional legal advisor in his capacity as such, (3) the communications relating to that purpose, (4) made in confidence (5) by the client, (6) are at his instance permanently protected (7) from disclosure by himself or by the legal adviser, (8) except the protection be waived.

8 Wigmore, *Evidence* § 2292 (McNaughton rev. ed. 1961). Note that the communication must concern legal advice from a lawyer and that the communication must be made "in confidence," which means that the client must intend that the communication be confidential. If, for example, a third party is present when the communication is offered, it is assumed that the client did not intend the communication to be confidential. Obviously, if the third party is an agent of the attorney (such as a legal assistant or secretary), the communication is still made in confidence. Thus, it is the client who defines the attorney-client privilege; ethical guidelines, which delineate most client communications as confidential, define confidentiality.

Unlike the concept of confidentiality, which is an ethical consideration, the attorney-client privilege finds its source in evidentiary rules. An evidentiary privilege is an immunity. The privilege is similar to the concept of confidentiality because it protects information given to the attorney by the client, but it differs in one important respect. Unlike the ethical consideration of confidentiality, which protects all disclosures, the privilege concerns only the compelled or involuntary disclosure of information. Thus, it is applied when an attorney or paralegal is being questioned by the police or in court. If the privilege applies, the lawyer or paralegal may refuse to answer. As soon as the attorney-client relationship begins, the privilege is created. Although the privilege ends when the representation ends, anything learned during the representation cannot be revealed.

Because this rule is grounded in policy considerations, it is not an ironclad one; rather, the privilege must be balanced against other valid interests. Those other interests are societal and personal interests, to be considered in the context of the privilege. Perhaps the most well-known example of this balancing approach, when it involves confidential communications, occurred in the *Tarasoff* case. *Tarasoff v. Regents of University of California,* 17 Cal. 3d 425, 551 P.2d 334, 131 Cal. Rptr. 14 (1976). In that case, a psychotherapist knew of his patient's plan to commit murder but did not reveal the information; a statutory privilege protected communications between therapist and patient. The California Supreme Court held that the need to protect the threatened individual, who actually was murdered by the psychotherapist's patient, overrode the necessity of protecting the communications. This same balancing approach was used by the Pennsylvania Appellate Court in *Pennsylvania v. Ferri,* 559 A.2d 208 (1991). In that case, the prosecution needed to establish a proper chain of custody to authenticate clothing worn by Ferri, a convicted murderer. To establish that chain, both Ferri's first attorney and his second attorney, a public defender, would have to testify concerning allegedly privileged information. Ferri argued that information concerning the clothing was privileged. The court, balancing the need to protect the defendant against the need to let the prosecution introduce incriminating physical evidence, decided to allow the defendant to stipulate as to the authenticity of the clothing. When the defendant refused such a stipulation, the trial court was correct, the appellate court found, in allowing testimony of Mr. Ferri's lawyers that was specifically tailored to cover the information needed for the chain of custody only.

Confidentiality, therefore, is the result of a balancing of interests, and the interests to be balanced are specific to each set of facts. In *Tarasoff,* it was the interest of the victim in being free from harm versus the confidentiality basic to therapist-patient relationships; in *Ferri,* it was the interest of the State in having a trial based on the facts versus the attorney-client privilege. Although the policy reasons supporting confidentiality must be weighed in each situation, the interest must generally be an overwhelming one to overcome the privilege; otherwise, the privilege would become useless.

3.3 WORK PRODUCT DOCTRINE

Another concept that goes hand in hand with that of privilege is the concept of work product. The work product doctrine was first articulated in *Hickman v. Taylor,* 329 U.S. 495 (1947) and has subsequently been codified as Rule 26(b)(3) in the Federal Rules of Civil Procedure, which is the basis for many state rules concerning work product. This doctrine covers the elements of work produced by an attorney or the attorney's agents during representation of the client and relates to both the mental impressions (thoughts, ideas, strategies) of the attorney and the information he or she compiles. For example, the attorney or paralegal may take notes during each client interview and maintain these notes in a file. An attorney or legal assistant may draft a memorandum to the file outlining legal arguments and trial strategies, or create charts or other models to be used as demonstrative evidence at trial. These items are protected from disclosure by the work product doctrine and are sometimes referred to as *materials prepared in anticipation of litigation*. Thus, if a criminal defense attorney interviews a witness to a crime, the district attorney's office cannot obtain a copy of the attorney's notes pertaining to that interview, because of the principle of work product.

However, like the evidentiary attorney-client privilege, the privilege covering materials prepared in anticipation of litigation is also subject to exceptions that permit disclosure. Although the private thoughts of the attorney are absolutely privileged, information itself receives only a qualified privilege. If the opposing counsel can show that the materials cannot be replicated and are essential to the case, sometimes the privilege is waived. For example, suppose that the lawyer claiming the privilege had interviewed a witness who subsequently died. If no one else had been able to speak to the witness, the attorney would probably have to produce the notes of that conversation.

One situation that frequently arises for paralegals who work in litigation concerns documents that are used in a case but were prepared routinely, not in anticipation of litigation. A police or insurance report might fall into this category; either would have been prepared whether or not litigation would follow. As these types of reports are not prepared in anticipation of litigation, but are merely prepared in the ordinary course of business, they would not be protected by the work product doctrine. Only documents prepared for and in anticipation of litigation are protected by the work product doctrine. Thus, in an employment discrimination suit, an employee's record of the various incidents that in her mind constituted employment discrimination, prepared in anticipation of filing suit, would be covered by the doctrine, but the same employee's evaluations would not.

The key to remembering what is and what is not covered by the work product doctrine is to ask yourself the simple question: "Was the document prepared for and in anticipation of litigating this matter and not just in the ordinary course of business?" If so, then the work product doctrine is applicable.

CASE STUDY: DO YOU HAVE TO PAY FOR CONFIDENTIALITY?

Legal assistant Lois is winding up her work for the day when she gets a call from an opposing attorney in the Lewis case. The opposing attorney wants to know the results of the independent medical evaluation that was scheduled for Lewis on behalf of Lois's firm. Lois knows that this information would normally be protected, but the Lewis case is being handled pro bono (no fee), and Lois thinks she remembers something about confidentiality not applying unless the client is a paying client. She then divulges the information to the opposing attorney.

Was Lois correct? Does a nonpaying client waive confidentiality by virtue of not paying for legal services? Regardless of whether she was correct, should Lois have revealed the information?

Special principles also apply to corporate clients when the issue of confidentiality arises. An attorney or paralegal representing a corporation owes the duty of confidentiality to the corporation but not to the corporate directors or officers. Thus, if during an interview, a corporate employee discloses information damaging to himself personally, but beneficial to the corporation, the attorney has no duty to keep that information confidential; the attorney's duty as counsel for the corporation is to the corporation, not to the individual. It is advisable for lawyers and paralegals involved in corporate representation to remind corporate officers of this to prevent problems.

Finally, it is important to acknowledge that issues of confidentiality may arise concerning intraoffice communications and confidences, rather than concern client confidences. In the course of working together, lawyers and paralegals will learn information, some personal and some professional, that the person might want to remain confidential. Such information might concern the "after-hours" activity of a married lawyer, the past activities or associations of colleagues, or a variety of other such information. It might concern using contacts or influence to gain supposedly confidential information, or it might involve an individual's further career development. As with many ethical issues, no clear guidelines exist concerning disclosure of personal information; each situation must be evaluated on its own merits, in its own context. Nonetheless, the issues presented in these situations are surely sticky ones. Use common sense when dealing with these situations. In most instances it is best to keep the information private, both inside and outside the office, so long as the activity does not adversely affect the workings of the office.

THE CASE OF ATTORNEY RICHARD'S RECOMMENDATIONS

Attorney Richards is a senior partner with a well-respected law firm. Two of his former legal assistants are being considered for new positions and their prospective employers want letters of recommendation from attorney Richards.

Paralegal Dena is an excellent paralegal seeking a position as a litigation paralegal in a small firm. She's bright, capable, and professional; it is also generally understood in the office that she is a lesbian. Some might say she is also a radical feminist, but she has never brought her political views to work. She has been spoken to about padding her billable hours, and that seems to have stopped, but as a litigation paralegal, she is first-rate.

Paralegal Max is seeking a position in the legal department of a real estate company. He has a fine military record and does a good job at work. Since he left his former position, Max has been convicted of drug possession, but attorney Richards does not know any details. Attorney Richards also knows that Max recently completed a probationary period stemming from his involvement in a kickback scheme at his former employer, but the evidence indicates that Max had been a pawn who was in the wrong place at the wrong time. Max is married, with two daughters and a dog, Bailey.

In his letters of recommendation, what should attorney Richards disclose about his two former assistants?

3.4 RULES AND GUIDELINES CONCERNING CONFIDENTIALITY

ABA Model Rules

Confidentiality is covered in Rule 1.6 of the Model Rules, which provides:

RULE 1.6 **Confidentiality of Information**

(a) A lawyer shall not reveal information relating to representation of a client unless the client consents after consultation, except for disclosures that are impliedly authorized in order to carry out the representation, and except as stated in paragraph (b).

(b) A lawyer may reveal such information to the extent the lawyer reasonably believes necessary:

(1) to prevent the client from committing a criminal act that the lawyer believes is likely to result in imminent death or substantial bodily harm; or

(2) to establish a claim or defense on behalf of the lawyer in a controversy between the lawyer and the client, to establish a defense to a criminal charge or civil claim against the lawyer based upon conduct in which the client was involved, or to respond to allegations in any proceeding concerning the lawyer's representation of the client.

The Rules designate more information to be confidential than does the Code, requiring only that the communication "relates . . . to the representation." This includes any information, whether acquired before or after representation, that relates to the subject of representation. In this respect, the Rules are broader than the Code. Thus, any and all information that the legal professional or her agents may gain relating to the representation of a client is covered and cannot be disclosed.

As to exceptions, however, the Rules are narrower than the Code. Under Rule 1.6(b), disclosure is permitted only to prevent a crime that is likely to result in imminent death or substantial bodily harm (not just any future crime), or to establish a claim or defense in a controversy between lawyer and client. The Code would require disclosure if a client told his attorney he was going to commit perjury, but under the Rules such disclosure would not be required because perjury is not likely to result in imminent death or substantial bodily harm. Even if the crime *is* likely to result in imminent death or substantial bodily harm, the attorney is cautioned in the Comment to the Rule to disclose only the amount of information, and no more, that the attorney believes necessary to prevent the crime. The Rules recognize in this respect that the free flow of information between attorney and client is even more important than preventing or disclosing some potential criminal acts. However, as the Comments to Rule 1.6 recognize, although the attorney may not have a duty to disclose this information, the attorney must not counsel or encourage a client to commit a criminal act. The Rules also provide that if a lawyer believes a client is using the attorney's services to materially further a course of criminal or fraudulent conduct, the lawyer should withdraw, but should not disclose any confidences or secrets of the client except those that are likely to result in imminent death or severe bodily harm.

The Rules provide that an attorney may disclose confidences and secrets to defend herself and her actions during the course of such proceedings as a malpractice or ethical complaint proceeding. Should a client file a malpractice suit or an ethical complaint, the attorney may once again use information gained while representing the client to defend against such accusations. For example, if the client gave the lawyer authority to settle a case and told the attorney, specifically against the attorney's advice, not to take a particular legal stand, the attorney could reveal those instructions to defend against a malpractice suit brought by that client. This exception can also lead to potential abuse, as professional basketball player Isaiah Thomas learned when the legal order that kept his 1985 paternity suit settlement confidential could not be respected because the child's mother later sued her lawyer. Jenni Dokes, the child's mother, alleged that the lawyer settled the case for too little money. One must wonder if ethical rules can sometimes be used for unethical (albeit legal) purposes.

If the client does not pay a legal bill, the attorney can file a lawsuit to collect the money and use information obtained while representing the client to collect the money. Some examples of such information are the client's place of employment (for garnishing wages), the client's bank account numbers (for garnishing checking accounts), and the client's Social Security number (to help a private investigator obtain additional information). Some commentators have remarked that this exception stems from the client's "sin" of not paying the lawyer's bill, suggesting that the need to collect a fee is not a great enough reason to reveal confidential communications. The attorney in these situations should make every effort to avoid unnecessary disclosure of client confidences.

It is important to remember that both the Rules and the Code permit an attorney to disclose information if the client has voluntarily and with informed knowledge waived the right to confidentiality. Consent to disclosure occurs, for instance, when the client gives the attorney permission to tell opposing counsel that the client will settle for a certain amount. Because the privilege of confidentiality belongs to the client, it is the client's to relinquish. The major issue in such a waiver is that the client be fully aware of what he or she is doing and the ramifications of those actions. If the waiver is an informed one, it will allow the attorney to breach the confidentiality of communications. Thus, if a divorce client tells you that you may disclose to anyone the fact that she had an affair with another man during her marriage, you may reveal this information. However, even if you believe the client has waived this privilege, the best practice is to get the waiver in writing or not reveal the information unless absolutely necessary.

ABA Model Code

Canon 4 of the Model Code states: "A Lawyer Should Preserve the Confidences and Secrets of a Client." The disciplinary rule that elaborates on this principle is DR 4-101.

DR-4-101 Preservation of Confidences and Secrets of a Client.

(A) "Confidence" refers to information protected by the attorney-client privilege under applicable law, and "secret" refers to other information gained in the professional relationship that the client has

You lawyers are so paranoid. Don't worry . . . no one can hear me.

requested be held inviolate or the disclosure of which would be embarrassing or would be likely to be detrimental to the client.

(B) Except when permitted under DR-4-101(C), a lawyer shall not knowingly:

(1) Reveal a confidence or secret of his client.

(2) Use a confidence or secret of his client to the disadvantage of the client.

(3) Use a confidence or secret of his client for the advantage of himself or of a third person, unless the client consents after full disclosure.

(C) A lawyer may reveal:

(1) Confidences or secrets with the consent of the client or clients affected, but only after a full disclosure to them.

(2) Confidences or secrets when permitted under Disciplinary Rules or required by law or court order.

(3) The intention of his client to commit a crime and the information necessary to prevent the crime.

(4) Confidences or secrets necessary to establish or collect his fee or to defend himself or his employees or associates against an accusation of wrongful conduct.

(D) A lawyer shall exercise reasonable care to prevent his employees, associates, and others whose services are utilized by him from disclosing or using confidences or secrets of a client, except that a lawyer may reveal the information allowed by DR 4-101(C) through an employee.

(Footnotes omitted.)

All communications from a client to an attorney are to be held in confidence, with the following exceptions:

1. The client has knowingly consented to such disclosure
2. The client has stated intent to commit a crime
3. To collect a fee
4. To defend against accusations of wrongdoing.

The second exception concerns the future commission of a crime and differs from the Rules. DR 4-101(C)(3) allows a lawyer to reveal "the intention of his client to commit a crime and the information necessary to prevent the crime." The operative word of this provision is "future"; only future criminal actions—not prior offenses of which the legal professional becomes aware in the course of representing the client—may be disclosed. Significantly, the Code relates to all crimes, while the Rules specifically delineate a crime that may result in death or significant bodily harm.

DR 4-101(D) concerns the duty of the attorney to use reasonable care to prevent disclosure of a client's confidences or secrets by the attorney's employees or associates. A lawyer must diligently ensure that associates and employees do not reveal or misuse confidential information. If a legal assistant divulged confidential information, therefore, the attorney might be in violation of this rule. This is another area where paralegals should be aware of the extent to which their actions affect lawyers.

Finally, the Code makes a distinction between client confidences and secrets. "Confidences," as defined by the Model Code, refers to information that would be precluded from disclosure under the applicable evidentiary privilege standards. "Secrets" refers to more than merely information which the attorney or her agents may be precluded from revealing under the applicable evidentiary privilege standard; anything that a client asks the lawyer to keep confidential, which if revealed would be embarrassing or detrimental to the client's interests, is protected from disclosure under the Model Code. In practice, it is best not to worry about this distinction. Instead, make a commitment that your professional work will be highly sensitive to the need to keep all client communications, whether confidences or secrets, confidential.

ABA Model Guidelines

Guideline 6 provides that: "It is the responsibility of a lawyer to take reasonable measures to ensure that all client confidences are preserved by a legal assistant." This language is very similar to that in the Code. As you may recall, DR 4-101(D) requires an attorney to take reasonable steps to ensure that employees do not disclose the confidences or secrets of clients. The Comment to Guideline 6 directs attorneys to educate their legal assistants that all information concerning the client, even the mere fact that the client is a client of the firm, must be strictly confidential. Likewise, the lawyer must take reasonable steps to ensure that paralegals do not make such disclosures. Examples of proper steps are having a secure computer system as well as having security measures for what may and may not be taken out of the office.

NALA

NALA also emphasizes the importance of client confidences and the duty for legal professionals to keep these communications confidential. Canon 7 of the NALA Code of Ethics states: "A legal assistant must protect the confidences of a client, and it shall be unethical for a legal assistant to violate any statute now in effect or hereafter to be enacted controlling privileged communications." As you can see from the language of this Canon, NALA's Code attempts to extend the evidentiary statutes defining privileged communications to legal assistants. In addition, the language of the Code is adamant: it is *"unethical"* to violate confidentiality laws. It is difficult to imagine stronger language than that to discourage violation of confidentiality provisions.

NFPA

The Affirmation of Responsibility from NFPA also emphasizes the importance of confidentiality for the paralegal. Considering that one of the six sections of the Affirmation is entirely devoted to client confidences, it is clear that NFPA places great importance on the ethical imperative to maintain client confidence. Like NALA's canon and the Code, the language in the NFPA Affirmation is clear and very straightforward: "A paralegal shall preserve client confidences and privileged communications." The discussion portion of Principle IV goes on to state: "Confidential information and privileged communications are a vital part of the attorney, paralegal, and client relationship. This importance of preserving confidential and privileged information is understood to be an uncompromising obligation of every paralegal." The use of the word "uncompromising" clearly means that NFPA believes that keeping and maintaining client confidences is an absolute prerequisite to being an ethical paralegal.

3.5 CONFIDENTIALITY AND THE PARALEGAL

Because most legal assistants work with clients daily, the issue of confidentiality is extremely important and relevant for paralegals. A good rule of thumb is to treat everything that a client tells you as a paralegal as confidential. If you have a question about the exceptions for confidentiality—when the client waives it, tells you he or she is about to commit a crime, to collect a fee, or to defend yourself against wrongdoing—the best course is to discuss such questions with your supervising attorney. Remember that you cannot take back what you have said; it is therefore best to say nothing until you are certain that it is perfectly correct to circulate certain information.

However, common sense is also important. If you are calling a client to set up a deposition date, the date the client tells you to give opposing counsel is of no significance to the case. Therefore, although the information comes from a client to an agent of an attorney and can be considered confidential, passing along this information in no way jeopardizes the client's case, so you may repeat it. On the other hand, a client's telling you to settle a case for a certain amount is confidential and could jeopardize the attorney's negotiating authority. Think first to help protect the client's absolute right to confidentiality.

Most importantly, you should never discuss the merits of a case outside the office, nor should you reveal that a particular person or entity is a client of the firm. You may be tempted to share the racy details of a divorce case with your best friend, or you may be so engrossed in the legal ramifications of a particular case that you feel compelled to share the information stemming from a particular representation. *Do not do it.* This urge is especially great if many of your social friends are in the profession; however, they are bound by the same ethical standards and they must respect your unwillingness to discuss cases in which you are involved. No matter the pressure or temptation, it is best to follow what Judge Don A. Langham, Judge of the Superior Court of Fulton County, Georgia, has informally called a "no possibility whatsoever" standard, meaning that a legal professional should not repeat anything if there is any possibility whatsoever, no matter how improbable, that what he or she says is breaching the duty of confidentiality. Respecting the confidentiality of a client's communications is at the heart of ethical lawyering; if you cannot fulfill this ethical commitment, you simply cannot work in the legal system.

A problem of confidentiality often arises when an attorney, paralegal, or other legal professional moves to another firm. Changing employment presents interesting issues of public policy, because the need to protect confidential communications must be balanced against the need of lawyers and legal assistants to change employment when they want. A balance between these competing interests is frequently struck by the implementation of policies, procedures, and checks and balances, so that the lawyer or paralegal can work at the new firm but at the same time be insulated from any information about or involvement with the case in question. Recent case law has specified the actions a firm must take to protect client confidences and avoid conflicts of interest when faced with this situation. These screening devices are referred to as a "Chinese Wall"; an effective Chinese Wall can help a firm in this situation avoid disqualification. This important topic is fully discussed in chapter 4, on conflict of interest, as it implicates that ethical issue as well.

If a new employee worked on a case at a previous firm, it is best to avoid working on that case at the new firm. This principle is called *disqualification.* Disqualification may also arise if one's spouse or relative is opposing counsel, or it may arise if an individual working in the public sector, as a consumer advocate or prosecutor, moves into the private sector to work for an industry or criminal defense firm. Although such a move would not disqualify the person per se from every case which his or her former employer handles, the person should not work on any cases that were pending at the time of separation, especially if the person worked on the case.

 ## THE CASE OF ELLEN THE EAGER ENTREPRENEUR

Ellen is a real estate paralegal with a large law firm, who has worked for the past five years in real estate law. Ellen is also a savvy businessperson who always looks for opportunities to invest her money profitably.

Ellen recently completed work on the Sydeman case, which involved sale of land in a rapidly growing area. The land sale is not general knowledge, and Ellen correctly figured that prices in the vicinity would rise because of the new development. Not being one to miss an opportunity, Ellen purchases land in the area. Is her purchase unethical because it was based on improper use of confidential information?

3.6 CASE LAW INTERPRETING CONFIDENTIALITY

The cases digested in this section will give you an idea of how the courts have looked at the issue of confidentiality.

In *Cabra,* the court examined the extent to which the doctrine of confidentiality applies to the notes taken by a legal assistant during the course of a trial.

UNITED STATES v. CABRA

United States Court of Appeals
622 F.2d 182 (5th Cir. 1980)

AINSWORTH, Circuit Judge:

This appeal raises the novel question [of] whether a district judge can impound notes taken during a criminal trial by a paralegal employed by defense counsel to assist in preparation of the defense. We hold that in this case, the district judge acted improperly in impounding the notes.

Appellants Edwin L. Cabra and Claude "Buddy" Leach were tried in district court on charges of vote buying in connection with the November 7, 1978 general election. After three weeks of trial, appellants were acquitted on all counts. Other charges against Leach alleging illegal receipt of campaign contributions are still pending.

During the trial, the district judge, on his own motion, called a bench conference to ask defense counsel if anyone associated with the defense was taking notes on the proceedings. Defense counsel informed the court that Ms. Mary Jane Marcantel, a paralegal employed by the defense, was taking shorthand notes of portions of the testimony. Counsel stated that

the purpose of the note-taking was to assist in the preparation of cross-examination, to provide summaries of testimony, and to aid in the preparation of the defense in anticipated criminal prosecutions in related cases. Ms. Marcantel was not present during the entirety of the trial and thus her notes did not reflect a complete account of the proceedings. The shorthand notes were not verbatim, but merely reflected, as accurately as possible, the substance of the testimony.

After ascertaining the character of the notes, the district judge, over defense counsel's objection, ordered that Ms. Marcantel could continue to take notes but that at the completion of the trial the notes were to be submitted to the court and sealed. After trial, the district judge sent a letter requesting compliance with the order. Appellants moved to vacate the order and filed a memorandum of law supporting their position. The district judge denied the motion, but stayed the order pending this appeal.

The district judge based the order on the court's duty "to insure the orderly process of a case." He stated that since the notes could be considered as an unofficial transcript the validity of the official transcript was at stake. "The court feels that there should only be one official transcript and that such unofficial transcripts should not be allowed. The court by this does not mean that these particular defendants would make any improper use of these notes. Rather this order is required to protect the integrity of the official court reporter's transcript." . . .

A district judge has the power to issue appropriate orders regulating conduct in the courtroom in order to assure an orderly trial. Often the basis of the power is the need to insure that a defendant obtains a fair trial free from unnecessary disruption.

This case is similar to the facts presented in *Columbia Broadcasting System.* There, the district court issued an order prohibiting any sketching of the proceedings. Sketches were made by artists employed by the media for subsequent showing on television news programs. This court, while acknowledging the district court's power to control its proceedings, rejected the order as overly broad. "We are unwilling . . . to condone a sweeping prohibition of in-court sketching when there has been no showing whatsoever that sketching is in any way obtrusive or disruptive." *Columbia Broadcasting System, supra,* 497 F.2d at 107 (footnote omitted). As in *Columbia Broadcasting System,* we cannot understand how Ms. Marcantel's note-taking resulted in any disruption of the courtroom proceedings. There is no evidence that her work had a disturbing or disruptive effect. It appeared that her actions did not differ from the note-taking activities of the press covering the trial or of opposing counsel. Certainly,

the note-taking did not interfere with or infringe appellants' rights to a fair trial as the task was performed on their behalf.

The district court placed great weight on the fact that Ms. Marcantel's notes were verbatim. There is no evidence, however, that this was true. Defense counsel state that the notes were incomplete and that while Ms. Marcantel strived for accuracy, the notes were not always taken in question and answer form. Even assuming that the notes were verbatim, however, we do not believe that the district judge's action was proper. Note-taking at trial is an acknowledged function of paralegals, *see* W.P. Statsky, *Introduction to Paralegalism,* 356 (West 1974). [First edition] A court should not penalize a party on account of the proficiency of its paralegal's performance. The district court's concern for the sanctity of the official transcript is misplaced. While it is the court's responsibility to assure that the official transcript is prepared in accordance with the Court Reporter's Act, 28 U.S.C Section 753, *see United States v. Garner,* 581 F.2d 481, 488 (5th Cir. 1978), the Act explicitly states that "[n]o transcripts of the proceedings of the court shall be considered as official except those made from the records taken by the reporter." Moreover, defense counsel stated that they had no intention of relying on the notes as an official summary of the testimony. Thus, the district court was operating under the mistaken assumption that the paralegal's notes challenged the validity of the official transcript.

Since the district court's reasons for impounding the notes were based on unwarranted concerns, the order was an improper exercise of the court's discretionary authority to control courtroom proceedings. Accordingly, the order is reversed.

REVERSED.

CASE QUESTIONS

1. How did the district court and the appellate court view the character of the notes taken by the paralegal?
2. What factors were considered in deciding whether to impound the notes?
3. Do you agree that these notes should be considered confidential?

In the *Mitchell* case, the court examined the circumstances surrounding the communication from a client to his attorney's employees to determine whether the statements were confidential.

PEOPLE V. MITCHELL

Court of Appeals of New York
448 N.E.2d 121 (N.Y. 1983)

SIMONS, Judge:

Defendant was a resident of Waterloo, New York, and, at the time these events occurred, he was under indictment for causing the stabbing death of his girlfriend, Audrey Miller, in February, 1976. He was represented on that charge by Rochester attorney Felix Lapine. In January, 1977, defendant went to Rochester to take care of some personal matters and registered at the Cadillac Hotel. On the evening of January 5, while sitting at the hotel bar, he met O'Hare McMillon. They had two or three highballs and then were seen to leave the bar about 11:00 p.m. and take the elevator to the floor on which Mitchell's room was located. No one saw either of them leave the defendant's room that night or the next morning, but in the afternoon of January 6, on a tip from attorney Lapine, the police went to defendant's hotel room and found the partially-clad, dead body of O'Hare McMillon on the bed. She had been stabbed 11-12 times in the face, chest and back. At least four of the wounds were sufficient to cause her death by exsanguination.

After leaving the hotel room that morning, defendant went to attorney Lapine's office. Lapine was not in but defendant met and spoke to a legal secretary, Molly Altman, in the reception area. She testified that he seemed nervous and as if he was looking for someone. Apparently he could not find whomever it was he was looking for, so he left, only to return a minute later and start telling her about what happened the night before. She testified that he said: "He wanted to go out and have a last fling . . . he had been out drinking and met a girl and then he woke up in the morning and she was dead. He had stayed there all night and then he walked out again."

While he was talking to Ms. Altman, Judith Peacock, another legal secretary, entered the reception area. She testified that the defendant was kind of rambling on but he said that: "He had laid next to someone all night and they didn't move, and he [was] in a bar and . . . in a hotel . . . this person who he had laid next to was black and he was worried because when the black people find out about it, they protect their own and he would be in danger." She also testified that he muttered something about a knife.

Ms. Pope-Johnson entered the room. She asked the defendant what was wrong and he told her: "that there was a dead body and he felt that he had done it and that the person was dead, that she was dead because of being stabbed."

Shortly thereafter, Lapine entered the office and talked privately with defendant. After defendant left, Lapine called the police and had them check defendant's hotel room. The body was discovered, defendant's identification learned from the hotel registration and defendant found and arrested at a bar near the courthouse.

On this state of the record, we conclude that the defendant has not met his burden of establishing that when he spoke to these unknown women in a common reception area, his statements were intended to be confidential and made to an employee of his attorney for the purpose of obtaining legal advice. The only evidence identifying the women came from Lapine, who responded to a question whether he had "any female employees" by saying "Yes", Robin Pope-Johnson. She, it turns out, was the last woman in the office to hear defendant's inculpatory statements and even if statements made to her at the time could have been privileged, the privilege was lost because of the prior publication to nonemployees and the utterance of the statements to Pope-Johnson in front of the nonemployees. Taking this view we need not consider whether the statements could be privileged because of an ongoing retainer between defendant and Lapine or if they could be privileged if made to an attorney's employee before a formal retainer was agreed upon.

When the *Mitchell* case was first heard on appeal at the New York Supreme Court, Appellate Division, that court, like the court above, found that the statements were not privileged. The dissent at that level is instructive.

PEOPLE V. MITCHELL

86 A.D.2d 976, 448 N.Y.S.2d 332 (1982)

. . . All concur, except CALLAHAN, J., who dissents and votes to reverse and grant a new trial in the following Memorandum:

I view existing precedent to mandate reversal and a new trial. . . .

Furthermore, I disagree with the majority that there was no error in the trial court's ruling with respect to the admission of certain statements made by defendant to personnel in the waiting room of his attorney's office. The record reveals that defendant telephoned the office of an attorney who was representing him on another pending charge and went to the office at their request. The trial court erroneously concluded that the attorney-client relationship did not exist until defendant's attorney arrived at his office. Contrary to the majority's view, it appears to be clear that defendant had gone to the attorney's office for the purpose of securing legal advice or assistance. Since the attorney-client privilege applies to "a confidential communication made between the attorney *or his employee* and the client in the course of professional employment" (CPLR 4503, subd. [a], emphasis added), I would remit for a further in camera hearing to determine (1) whether the two secretaries and a paralegal were, in fact, "employees" of defendant's attorney and (2) whether such statements were made in the "presence of strangers" (there being unsubstantiated claims that an unnamed third party was present) which would take the statements outside the privilege. Although the burden of proving each element of the claimed privilege rests upon the defendant, the trial court's erroneous ruling precluded defendant from offering proof to support his claim of privilege.

CASE QUESTIONS

1. Do you agree with the majority that Mitchell did not have an expectation of privacy?
2. Could the attorney's employees have done anything to provide better protection for Mitchell? Should they have done so?
3. Does the fact that Mitchell was a criminal defendant affect the analysis of the communication?

In the *Canfield* case, the court examined the reasons behind the doctrine of confidentiality in deciding whether a financial statement should be considered a confidential communication.

The PEOPLE
v.
Corinthians CANFIELD

**Supreme Court of California,
En Banc
527 P.2d 633 (Cal. 1974)**

McCOMB, Justice.

Defendant appeals from a judgment (order granting probation) of conviction entered upon a jury verdict finding him guilty of auto theft.

Facts: On the afternoon of October 6, 1971, Joan Petroni parked and locked her 1967 green Buick automobile in front of her home in San Jose and took the keys into the house. The following morning, the Buick was gone.

Officer Robert Arnold, of the California Highway Patrol, testified that early on the morning of October 7, 1971, he observed two automobiles apparently racing each other at speeds of approximately 100 miles an hour. One of them was a green Buick. The officer immediately gave chase, activating his rear amber and front red lights. After he had followed the cars for about eight miles, both of them pulled off the roadway onto the dirt shoulder. The officer got out of his vehicle and started toward the green Buick. The driver of that car looked directly at the officer and then sped away. The officer ran back to his car at once and again gave chase. After traveling another mile and a half, at speeds of up to 115 miles an hour, the Buick turned onto a side road and eventually spun out of control and into the Delta Mendota Canal. Miraculously, the driver (defendant) was uninjured.

The Buick was the one which belonged to Ms. Petroni. Following its removal from the canal, Officer Arnold examined it and, after observing that there was no key in the ignition, discovered that it had been hot-wired.

Defendant testified that he had purchased the Buick around 3 a.m. on October 7, 1971, for $1,300 in cash from one Levicks at Mickey's Blue Room, a bar in East Palo Alto. He said that he had brought a little over $500 with him to the bar around 1 p.m. on October 6, 1971; that he gambled there and had about $1,900 at the time he bought the car; and that later, after buying the car, he left $600 with his girlfriend at her home and retained only $10 in his pocket. He said that he then set out for Fresno, where he had formerly lived.

According to Officer Arnold's testimony, defendant told him shortly after his arrest that he had seen in the *San Jose Mercury* on October 6, 1971, an advertisement of the car for sale and that he later purchased it from a man

named "Levitts" at Mickey's Blue Room. At his trial, defendant admitted that that was what he had told the officer; but he said that it was not true, explaining that he had thought he would be released from jail sooner if he lied than if he told the truth.

Defendant testified that he had never met Levicks prior to the night he bought the car, but said that he had let people know some time before that he was interested in buying a car and that one of his friends had told him about the car Levicks had for sale and arranged for the two to meet at Mickey's Blue Room. The car supposedly belonged to Levicks' brother, who, defendant was told, was in the service in Texas at that time. Defendant drove the car around the block to test it. Then, after being assured by Levicks that it was not a stolen vehicle and that the brother would send him the automobile registration and the trunk key by mail, he completed the transaction, paying the full amount of the purchase price in cash. Defendant had been driving the car for five and one-half hours by the time it spun out of control and went into the canal; and he testified that during all that time he never once turned the motor off, because he was afraid he would not be able to get it started again.

Defendant further testified that just after the car went into the canal, he grabbed the key out of the ignition, put it in his pocket, and swam to the shore and that while he was at the jail he turned the key over to an unknown officer there. He denied that the car had been hot-wired.

In explaining why he had sped off after stopping the car on Officer Arnold's signals to stop, defendant testified that although he knew he was speeding, he had no idea why the officer had been chasing him; that he recalled he had had trouble with the San Matco Police Department; and that the officer had his hand quite close to his gun, and he was afraid the officer might kill him.

On cross-examination, defendant was asked how much he had won at gambling between March (when he moved to the Bay Area from Fresno) and October of 1971. Defendant gave an estimate of $75,000 and said that he had spent some of the money on expenses, such as clothing and jewelry, and had lost the rest in gambling. Defendant was then asked if he had ever filled out a financial eligibility statement. Following a conference at bench, the trial court ruled that defendant could be impeached by the form he had signed for the public defender pursuant to section 27707 of the Government Code.

Defendant had initially been interviewed at the jail by a legal aide named John Porter, who was a recent law school graduate working for the public defender while awaiting the results of the bar examination. Mr. Porter had asked whether defendant could afford private counsel and was told that he could not. After noting that defendant owned little more than a 1954 Oldsmobile, Mr. Porter asked him to sign the financial eligibility form. The form provided that the statement was being made under penalty of perjury, but at no time did Mr. Porter read the form to defendant or explain that he was signing under oath.

Defendant was charged with auto theft and receiving stolen property. He was, as hereinabove noted, found guilty of the auto theft charge, but he was acquitted on the other. He was granted three years' probation, contingent upon his serving one year in the county jail.

Is defendant's financial eligibility statement protected by the lawyer-client privilege?

Yes. It is clear from the circumstances under which the statement was given that it was given in confidence (see Evid.Code, section 952) and that defendant's purpose was to retain the public defender to represent him in the criminal proceedings against him. Under sections 951 and 954 of the Evidence Code, therefore, any disclosures made by defendant in the course of the interview were privileged and could not be revealed without his consent.

The lawyer-client privilege is, indeed, so extensive that where a person seeks the assistance of an attorney with a view to employing him professionally, any information acquired by the attorney is privileged whether or not actual employment results.

In indicating the reasons for the privilege, this court said in *City and County of San Francisco v. Superior Court,* 37 Cal.2d 227, 235 [12], 231 P.2d 26, 30: "The privilege is given on grounds of public policy in the belief that the benefits derived therefrom justify the risk that unjust decisions may sometimes result from the suppression of relevant evidence. Adequate legal representation in the ascertainment and enforcement of rights or the prosecution or defense of litigation compels a full disclosure of the facts by the client to his attorney. 'Unless he makes known to the lawyer all the facts, the advice which follows will be useless, if not misleading; the lawsuit will be conducted along improper lines, the trial will be full of surprises, much useless litigation may result. Thirdly, unless the client knows that his lawyer cannot be compelled to reveal what is told him, the client will suppress what he thinks to be unfavorable facts.' [Citation omitted.] Given the privilege, a client may make such a disclosure without fear that his attorney may be forced to reveal the information confided to him. '[T]he absence of the privilege would convert the attorney habitually and inevitably into a mere informer for the benefit of the opponent.'"

A relationship of trust and confidence between an indigent defendant and his attorney is now, in view of this court's determination that a defendant has no constitutional right to defend *pro se* at his trial, considered indispensable. And it is clear that if an accused is informed that the first information he provides his attorney is not privileged, he would not have the trust in his counsel so essential in providing effective representation. The problem is particularly serious with respect to indigents represented by the public defender, there apparently being a tendency on the part of many such defendants to regard the public defender as an arm of the state working closely with the prosecutor. . . .

The trial court ruled that under section 27707 of the Government Code a defendant's financial eligibility statement became a public record and that it was therefore not protected by the lawyer-client privilege. This ruling, however, is erroneous. Although section 27707 provides that "the court or the public defender may require a defendant or person requesting services of the public defender to file a financial statement under penalty of perjury," there is nothing in the section to require that the public defender turn over to the court a financial eligibility statement obtained by him. Presumably, if there is doubt that the defendant is eligible to have the public defender represent him, the court, which is empowered to make the final determination, may make oral inquiry of the defendant with respect to his assets or, even if the defendant has given a financial eligibility statement to the public defender, require that he give another to the court. But the language of section 27707 does not reveal an intention by the Legislature that the lawyer-client privilege be abrogated with respect to any financial eligibility statement given by a defendant in confidence to the public defender, as was the case here. In any event, even if it were held that the court could require the public defender to turn over to it a financial eligibility statement given by a defendant, the sole use which the court could make of the statement would be to enable it to determine whether the defendant was eligible for the services of the public defender and not, as here, to turn the statement over to the People to use in the prosecution of the case in chief against the defendant.

In view of our conclusion that defendant's financial eligibility statement is protected by the lawyer-client privilege, we deem it unnecessary to discuss his further contentions that forcing disclosure of the statement at his trial was a violation of his rights under the Fifth and Sixth Amendments of the United States Constitution, as well as article I, section 13, of the California Constitution, and also denied him equal protection of the laws.

Should the judgment (order granting probation) of conviction entered upon the jury verdict finding defendant guilty of auto theft be reversed?

No. Defendant, it will be recalled, was apprehended in a stolen, hot-wired vehicle after driving at speeds in excess of 100 miles an hour in an attempt to avoid being captured by the pursuing police officer. Furthermore, his testimony that he purchased the car for $1,300 cash in a bar from a total stranger, with the understanding that the automobile registration and the trunk key would be sent to him by mail at a later date, is inherently incredible. Under the circumstances, there being no reasonable probability that the jury would have reached a verdict favorable to defendant had his statement not been received in evidence, the error was harmless, and affirmance of the judgment is required. Moreover, even if we were to conclude that the admission of the statement violated defendant's rights under the federal Constitution, we are convinced that the error was harmless beyond a reasonable doubt.

The judgment (order granting probation) is affirmed.

WRIGHT, C.J., and TOBRINER, MOSK and BURKE, JJ., concur.

SULLIVAN, Justice (concurring).

I concur and I agree generally with the rationale by which the majority dispose of the case before us. But I do not agree with the broad holding that the majority opinion appears to announce and therefore feel I should emphasize my own views.

I agree that under the particular circumstances of this case, the financial eligibility statement signed by defendant and the communications between defendant and Mr. Porter (the public defender's legal assistant) relating to defendant's financial eligibility are protected by the attorney-client privilege. These communications took place in the privacy of an interviewing room in the Santa Clara County jail. Defendant then and there apparently believed that he was being represented by the public defender and therefore, in response to Mr. Porter's questions, freely and readily provided the information appearing on the statement. He was not told at any time that the purpose of the document was to determine whether or not he qualified for the appointment of a public defender as counsel for his defense on the basis of his indigency. During his interview with Mr. Porter, who was not a member of the State Bar, defendant was not aware, nor was he ever made aware, of the fact that his communications with the interviewer were other than those of a confidential nature, made in the course of an attorney-client relationship. Under those circumstances, it is apparent that defendant thought that the communications were confidential and he had a reasonable expectation that they would remain so.

On the other hand, if the procedures followed in situations like the present one are such that the defendant is made aware of their nature and purpose and understands that he will not be represented by the public defender until he has established his indigency, then any information given by him either orally or in writing for that purpose cannot properly be considered a "confidential communication" covered by the attorney-client privilege. Under such circumstances, information given by the defendant to establish his financial eligibility for free legal assistance, in my view, would not constitute "information transmitted between a client and his lawyer *in the course of that relationship . . .*" (Evid.Code, section 952 (emphasis added)). However, as previously stated, the particular circumstances of the case at bench do not warrant the conclusion that defendant was aware of the precise purpose of his interview with Mr. Porter. Accordingly, I think that we should emphasize that our holding herein is limited to the specific facts of the case before us.

CLARK, J., concurs.

CASE QUESTIONS

1. What is the distinction between the majority analysis and the concurrence?
2. Do you believe that financial eligibility information sheets should be absolutely protected from disclosure?
3. Do you think that Canfield had an expectation of privacy when he signed the financial eligibility statement?

Although the *Widger* case is long, it provides an excellent overview of the rules concerning changing employment as well as an articulate discussion of the policy reasons behind the doctrine of confidentiality.

In re COMPLEX ASBESTOS LITIGATION
Floyd W. WIDGER, et al., Plaintiffs and Appellants
v.
OWENS-CORNING FIBERGLAS CORPORATION, et al., Defendants and Respondents
Jeffrey B. Harrison, et al., Objectors and Appellants
[and eight other cases.]
Court of Appeal, First District, Division 3
283 Cal. Rptr. 732 (Ct. App. 1991)

CHIN, Associate Justice.

Attorney Jeffrey B. Harrison, his law firm, and their affected clients appeal from an order disqualifying the Harrison firm in nine asbestos-related personal injury actions. The appeal presents the difficult issue of whether a law firm should be disqualified because an employee of the firm possessed attorney-client confidences from previous employment by opposing counsel in pending litigation. We hold that disqualification is appropriate unless there is written consent or the law firm has effectively screened the employee from involvement with the litigation to which the information relates.

Respondents cross-appeal from the trial court's order, contending that the Harrison firm should have been disqualified in all asbestos cases throughout the state. We hold that a trial court does not have authority to disqualify counsel in proceedings pending in other courts. Further, the trial court did not abuse its discretion by not disqualifying the Harrison firm in all asbestos cases before the court. Therefore, we affirm the order of the trial court.

FACTS

Michael Vogel worked as a paralegal for the law firm of Brobeck, Phleger & Harrison (Brobeck) from October 28, 1985 to November 30, 1988. Vogel came to Brobeck with experience working for a law firm that represented defendants in asbestos litigation. Brobeck also represented asbestos litigation defendants, including respondents. At Brobeck, Vogel worked exclusively on asbestos litigation.

During most of the period Brobeck employed Vogel, he worked on settlement evaluations. He extracted information from medical reports, discovery responses, and plaintiffs' depositions for entry on "Settlement Evaluation and Authority Request" (SEAR) forms. The SEAR forms were brief summaries of the information and issues used by the defense attorneys and their clients to evaluate each plaintiff's case. The SEAR forms were sent to the clients.

Vogel attended many defense attorney meetings where the attorneys discussed the strengths and weaknesses of cases to reach consensus settlement recommendations for each case. The SEAR forms were the primary informational materials the attorneys used at the meetings. Vogel's responsibility at these meetings was to record the amounts agreed on for settlement recommendations to the clients. Vogel sent the settlement authority requests and SEAR forms to the clients. He also attended meetings and telephone conferences where attorneys discussed the recommendations with clients and settlement authority was granted. Vogel recorded on the SEAR forms the amount of settlement authority granted and distributed the information to the defense attorneys.

The SEAR form information was included in Brobeck's computer record on each asbestos case. The SEAR forms contained the plaintiff's name and family information, capsule summaries of medical reports, the plaintiff's work history, asbestos products identified at the plaintiff's work sites, and any special considerations that might affect the jury's response to the plaintiff's case. The SEAR forms also contained information about any prior settlements and settlement authorizations. Information was added to the forms as it was developed during the course of a case. Vogel, like other Brobeck staff working on asbestos cases, had a computer password that allowed access to the information on any asbestos case in Brobeck's computer system.

Vogel also monitored trial events, received daily reports from the attorneys in trial, and relayed trial reports to the clients. Vogel reviewed plaintiffs' interrogatory answers to get SEAR form data and to assess whether the answers were adequate or further responses were needed.

In 1988, Vogel's duties changed when he was assigned to work for a trial team. With that change, Vogel no longer was involved with the settlement evaluation meetings and reports. Instead, he helped prepare specific cases assigned to the team. Vogel did not work on any cases in which the Harrison firm represented the plaintiffs.

During the time Vogel worked on asbestos cases for Brobeck, that firm and two others represented respondents in asbestos litigation filed in Northern California. Brobeck and the other firms were selected for this work by the Asbestos Claims Facility (ACF), a corporation organized by respondents and others to manage the defense of asbestos litigation on their behalf. The ACF dissolved in October 1988, though Brobeck continued to represent most of the respondents through at least the end of the year. Not long after the ACF's dissolution, Brobeck gave Vogel two weeks' notice of his termination, though his termination date was later extended to the end of November.

Vogel contacted a number of firms about employment, and learned that the Harrison firm was looking for paralegals. The Harrison firm recently had opened a Northern California office and filed a number of asbestos cases against respondents. Sometime in the second half of November 1988, Vogel called Harrison to ask him for a job with his firm.

In that first telephone conversation, Harrison learned that Vogel had worked for Brobeck on asbestos litigation settlements. Harrison testified that he did not then offer Vogel a job for two reasons. First, Harrison did not think he would need a new paralegal until February or March of 1989. Second, Harrison was concerned about the appearance of a conflict of interest in his firm's hiring a paralegal from Brobeck. Harrison discussed the conflict problem with other attorneys, and told Vogel that he could be hired only if Vogel got a waiver from the senior asbestos litigation partner at Brobeck.

Vogel testified that he spoke with Stephen Snyder, the Brobeck partner in charge of managing the Northern California asbestos litigation. Vogel claimed he told Snyder of the possible job with the Harrison firm, and that Snyder later told him the clients had approved and that Snyder would provide a written waiver if Vogel wanted. In his testimony, Snyder firmly denied having any such conversations or giving Vogel any conflicts waiver to work for Harrison. The trial court resolved this credibility dispute in favor of Snyder.

While waiting for a job with the Harrison firm, Vogel went to work for Bjork, which represented two of the respondents in asbestos litigation in Northern California. Vogel worked for Bjork during December 1988, organizing boxes of materials transferred from Brobeck to Bjork. While there, Vogel again called Harrison to press him for a job. Vogel told Harrison that Brobeck had approved his working for Harrison, and Harrison offered Vogel a job starting after the holidays. During their conversations, Harrison told Vogel the job involved work on complex, nonasbestos civil matters, and later would involve processing release documents and checks for asbestos litigation settlements. Harrison did not contact Brobeck to confirm Vogel's claim that he made a full disclosure and obtained Brobeck's consent. Nor did Harrison tell Vogel that he needed a waiver from Bjork.

Vogel informed Bjork he was quitting to work for the Harrison firm. Vogel told a partner at Bjork that he wanted experience in areas other than asbestos litigation, and that he would work on securities and real estate development litigation at the Harrison firm. Initially, Vogel's work for the Harrison firm was confined to those two areas.

However, at the end of February 1989, Vogel was asked to finish another paralegal's job of contacting asbestos plaintiffs to complete client questionnaires. The questionnaire answers provided information for discovery requests by the defendants. Vogel contacted Bjork and others to request copies of discovery materials for the Harrison firm. Vogel also assisted when the Harrison firm's asbestos trial teams needed extra help.

In March 1989, Snyder learned from a Brobeck trial attorney that Vogel was involved in asbestos litigation. In a March 31 letter, Snyder asked Harrison if Vogel's duties included asbestos litigation. Harrison responded to Snyder by letter on April 6. In the letter, Harrison stated Vogel told Snyder his work for the Harrison firm would include periodic work on asbestos cases, and that Harrison assumed there was no conflict of interest. Harrison also asked Snyder to provide details of the basis for any claimed conflict. There were no other communications between Brobeck and the Harrison firm concerning Vogel before the disqualification motion was filed.

In June, a Harrison firm attorney asked Vogel to call respondent Fibreboard Corporation to see if it would accept service of a subpoena for its corporate minutes. Vogel called the company and spoke to a person he knew from working with Brobeck. Vogel asked who should be served with the subpoena in place of the company's retired general counsel. Vogel's call prompted renewed concern among respondents' counsel over Vogel's involvement with asbestos litigation for a plaintiff's firm. On July 31, counsel for three respondents demanded that the Harrison firm disqualify itself from cases against those respondents. Three days later, the motion to disqualify the Harrison firm was filed; it was subsequently joined by all respondents.

The trial court held a total of 21 hearing sessions on the motion, including 16 sessions of testimony. During the hearing, several witnesses testified that Vogel liked to talk, and the record indicates that he would volunteer information in an effort to be helpful.

A critical incident involving Vogel's activities at Brobeck first came to light during the hearing. Brobeck's computer system access log showed that on November 17, 1988, Vogel accessed the computer records for 20 cases filed by the Harrison firm. On the witness stand, Vogel at first flatly denied having looked at the case records, but when confronted with the access log, he admitted reviewing the records "to see what kind of cases [the Harrison firm] had filed." At the time, Vogel had no responsibilities for any Harrison firm cases at Brobeck. The date Vogel reviewed those computer records was very close to the time Vogel and Harrison first spoke. The access log documented that Vogel opened each record long enough to view and print copies of all information on the case in the computer system.

The case information on the computer included the SEAR form data. Many of the 20 cases had been entered on the computer just over a week earlier, though others had been on the computer for weeks or months. The initial computer entries for a case consisted of information taken from the complaint by paralegals trained as part of Brobeck's case intake team. Vogel denied recalling what information for the Harrison firm's cases he saw on the computer, and Brobeck's witness could not tell what specific information was on the computer that day.

Vogel, Harrison, and the other two witnesses from the Harrison firm denied that Vogel ever disclosed any client confidences obtained while he worked for Brobeck. However, Harrison never instructed Vogel not to discuss any confidential information obtained at Brobeck. Vogel did discuss with Harrison firm attorneys his impressions of several Brobeck attorneys. After the disqualification motion was filed, Harrison and his office manager debriefed Vogel, not to obtain any confidences but to discuss his duties at Brobeck in detail and to assess respondents' factual allegations. During the course of the hearing, the Harrison firm terminated Vogel on August 25, 1989.

The trial court found that Vogel's work for Brobeck and the Harrison firm was substantially related, and that there was no express or implied waiver by Brobeck or its clients. The court believed there was a substantial likelihood that the Harrison firm's hiring of Vogel, without first building "an ethical wall" or having a waiver, would affect the outcome in asbestos cases. The court also found that Vogel obtained confidential information when he accessed Brobeck's computer records on the Harrison firm's cases, and that there was a reasonable probability that Vogel used that information or disclosed it to other members of the Harrison firm's staff. The court refused to extend the disqualification beyond those cases where there was tangible evidence of interference by Vogel, stating that on the rest of the cases it would require the court to speculate.

The trial court initially disqualified the Harrison firm in all 20 cases Vogel accessed on November 17, 1988, which included 11 cases pending in Contra Costa County. However, on further consideration, the trial court restricted its disqualification order to the 9 cases pending in San Francisco. The Harrison firm timely noticed an appeal from the disqualification order, and respondents cross-appealed from the denial of disqualification in the Contra Costa County cases and all asbestos litigation. . . .

Concerns Raised by Disqualification Motions

Our courts recognize that a motion to disqualify a party's counsel implicates several important interests. These concerns are magnified when, as here, disqualification is sought not just for a single case but for many and, indeed, an entire class of litigation. When faced with disqualifying an attorney for an alleged conflict of interest, courts have considered such interests as the clients' right to counsel of their choice, an attorney's interest in representing a client, the financial burden on the client of replacing disqualified counsel, and any tactical abuse underlying the disqualification proceeding.

An additional concern arises if disqualification rules based on exposure to confidential information are applied broadly and mechanically. In the era of large, multioffice law firms and increased attention to the business aspects of the practice of law, we must consider the ability of attorneys and their employees to change employment for personal reasons or from necessity. . . . Persons going into business for themselves must not carry into it the secrets of their employers; but on the other hand, we think it our duty to take care that they not be prevented from engaging in any business they may obtain fairly and honorably.

Accordingly, judicial scrutiny of disqualification orders is necessary to prevent literalism from possibly overcoming substantial justice to the parties. . . . The issue ultimately involves a conflict between the clients' right to counsel of their choice and the need to maintain ethical standards of professional responsibility. The paramount concern, though, must be the preservation of public trust in the scrupulous administration of justice and the integrity of the bar. The recognized and important right to counsel of one's choosing must yield to considerations of ethics that run to the very integrity of our judicial process. . . .

Confidentiality and the Nonlawyer Employee

The courts have discussed extensively the remedies for the ethical problems created by attorneys changing their employment from a law firm representing one party in litigation to a firm representing an adverse party. Considerably less attention has been given to the problems posed by nonlawyer employees of law firms who do the same. The issue this appeal presents is one of first impression for California courts. While several Courts of Appeal have considered factual situations raising many of the same concerns, as will be discussed below, the decisions in those cases hinged on factors not present here. In short, this case is yet another square peg that does not fit the round holes of attorney disqualification rules.

Our statutes and public policy recognize the importance of protecting the confidentiality of the attorney-client relationship. The obligation to maintain the client's confidences traditionally and properly has been placed on the attorney representing the client. But nonlawyer employees must handle confidential client information if legal services are to be efficient and cost-effective. Although a law firm has the ability to supervise its employees and assure that they protect client confidences, that ability and assurance are tenuous when the nonlawyer leaves the firm's employment. If the nonlawyer finds employment with opposing counsel, there is a heightened risk that confidences of the former employer's clients will be compromised, whether from base motives, an excess of zeal, or simple inadvertence.

Under such circumstances, the attorney who has traditionally been responsible for protecting the client's confidences—the former employer—has no effective means of doing so. The public policy of protecting the confidentiality of attorney-client communications must depend upon the attorney or law firm that hires an opposing counsel's employee. Certain requirements must be imposed on attorneys who hire their opposing counsel's employees to assure the attorney-client confidences are protected. . . .

The Harrison firm argues that conflict of interest disqualification rules governing attorneys should not apply to the acts of non-lawyers, citing [two cases]. The courts in both cases refused to disqualify attorneys who possessed an adverse party's confidences when no attorney-client relationship ever existed between the party and the attorney sought to be disqualified. . . .

We believe the *Maruman* court's conclusions are appropriate for the factual situation that case represented. Mere exposure to the confidences of an adversary does not, standing alone, warrant disqualification. Protecting the integrity of judicial proceedings does not require so draconian a rule. Such a rule would nullify a party's right to representation by chosen counsel any time inadvertence or devious design put an adversary's confidences in an attorney's mailbox. Nonetheless, we consider the means and sources of breaches of attorney-client confidentiality to be important considerations.

The salient fact that distinguishes the present appeal from *Maruman* and *Cooke* is the person who disclosed the adverse party's attorney-client communications. If the disclosure is made by the attorney's own client, disqualification is neither justified nor an effective remedy. A party cannot "improperly" disclose information to its own counsel in the prosecution of its own lawsuit. Even if counsel were disqualified, the party would be free to give new counsel the information, leaving the opposing party with the same situation. However, preservation of open communication between attorney and client is endangered when an attorney's employee discloses client confidences. . . .

The integrity of judicial proceedings was threatened not by attorney misconduct, but by employee misconduct neither sanctioned nor sought by the attorney. The Harrison firm's disqualification is required not because of an attorney's affirmative misconduct, but because errors of omission and insensitivity to ethical dictates allowed the employee's misconduct to taint the firm with a violation of attorney-client confidentiality.

Protecting Confidentiality—The Cone of Silence

Hiring a former employee of an opposing counsel is not, in and of itself, sufficient to warrant disqualification of an attorney or law firm. However, when the former employee possesses confidential attorney-client information, materially related to pending litigation, the situation implicates " '. . . considerations of ethics which run to the very integrity of our judicial process.' [Citation omitted.]" Under such circumstances, the hiring attorney must obtain the informed written consent of the former employer, thereby dispelling any basis for disqualification. Failing that, the hiring attorney is subject to disqualification unless the attorney can rebut a presumption that the confidential attorney-client information has been used or disclosed in the new employment.

A law firm that hires a nonlawyer who possesses an adversary's confidences creates a situation, similar to hiring an adversary's attorney, which suggests that confidential information is at risk. We adapt our approach, then, from cases that discuss whether an entire firm is subject to vicarious disqualification because one attorney changed sides. The courts disagree on whether vicarious disqualifications should be automatic in attorney conflict of interest cases, or whether a presumption of shared confidences should be rebuttable. An inflexible presumption of shared confidences would not be appropriate for non-lawyers, though, whatever its merits when applied to attorneys. There are obvious differences between lawyers and their nonlawyer employees in training, responsibilities, and acquisition and use of confidential information. These differences satisfy us that a rebuttable presumption of shared confidences provides a just balance between protecting confidentiality and the right to chosen counsel.

The most likely means of rebutting the presumption is to implement a procedure, before the employee is hired, which effectively screens the employee from any involvement with the litigation, a procedure one court aptly described as a "cone of silence." Whether a potential employee will require a cone of silence should be determined as a matter of routine during the hiring process. It is reasonable to ask potential employees about the nature of their prior legal work; prudence alone would dictate such inquiries. Here, Harrison's first conversation with Vogel revealed a potential problem—Vogel's work for Brobeck on asbestos litigation settlements. . . .

Protecting Confidentiality—The Rule for Disqualification

Absent written consent, the proper rule and its application for disqualification based on nonlawyer employee conflicts of interest should be as follows. The party seeking disqualification must show that its present or past attorney's former employee possesses confidential attorney-client information materially related to the proceedings before the court. The party should not be required to disclose the actual information contended to be confidential. However, the court should be provided with the nature of the information and its material relationship to the proceeding.

Once this showing has been made, a rebuttable presumption arises that the information has been used or disclosed in the current employment. The presumption is a rule by necessity because the party seeking disqualification will be at a loss to prove what is known by the adversary's attorneys and legal staff. To rebut the presumption, the challenged attorney has the burden of showing that the practical effect of formal screening has been achieved. The showing must satisfy the trial court that the employee has not had and will not have any involvement with the litigation, or any communication with attorneys or coemployees concerning the litigation, that would support a reasonable inference that the information has been used or disclosed. If the challenged attorney fails to make this showing, then the court may disqualify the attorney and law firm.

The Trial Court Properly Exercised Its Discretion

With the foregoing principles in mind, we turn to the trial court's exercise of discretion. The Harrison firm devotes a substantial portion of its arguments to challenging the sufficiency of the evidence to support disqualification. . . . Under the familiar rules, we must consider the evidence in the light most favorable to the prevailing party and take into account every reasonable inference supporting the trial court's decision.

The Harrison firm's primary contention on appeal is that respondents failed to show the Vogel possessed any specific client confidences. The Harrison firm's repeated invocation of *specific* confidences misses the point and underscores the futility of its factual argument. Vogel admitted reviewing the Harrison firm's cases on Brobeck's computer to see "what kind of cases [the Harrison firm] had filed." The plain inference is that Vogel used his training in asbestos litigation to make a rough analysis of his prospective employer's cases. Vogel acknowledged that because of his experience in looking at SEAR forms, he knew that some cases have more value than others. He also testified that the SEAR forms are used as the basis for evaluating cases. The SEAR form information Vogel obtained about the Harrison firm's cases was part of a system of attorney-client communications.

There can be no question that Vogel obtained confidential attorney-client information when he accessed the Harrison firm's case files on Brobeck's computer. Respondents need not show the specific confidences Vogel obtained; such a showing would serve only to exacerbate the damage to the confidentiality of the attorney-client relationship. As discussed above, respondents had to show only the nature of the information and its material relationship to the present proceedings. They have done so.

To blunt the impact of Vogel's misconduct, the Harrison firm argues that the cases on the computer were newly filed and that no evidence showed the computer information to be more than appeared on the face of the complaints, which are public records. The argument is wrong on both points. While many of the cases were entered on the computer little more than a week earlier, others were entered weeks or months before Vogel looked at them. Moreover, the fact that some of the same information may appear in the public domain does not affect the privileged status of the information when it is distilled for an attorney-client communication. Therefore, there was substantial evidence that Vogel possessed confidential attorney-client information materially related to the cases for which the trial court ordered disqualification.

The Harrison firm also argues that there was no evidence that Vogel disclosed any confidences to any member of the firm, or that any such information was sought from or volunteered by Vogel. Harrison testified that he never asked Vogel to divulge anything

other than impressions about three Brobeck attorneys. Harrison and his office manager also testified that Vogel was not involved in case evaluation or trial tactics discussions at the Harrison firm. However, this evidence is not sufficient to rebut the presumption that Vogel used the confidential material or disclosed it to staff members at the Harrison firm. Moreover, there was substantial evidence to support a reasonable inference that Vogel used or disclosed confidential information.

Despite Harrison's own concern over an appearance of impropriety, Harrison never told Vogel not to discuss the information Vogel learned at Brobeck and did not consider screening Vogel even after Brobeck first inquired about Vogel's work on asbestos cases. The evidence also amply supports the trial court's observation that Vogel was "a very talkative person, a person who loves to share information." Further, Vogel's willingness to use information acquired at Brobeck, and the Harrison firm's insensitivity to ethical considerations, were demonstrated when Vogel was told to call respondent Fibreboard Corporation and Vogel knew the person to contact there.

The trial court did not apply a presumption of disclosure, which would have been appropriate under the rule we have set forth. The evidence offered by the Harrison firm is manifestly insufficient to rebut the presumption. Beyond that, though, substantial evidence established a reasonable probability that Vogel used or disclosed to the Harrison firm the confidential attorney-client information obtained from Brobeck's computer records. Accordingly, the trial court was well within a sound exercise of discretion in ordering the Harrison firm's disqualification. . . .

CONCLUSION

We realize the serious consequences of disqualifying attorneys and depriving clients of representation by their chosen counsel. However, we must balance the important right to counsel of one's choice against the competing fundamental interest in preserving confidences of the attorney-client relationship. All attorneys share certain basic obligations of professional conduct, obligations that are essential to the integrity and function of our legal system. Attorneys must respect the confidentiality of attorney-client information and recognize that protecting confidentiality is an imperative to be obeyed in both form and substance. A requisite corollary to these principles is that attorneys must prohibit their employees from violating confidences of former employers as well as confidences of present clients. Until the Legislature or the State Bar choose to disseminate a different standard, attorneys must be held responsible for their employees' conduct, particularly when that conduct poses a clear threat to attorney-client confidentiality and the integrity of our judicial process.

The order of the trial court is affirmed. Each party shall bear its own costs.

WHITE, P.J., and STANKMAN, J., concur.

CASE QUESTIONS

1. What actions should the Harrison firm have taken to prevent disqualification?
2. Did Vogel have a duty which he violated?
3. What would you have advised Vogel to do when he applied for a position with the Harrison firm?

3.7 RECOGNIZING AND RESOLVING CONFIDENTIALITY PROBLEMS

Case law, ABA Model Rules, ABA Model Code, ABA Model Guidelines, NALA's Code, NFPA's Affirmation, and evidentiary principles all stress the importance of confidentiality in the legal profession. As a paralegal, you may wonder how to resolve day-to-day ethical considerations about maintaining client confidences and secrets. The best and general rule is: *Never talk about any matter in a case outside the office.* No matter how "juicy" or interesting a particular case or client might be, you would not be a very effective legal professional if you became the equivalent of a scandal sheet for your friends. Think of whether they would hire your firm if they knew that you talked about cases.

Also, rely on the discretion and advice of your supervising attorney should you believe that some information must be disclosed. The supervising attorney is in the best possible position to judge the ramifications and the ethical problems surrounding a certain piece of information. Remember that the attorney is responsible for the work and actions of his or her assistants and may be vicariously liable for their negligence.

Should you be subpoenaed or questioned by the police, it may be best not to disclose anything. In real-life situations, if you are called to testify in court and the information sought is confidential and privileged, the attorney will most likely make a motion to quash the subpoena, protecting you from testifying under the principle of privileged communications. Many state legislatures have passed statutes that protect communications not only with one's attorney, but also with agents of the lawyer, such as secretaries and legal assistants.

THE CASE OF THE WAYWARD WAIVER

Attorney Grady and legal assistant Stephenson are defending Moose van Pimplebottom, who has been accused of first-degree murder, kidnapping, and rape. In conversations with Moose, Stephenson learned that he did in fact commit those crimes, in a rage of unrequited love. Moose calls the office one afternoon, asking to speak to Grady. Because Grady is unavailable and he knows the legal assistant well, Moose asks to talk to Stephenson. Moose then tells Stephenson that he knows he did a terrible thing and that he does not want to keep secrets from the district attorney any longer. Moose says he understands that this means he will go to jail, probably for a very long time, but he just wants to tell the truth.

After Moose hangs up, district attorney James calls Stephenson the legal assistant and says, "I'd sure like to dispose of the van Pimplebottom case; Moose is guilty as hell—I just need to prove it. You got any new information for me?"

Has Moose waived his right to confidentiality? Should Stephenson reveal Moose's guilt?

In his guest editorial, Roy Sobelson explores a new approach to the issue of confidentiality.

GUEST EDITORIAL

EXPLAINING "CONFIDENTIALITY"— A NEW APPROACH

by Roy Sobelson

In light of the many exceptions, it is clearly misleading to suggest to a client that "everything is confidential." The reasons for this have been detailed above.

Given all of this, what should the lawyer say? The lawyer must find some way of accommodating two very important needs. First, he must make sure that the disclosure is truthful, accurate, and complete enough to be appreciated by the client. Second, the disclosure must not be so complicated and frightening that it unduly chills the open and honest exchange of information. Because a truly accurate disclosure is so important, and likely to be fairly lengthy, to the extent possible it should be made in a written form, submitted to the client prior to the interview, complete with a space for the client to indicate his understanding of the terms. The form might look and sound something like this.

CONFIDENTIALITY: YOUR RIGHTS AND YOUR LAWYER'S DUTIES

NOTE: THIS DOCUMENT STATES IMPORTANT LEGAL RIGHTS. IT IS ESSENTIAL THAT YOU READ AND SIGN IT ALL BEFORE YOU CONFER WITH OUR ATTORNEY. IF YOU HAVE QUESTIONS ABOUT IT, ASK THE ATTORNEY BEFORE YOU SIGN IT. YOUR SIGNATURE AT THE END WILL SIGNIFY YOUR UNDERSTANDING OF THE MATTERS STATED HERE.

1. In order to represent you competently, it is essential that you and I speak openly and honestly, even about information which is damaging to your case or embarrassing. Any deletion, alteration, or concealment of relevant information could do great harm to your case and to our professional relationship. To encourage open communication, the law has developed rules of "confidentiality." CONFIDENTIALITY HAS LIMITS, HOWEVER, AND THESE ARE DISCUSSED IN THIS DOCUMENT.

2. Whether you end up hiring me or not, I have a duty of "confidentiality" to you which forbids me (even after any relationship between us ends) to voluntarily disclose information about your case or use it to your disadvantage. There are limitations on this, however, such as the following:

   (a) Information is normally shared with other members of this firm, all of whom are bound by confidentiality. Upon your request, specific information will not be shared, as long as it is still possible to represent you competently.

   (b) Secretaries, paralegals, and other essential nonlawyer personnel are also exposed to confidential information; these persons are admonished not to reveal this information. Upon your request, this will be limited, as long as it is still possible to represent you competently.

   (c) Lawyers are occasionally required by the law to give statistical, bookkeeping, and similar information to regulatory agencies such as the state bar, consumer protection agencies, and even the Internal Revenue Service. To the extent possible, this information will be submitted anonymously, but that is not always possible.

   (d) This firm uses data processing services for bookkeeping and statistical purposes; these services must be given access to limited information in your file. You have the right to prohibit dissemination of information, as long as it is still possible to represent you competently.

   (e) In representing you, we are sometimes required to reveal to a court or other party information about your case, such as medical records, facts of an accident or occurrence, names of available witnesses, and the like. This information may come directly from you, or it may be learned while working for you. You may request that certain items not be revealed, but it may not be possible to honor that request and still represent you competently.

3. From the first moment we speak, you have a legal right to PROHIBIT me from disclosing any of our COMMUNICATIONS (oral or written). This prohibits me from disclosing anything you tell me about acts you may have engaged in before you consult with me. Except in rare circumstances, this prohibition *does not apply* to certain things, such as:

   (a) The fact and terms (such as fee) of our relationship;

   (b) Information such as your name, address, and phone number, and things that I may observe during our relationship, such as your appearance;

   (c) Information conveyed to me for purposes other than obtaining legal advice; an example is information conveyed for PURELY personal or business purposes. (Business or personal information conveyed in the context of legal consultation is protected);

   (d) Communications made for the purposes of having me participate or aid in criminal, fraudulent, or wrongful activity;

(e) Tangible objects you give to or leave with me. (It does, however, cover anything you tell me ABOUT those objects.)

4. Despite my obligations of confidentiality, I may be FORCED to reveal information under the following circumstances:

(a) If a court orders me to;

(b) If certain laws require me to;

(c) If you intend to commit a crime or fraud in the future;

(d) If you commit a fraud, such as perjury, while I am your lawyer.

5. If any question is raised about the quality, legality, or value of my legal services to you, I may reveal information to the extent necessary to defend or otherwise protect myself. If I am forced to take legal action against you to collect fees I have earned, I may reveal information necessary to prove and collect my claim against you.

6. YOUR RIGHTS UNDER THESE RULES MAY BE WAIVED (FORFEITED) BY REVEALING ANY INFORMATION TO OTHERS. UNLESS YOU HAVE CONFERRED WITH ME FIRST, PLEASE CONFINE ALL DISCUSSION OF YOUR CASE TO OUR CONVERSATIONS. IF ANY PERSON ASKS YOU ABOUT YOUR CASE OR MATTERS RELATED TO IT, PLEASE DIRECT SUCH INQUIRIES TO ME.

7. IF YOU HAVE READ THE ABOVE DOCUMENT AND AGREE TO BE BOUND BY ITS TERMS, PLEASE SIGN BELOW.

_____   _____
Date   Signature of Client

Some would argue that this disclosure will scare clients. There are two reasons why this is not a legitimate objection. First of all, the lawyer has a duty to inform his client of these important rights. The fact that the information is complicated or frightening is no excuse for hiding it. Second, while giving the client either no information or inaccurate information about confidentiality may result in greater disclosure by the client, it may also cause him to expose information he has the absolute right to keep secret, even if complete secrecy can only be accomplished by refusing to consult with an attorney. A client has a right to decide that some information is so sensitive that he does not wish to entrust it to a lawyer who will reveal it if, for instance, a court order (even one which is arguably invalid) compels him to.

Others may object that this disclosure will give the wrong message to clients; it will cause clients bent on using the lawyer for illegal purposes or who are unsure about the legality of their actions to hide information. This most likely happens already, if for no other reason other than that clients may fear a loss of respect from their lawyer if they should reveal their real motives or purposes. Selective disclosure should be unavailing; the lawyer acting on incomplete information will be unable to handle the matter with complete competence, while the client whose lawyer later discovers he has been deliberately misled deserves no protection from the rules of confidentiality.

Furthermore, if clients refuse to reveal their true intentions, then at least the lawyers would not be knowing instruments of crime. Once a lawyer explains the limitations of confidentiality, his clients will realize they will not be aided in improper actions by the attorney. If all attorneys comply with their duty to explain the rules, lawyer shopping will be futile and clients will become acutely aware that lawyers are not willing instruments of crime.

Finally, some will argue that this disclosure is too onerous for attorneys. However, if all attorneys are required to make the disclosures, they will all be on equal footing. At the same time, universal disclosure will make confidentiality documents more widely known. This could have several effects; it could inform the public, it could make attorneys who participate in illegal acts more noticeable, and it could inspire a frank and thorough reconsideration of all the doctrines of confidentiality, both ethical and legal.

■ Roy Sobelson is Associate Professor of Law at Georgia State University School of Law. This article was excerpted with permission from "Lawyers, Clients and Aspects of Confidentiality: Lawyers Talking without Speaking, Clients Hearing without Listening," 1 *Georgetown Journal of Legal Ethics*, 771–74 (No. 4, Spring 1988).

3.8 THE PARALEGAL, THE LAWYER, AND CONFIDENTIALITY: A SUMMARY

Maintaining confidences and secrets is one of the very foundations of the American legal system. Without the protection of communications from a client to the attorney and the agents of the attorney, it is very likely that most individuals would not receive or seek legal representation when they most needed it. Paralegals who fail to maintain confidentiality are undermining the role of the legal assistant. As the supervising attorney begins to know and trust you more, as he or she sees you maintaining confidentiality of communications, your prestige and respect within the firm will increase. We have previously referred to the similarity of the legal profession and the medical profession. Like the legal profession, the medical profession is also bound by patient confidentiality provisions. The reasons for this restraint on third-party communications with one's health care provider, like the restraints on one's legal representative, are to ensure that the client/patient is free to discuss all problems with the professional to ensure that the client/patient receives the best assistance possible. As a paralegal, a trusted and involved member of the legal team, it is your ethical duty to provide the very best representation for your client. This right to zealous, effective representation is the basis for the ethical mandates of the prohibition against disclosure of confidential information. By respecting the ethical guidelines concerning confidentiality, the paralegal can make a significant contribution to the ethical representation of clients.

REVIEW QUESTIONS

1. What kinds of lawyer-client communications are confidential?
2. Why should some communications be confidential?
3. What is the attorney-client privilege?
4. What is the work product doctrine?
5. How do the Rules and the Code differ on the issue of confidentiality?

QUESTIONS FOR THOUGHT AND DISCUSSION

1. In your opinion, do the Rules or the Code provide greater protection of a client's right to confidentiality?
2. Are there any arguments *against* protecting client confidences and secrets? What are they?
3. You are a paralegal with the firm of Bibeau and Kashinsky. The firm has recently been retained by Sarah Hinson, your husband's ex-fiancée.

Would you violate ethical standards of confidentiality if you told your husband that Sarah was a client, without revealing any specifics of her representation?

4. You are a paralegal; your roommate is a lawyer. You work for different firms. While working on a brief, you decide to call your roommate to get feedback on your legal arguments. How can you ensure that you do not violate your ethical obligation of confidentiality during this conversation?

5. Debbie is asked by her supervising attorney to contact Ms. Meloncamp at her office to obtain the information necessary to complete the financial affidavit for Ms. Meloncamp's divorce. Ms. Meloncamp works at the post office, and the phone book indicates that there is surveillance equipment on the telephones. Would Debbie's conversation with Ms. Meloncamp be protected communication? Why or why not?

LAW, LITERATURE, AND ETHICS

From Presumed Innocent
By Scott Turow

"Now, let's talk about this motion to disqualify Mr. Molto." This is our request to prevent Tommy Molto from acting as one of the trial lawyers on the case, because Nico has said Molto may be a witness.

Nico starts right in. To disqualify one of the prosecutors with three weeks to trial would be an onerous burden. Impossible. The state could never be ready. I do not know if Nico is looking for more time, or trying to defeat the motion. He is probably not sure himself.

"Well, look now, Mr. Della Guardia, I'm not the person who told you to put Mr. Molto on your witness list," Judge Lyttle says. "I cannot imagine how you thought you were going to proceed with a prosecutor who might be a witness. A lawyer may not be an advocate and a witness in the same proceeding. We've been doing business in our courts the same way for about four hundred years now. And I do not intend to change it for this trial, no matter how important it is to any of the participants, no matter how many reporters show up from *Time* or *Newsweek* or anyplace else." Judge Lyttle pauses and squints toward the reporters' gallery, as if he only now had noticed them there.

"But let me say this—" Larren stands up, and wanders behind the bench. Five feet off the ground to start with, he speaks from an enormous height. "Now, I take it, Mr. Delay Guardia, that the statement you are speaking of is the one where Mr. Sabich responds to Mr. Molto's accusation of murder by saying, 'You're right.'"

"'Yeah, you're right,'" says Nico.

Larren accepts the correction, bowing his large head.

"All right. Now, the state has not offered the statement yet. However, you've indicated your intentions and Mr. Stern has made his motion for that reason. But this is what occurs to me. I really am not sure that statement will come into evidence. Mr. Stern hasn't made any objection yet. He would rather see Mr. Molto disqualified first. But I imagine, Mr. Delay Guardia, that when we get there Mr. Stern is gonna say that this statement is not relevant." This is one of Larren's favorite means of assisting the defense. He predicts objections he is likely to hear. Some of them—like this one—are clearly going to come. Others never would have occurred to defense counsel. In either event, when formally made, the objections foretold inevitably succeed.

"Your Honor," says Nico, "the man admitted the crime."

"Oh, Mr. Delay Guardia," says Judge Lyttle. "Really! You see, that is my point. You tell a man he's engaged in wrongdoing and he says, 'Yeah, you're right.' Everyone recognizes that's facetious. We all are familiar with that. Now, in my neighborhood, had Mr. Sabich come from those parts, he would have said, 'Yo' momma.'"

There is broad laughter in the courtroom. Larren has scored again. He sits on the bench, laughing himself.

"But you know, in Mr. Sabich's part of town, I would think people say, 'Yeah, you're right,' and what they mean is 'You are wrong.'" Pausing. "To be polite."

More laughter.

"Your Honor," Nico says, "isn't that a question for the jury?"

"On the contrary, Mr. Delay Guardia, that is initially a question for the court. I have to be convinced this evidence is relevant. That it makes the proposition for which it is offered more probable. Now, I am not ruling yet, but, sir, unless you are a good deal more persuasive than you have been so far, I expect that you will find me ruling that this evidence is not relevant. And you might want to keep that in mind in addressing Mr. Stern's motion, because if you're not going to be offering that evidence, or relying on it in cross-examination of the defendant, why then, I'd have to deny the defendant's motion."

Larren smiles. Nico, of course, is screwed. The judge has as much as told him that the statement will not be admitted. Nico's choice is to lose Molto and make a futile effort to introduce the evidence, or to keep Tommy and abandon the proof. It is really no choice at all for him—better to take half a loaf. My statement to Molto has just disappeared from this case.

Molto approaches the podium. "Judge—" he says, and gets no further. Larren interrupts. His face drains of all good humor.

"Now, Mr. Molto, I will not listen to you address the admissibility of your own testimony. Maybe you can convince me that that time-honored rule prohibiting a lawyer from being a witness in a case he tries shouldn't be applied here, but until you do, I will not hear further from you, sir."

Larren closes business quickly. He says he will see us for trial on August 18. With one more glance toward the reporters, he leaves the bench.

Molto is still standing there, his look of disgruntlement plain. Tommy's always had a bad habit for a trial lawyer of allowing his dissatisfaction to be evident. But Judge Lyttle and he have been going at each other now for many years. I may not have recalled Carolyn's service in the North Branch, but I could never have forgotten Larren and Molto. Their disputes were notorious. Exiled by Bolcarro to that judicial Siberia, Judge Lyttle applied his own rough justice. The cops were guilty of harassment, unless proven otherwise. Molto, beleaguered and bitterly unhappy, used to claim that the pimps and junkies and sneak thieves, some of whom made daily appearances in Larren's courtroom, would rise to applaud him when he assumed the bench for the morning call. The police despised Judge Lyttle. They invented racial epithets that showed the same imagination which put humankind upon the moon. Larren had been downtown for years by the time I finished the Night Saints investigation and Lionel

Kenneally was still complaining whenever he heard Larren's name. There was one story Kenneally must have told me ten times about a battery case, brought by a cop who claimed that the defendant had resisted arrest. The cop, named Manos, said he and the defendant had gotten into a tussle shortly after the defendant called the cop a name.

What name? Larren asked him.

Here in court, said Manos, I'd rather not say, Judge.

Why officer, are you afraid you might offend those present? Larren gestured toward the forward benches, where the defendants on the morning call were seated, an assemblage of hookers, pickpockets, and junkie thieves. Speak freely, Judge Lyttle said.

He called me motherfucker, Your Honor.

From the benches there were whistles, catcalls, lots of joviality. Larren gaveled silence, but he was laughing, too.

Why officer, said Larren again, still smiling, didn't you know that is a term of endearment in our community?

The folks on the benches went wild: black-power salutes and a frenzy of stroking palms. Manos took all of this in silence. A minute later, when Molto rested, Larren directed a verdict for defense.

'And the great part,' Kenneally told me, 'is that Manos comes up to the bench, stands there with his hat in his hand, and says to Lyttle, sweet as a school kid, "Thank you, motherfucker," before he walks away.'

I have heard this story from two other people. They agree on the final exchange. But both of them swear the last remark came from the bench.

■ Excerpt from *PRESUMED INNOCENT* by Scott Turow. Copyright © 1987 by Scott Turow. Reprinted by permission of Farrar, Strauss & Giroux, Inc.

CHAPTER 4
Conflict of Interest

CHAPTER OVERVIEW

In this chapter you will learn about the ethical issues that arise when conflicts of interest develop. You will learn how to identify potential conflicts and discuss how they might impair legal professionals from fulfilling their professional responsibility to clients. You will also consider how ethical regulations and case law affect the work of the paralegal.

THE CASE OF THE CONFUSED CIA PARALEGAL

Nicole, a paralegal with the CIA, signed a pact of secrecy prior to her employment with the CIA, in which she promised not to reveal any information relative to her work with the agency. She has worked for at least 10 years for Clark Kent, who seemed to be an irreproachable and totally ethical boss; yet he was allegedly involved in selling arms to Iran in return for American hostages, an illegal activity. After this was discovered, Nicole was subpoenaed to testify before the Senate Arms Committee. Should she answer the questions asked of her by the committee?

THE CASE OF THE NO-TELL MOTEL

Peggy is a paralegal with a firm specializing in domestic relations. She has worked in this field for many years and is currently working with Mike Hart, who is well-known as the best divorce lawyer in that area. Because of that reputation, he represents many wealthy clients.

The firm has an outdated telephone system, making it is easy to pick up on a telephone conversation in progress, because the lights do not always show that someone is on the line. One day, Peggy picks up on a line that appears available and she hears Hart say: "I know you can't afford to pay for your divorce, but if you meet me at the No-Tell Motel at 10:00 p.m. tonight, I'll do your divorce free." What should Peggy do?

4.1 CONFLICT OF INTEREST: AN INTRODUCTION

The concept of conflict of interest is not particularly different in the context of law than in other social, political, or business contexts. Essentially, conflicts of interest occur when a person is in a situation where his or her loyalties are divided, thus impairing his or her ability to make decisions or take actions in an unbiased, objective fashion. In the legal environment, attorneys face conflict-of-interest issues when their own interests or the interests of their firms, families, or other clients are affected by the outcome of a case. It is an attorney's professional responsibility to represent a client as effectively as possible; when that ability is compromised, even in what might appear to be a minor way, problems with conflict of interest may arise.

This provision of ethical conduct is derived from other fundamental ethical considerations. First, it relates to the concept of preserving client secrets and confidences, for it is intended to assure the party sharing confidential information that the information will indeed remain confidential. For example, if you have a duty to one client to communicate all relevant information, and you possess relevant (but supposedly confidential) information received from another client, you cannot fulfill your conflicting duties of confidentiality and effective representation to both clients. The rules concerning conflict of interest thereby promote the confidentiality of communications. Second, the duty of absolute loyalty to the client and zealous representation are related to conflicts of interest. Obviously, if attorneys are obligated to represent their clients fully and completely, they cannot do so if their interests or loyalties are divided.

Simultaneous Representation

Conflicts of interest occur most clearly when an attorney simultaneously represents two clients with opposing interests. The following example illustrates how preserving client secrets and confidences is related to conflict of interest:

> Attorney Gail Gibson represents the Atlanta Power Company in rate cases before the Georgia Public Service Commission. In these cases, the Atlanta Power Company files a petition with the Commission and requests that its rates be increased by a certain amount. Gail Gibson has been representing the Atlanta Power Company for five years and is intimately familiar with the workings of the company.
> Rita Ratepayer, a residential customer of Atlanta Power Company, contacts attorney Gibson and asks that she represent Rita Ratepayer in a case. The purpose of Gibson's representation of Rita Ratepayer is to try to make sure that Atlanta Power Company's rates are not increased.

This scenario is an obvious example of conflict of interest, and it also demonstrates how a conflict of interest might affect the ethical duty of confidentiality. Simultaneous representation of adverse interests always raises a conflict-of-interest problem. Attorney Gibson is bound to preserve the confidences and secrets of her client, Atlanta Power Company. She cannot represent an adverse party in the same case, because she would have to jeopardize the confidences and secrets of her client, Atlanta Power Company. When an attorney simultaneously represents adverse interests, there is a strong presumption that such representation raises an impermissible conflict of interest. Both the Code and the Rules use a stringent two-part test, allowing such a representation only if the attorney can adequately represent both parties and the clients consent to the situation.

In addition to the representation of adverse parties, simultaneous conflict issues arise when one attorney is retained by a divorcing couple or by more than one party during the probate of an estate. Another example would be if a lawyer represented several clients in the same case. Think of the conflicts that would exist if an attorney represented 10 plaintiffs in a joint lawsuit against a contractor for negligence when the plaintiffs' condominiums burned to the ground because of faulty wiring. What if 8 of the 10 wanted to settle, but the other 2 would not accept the settlement?

Simultaneous-representation conflicts of interest also arise when firms specialize in representing a specific class of client. Thus, an insurance defense firm would find it difficult to represent a plaintiff in a lawsuit against an insurance company the firm had previously represented; a labor law firm that represents companies would find it difficult to represent a plaintiff in a labor dispute with a company it represented; a construction law firm would find it difficult to represent a subcontractor against a client contractor. These types of conflicts are conflicts not of clients but of issues. The Comment to Rule 1.7 does not prohibit a lawyer's representing two clients who are asserting opposing legal arguments, but suggests that such employment may be improper when the cases are pending in the same trial court or pending at the same time in an appellate court.

Absolute Loyalty

Another aspect of conflict of interest is the duty of absolute loyalty to one's client. The duty of absolute loyalty exists even if there is no disclosure of a client's secrets or confidences. Further, every attorney is expected to represent every client to the very best of that attorney's abilities, within the bounds of the law. Consider the following situation:

> Carl Collision's automobile insurance company is Smash Insurance Company. On November 18, 1990, Carl has an automobile accident in which he runs a tractor-trailer owned by Ryder off the road. Ryder files a lawsuit against Carl Collision and Carl calls Smash Insurance Company to represent him in the lawsuit. (When one is insured and files a claim under the insurance policy, the insurance company chooses the attorney. Although the attorney represents the one insured by the policy, the insurance company chooses and pays the attorney.)
>
> Smash's insurance adjuster calls their regular attorney, Greene Bush, and asks him to handle the case. The insurance adjuster tells Bush that this is Carl's 10th accident and they want to cancel his insurance. Ryder has alleged, in its complaint against Collision, that the accident was intentional, because Collision had been trying for several miles to run the tractor-trailer off the highway. Collision allegedly hates Ryder trucks, for some unknown reason. The insurance adjuster tells Bush not to dispute this claim of intentional conduct, because if the conduct was intentional, then Smash Insurance Company will not be liable.

In this instance, there is no direct conflict of interest, because the attorney has not been called upon to represent adverse parties; however, a conflict nevertheless exists. Although the insurance company is paying Bush's legal expenses, Bush is the attorney for Collision and owes his total loyalty to Collision. The fact that the insurance adjuster has asked Bush not to defend against the plaintiff's claim that Collision acted intentionally raises doubts as to whether Bush can effectively represent Collision. Bush's loyalties as the regular attorney for Smash Insurance Company may raise doubt about Bush's ability to zealously represent his client, Collision. Here, there is a conflict between the client (Carl Collision) and the entity paying for the legal expenses (Smash Insurance Company), which calls into question whether Bush will represent Collision to the best of Bush's abilities within the bounds of the law. This conflict is more subtle than the case of attorney Gibson and the Atlanta Power Company, but is one that occurs often in the real world.

Business Interests

Besides these two common examples of conflict of interest, there are several other circumstances under which conflict-of-interest issues frequently arise. First, conflicts between a client's and attorney's business interests could exist. Even though a legal professional must put aside her personal interests when representing a client, sometimes it is difficult to do so. For example, the attorney could own the majority of stock in a company and have a client who wants to sue that company. Arguably, the lawyer would, from a personal perspective, not want to see the claim succeed, because it might reduce the dividends the company paid for that quarter. Whether a conflict of interest truly exists in this situation depends partly on how much stock the attorney owns. If the lawyer owns 10 shares, a conflict of interest might not exist. On the other hand, if she owns 100,000 shares, a conflict of interest probably would exist. Additionally, consider that even if

"I'm a lawyer. I'd be happy to defend you."

the attorney owns only 10 shares, a conflict of interest probably would exist if the lawsuit sought $300 billion rather than $200,000. Thus, in conflict-of-interest situations in which an attorney's business interests might fly in the face of the client's needs, the particular facts of the case will determine whether, in fact, the attorney's representation of the client would be hindered by the attorney's business interests.

Successive Representation

Conflicts between the client and a current or previous client present conflict-of-interest problems. These situations arise when a client requests that an attorney represent her, but her interests are contrary to those of a previous or current client. This would occur if the present client, who is the ex-wife of the ex-husband the attorney represented in an earlier divorce proceeding, wants to file a lawsuit arising out of the divorce settlement. This is called *successive representation*—the conflict is between a current and a former client. Successive conflicts of interest might well occur if a legal professional changes firms. In these situations, the hiring firm must ensure that the entire firm is not disqualified from representation merely because of a new employee who may not have actually worked on the case, but was formerly an employee of an opposing party's legal representative. By not working on, participating in any discussions about, or having anything to do with a case that may involve a conflict, you can usually prevent conflict-of-interest allegations. Usually in these cases, only if the clients have truly adverse interests and the matter being handled is substantially the same will an actual conflict of interest arise. In the preceding example, if the ex-wife came to the ex-husband's attorney and requested assistance on a real estate closing, a conflict of interest probably would not exist. The test applied is this: Are the interests truly adverse, and is the matter being handled substantially the same? This *substantially related* test, which has been adopted by most jurisdictions, can be applied to both the facts and the law. Thus, if the former case was a divorce and the present one is a real estate closing, the fact test would question whether the property being closed was disputed in the divorce. The legal test, on the other hand, would look to see if real estate closing and domestic relations cases have similar issues.

Personal Interests

Conflicts of interest can arise when the client and the attorney have opposing personal interests. Although a competent legal professional should not let personal preferences interfere with representation of a client, some personal beliefs and choices cannot be overcome; therefore, it is better to refer a case to another lawyer than to jeopardize the client. A good example of such a conflict would be if the attorney is a devout Catholic who does not believe in divorce, and the client wants the attorney to represent him in a divorce. Clearly, the lawyer would have a difficult, if not impossible, task in fully advocating his client's wishes if the attorney could not overcome personal feelings about divorce.

Sexual relations between attorney and client also present conflict-of-interest problems and frequently stand as examples of unethical behavior. In *Florida Bar v. Samaha,* 557 So. 2d 1349 (Fla. 1990), a lawyer was suspended for sexual touching of a female client and taking seminude photographs under the guise that they were needed to assess a personal injury claim. In *Carter v. Kritz,* 560 A.2d 360 (R.I. 1989), a lawyer offered some clients the opportunity to pay their fees by posing nude or seminude for photographs. In *In re Ridgeway,* 158 Wis. 2d 452, 462 N.W.2d 671 (1990), a public defender was disciplined for giving beer to an alcoholic client, in violation of her probation, and engaging in sex with her. In *In re Rudnick,* 1992 WESTLAW 42465 (N.Y. App. Div., Mar. 2, 1992), a lawyer threatened to abandon his female client's case, causing her to lose custody of her child, unless she continued to have an intimate relationship with him.

Sexual conflicts were previously viewed in light of prohibitions against the appearance of impropriety or as personal interest conflicts; they have also been seen as a lack of competence, violations of advocate-witness prohibitions, or breaches of general "fitness to practice." The seriousness and frequency of this problem have created a trend toward developing specific ethical provisions concerning sexual interest conflicts. Several states have proposed ethical rules dealing with sex between attorney and client. Illinois' proposed Rule 1.17 states:

(a)   A lawyer shall not, during the representation of a client, engage in sexual relations with the client if:

(1)   The sexual relations are the result of duress, intimidation, or undue influence by the lawyer; or

(2)   The lawyer knows or reasonably should know that the client's ability to decide whether to engage in sexual relations is impaired by the client's emotional or financial dependency, or some other reason.

(b)   Where a lawyer in a firm has sexual relations with a client, the other lawyers in the firm shall not be subject to discipline solely because of the occurrence of such sexual relations.

Oregon's proposed rule, DR 5-110, which was defeated, read:

(A)   A lawyer shall not have sexual relations with a current client of the lawyer if the sexual relations would, or would likely, damage or prejudice the client.

(B)   A lawyer shall not expressly or impliedly condition the performance of legal services for a current or prospective client upon that client's willingness to engage in sexual relations with the lawyer.

(C)   In all other circumstances, a lawyer may have sexual relations with a current client only if (1) the sexual relationship began prior to the attorney-client relationship, (2) the lawyer and client are married or are in an equivalent domestic relationship, or (3) prior to the beginning of the sexual relationship, the client consents after full disclosure.

(D)   "Sexual relations" shall mean:

(1)   Sexual intercourse; or

(2)   Any touching of the sexual or other intimate parts of a person or causing such person to touch the sexual or other intimate parts of the actor for the purpose of arousing or gratifying the sexual desire of either party.

The development of proposed rules concerning sexual interest conflicts reflects the growing concern of bar associations to confront this area directly, as it is a serious problem that directly affects the public's perception of the ethical standards of lawyers. Future developments will likely include efforts by bar associations and other organizations to develop strict ethical guidelines on sexual relationships between lawyers and clients.

Advocate as Witness

As the Law, Literature, and Ethics section at the beginning of this chapter illustrated, the attorney who acts as a witness in a proceeding in which he or she is appearing as an advocate also faces conflict-of-interest issues. This conflict would also exist if another member of the advocate's firm were called as a witness. This is a conflict because, as a witness, the person testifying has an absolute duty to tell the truth, and this duty to testify truthfully might be jeopardized by the advocate's financial incentives. Further, testimony by an advocate or law firm contrary to the position of the client would pose obvious problems. Even testimony favorable to the client might cause the factfinder to be unduly harsh when weighing that evidence. Ethical rules prohibit advocate/witness situations except when the testimony concerns an uncontested matter (such as attorney fee amounts) or some other matter in which there will be no opposition, such as chain-of-custody testimony.

There are an infinite number of variations on situations which present conflict-of-interest issues, but these examples represent the most frequent situations where conflict arises.

Waiver

Although it is the legal professional who has the conflict of interest, it is the client who has the choice to waive the conflict of interest. However, this waiver must be freely and voluntarily given and should be in writing. Two states, Wisconsin and Washington, have gone beyond the requirements of the Code and Rules and made it mandatory that such waivers be in writing. Because a conflict of interest so directly affects effective representation, the consent given must be *informed consent.* As the court said in *In re Boivin,* 271 Or. 419, 533 P.2d 171, 174 (1975):

To satisfy the requirement of full disclosure by a lawyer before undertaking to represent conflicting interests, it is not sufficient that both parties be informed of the fact that the lawyer is undertaking to represent both of them, but he must explain to them the nature of the conflict of interest in such detail so that they can understand the reasons why it may be desirable for each of them to have independent counsel, with undivided loyalty to the interest of each of them.

A conflict of interest is therefore present when something or someone prevents an attorney or any member of the legal team from either maintaining a client's secrets or confidences or undermines the zealous representation of the client. Whenever it appears that an attorney's professional judgment may be compromised, there is probably a conflict-of-interest problem.

THE CASE OF CLAUDETTE'S CONFLICTS

Legal assistant Claudette has recently begun working for Michael Spero, a sole practitioner specializing in domestic relations and criminal defense. Spero has briefed Claudette on the active files. These include a tort case against Sam Spade, a Jungian psychotherapist who saw Claudette professionally, for about six months, two years ago; a real estate closing in which Spero will represent both buyer and seller and be paid by the seller; and a sexual discrimination suit against Chez Louis, a French restaurant managed by Claudette's uncle.

Which of these conflicts should Claudette discuss with attorney Spero? Which of these conflicts should prevent her working on the case?

4.2 RULES AND GUIDELINES CONCERNING CONFLICT OF INTEREST

ABA Model Rules

Model Rule 1.7 provides the guidelines for judging conflicts of interest.

RULE 1.7 Conflict of Interest: General Rule

(a) A lawyer shall not represent a client if the representation of that client will be directly adverse to another client, unless:
(1) the lawyer reasonably believes the representation will not adversely affect the relationship with the other client; and
(2) each client consents after consultation.
(b) A lawyer shall not represent a client if the representation of that client may be materially limited by the lawyer's responsibilities to another client or to a third person, or by the lawyer's own interests, unless:
(1) the lawyer reasonably believes the representation will not be adversely affected; and

(2) the client consents after consultation. When representation of multiple clients in a single matter is undertaken, the consultation shall include explanation of the implications of the common representation and the advantages and risks involved.

It is more strict than the requirements set forth in the corresponding code section, DR 5-105(A). Unlike the Code, Rule 1.7 requires that an attorney not represent a client if that representation of that client will be directly adverse to another client unless the client not only consents, but the attorney is also reasonably assured, apart from that consultation, that the lawyer's interests would not detrimentally affect the client. This imposes a higher burden on the lawyer, because client consent must be combined with an objective decision that the client's representation will not be impaired.

The second section of Rule 1.7 provides that a lawyer not represent a client if the representation of that client may be materially limited by the attorney's responsibilities to another client or third person, or by the lawyer's own interest. The same two requirements—that the attorney reasonably believe the representation will not be adversely affected and that the client consent after full disclosure—are mandated before the attorney can accept the new client.

The Comments to Rule 1.7 recognize that "[l]oyalty is an essential element in the lawyer's relationship to the client." This concept of loyalty prohibits undertaking representation adverse to that client's interests without the client's consent. Conflicts of interest impair this loyalty because the lawyer is unable to consider, recommend, or carry out an appropriate course of action for the client, because of the lawyer's other responsibilities or interests. Thus, anything that materially interferes with an attorney's independent professional judgment would be a conflict and should be avoided.

The Rules also set forth very specific examples of transactions between attorney and client that are prohibited by the strictures against conflicts of interest. These situations arise when an attorney has a pecuniary interest adverse to the client. In these situations, the attorney cannot hold such an interest unless the transaction is fair and reasonable and fully disclosed to the client, the client is given a reasonable opportunity to seek independent counsel, and the client consents in writing. Further, Rule 1.8 provides that an attorney shall not use information relating to representation of the client to the detriment of that client.

RULE 1.8 Conflict of Interest: Prohibited Transactions

(a) A lawyer shall not enter into a business transaction with a client or knowingly acquire an ownership, possessory, security or other pecuniary interest adverse to a client unless:

(1) the transaction and terms on which the lawyer acquires the interest are fair and reasonable to the client and are

fully disclosed and transmitted in writing to the client in a manner which can be reasonably understood by the client;

(2)   the client is given a reasonable opportunity to seek the advice of independent counsel in the transaction; and

(3)   the client consents in writing thereto.

(b)   A lawyer shall not use information relating to representation of a client to the disadvantage of the client unless the client consents after consultation.

(c)   A lawyer shall not prepare an instrument giving the lawyer or a person related to the lawyer as parent, child, sibling, or spouse any substantial gift from a client, including a testamentary gift, except where the client is related to the donee.

(d)   Prior to the conclusion of representation of a client, a lawyer shall not make or negotiate an agreement giving the lawyer literary or media rights to a portrayal or account based in substantial part on information relating to the representation.

(e)   A lawyer shall not provide financial assistance to a client in connection with pending or contemplated litigation, except that:

(1)   a lawyer may advance court costs and expenses of litigation, the repayment of which may be contingent on the outcome of the matter; and

(2)   a lawyer representing an indigent client may pay court costs and expenses of litigation on behalf of the client.

(f)   A lawyer shall not accept compensation for representing a client from one other than the client unless:

(1)   the client consents after consultation;

(2)   there is no interference with the lawyer's independence of professional judgment or with the client-lawyer relationship; and

(3)   information relating to representation of a client is protected as required by Rule 1.6.

(g)   A lawyer who represents two or more clients shall not participate in making an aggregate settlement of the claims of or against the clients, or in a criminal case an aggregated agreement as to guilty or nolo contendere pleas, unless each client consents after consultation, including disclosure of the existence and nature of all the claims or pleas involved and of the participation of each person in the settlement.

(h)   A lawyer shall not make an agreement prospectively limiting the lawyer's liability to a client for malpractice unless permitted by law and the client is independently represented in making the agreement, or settle a claim for such liability with an unrepresented client or former client without first advising that person in writing that independent representation is appropriate in connection therewith.

(i)   A lawyer related to another lawyer as parent, child, sibling or spouse shall not represent a client in a representation directly adverse to a person who the lawyer knows is represented by the other lawyer except upon consent by the client after consultation regarding the relationship.

(j)   A lawyer shall not acquire a proprietary interest in the cause of action or subject matter of litigation the lawyer is conducting for a client, except that the lawyer may:

(1) acquire a lien granted by law to secure the lawyer's fee or expenses; and

(2) contract with a client for a reasonable contingent fee in a civil case.

As for gifts, a lawyer has a duty not to prepare any document which gives the attorney or anyone related to the attorney a substantial gift from the client unless the client is related to the person to whom the gift is given. However, as the Comments to Rule 1.8 suggest, this does not preclude a client from giving an attorney a token gift, such as flowers or a small Christmas gift; it is only when the gift is substantial that the attorney cannot personally draft the conveying document. Remember, this Rule does not preclude a lawyer from accepting substantial gifts from a client; it merely precludes the lawyer from drafting the conveying instrument. A contemporary portion of Rule 1.8, which concerns an increasingly common occurrence, is the granting of literary or media rights to a particular case. Under Rule 1.8, such rights cannot be given by the lawyer until the conclusion of the representation.

The Rules are less stringent when it comes to an attorney being a witness, requiring that the attorney be a "necessary witness" to the case (Rule 3.7). If the attorney's testimony is not significant, material, or unique, the Rules do not designate this situation as a conflict of interest that must be alleviated. Thus, an advocate is prohibited from acting as a witness only if the combination of roles prejudices the opposing party's rights in the litigation.

RULE 3.7 Lawyer as Witness

(a) A lawyer shall not act as advocate at a trial in which the lawyer is likely to be a necessary witness except where:

(1) the testimony relates to an uncontested issue;

(2) the testimony relates to the nature and value of legal services rendered in the case; or

(3) disqualification of the lawyer would work substantial hardship on the client.

(b) A lawyer may act as advocate in a trial in which another lawyer in the lawyer's firm is likely to be called as a witness unless precluded from doing so by Rule 1.7 or Rule 1.9.

The Rules also adopt a more liberal view concerning a lawyer who helps a client with the expenses of litigation. Rule 1.8(e) permits repayment of funds to be contingent on the result of the case, and allows a lawyer to pay court costs and expenses of litigation for an indigent client, neither of which is permitted under the Code. Some states have refused to go this far by adopting the Rules without including these two provisions.

Rule 1.9 concerns conflicts between a present client and a former client.

RULE 1.9 Conflict of Interest: Former Client

A lawyer who has formerly represented a client in a matter shall not thereafter:

(a) represent another person in the same or a substantially related matter in which that person's interests are materially adverse to the interests of the former client unless the former client consents after consultation; or

(b) use information relating to the representation to the disadvantage of the former client except as Rule 1.6 would permit with respect to a client or when the information has become generally known.

This Rule adopts the "substantially related" test, which states that a conflict exists only if the interests of the two clients are substantially related and adverse. This test is designed to protect the loyalty that a lawyer owes a former client without unduly burdening that lawyer's ability to accept new clients. The Rules therefore permit representation in situations in which previously the courts would have found a conflict.

Rule 1.10 provides for *imputed disqualification,* which means that if an attorney is disqualified from a case, the attorney's firm will also be prohibited from representing that client.

RULE 1.10 Imputed Disqualification: General Rule

(a) While lawyers are associated in a firm, none of them shall knowingly represent a client when any one of them practicing alone would be prohibited from doing so by Rules 1.7, 1.8(c), 1.9 or 2.2.

(b) When a lawyer becomes associated with a firm, the firm may not knowingly represent a person in the same or a substantially related matter in which that lawyer, or a firm with which the lawyer was associated, had previously represented a client whose interests are materially adverse to that person and about whom the lawyer had acquired information protected by Rules 1.6 and 1.9(b) that is material to the matter.

(c) When a lawyer has terminated an association with a firm, the firm is not prohibited from thereafter representing a person with interests materially adverse to those of a client represented by the formerly associated lawyer unless:

(1) the matter is the same or substantially related to that in which the formerly associated lawyer represented the client; and

(2) any lawyer remaining in the firm has information protected by Rules 1.6 and 1.9(b) that is material to the matter.

(d) A disqualification prescribed by this Rule may be waived by the affected client under the conditions stated in Rule 1.7.

This is applicable not only to attorneys in private firms, but also to attorneys in corporate legal departments or legal service organizations. The rules are less stringent for paralegals than for attorneys when it comes to imputed disqualification, as is discussed in later sections on Chinese Walls.

ABA Model Code

Canon 5 of the Model Code deals with conflicts of interest. The language of the Canon states: "A Lawyer Should Exercise Independent Professional Judgment on Behalf of a Client." Conflict of interest is handled by several Disciplinary Rules, DR 5-101 through DR 5-107.

DR 5-101   Refusing Employment When the Interests of the Lawyer May Impair His Independent Professional Judgment.

(A)   Except with the consent of his client after full disclosure, a lawyer shall not accept employment if the exercise of his professional judgment on behalf of his client will be or reasonably may be affected by his own financial, business, property, or personal interests.

(B)   A lawyer shall not accept employment in contemplated or pending litigation if he knows or it is obvious that he or a lawyer in his firm ought to be called as a witness, except that he may undertake the employment and he or a lawyer in his firm may testify:

(1)   If the testimony will relate solely to an uncontested matter.

(2)   If the testimony will relate solely to a matter of formality and there is no reason to believe that substantial evidence will be offered in opposition to the testimony.

(3)   If the testimony will relate solely to the nature and value of legal services rendered in the case by the lawyer or his firm to the client.

(4)   As to any matter, if refusal would work a substantial hardship on the client because of the distinctive value of the lawyer or his firm as counsel in the particular case.

DR 5-102   Withdrawal as Counsel When the Lawyer Becomes a Witness.

(A)   If, after undertaking employment in contemplated or pending litigation, a lawyer learns or it is obvious that he or a lawyer in his firm ought to be called as a witness on behalf of his client, he shall withdraw from the conduct of the trial and his firm, if any, shall not continue representation in the trial, except that he may continue the representation and he or a lawyer in his firm may testify in the circumstances enumerated in DR 5-101(B)(1) through (4).

(B)   If, after undertaking employment in contemplated or pending litigation, a lawyer learns or it is obvious that he or a lawyer in his firm may be called as a witness other than on behalf of his client, he may continue the representation until it is apparent that his testimony is or may be prejudicial to his client.

DR 5-103 Avoiding Acquisition of Interest in Litigation.

(A) A lawyer shall not acquire a proprietary interest in the cause of action or subject matter of litigation he is conducting for a client, except that he may:

(1) Acquire a lien granted by law to secure his fee or expenses.

(2) Contract with a client for a reasonable contingent fee in a civil case.

(B) While representing a client in connection with contemplated or pending litigation, a lawyer shall not advance or guarantee financial assistance to his client, except that a lawyer may advance or guarantee the expenses of litigation, including court costs, expenses of investigation, expenses of medical examination, and costs of obtaining and presenting evidence, provided the client remains ultimately liable for such expenses.

DR 5-104 Limiting Business Relations with a Client.

(A) A lawyer shall not enter into a business transaction with a client if they have differing interests therein and if the client expects the lawyer to exercise his professional judgment therein for the protection of the client, unless the client has consented after full disclosure.

(B) Prior to conclusion of all aspects of the matter giving rise to his employment, a lawyer shall not enter into any arrangement or understanding with a client or a prospective client by which he acquires as interest in publication rights with respect to the subject matter of his employment or proposed employment.

DR 5-105 Refusing to Accept or Continue Employment if the Interests of Another Client May Impair the Independent Professional Judgment of the Lawyer.

(A) A lawyer shall decline proffered employment if the exercise of his independent professional judgment in behalf of a client will be or is likely to be adversely affected by the acceptance of the proffered employment, or if it would be likely to involve him in representing differing interests, except to the extent permitted under DR 5-105(C).

(B) A lawyer shall not continue multiple employment if the exercise of his independent professional judgment in behalf of a client will be or is likely to be adversely affected by his representation of another client, or if it would be likely to involve him in representing differing interests, except to the extent permitted under DR 5-105(C).

(C) In the situations covered by DR 5-105(A) and (B), a lawyer may represent multiple clients if it is obvious that he can adequately represent the interest of each and if each consents to the representation after full disclosure of the possible effect of such representation on the exercise of his independent professional judgment of behalf of each.

(D) If a lawyer is required to decline employment or to withdraw from employment under a Disciplinary Rule, no partner or associate, or any other lawyer affiliated with him or his firm may accept or continue such employment.

DR 5-106 Settling Similar Claims of Clients.

(A) A lawyer who represents two or more clients shall not make or participate in the making of an aggregate settlement of the claims of or against his clients, unless each client has consented to the settlement after being advised of the existence and nature of all the claims involved in the proposed settlement, of the total amount of the settlement, and of the participation of each person in the settlement.

DR 5-107 Avoiding Influence by Others Than the Client.

(A) Except with the consent of his client after full disclosure, a lawyer shall not:

(1) Accept compensation for his legal services from one other than his client.

(2) Accept from one other than his client any thing of value related to his representation of or his employment by his client.

(B) A lawyer shall not permit a person who recommends, employs, or pays him to render legal services for another to direct or regulate his professional judgment in rendering such legal services.

(C) A lawyer shall not practice with or in the form of a professional corporation or association authorized to practice for a profit, if:

(1) A non-lawyer owns any interest therein, except that a fiduciary representative of the estate of a lawyer may hold the stock or interest of the lawyer for a reasonable time during administration;

(2) A non-lawyer is a corporate director or officer thereof; or

(3) A non-lawyer has the right to direct or control the professional judgment of a lawyer.

These rules deal with situations in which a conflict might emerge from the lawyer's interests (DR 5-101), the lawyer being called as a witness (DR 5-102), the lawyer acquiring a proprietary interest in the litigation (DR 5-103), business relations with a client (DR 5-104), another of the lawyer's clients (DR 5-105), multiple clients (DR 5-106), and third-party influence (DR 5-107). DR 5-101 provides that an attorney should not accept employment without full disclosure that his professional judgment in the case would be affected by his own financial, business, property, or personal interests, and the consent of the client. This provision is less restrictive than the Rules. DR 5-105 precludes an attorney from representing adverse interests unless the client consents after full disclosure. The Rules parallel to these two Code sections go beyond the requirements of the Code: the Code only requires that the client consent to the representation, whereas the Rules require that, in addition to the consent, the attorney must judge that her representation of the adverse interest will not adversely affect the client.

The Ethical Considerations under Canon 5 deal with specific situations in which an attorney's independent professional judgment may be questioned and a conflict of interest may arise. Like the Rules, EC 5-1 defines the loyalty an attorney owes the client and considers loyalty a reason conflict-of-interest issues should not be taken lightly. Specifically, EC 5-1 provides that:

> The professional judgment of a lawyer should be exercised, within the bounds of the law, solely for the benefit of his client and free of compromising influences and loyalties. Neither his personal interests, the interests of other clients, nor the desires of third persons should be permitted to dilute his loyalty to his client.

This Ethical Consideration provides a good general overview of when conflicts of interest arise. Whenever attorneys feel that their decisions for clients are not determined by what is best for those clients in those particular situations, conflicts of interest probably exist.

The rest of the Ethical Considerations under Canon 5 deal with specific situations in which conflicts of interest arise. EC 5-2 states that an attorney should avoid acquiring property rights or assuming a position that would make his judgment less protective of his client. EC 5-3 states that an attorney's judgment on behalf of her client may be impaired if the attorney has a property interest in the same property as her client. It is important to remember that, in the eyes of the law, property includes not only land (defined as real property), but also patents, corporate stock, business ownership, and the like. Thus, this Ethical Consideration states that an attorney probably should not accept employment from a client who has ownership in the same property as the attorney. Nor should the attorney acquire, after accepting representation, property interests which are the same as those of his client. Further, an attorney should not try to influence her client to permit the attorney to invest in a venture (such as a new business or new corporation) started by the client. For example, attorney Jeanette is asked by client Morris to form a corporation for him. The corporation's purpose is to market private homes to individuals during the 1996 Olympics in Atlanta. After incorporating "Olympic Domiciles," attorney Jeanette should not now attempt to become a major stockholder in Olympic Domiciles. Once the corporation has gone public, attorney Jeanette might be permitted to invest in the corporation, as long as she did not use any inside information or knowledge gained from the representation.

A rather interesting situation is addressed by EC 5-4. During the course of the Watergate trials, several defendants contracted with publishers to publish memoirs of the events leading to those trials. This Ethical Consideration deals with the situation in which an attorney or his agent, especially during the course of a criminal case, receives television, radio, motion picture, magazine, or book rights with respect to the case. Although this Ethical Consideration does not prohibit the attorney from obtaining such rights, it requests that an attorney avoid entering into this type of relationship with her client until the case has been totally terminated. Compare this requirement to that set forth in Rule 1.8. If Charles Manson had entered into a contract with Murder Motion Pictures for the story of his life of crime, the attorney representing Manson should not obtain a percentage of this contract until Manson has either fired the attorney or exhausted all the appeals he wishes to pursue.

Both etiquette and EC 5-5 require that an attorney not suggest to his client that the client present him with gifts, such as bequests or devises under wills. As a companion to EC 5-5, EC 5-6 precludes an attorney from consciously influencing her client to name her as an executor, trustee, or lawyer under the client's will. EC 5-7 deals with an attorney's obtaining a financial stake in the litigation case of the client. Although EC 5-7 specifically condones contingency agreements (in which an attorney accepts a case for a certain percentage of the amount recovered plus expenses, rather than for a certain amount per hour), the attorney is cautioned to enter only into contingency agreements that are in the best interests of the client.

A companion to this principle is EC 5-8, which specifically addresses the question of expenses and advances for expenses in contingency cases. EC 5-8 precludes an attorney from financing a client's case by paying all of the expenses for the client. An attorney may advance the client certain sums of money, such as a sum to cover the cost of a deposition, so long as the client is ultimately responsible for these expenses. Consider the situation of the indigent widow whose husband was killed when a large manufacturing plant owned and operated by Acme Products exploded. The explosion occurred after Acme Products failed to correct fire safety violations that had been brought to its attention two months before by the local fire marshal. Clearly, Acme Products would be liable in this case, however, because she cannot pay, the widow may not be able to collect for her husband's death without a contingency agreement for legal fees. To prove the case, the attorney would have to take the depositions of the officials of Acme Products, well as the deposition of the local fire marshal. Since the widow is indigent, she cannot pay for these depositions until she recovers for her husband's death. Therefore, the attorney could advance the depositions' costs, as long as long as they had an agreement which would make the widow ultimately responsible for these expenses. Without question, Rule 1.8(e) is much more liberal, because it permits attorneys to pay the court costs and expenses for indigent clients.

EC 5-9 precludes an attorney from appearing as a witness and an advocate in the same case. For example: Attorney Frank witnesses an automobile accident, and the injured party immediately asks, "Is there an attorney in the house?" Frank should not accept the case, for he would probably be called as a witness in the case. EC 5-10 elaborates on the problems of an attorney being both an advocate and a witness. An attorney may accept a case in which she may be called as a witness if she determines, in her own judgment, that her testimony as a witness goes only to an uncontested matter or is merely a summary of other witnesses' testimony. Whether in such cases an attorney should withdraw from representation of the client depends on whether withdrawal would prejudice the client.

THE CASE OF THE RECOVERABLE ATTORNEY'S FEES

David Cowles, an attorney with Walter, Marvin, Lovett, and Junior, represents Noreen Nicelady in a sexual discrimination suit against a major corporation. He and his assistant Latrice have expended many hours on the Nicelady case, but they now find themselves testifying as to their fees in the case.

Latrice has never faced this situation before, and she is concerned about the attorney being both an advocate and a witness in the same case; she thinks that the situation might present a conflict of interest. However, she is also aware of the legal principle that, because attorney's fees are a recoverable damage in a sexual discrimination suit, the amount of attorney's fees earned by David Cowles must be admitted into evidence. Proud of her reputation as an ethical paralegal who is sensitive to ethical issues, Latrice goes into David's office and asks whether he is permitted to take the witness stand and permissibly testify as to the amount of legal expenses he has incurred in the representation of Noreen Nicelady.

Does this present a conflict of interest?

EC 5-11 through 5-13 deal with the problems of conflicts of interest associated with the employment of co-counsel. Specifically, EC 5-12 states that an attorney should suggest that a client employ co-counsel if the employment of co-counsel is in the client's best interests. When co-counsel disagree on vital matters in the representation of their client, the disagreement should be resolved by the client. EC 5-13 deals with the membership of an attorney in an organization. The lawyer should not let membership in any organization influence representation of the client.

EC 5-14 through EC 5-20 deal with the problems of conflicts of interest in the representation of multiple clients. EC 5-14 emphasizes that there are almost no situations in which an attorney can effectively represent multiple clients with differing interests in litigation and urges attorneys to err on the side of declining such representation. However, this Ethical Consideration recognizes that in nonlitigation settings, such representation may be possible. EC 5-15 states that even if an attorney's judgment would not be impaired by representation of multiple clients, he or she should explain fully to the clients the ramifications of such representation and give them an opportunity to seek other counsel. EC 5-17 sets forth the most common situations in which a lawyer may be asked to represent multiple clients: co-defendants in a criminal case; co-plaintiffs in a personal injury action (an insured and the insuror); and the beneficiaries of a decedent's estate. This ethical consideration states that the question of whether a conflict of interest exists in these situations should be analyzed on a case-by-case basis.

Attorney representation of a corporation is also a common source of conflict-of-interest problems, as recognized by EC 5-18. When a lawyer represents a corporation, her allegiance and total loyalty are to the corporation, not the board of directors or officers of the corporation.

EC 5-19 sets forth the principle that even though an attorney believes he can represent multiple clients without a conflict of interest, if even one client believes such a conflict exists or would arise, the attorney should defer to the wishes of the client and withdraw from representation.

Ethical Consideration 5-20 deals with the attorney as a mediator or arbitrator. A lawyer may mediate or arbitrate a case involving former clients if she discloses the nature of the former relationship. However, after the mediation or arbitration, the lawyer is precluded from representing, in the particular matter arbitrated or mediated, the parties involved in that mediation or arbitration.

The remaining Ethical Considerations under Canon 5, EC 5-21 through 5-24, deal with the wishes of third parties and how these wishes may develop into conflict-of-interest problems. EC 5-21 states that an attorney should disclose to the client any pressures from third parties paying for the legal expenses which might undermine the attorney's representation of the client. EC 5-22 is an acknowledgement of the common problem that an attorney may feel a conflict of interest when a third party is compensating her for representing the client. EC 5-23 recognizes that when an attorney is employed by a third party to represent another, the lawyer must be constantly on guard not to be influenced by the wishes of this third party. EC 5-24 suggests that an attorney not be involved in a corporate entity with a nonlawyer for the purposes of practicing law.

As you can see, these Ethical Considerations attempt to define specific types of situations that may present conflicts of interest for attorneys. Paralegals, like attorneys, need to be fully aware of conflicts of interest pertaining to them in order to maintain the integrity of the legal team working on a case. Additionally, ethical paralegals should analogize from the ethical guidelines for attorneys to determine their own ethical behavior. For example, the Ethical Consideration prohibiting involvement of a lawyer with a client in a business venture should be seen as applicable to both lawyer and legal assistant. Similarly, the rules concerning attorneys appearing as witnesses apply to paralegals as well.

THE CASE OF THE GENEROUS GIFT

Jana King is an energetic, bright, bubbly, enthusiastic, highly professional, highly competent, and highly attractive paralegal, who assists attorney Taylor Lindsey in a wills, trusts, and estate practice. For the past several months, Jana has been working on Mr. Collier's will and estate plan. Mr. Collier, now 85 years old, is a multimillionaire who made his fortune in real estate. Mrs. Collier died several years ago, and Mr. Collier went into a deep depression; after all, they had been married for nearly 60 years. His depression lifted just about the time he was introduced to Jana.

Everyone could see that Mr. Collier was "sweet" on Jana, but in a paternal way—Jana was only 26 years old. One day, Mr. Collier comes into the office to sign a new version of his will. "I have another provision I want to add," he announces. "I want to leave $150,000 to my friend Jana King, who has made me smile again. Please add that provision to my will."

Are there any ethical issues relating to this gift?

ABA Model Guidelines

Guideline 7 provides that: "A lawyer should take reasonable measures to prevent conflicts of interest resulting from a legal assistant's other employment or interests insofar as such other employment or interests would present a conflict of interest if it were that of the lawyer." The Comments to the Guideline recognize that paralegals should inform attorneys if a conflict exists in the particular case. As the Comments suggest, the "other employment" of the Guideline takes into account the fact that some paralegals may be employed by more than one law firm at the same time or may have switched jobs. The Comments further recognize that it is possible to implement a Chinese Wall if a paralegal has a conflict of interest, so that, unlike an attorney conflict, the entire firm will not be disqualified from the case. Although the Guidelines state that it is the attorney's responsibility to ensure that such conflicts do not exist, in reality a good paralegal should inform the supervising attorney if there may be a conflict of interest between the legal assistant and a particular case or client.

NALA and NFPA

Although NALA and NFPA rules do not directly address the question of conflict of interest, both the Code and the Affirmation indirectly forbid conflicts of interests by requiring that legal assistants preserve client secrets and confidences. This principle is set forth in Canon 7 of the Code: "A legal assistant must protect the confidences of a client, and it shall be unethical for a legal assistant to violate any statute now in effect or hereafter to be enacted controlling privileged communications." Likewise, the Affirmation states: "A paralegal shall preserve client confidences and privileged communications." As previously discussed, preserving client confidences is one of the bases of the conflict-of-interest principle.

4.3 CONFLICT OF INTEREST AND THE PARALEGAL

Conflict-of-interest problems and issues can arise in several ways for the paralegal. First, paralegals frequently have responsibility for distributing and analyzing conflict-of-interest checks. *Conflict-of-interest checking* is the process of ascertaining whether any firm members have conflicts of interest with any party in new matters. Checking for conflicts of interests is a lawyer or firm's ethical duty under the Model Rules; the Comment to Rule 1.7 asserts that "[l]oyalty is an essential element in the lawyer's relationship to a client . . . . The lawyer should adopt reasonable procedures, appropriate for the size and type of firm and practice, to determine in both litigation and non-litigation matters the parties and issues involved and to determine whether there are any actual or potential conflicts of interest." Many firms today have developed conflict-of-interest databases, which use computer technology to check for conflicts in representation. Each firm will have established procedures to perform conflict-of-interest checks; very often, it is the first process initiated concerning a potential new client. (See figure 4-1.) Whether that procedure is manual or computerized, it is essential that it be effective in order to comply with this ethical mandate.

A conflict-of-interest check might involve the following questions:

1. Does the lawsuit involve a party who was previously sued or represented by someone in the firm?
2. Does anyone in the firm own any interest in an entity to be sued by the firm?
3. Has an attorney or paralegal in the firm worked on cases involving the party to be sued?
4. In the case of an existing lawsuit, has anyone in the firm worked for the firm representing the adverse party or worked for the adverse party?
5. Has the firm previously represented insurance companies and is it now representing an individual who is suing an insurance company?
6. In the case of multiple clients whose interests are not diverse and who are on the same side in a lawsuit, are the parties' interests so similar that there would not be a conflict of interest?
7. Is the attorney or paralegal personally involved in the lawsuit, i.e., was the attorney or paralegal a witness to the automobile accident and could be called as a witness?

DREW, ECKL & FARNHAM

REQUEST FOR CONFLICT SEARCH

THIS FORM MUST BE TYPED

TO: RECORDS CENTER

DATE/TIME NEEDED: 1/16/91 - 10:00 a.m.

FROM: Jane Johnson Ext. 3100
Attorney Name

DATE/TIME SUBMITTED: 1/15/91 - 10:00 a.m.

REQUEST IS IN REGARD TO: [XX] Proposed Client–Matter [ ] Existing Client–Matter

File I.D. Number: No number - a proposed client

Client Name: Friendly Insurance Company

Matter Name: Wendell Pate

SEARCH FOR THE FOLLOWING INDIVIDUALS OR ENTITIES: Pick-A-Pair and Wendell Pate

WHITE COPY: RECORDS CENTER, YELLOW COPY: SEE CONFLICTS REPORT

FIGURE 4-1 Sample conflict-of-interest check form.

When checking for conflicts of interest, it is wise to check names against all spellings and variations. It would be truly embarrassing and damaging for the firm if you failed to pick up *Smith* when Smith was put into the file as Smyth. This task requires much attention to detail, and it also must be done expeditiously, not only for the benefit of the firm, but also for the client. A firm may undertake representation of a client only after it has ascertained that there are no conflicts of interest that might threaten the integrity of its representation of the case, so conflict-of-interest checks are performed regularly on all prospective clients and on all new matters.

A second important area which raises conflict-of-interest issues for paralegals concerns their prior employment and associations. It is one of the most important issues for paralegals, because it frequently arises, and because case law has delineated the proper steps to deal with the situation effectively.

To avoid potential career conflicts of interest, it is imperative that, during a job interview, you fully disclose all previous employers and potential conflicts of interest. Even though it may not be apparent or likely that a conflict exists, it is far better to disclose all relevant information; failure to disclose essential information can cause not only embarrassment but also potential liability. If your prospective firm has the relevant information, they still may be able to handle the case by screening you from all activities and information relating to that case. Chapter 3's excerpt from the *In re Complex Asbestos Litigation* case concerned this very issue; in that case, the court held not only that the paralegal revealed client confidences and secrets as a result of his prior employment, but also that the legal assistant's new firm, which represented plaintiffs in asbestos litigation, should have set up a Chinese Wall to prevent the paralegal from having a conflict of interest.

When a conflict arises from the changed employment of a legal assistant, it is not necessary that the firm disqualify itself from the case, although in some cases disqualification would be proper. Rather, the firm can adopt procedures and policies that effectively screen the paralegal from any contact with the case at issue. This screening process, which is also referred to as erecting a *Chinese Wall* or *cone of silence,* can ensure compliance with ethical concerns while preserving job mobility for legal assistants. It is interesting to note that ABA Opinions have required stricter guidelines for attorneys than for legal assistants. If faced with this conflict, an attorney's new firm will be disqualified unless the attorney had no contact with the case at all; even an effective screen might not prevent disqualification. For paralegals, on the other hand, an effective screening process will protect the firm from disqualification; according to ABA Opinion 88-1521, restrictions on nonlawyer employees must be minimal to facilitate employment mobility while still protecting client confidences. Additionally, some jurisdictions have ruled that screening mechanisms for paralegals do not even have to be formal or institutionalized; they must merely protect confidentiality. In *Kapko Manufacturing Co. v. C&O Enterprises, Inc.,* 637 F. Supp. 1231 (N.D. Ill. 1985) (excerpted later in this chapter), the court found that informal methods, which were enough to ensure against sharing of confidential information, would also prevent imputed disqualification of the firm. In that case, also, the court felt that the motion to disqualify was really a "means of retaliation against an opposing counsel and a former secretary," thus making it easier to find that the screening methods employed were sufficient to comply with ethical concerns.

When a law firm finds that one of its new employees possesses confidential information and therefore has a conflict of interest with one of the firm's cases or clients, the firm can avoid imputed disqualification by following certain procedures. These safeguards include:

1. Limiting access to documents, files, computers, and other sources that might have information about the case in question
2. Physically separating the person from others working on the case that presents the conflict
3. Notifying office employees of the conflict
4. Creating a wall of silence, so that no person talks to the new employee about the case
5. Establishing and documenting the screening procedures before the person begins work at the new firm
6. Developing and disseminating a policy statement emphasizing the importance of maintaining confidentiality
7. Having new employees complete a questionnaire concerning their former associations and involvements
8. Notifying the client about the potential conflict.

"And here is our Chinese Wall . . . quite extensive, don't you think?"

The guest editorial following this section does an excellent job of addressing the ethical implications that arise when legal assistants change jobs and describing the procedures to be taken to avoid disqualification when this type of conflict arises.

Conflict of interest can also arise for legal assistants because of personal relationships and relatives. Sometimes paralegals have spouses who are attorneys. Arguably, the spouse could at sometime work on the opposite side of a case from the paralegal. Even though prohibited, it is likely that spouses employed in the same profession discuss and compare notes. Be aware that when such situations exist, both parties must be absolutely strict about revealing any information whatsoever, no matter how insignificant, to the other. Conflicts also arise because of a legal assistant's relatives. Suing a legal assistant's mother may be unwise, for obvious reasons. Like most conflict-of-interest issues involving paralegals, setting up a cone of silence or Chinese Wall may handle this potential conflict sufficiently. However, every situation should be judged on a case-by-case basis while still using common sense. As in the example of the firm suing a paralegal's mother, it is unlikely that even setting up a Chinese Wall would alleviate the conflict-of-interest problem or the very real personal problem that could exist in the firm.

THE CASE OF JOYCE'S JOB OFFER

Joyce is an experienced paralegal who has worked in the malpractice section of a large firm for 20 years. Her supervising attorney, Gary Vogel, is a highly successful specialist in physician defense work. Gary's client is the largest insurer of professional malpractice insurance for physicians. Michael Rickles, a renowned plaintiff's lawyer specializing in medical malpractice actions, knows Joyce from her work with Gary on several cases. He respects her work and thinks of her as the best legal assistant an attorney could want. Michael approaches Joyce and offers her three times her current salary if she will work for him. Joyce needs the money, as she is recently divorced; however, she also knows that most of her work will be against the insurance company that Gary represents.

Should she take the job? What would you advise her to tell both Gary and Michael? Should she tell the insurance company of her plans? Would the situation be different if Joyce were a legal secretary? What if she were an attorney associate of Gary's?

In her guest editorial, Vicki Voisin examines methods of handling conflicts of interest that arise when a legal assistant changes employment.

GUEST EDITORIAL

CHANGING JOBS: ETHICAL CONSIDERATIONS FOR LEGAL ASSISTANTS

By Vicki Voisin, CLA, NALA Ethics Chairman

When a legal assistant changes jobs, conflicts of interest may arise if the former employer and the new employer have cases and clients in common.

ABA OPINION

To avoid such conflicts, the American Bar Association's Committee on Ethics and Professional Responsibility has recently issued an opinion which states:

A law firm that hires a non-lawyer employee, such as a paralegal, away from an opposing law firm may save itself from disqualification by effectively screening the new employee from any participation in the case the two firms have in common. ABA Opinion No. 88-1526 (6/22/88).

The ABA Opinion notes that a "confidence" is by definition that "information protected by the attorney-client privilege under applicable law." "Secrets" are defined as "other information gained in the professional relationship that the client has requested be held inviolate, or the disclosure of which would be embarrassing or would be likely to be detrimental to the client." The Opinion specifically states that "the term used in Model Rule 1.6 'information relating to the representation of a client,' though not specifically defined, plainly encompasses, in addition to confidences and secrets, all information which pertains to the attorney-client relationship, even though it was not learned during the relationship, and even though disclosure would not embarrass or be detrimental to the interests of the client." This would include analyses, strategies, and any other information gathered in the course of preparing the client's case.

By the very nature of their work, legal assistants must be both familiar with, and extensively involved in, cases handled by their employers. Therefore, it stands to reason that the legal assistant would have knowledge of most of the facts surrounding a case, including analyses and strategies to be used against the adversary.

ETHICAL GUIDELINES

Professional association ethical guidelines point out the potential for conflicts of interest and the sanctity of confidential information. Certified legal assistants are bound by the Code of Ethics of the National Association of Legal Assistants (NALA). That Code states at Canon 7:

A legal assistant must protect the confidences of a client, and it shall be unethical for a legal assistant to violate any statute now in effect or hereafter to be enacted controlling privileged communications.

The Model Standards and Guidelines for Utilization of Legal Assistants Annotated (1985) published by NALA states at Section V. that:

The attorney should exercise care that the legal assistant preserves and refrains from using any confidence or secrets of a client and should instruct the legal assistant not to disclose or use any such confidences or secrets.

Further, Canon 12 of NALA's Code of Ethics states:

A legal assistant is governed by the American Bar Association Model Code of Professional Responsibility and the American Bar Association Model Rules of Professional Conduct.

While a legal assistant is not subject to professional discipline and has no direct responsibility under the ABA Code of Responsibility, the lawyer does, and the courts have generally held lawyers responsible for the conduct of non-lawyer employees. DR4-101(D) of the ABA Code of Professional Responsibility provides in part that:

A lawyer shall exercise reasonable care to prevent his employees, associates and others whose services are utilized by him from disclosing or using confidences or secrets of a client.

The obligation is emphasized in ABA Ethical Consideration 4-2:

It is a matter of common knowledge that the normal operation of a law office exposes confidential professional information to non-lawyer employees of the office, particularly secretaries and those having access to files: this obligates the lawyer to exercise care in selecting and training his employees so that

the sanctity of all confidences and secrets of his clients may be preserved.

Therefore, the former employer, the new employer, and the legal assistant all have a responsibility to their clients to protect confidences and secrets.

COURT TREATMENT OF NON-LAWYER CONFLICTS OF INTEREST

Several courts have already been faced with requests for disqualification of law firms on the basis of assorted conflicts of interests by non-lawyers.

In *Kapco Manufacturing Co., Inc. v. C&O Enterprises, Inc.*, 637 F. Supp. 1231 (N.D. Ill. 1985), the court considered whether a law firm must be disqualified from representing a defendant in litigation following the employment of the office manager-secretary of plaintiff's counsel. The motion to disqualify was based on the assumption that the employee had had access to a great deal of confidential information about plaintiff's case while working with her former employer.

While the court in *Kapco* did find that the office manager had knowledge of confidential information, the court also found that the new employer had taken action to be sure that the office manager did not work on defendant's case and that no discussion about the case took place with the employee. On this basis, the motion to disqualify was denied.

In *Williams v. Trans World Airlines, Inc.*, 588 F. Supp. 1037 (W.D. Mo. 1984), the court took a harsher approach and ordered disqualification of a firm in a case where a non-lawyer had previously assisted the defendant's attorney with the defense against plaintiff's firm. The court in *Williams* specifically noted that the individual had (1) never been cautioned not to reveal any confidential information acquired while working for the defendant; and (2) there was no subsequent attempt to insulate her to avoid imparting to plaintiffs the knowledge she gained in assisting the defense. In so holding, the court stated:

Non-lawyer personnel are widely used by lawyers to assist in rendering legal services. Paralegals, investigators, and secretaries must have ready access to client confidences in order to assist their attorney employers. If information provided by a client in confidence to an attorney for the purpose of obtaining legal advice could be used against the client because a member of the attorney's non-lawyer support staff left the attorney's employment, it would have a devastating effect both on the free flow of information between client and attorney and on the cost of quality of the legal services rendered by an attorney. Every departing secretary, investigator, or paralegal would be free to impart confidential information to the opposition without effective restraint. The only practical way to assure that this will not happen and to preserve public trust in the scrupulous administration of justice is to subject these "agents" of lawyers to the same disability lawyers have when they leave legal employment with confidential information.

588 F. Supp. at 1044. The court granted the motion to disqualify based on this reasoning. The same result was reached by the court in *Glover Bottled Gas Corp. v. Circle M. Beverage Barn, Inc.*, 514 N.Y.S.2d 440 (App. Div. 2d Dep't 1987), where a New York appellate court ordered disqualification of defendant's firm when a legal assistant previously employed by plaintiff was hired by the defendant. The paralegal worked on the litigation between the parties and had even interviewed plaintiff's manager concerning the facts of the case. Although noting the Code of Professional Responsibility did not apply to non-lawyers, the court stated it still placed a burden on the attorneys to ensure employees' conduct was in accord with the code.

However, in *Esquire Care, Inc. v. Maguire*, 532 So. 2d 740 (Fla. Dist. Ct. App. 1988), a Florida court denied a request to disqualify a firm when a secretary changed jobs and ended up on the opposite side in a personal injury case. The former employer asserted that because the secretary had responsibility for and access to the file during her employment and in the interim period after she had accepted the new position, the new employer should be disqualified. The court noted, though, that the secretary had no responsibility on the file with her new employer, and that they had specifically instructed her not to discuss her knowledge of the case. The court suggested a two-step procedure in evidentiary hearings to determine first if an ethical violation has occurred, and second, whether as a result one party has obtained an unfair advantage over the other. The court thus distinguished the situations involving non-lawyers from those involving lawyers, since in the latter instances, there is a presumption in favor of disqualification.

THE ABA REASONING

The ABA opinion noted that other courts and ethics committees have used the rationale of *Kapco* (and that employed by the *Esquire* court) to allow law firms to continue representation in cases where screening is effectively used to prevent disclosure by newly hired employees of confidential information relating to clients of their former employers. In contravention of this rationale is the State Bar of Michigan Opinion C1-1096 (1985), wherein the informed consent of all opposing clients is required, and New Jersey Opinion 546 (1982), which states that the presumption that confidences have been exchanged is irrebuttable, and disqualification is automatic.

The ABA opinion, however, distinguished non-lawyer employees from lawyers who move from one firm to another which is on the opposite side of a matter. In the case of lawyers, disqualification is required in all events *except* where the newly employed lawyer has no knowledge of confidential information and was not directly involved in the matter while with the former employer.

The ABA committee found that in the instance of non-lawyers, the analysis in *Kapco* is superior to the automatic disqualification presumption utilized for lawyer conflicts, because this requirement would limit employment opportunities for non-lawyers, possibly requiring them to abandon their careers. Therefore, the ABA Committee's opinion maintains that while there should be restrictions on the non-lawyer's employment, those restrictions should be kept to the minimum required to protect the confidence of the client.

THE SCREENING PROCESS AND PROTECTIVE MEASURES

Neither the opinion issued by the ABA Committee nor the court in *Kapco* specifies exactly what "screening measures" should be used. During testimony in *Kapco*, the office manager-secretary stated that she had no discussion with her new employer (or anyone in that firm) about the case, that no one from the new firm had asked her any questions about the case, that she had volunteered no information about the case to anyone at the new firm, and that she had never seen the new firm's file on the case, nor did she know where the file was located.

Further, the new employer stated that he had talked with all of the lawyers and employees in the firm and told them not to discuss the case with the new employee.

He also testified that no confidences had come to his attention with regard to the case.

The *Kapco* court admitted that it would be difficult, if not impossible, to imagine what sort of formal screening mechanisms could be established, particularly in a small law firm, beyond those entered in testimony.

Absent more absolute guidelines from either the courts or from the ABA Committee itself, law firms should be responsible for instituting whatever procedures might be required to screen a legal assistant from cases with which he/she was involved in previous employment. At the very least, those measures should be consistent with those entered in testimony in the *Kapco* case and, perhaps, might also include other special procedures instituted on a case-by-case, firm-by-firm basis.

While legal assistants must have mobility in employment opportunities, so must the protection of privileged information relating to clients remain in tantamount importance. With special procedures and precautions, the transition from one employer to another may be accomplished without jeopardizing the mobility of the legal assistant or requiring any disqualification of the new employer, and, most important, without compromising the confidence of the clients.

Lawyers must supervise all of their employees (including, but certainly not limited to, legal assistants) and this supervision must include reasonable efforts to assure that the actions of the employees are in keeping with the professional obligations of the lawyer. To this end, the lawyer should give instructions to all support staff—legal assistants, secretaries, accountants, office administrators, investigators, law clerks, etc.—not to disclose information relating to representation of a client. When a new employee who formerly worked for another law firm is hired, the instructions should include a warning to watch for any matters in which any client of the former employee may be involved.

The ABA Committee recommends that the legal assistant must be warned (1) not to divulge any information relative to the representation of a client of the former employer; and (2) not to be involved in any way in any case on which the legal assistant worked in prior employment.

When the new employer learns of this prior involvement, steps must be taken to be sure the legal assistant is never involved with those cases. If any information is ever revealed or if the screening process would be ineffective, the ABA committee has found that the firm must be disqualified or must withdraw from representing the client.

The obligation of a lawyer to take measures to assure that legal assistants do not disclose confidential information extends even after the employment ends. When a legal assistant resigns from employment in a law firm, the lawyer should advise the legal assistant that he/she must not, in future employment at another firm, work on any matter or reveal any information learned in prior employment. Absent satisfaction that this is done, the former employer should take steps to disqualify the new employer from representing the opposing client.

Proper admonitions to the legal assistant by both the former employer and the new employer not to disclose privileged communications, along with screening measures which prevent the legal assistant from participating in any way in any cases which the firms have in progress when the change in employment occurs, or might have in common in the future, should adequately assure protection of client confidences, and prevent disqualifications on the basis of conflicts of interest.

This policy will insure that legal assistants will have the ability to change jobs. The ability is of paramount importance to the career legal assistant who must remain able to seek new employment, improved working conditions, and higher salaries, if that career is to flourish.

■ Vicki Voisin, CLAS, is a legal assistant with Simpson & Moran, P.C., in Charlevoix, Michigan. She is the treasurer for the National Association of Legal Assistants (NALA) and is on NALA's Board of Directors. This article is reprinted with permission of Vicki Voisin, CLAS, and the National Association of Legal Assistants, Inc., Tulsa, Oklahoma. The article originally appeared in the 1989 *Career Chronicle,* a special edition of 16 FACTS & FINDINGS, Issue 3 (Fall 1989).

4.4 CASE LAW CONCERNING CONFLICT OF INTEREST

The following cases will give you insight into how courts have looked at conflict-of-interest problems.

In the *Kapco* case, you can see how a law firm can effectively deal with conflicts that may emerge as a result of nonlawyer personnel changing employment.

KAPCO MANUFACTURING COMPANY, INC.,
v.
C & O ENTERPRISES, INC.,

United States District Court,
N.D. Illinois, E.D.
637 F. Supp. 1231 (N.D. Ill. 1985)

MEMORANDUM OPINION AND ORDER
ROVNER, District Judge.

Presently pending before this Court is the motion of plaintiff Kapco Manufacturing Company, Inc. ("Kapco") to disqualify the attorneys representing defendants C & O Enterprises, Inc. ("C & O"), Tom Carter, and Jack O'Neill. Eugene F. Friedman of the firm of Eugene F. Friedman, Ltd. represents Kapco. The law firm sought to be disqualified is Alexander, Unikel, Bloom, Zalewa & Tenenbaum, Ltd. ("the Alexander firm"), and the attorney whose disqualification is directly at issue is a partner in that firm, Marvin M. Tenenbaum. Kapco has also requested an injunction against all of the employees of the firm, prohibiting them from disclosing or discussing any information they may have in this suit with anyone.

The procedural history of this case and the flurry of motions filed by Kapco are adequately set forth in the published opinions, and for the sake of economy, will not be repeated here. Suffice it to state for present purposes that . . . Kapco filed the instant motion to disqualify Tenenbaum and the Alexander firm and for an injunction on May 15, 1985.

After full briefing on the motion to disqualify was completed, this Court held an evidentiary hearing on October 3 and 4, 1985. For the reasons stated below, the motion to disqualify and for an injunction is denied.

Facts

Friedman's firm presently numbers two attorneys, himself and an associate, Bruce W. Craig. Although the Friedman firm shares office space with another small firm, it is separate and distinct from that firm, with separate files and office personnel.

Ms. Patricia C. Wyatt was Friedman's main secretary and office manager from December 3, 1981, to sometime in April 1985. On May 6, 1985, Ms. Wyatt began working full time as a secretary for partner Richard Alexander of the Alexander firm. Until approximately December 1980, she had previously worked as a secretary for Mr. Alexander prior to her employment with Friedman in December 1981.

As Friedman's secretary, her duties were wide ranging. She testified that she did everything for Friedman, from secretarial and clerical duties to filing papers in court and acting as a messenger. There is no testimony, however, that she ever performed services such as legal or fact investigation, research, or analysis. In any event, she had complete and free access to Kapco's files, which were numerous because Kapco is or had been involved in approximately 10 to 15 cases as a plaintiff or defendant since its inception several years ago. Friedman acts as Kapco's counsel on all litigated matters and on most general matters. Kenneth Rubel, Kapco's president and sole shareholder, engaged Friedman's services approximately three years ago.

According to Friedman, Craig, and Rubel, Ms. Wyatt received substantial amounts of confidential information concerning Kapco and this litigation while she worked for Friedman. Ms. Wyatt did not contest this assertion. In particular, Friedman, Rubel, and Craig testified that she attended a luncheon with them on March 25, 1985 at the Italian Village Restaurant in Chicago at which they discussed Kapco's possible courses of action on several motions pending before Judge Bua. At that time, they discussed the possibility of taking an appeal, and they discussed strategy in other cases in which Kapco was involved.

At least until early 1985, Friedman and Ms. Wyatt apparently enjoyed a cordial professional relationship and a personal friendship as well. Although Friedman had occasion to reprimand her for using his word processing equipment to do typing for one of his clients after hours without informing him that she was doing so, and also without informing Friedman that she had dated this client, he gave her regular raises. Friedman and Ms. Wyatt also met on occasion after work for drinks, he lent her $3,000 when she needed money during her custody battle, she called him and his wife to discuss personal matters at home, and she borrowed books from him occasionally. In mid-February, 1985, Friedman and Ms. Wyatt had a dispute over her salary raise and

vacation time. During the course of their discussions, Ms. Wyatt told Friedman that she had a job offer from another firm, the name of which she did not divulge to him. Bruce Craig, Friedman's associate, subsequently engaged in a discussion with Ms. Wyatt in an effort to convince her not to leave the Friedman firm. During that conversation, she told Craig that she had a job offer from the Alexander firm, but that Tenenbaum "threw a fit" when he learned that the Alexander firm might hire her because of the potential conflicts regarding this on-going litigation.

Sometime in late February or early March 1985, Ms. Wyatt told Friedman that she would remain in his employment. She continued to work on Kapco matters—including attending the March 25, luncheon described above—until April 11, 1985, when she informed Friedman that she would leave his employment effective April 30, 1985. She refused to tell Friedman or Craig where she would be working despite Friedman's specific inquiries, explaining only that she did not want Friedman to call her during business hours to find out where various items and files were located in the office. She also refused to answer his direct questions as to whether she would be working for anyone having any connection with any matters handled by his office. Indeed, she even refused to answer when Friedman asked her directly whether she would be working with the Alexander firm because he knew that she was personally friendly with one of the partners of that firm, James Zalewa. She gave instructions to her family and friends not to tell Friedman where she would be employed. No one at the Alexander firm informed him of Ms. Wyatt's impending employment with that firm.

Tenenbaum testified that he was indeed concerned when he first learned in early 1985 from his partners that the Alexander firm was considering hiring Ms. Wyatt as the secretary to Mr. Alexander. He told his partners that he had settled the *Kapco* case with Friedman but that because Friedman's motion to reinstate was pending, it was "inadvisable" to offer her employment. They agreed. On March 26, 1985, Judge Bua denied the motion to reinstate, and Tenenbaum told his partners that, although he continued to have concerns, they could extend an offer of employment to Ms. Wyatt because Mr. Alexander needed a secretary. His concerns now centered not around any potential conflict of interest but around what Friedman might do to Ms. Wyatt or to his firm if he found out she was employed by the Alexander firm.

Ms. Wyatt stated that she too was concerned because Mr. Friedman specifically told her when she left his office that from now on, she would be "fair game." She also stated that, aside from disputes over a salary raise and vacation time, she decided in early 1985 to seek employment elsewhere because Friedman frequently used foul language in the office, made crude remarks about women, told off-color jokes, and referred to opposing counsel, including Tenenbaum, in profane terms. She telephoned the Alexander firm in early 1985 to ask if they had a position available, and the firm responded negatively. She subsequently obtained a tentative offer from them that, she testified, wasn't confirmed until April, whereupon she accepted the offer and gave Friedman notice that she was leaving.

On May 6, 1985, she began to work full time as a secretary to Richard Alexander of the Alexander firm. Tenenbaum helped organize that firm in August, 1983, and it now consists of approximately 15 lawyers, only three of whom work in its litigation section. Ms. Wyatt continued to work full time until August 14, 1985, when she began to attend college full time and to work only part time for the Alexander firm.

Ms. Wyatt testified that she has had no discussions with anyone at the Alexander firm regarding Kapco or this case; that she has done no work for the Alexander firm on Kapco or this case; that no one from that firm ever has asked her any questions regarding Friedman, Kapco, this case, or Rubel; that she has volunteered no information to anyone at the firm regarding Kapco or this case; and that she has never seen the Alexander firm's file on this case and indeed does not even know where it is located.

Tenenbaum confirmed that he has had no discussions with Ms. Wyatt regarding Kapco and this case except two. The first occurred before Ms. Wyatt began her employment with the firm when she indicated to him her concerns over what Friedman might do when he discovered her new place of employment. Tenenbaum told her not to worry. The second occurred several months ago when she asked him the status of this case, and he told her only that it was still pending. Tenenbaum also stated that he has talked to all the lawyers and employees of his firm, told them not to discuss anything regarding Kapco or this case with Ms. Wyatt, and they have not engaged in any such discussions with Ms. Wyatt. In any event, no Kapco confidences have come to his attention or to that of Mr. M. Marshall Seeder, the only other attorney at his firm working on the case, via Ms. Wyatt. Finally, Tenenbaum testified that his clients would be prejudiced if the motion to disqualify were granted.

On May 8, 1985, Friedman learned through a circuitous method, the details of which are not important here, that Ms. Wyatt was employed by the Alexander firm. He subsequently learned from the new secretary that he hired to replace Ms. Wyatt, Ms. Lynn

DeHeer, that Ms. Wyatt had been working on a part time basis in the evenings as a secretary to the Alexander firm at least until May 1984. Ironically, Ms. DeHeer, whom Friedman hired to replace Ms. Wyatt, was a secretary at the Alexander firm until May 1984, when she left to become the secretary of a Mr. Meyers, who had once been associated with that firm but then left to practice law on his own.

One week after he learned of Ms. Wyatt's current employment at the Alexander firm, and after Rubel indicated that he was very much concerned about the possible disclosure of Kapco's confidential information to the Alexander firm, Friedman filed his "emergency motion to disqualify and for an injunction" in this Court on May 15, 1985.

Discussion

The Seventh Circuit has noted repeatedly "two important considerations invoked in motions to disqualify counsel and emphasized the delicacy of the balance that must be maintained between them: the sacrosanct privacy of the attorney-client relationship (and the professional integrity implicated by that relationship) and the prerogative of a party to proceed with counsel of its choice." Because disqualification is a "drastic measure which courts should hesitate to impose except when absolutely necessary," *Freeman,* 689 F.2d at 721, the Seventh Circuit has adopted a three step analysis for disqualification motions in cases involving the transfer of an attorney from one firm to another.

> First, we must determine whether a substantial relationship exists between the subject matter of the prior and present representations. If we conclude a substantial relationship does exist, we must next ascertain whether the presumption of shared confidences with respect to the prior representation has been rebutted. If we

conclude this presumption has not been rebutted, we must then determine whether the presumption of shared confidences has been rebutted with respect to the present representation. Failure to rebut this presumption would also make disqualification improper.

Schiessle, 717 F.2d at 420 (footnote omitted).

With these principles in mind, the first question which this Court must confront is whether to apply this analysis to a situation in which an attorney is sought to be disqualified not because a lawyer from the opposing camp has now become associated with him in some way but because a secretary-office manager has switched sides in the midst of contested litigation. In its brief in support of the motion to disqualify, Kapco cited no federal case law which addresses this fact situation. In its answering brief, C & O has raised the spectre of the possibility that every time a secretary, office manager, docket clerk, or messenger leaves a law firm to join a firm representing an opponent of the clients of the first firm, a disqualification motion will be brought. Although this concern ordinarily would make this Court reluctant to analyze the secretary-transfer situation just as the Seventh Circuit has mandated the attorney-transfer situation must be analyzed, this case is unique. Contrary to C & O's characterization of this case, here a relatively minor employee from a large law firm has not left to join another large law firm after litigation between clients of each firm has essentially ceased; here, a key employee, who has had access to and admittedly has received confidential client communications from a two-lawyer law firm has left to become the secretary to a partner of the opposing law firm, which is also small, in the heat of litigation. The fact situation presented by this case is unusual, and this Court believes that the same potential, if not actual, conflict of interest problems are posed by this case as in the typical attorney-transfer disqualification case. Accordingly, this Court will apply the analysis of the Seventh Circuit as set forth above in *Schiessle* to decide the motion to disqualify.

The Seventh Circuit's three step analysis requires first that the court determine whether a substantial relationship exists between the subject matter of the "prior and present representations." In this case, there is no doubt that a substantial relationship exists because the "prior and present representations" concern the same ongoing litigation. Thus, there can be no real dispute that there is a substantial relationship between the prior and present representations.

The second step in the analysis requires the Court to ascertain whether the presumption of shared confidences with respect to the prior representation, or relationship, has been rebutted. The Seventh Circuit has held that the existence of a substantial relationship gives rise to a presumption of shared confidences with respect to the prior representation. Kapco presented substantial evidence that Ms. Wyatt obtained confidential information regarding Kapco during the course of her varied duties as Friedman's secretary-office manager, and Ms. Wyatt did not deny this assertion. Accordingly, the presumption of shared confidences with respect to the prior representation has not been rebutted.

This Court must next proceed to the third step of the Seventh Circuit's analysis in *Schiessle, supra: i.e.* whether the presumption of shared confidences has been rebutted with respect to the present representation, or, in this case, relationship. C & O orally moved the Court at the close of Kapco's case to deny Kapco's motion to disqualify because Kapco failed to present any evidence that Ms. Wyatt

disclosed Kapco's confidences to the Alexander firm. In support of its argument that C & O should not be required to rebut a presumption in which no evidence had been presented, C & O argued that this Court should not apply the presumption in the first place.

The application of the presumption of shared confidences is proper under the unique facts of this case.

The evidence presented to rebut the presumption of shared confidences must "clearly and effectively" demonstrate that the attorney whose disqualification is at issue did not in fact possess any confidential information: he must prove that he did not have knowledge of the confidences of the client. After reviewing all of the evidence, this Court finds that C & O has clearly and effectively rebutted the presumption of shared confidences with respect to the present relationship between Ms. Wyatt and the Alexander firm and that Kapco has not met its burden of persuading this Court that in fact Ms. Wyatt has disclosed confidential information to the Alexander firm or is likely to do so in the future.

Kapco contends that to adequately rebut the presumption of shared ·confidences with respect to the present representation, C & O was required to and did not prove that "specific institutional mechanisms" (e.g., "Chinese Walls") had been implemented to effectively insulate against any flow of confidential information from Ms. Wyatt to the Alexander firm. As the Seventh Circuit stated in *Schiessle:*

> Such a determination can be based on objective and verifiable evidence presented to the trial court and must be made on a case-by-case basis. Factors appropriate for consideration by the trial court might include, but are not limited to, the size and structural divisions of the law firm involved, the likelihood of contact between

the "infected" attorney and the specific attorneys responsible for the present representation, the existence of rules which prevent the "infected" attorney from access to relevant files or other information pertaining to the present litigation or which prevent him from sharing in the fees derived from such litigation.

717 F.2d at 421 (citation omitted).

The Federal Circuit, expressly analyzing and applying the law of the Seventh Circuit on attorney disqualification, rejected precisely the same argument in *Panduit, supra:*

Nowhere in Seventh Circuit opinions has proof of *formal screening* been delineated as the *sine qua non* of establishing the nonexistence of the presumed fact that confidences have been shared. Within the factual context of *LaSalle Bank,* 703 F.2d at 259, the court merely opined that a *timely* screening arrangement might have prevented disqualification in that case.

* * *

A rule that screening is the exclusive means of rebutting the presumption that confidences have been shared, *regardless of independent evidence,* cannot [survive] *La Salle* or *Schiessle.*

744 F.2d at 1580–81 (emphasis in original).

Given that this Court has found as a matter of fact that neither Tenenbaum nor the Alexander firm has received any of Kapco's confidential information from Wyatt, this Court holds that the absence of formal, institutionalized "Chinese Walls" type mechanisms in the Alexander firm does not require disqualification. Indeed, it is difficult if not impossible to imagine what sort of formal mechanisms could be established to erect the "Chinese Wall" in a firm as small as the Alexander firm that are not already present. Tenenbaum testified that he has instructed everyone in the firm not to discuss Kapco with Ms. Wyatt and that he did so prior to her employment in

May 1985. Ms. Wyatt testified she has discussed Kapco with no one at the Alexander firm; that she has not performed any work on Kapco matters; that she does not work with Tenenbaum or Seeder, his associate; that she has never looked at the Alexander firm's Kapco files and that she does not even know where it is located. As the court in *Panduit, supra,* 744 F.2d at 1579, stated: "An *absolute* finding of no *possible* inadvertent sharing of confidences is not required to establish an effective rebuttal." (Emphasis in original.) Thus, with Tenenbaum's assurances that he has done all that is necessary to guard against the receipt of Kapco's confidences through Ms. Wyatt, this Court concludes that C & O has clearly and effectively rebutted the presumption of shared confidences with respect to the present relationship between Ms. Wyatt and the Alexander firm.

The Seventh Circuit has repeatedly admonished courts to guard against lightly disqualifying the attorney of a party's choice partly because of the prejudice inevitably resulting from such disqualification. This factor is particularly persuasive here because Tenenbaum has not only been involved in this litigation from its inception at considerable expense to C & O, but he was also personally involved in negotiating the December 20, 1984, settlement agreement, the substance and meaning of which Kapco has now put in issue. As such, Tenenbaum is virtually indispensable to C & O's position in the current litigation. The Seventh Circuit has also cautioned district courts to guard against the increasing use of disqualification motions in the arsenal of litigation tactics. Although this Court recognizes that an employee who has shared a client's confidences should not be able to switch to the opposing camp mid-litigation with impunity, the Court cannot ignore the obvious animus that exists between Friedman and Tenenbaum and between Friedman and Ms. Wyatt. Although Kapco's concerns that its confidences not be disclosed to its opponents are legitimate, this Court will not condone its use of the attorney disqualification tactic as a means of retaliation against an opposing counsel and a former secretary.

Conclusion

For the reasons stated above, Kapco's "emergency motion to disqualify and for injunction" is denied. The request of all parties for attorney's fees and costs incurred in prosecuting and defending against the motion is also denied; each party is to bear its own costs and attorneys' fees.

CASE QUESTIONS

1. Why did the court refuse to disqualify the law firm?
2. Would the court's decision have been different if it had been an attorney, rather than a secretary, who had changed firms?
3. What factors distinguish this case from the asbestos case excerpted in chapter 3?

The *Herron* case concerns a possible conflict of interest arising out of a legal secretary's changing employment. Note that the court considers the extent to which the secretary was screened from confidential information, but that the analysis proceeds from a concern for the "appearance of impropriety" rather than the rules concerning confidentiality or conflict of interest.

Jerry M. HERRON, Appellant,
v.
James JONES, III, et. al., Appellees

Supreme Court of Arkansas
637 S.W.2d 569 (Ark. 1982)
July 12, 1982

GEORGE ROSE SMITH, Justice.

This medical malpractice suit was brought by the appellees, the surviving husband and minor children of Shirley L. Jones, whose death is alleged to have been caused by the negligence of the appellant, a physician. In December 1981, the suit had been pending for 16 months, all discovery had been completed, and the case was set for a four-day trial in February. On December 16 the plaintiffs' attorneys, Henry & Duckett, filed a motion asking that all defense counsel—the firm of Friday, Eldredge & Clark, Phillip Malcom (the member of the Friday firm handling the case), and a Texas law firm acting as co-counsel—be disqualified from further participation in the case because Pat Brown Damon, a legal secretary who had worked for Henry & Duckett for eleven months, had become a secretary for the Friday firm, and particularly for Malcom, in November 1981. The motion for disqualification asserted that Canons 4 and 9 of the Code of Professional Responsibility, 33 *Ark. L. Rev.* 643 (1980) would be violated by the lawyers' continued participation in the case.

The trial judge, relying primarily on *State of Arkansas v. Dean Foods Products Co.,* 605 F.2d 380 (8th Cir. 1979), ruled that defense counsel were all disqualified from proceeding further in the case, not because there was any actual impropriety, but because there was a violation of Canon 9: "A Lawyer Should Avoid Even the Appearance of Professional Impropriety." The case comes to this court for an interpretation of our Code of Professional Responsibility Rule 29(1)(c).

On the merits, the proof is that before Mrs. Damon left Henry & Duckett she was cautioned not to disclose confidential information about this case. When she became a secretary at the Friday firm, she was told at the outset that she would have nothing to do with this case, for which the file was kept in Malcom's own office. Mrs. Damon herself stated in an affidavit that she had had no contact with the case since being employed by the Friday firm, had not spoken to anyone in the firm about the case, and would not do so in the future.

Thus there is no suggestion of impropriety in fact. Instead, the appellees emphasize the language of Canon 9, that a lawyer must avoid even the appearance of impropriety. Granted. But we must keep in mind that the *Dean Foods* case and similar decisions have all dealt with the situation in which the lawyer himself has changed from one firm to another, with a possible conflict of interest. Here, however, it was not a lawyer but a legal secretary who changed her employment. We have no doubt that the Canon 4 duty to preserve the confidences of a client applies to all the employees of a law firm, but Canon 9 is directed specifically to lawyers and to no one else. Counsel for the appellees conceded at the oral argument that they have found no case in which a lawyer has been disqualified in circumstances similar to those now presented.

The proof demonstrates beyond question that every precaution was taken to avoid any disclosure of confidential information by Mrs. Damon and that no such disclosure occurred. Moreover, there is much testimony that temporary secretarial help is continually found to be necessary by many law firms in Pulaski County. The representative of a concern engaged in the business testified that her firm provides the temporary services of experienced legal secretaries on a regular basis to between forty and fifty law offices in the community. Twenty percent of that company's secretaries work for from two to eight firms in a year. There was also testimony that law firms prefer to employ legal secretaries with prior experience, so that permanent secretaries as well as temporary ones frequently move from one law office to another. Thus complete avoidance of a situation like that now presented is impossible.

We need not detail the abundance of similar testimony, which was uncontradicted. We are convinced that any appearance of impropriety, any presumption of impropriety, that might have arisen from Mrs. Damon's change of jobs was effectively overcome by the undisputed testimony. The trial judge was mistaken in sustaining the motion to disqualify defense counsel.

Reversed.

CASE QUESTIONS

1. What actions did the law firm take to screen Mrs. Damon?
2. In what way is the court's analysis different from the court's analysis in *Kapco?*

The *Blalock* case considers whether an attorney's having had sexual relations with the complaining witness in a sexual assault case constitutes a violation of the rules against conflict of interest. The court also asserts that a conflict of interest can lead to a claim of ineffective assistance of counsel.

The PEOPLE of the State of Colorado, Plaintiff-Appellant,

v.

Hugh BLALOCK, Defendant-Appellee

No. 27802
592 P.2d 406 (Colo. 1979)
Supreme Court of Colorado, En Banc
March 26, 1979

ERICKSON, Justice.

The district attorney has filed a direct appeal from a district court order which granted the defendant's motion for post-conviction relief, pursuant to Crim.P. 35(b), and ordered a new trial. We affirm.

Blalock was charged in a three-count information with attempted murder, first-degree sexual assault, and second-degree kidnapping. The defendant pled not guilty and trial was to a jury.

Before the case was submitted to the jury, the attempted murder charge was dismissed, and the defendant was convicted by the jury of first-degree sexual assault and second-degree kidnapping. A concurrent sentence of not less than eight nor more than twelve years in the Colorado state penitentiary was

imposed. The defendant has served more than two years of his sentence. He was released on bail after a new trial was ordered.

The defendant's motion for post-conviction relief was based upon the fact that his defense counsel had sexual intercourse with the complaining witness prior to the time that he undertook to represent the defendant and had a conflict of interest which denied the defendant effective assistance of counsel. *U.S. Const.,* Amend. VI.

The lawyer, Lawrence C. Rotenberg, after his second interview with the defendant, advised him of his prior sexual relations with the complaining witness or victim and told the defendant that under no circumstances could the sex history of the victim be gone into in the defense of his case. However, he expressed the opinion that his previous affair with the victim would be an advantage when it came to cross-examination and the overall defense of the case.

Three different district judges have reviewed the conduct of defense counsel. At an early stage, the Honorable Robert Fullerton pointed out the obvious impropriety and the conflict to Rotenberg. Rotenberg's background with the victim came to the attention of the court after Rotenberg interviewed the victim. Rotenberg contacted the victim at her place of employment, late at night, without notice, and discussed the charges which were pending against the defendant. In the course of the interview, he attempted to capitalize on his previous relationship with the victim and tried to persuade her to contact the district attorney and have the charges against the defendant reduced. The victim became hysterical and contacted the district attorney. The district attorney brought the matter to the attention of Judge Fullerton, and a hearing was held.

At the *in camera* hearing before Judge Fullerton, Rotenberg insisted that he had the right to represent the defendant and that he was the counsel that the defendant had chosen. Judge Fullerton, after a hearing, advised Rotenberg that if he continued to represent the defendant, a grievance would be filed with the grievance committee of this court. Rotenberg withdrew from the case over the defendant's objection and assertion that he had the right to counsel of his own choice.

During the week following Rotenberg's withdrawal, the defendant attempted to obtain new counsel. He was handicapped, however, by his retainer agreement with Rotenberg. He had agreed to pay Rotenberg $1,500 for defending the case. At the time he withdrew, Rotenberg had interviewed the complaining witness and done little more. At that time, the defendant had paid him $800 or $900. However, when the defendant asked Rotenberg to return some part of the fee so that he could retain another lawyer, Rotenberg refused. Rotenberg told the defendant he would wipe the slate clean if the defendant did not want him to represent him further, but would not make any refund. While the defendant was attempting to secure other counsel, defendant's case was assigned to a different division for trial. With a new judge presiding, Rotenberg agreed to again enter his appearance and defend the case if the defendant would pay Rotenberg $1,500. The economic pressure applied by Rotenberg influenced the defendant to agree to Rotenberg's demands. The economic pressure applied by Rotenberg was improper.

When the district attorney learned of Rotenberg's decision to defend the case, the conflict of interest was brought to the attention of a second district judge, and a second *in camera* hearing was held. Rotenberg asserted at that hearing that he would not go into the sexual background of the victim and again asserted that the defendant wanted him to be his lawyer. The district judge concluded that she could not deny the defendant's request to have Rotenberg represent him and did not require Rotenberg to withdraw.

At the time of trial, a third judge was assigned to hear the case. He was not apprised of Rotenberg's conflict of interest and did not become aware of the full extent of the conflict until after a motion for post-conviction relief was filed by a different lawyer. Rotenberg cross-examined the victim and asked some questions which might not have been asked if his relationship with the witness was not buttressed by a background of sexual intimacy. However, Rotenberg did not attempt to explore the sexual history of the victim.

When the post-conviction proceedings were held, the trial judge heard extended testimony and concluded that the conduct of defense counsel not only reflected an appearance of impropriety, but also constituted a deprivation of the effective assistance of counsel. A court must determine, when faced with a claim of ineffective assistance of counsel, "whether the advice was within the range of competence demanded of attorneys in criminal cases," *McMann v. Richardson, supra,* 397 U.S. at 771, 90 S. Ct. at 1449, and whether the assistance rendered by the attorney demonstrates "faithful representation of the interest of his client," *Tollett v. Henderson, supra,* 411 U.S. at 268, 93 S. Ct. at 1608 . . . . Our examination of the entire record indicates that there was a denial of effective assistance of counsel. The conflict of interest arising out of Rotenberg's previous sexual liaison with the victim is apparent.

* * *

Any jury would have been incensed by the testimony that was presented. The defendant was not provided reasonably effective assistance of counsel.

At the Crim.P. 35(b) hearing, Judge Fullerton, who first confronted Rotenberg with what we would identify as a clear conflict of interest, said that he did not believe that the defendant understood the consequences of his election to have Rotenberg represent him. The defendant testified that representation by Rotenberg also occurred because the defendant could not obtain the funds to employ other counsel. In granting the defendant's motion for post-conviction relief, the trial judge found that the defendant had not given his informed consent to a waiver of his right to the effective assistance of counsel and that the defendant had been denied that assistance. The representation in this case not only failed to meet our standard which requires reasonably effective assistance of counsel, but also falls in that category of representation that has been described as being a sham and a farce.

The same district court judge presided over both defendant's trial and the Crim.P. 35(b) hearing. If we were to reverse the trial court that granted post-conviction relief, we would have to overrule the trial court's conclusion that there was ineffective assistance of counsel. The right to effective assistance of counsel is among those "constitutional rights so basic to a fair trial that their infraction can never be treated as a harmless error."

We cannot say that the record does not support the trial court's conclusion and was not in accordance with the weight of the evidence.

Accordingly, we affirm.

PRINGLE and CARRIGAN, JJ., do not participate.

CASE QUESTIONS

1. What was the nature of the conflict in this case?
2. How would the Rules and the Code differ on the attorney's duty when faced with this type of conflict?
3. How is the claim of ineffective assistance of counsel related to the conflict of interest?
4. How would you have advised Rotenberg in this case?

The *Lewis* case is an example of a sexual conflict of interest in a jurisdiction that does not yet have a specific standard concerning sexual relations between attorneys and clients. There was strong disagreement, not only among the justices but also in the public and bar, as to the propriety of the court's punishment.

IN THE MATTER OF JAMES WOODROW LEWIS

Supreme Court of Georgia
262 Ga. 37 (1992)

PER CURIAM.

The State Bar of Georgia filed a formal complaint against James Woodrow Lewis charging him with violations of Standards 3, 4, 28, 30, 45(d), and 45(e) of State Bar Rule 4-102. Following limited discovery and prior to any evidentiary hearing, the State Bar and Lewis filed cross-motions for summary judgment. The special master granted to Lewis partial summary judgment on the charges alleging violations of Standards 4 and 28 and granted to the State Bar partial summary judgment on the charges alleging violations of Standards 30 and 45(d). The review panel of the state disciplinary board adopted the special master's findings and found also that Lewis had violated Standard 45(e).

We are limited to the record before this court, which is based on a summary proceeding. The parties have not taken depositions or presented evidence at a hearing before the special master. The State Bar contends, and Lewis concedes, that he engaged in sexual intercourse with a client. Lewis contends that he had a sexual relationship with the individual concerned several years before she became his client. He further contends that he accepted representation as a service for a friend, with no expectation of receiving a fee and without any demand of personal favors,

and that the relationship was consensual through its entire existence. He insists also that his conduct has not affected adversely his client's cause, as the trial court awarded her custody of her child. He supports his contentions with an affidavit from his client's sister, who also states that her sister continued to see and telephone Lewis after he no longer represented her in the divorce action. The State Bar counters that the client objected to the sexual activities.

1. This proceeding is the first time that we have considered whether a lawyer who has a sexual relationship with a client should be disciplined. Standard 30 provides:

> Except with the written consent or written notice to his client after full disclosure a lawyer shall not accept or continue employment if the exercise of his professional judgment on behalf of his client will be or reasonably may be affected by his own financial, business, property or personal interests.

Notwithstanding the many circumstances that are in sharp dispute, Lewis acknowledged that he had engaged in sexual intercourse with a client while representing her in a contested divorce and custody action. Thereby—under the circumstances of *this* case—he has admitted to violating Standard 30, in that "his professional judgment on behalf of his client will be or reasonably may be affected by his own . . . personal interests." In the context of an action for divorce and custody, that conduct in se is a violation of Standard 30. Every lawyer must know that an extramarital relationship can jeopardize every aspect of a client's matrimonial case—extending to forfeiture of alimony, loss of custody, and denial of attorney fees. Thus, where, as in this case, there has been no testimony and no findings to resolve disputed factual contentions, the admission by Lewis of sexual intercourse with his client authorized the entry of summary judgment against him on the charge brought under Standard 30.

2. The same admission warrants summary judgment adverse to Lewis as to Standard 45(d) and 45(e). Lewis's admission establishes without issue that he participated with "his client in conduct that the lawyer knows to be illegal" and that Lewis did "knowingly engage in . . . conduct contrary to a disciplinary rule."

3. As a sanction for these violations—based upon Lewis's admission as to a single factual matter—we order that he be suspended from the practice of law for a period of three years. Additionally, we direct that Lewis notify his clients of this action and take all actions necessary to protect their respective interests as required by State Bar Rule 4-219 (c).

4. (a) The special master and the review panel denied the State Bar's motion for summary judgment on the charge that Lewis violated Standard 3, which prohibits a lawyer from engaging in illegal professional conduct involving moral turpitude. Both the special master and the review panel rejected the State

Bar's argument that it had established as a matter of law that Lewis extracted sexual conduct from his client as a condition of his legal representation. We agree that the affidavits create genuine issues of material fact concerning the crucial questions of whether Lewis made an inappropriate bargain with his client, i.e., services for sex, and whether he coerced his client into having sexual intercourse as a condition for his continued legal representations.

(b) Hence, these issues are not now before us, and their resolution must await the completion of further proceedings before the special master, in which testimony may be heard from Lewis and his client. We will accord to members of the State Bar of Georgia one of the guarantees that American jurisprudence traditionally has extended to the basest of common criminals: the right to be heard.

5. We note that subsequent proceedings may be completed in the usual manner and subjected to final review well within the three-year suspension period. Hereafter, should the special master or the review panel find it appropriate, recommendations as to additional discipline, including disbarment, may be submitted in the regular order.

Suspended for three years. All the Justices concur, except Clarke, C.J., Benham and Sears-Collins, JJ., who would order disbarment.

BENHAM, Justice, dissenting.

I would follow the recommendation of the Review Panel and disbar James Woodrow Lewis.

I am authorized to state that Chief Justice Clarke and Justice Sears-Collins join in this dissent.

CASE QUESTIONS

1. Do you agree with the majority or the dissent as to the appropriate punishment?
2. Should the consent of the client be a mitigating factor in a sexual conflict-of-interest case?
3. Should jurisdictions pass specific statutes concerning sexual relations with a client?

4.5 RECOGNIZING AND RESOLVING CONFLICT-OF-INTEREST PROBLEMS

Although conflicts of interest seem obvious, in actuality they are sometimes difficult to detect. For this reason, conflict-of-interest checking, as previously discussed, should be performed in every situation involving representation. This would include communicating with all attorneys and checking old files and databases to determine if the firm or any attorney or employee of the firm ever represented the client, sued the new client, or represented the party to be sued. This practice is necessary to run an effective and ethical law firm; nothing could be more embarrassing than for a lawyer to sue a former client. By participating in the conflict-of-interest checks performed in your firm, you will help the firm identify any conflict of interest that might impair its ability to represent a client ethically.

Once you recognize that a conflict of interest exists, you must decide how to handle it. Naturally, each situation is unique, and your response will depend on the relevant circumstances, but when faced with a conflict of interest, you might consider the following courses of action.

1. Advise your supervising attorney that a potential conflict of interest may exist.
2. If the conflict only involves you (the paralegal), work with your supervising attorney to effectively screen yourself from the case. Do nothing on the case; do not even make an ordinary phone call or sign a simple letter giving the client information.
3. If you are in doubt as to whether a conflict exists, take the conservative position. Then discuss it with the paralegal supervisor or your supervising attorney.

4.6 CONFLICT OF INTEREST: A SUMMARY

In practicing law, there inevitably arise situations where lawyers and paralegals might be faced with conflicting loyalties. The ethical considerations concerning conflict of interest directly relate to the necessity for confidentiality of client communications and zealous representation of the client's interests. By making it unethical and inappropriate for attorneys to work in situations where they serve two masters, the Codes attempt to ensure that legal clients are afforded their right of full, vigorous, confidential representation.

Paralegals must be acutely aware of the impropriety of conflict-of-interest situations. By understanding their importance and analyzing your work and involvement for potential conflict-of-interest situations, you will successfully avoid problems in this area. As you become more sensitive to conflicts of interest, you will learn appropriate responses to difficult situations. By communicating effectively with appropriate people on your job, you will be able to recognize and resolve ethical dilemmas arising from conflict of interest.

REVIEW QUESTIONS

1. What situations generally cause a conflict of interest?
2. What is a Chinese Wall?
3. What steps should a firm take to effectively screen a paralegal who is starting in a new position?

QUESTIONS FOR THOUGHT AND DISCUSSION

1. Paralegal John worked in-house for Delta Industries, Inc. Delta regularly employed attorney Mick to do most of its legal work. Can John work for attorney Mick after leaving Delta Industries?
2. Robert, the paralegal, is married to Cynthia, the attorney. His firm represents the plaintiff in a case in which Cynthia's firm represents the defendant. Is this a conflict of interest?
3. Attorney Trey incorporates BigC, Inc., and is paid for his legal services by the majority shareholder, Ms. Sanford. Because Trey did such a great job, Ms. Sanford gives him 25 percent of the shares of BigC, Inc. Are there any ethical problems with this?
4. Philip was a criminal defense lawyer who represented Jim Joint in his drug trial. Joint was subsequently found not guilty by the jury. Philip has been offered a position with the district attorney's office. Joint is arrested and indicted on murder charges and Philip is assigned to be the prosecutor on the case.
   a. Can Philip prosecute Joint?
   b. What if Joint gave Philip oral permission to prosecute him? What about written permission?
   c. Does it make a difference that Philip represented Joint on drug charges, and now Joint is being prosecuted for murder?

    d. Would it make a difference if Philip had not represented Joint in a previous criminal case, but rather had prepared a will for Joint?

    e. What action would you advise Philip to take?

5. Your personal physician is being sued for malpractice. The firm that employs you as a legal assistant is defending the doctor. Should you work on the case?

Chapter 5 Feature: The Unauthorized Practice of Law

LAW, LITERATURE, AND ETHICS

From Helter Skelter
By Vincent Bugliosi

On December 17, Manson appeared before Judge Keene and asked to have the Public Defender dismissed. He wanted to represent himself, he said.

Judge Keene told Manson that he was not convinced that he was competent to represent himself, or, in legal jargon, to proceed "in pro per" (in propria persona).

MANSON: "Your Honor, there is no way I can give up my voice in this matter. If I can't speak, then our whole thing is done. If I can't speak in my own defense and converse freely in this courtroom, then it ties my hands behind my back, and if I have no voice, then there is no sense in having a defense."

Keene agreed to reconsider Manson's motion on the twenty-second.

Manson's insistence that only he could speak for himself, as well as his obvious enjoyment at being in the spotlight, led me to one conclusion: when the time came, he probably wouldn't be able to resist taking the stand.

I began keeping a notebook of questions I intended to ask him on cross-examination. Before long there was a second notebook, and a third.

On the nineteenth Leslie Van Houten also asked to have her present attorney, Donald Barnett, dismissed. Keene granted the motion and appointed Marvin Part to be Miss Van Houten's attorney of record.

Only later would we learn what was happening behind the scenes. Manson had set up his own communications network. Whenever he heard that an attorney for one of the girls had initiated a move on behalf of his client which could conceivably run counter to Manson's own defense, within days that attorney would be removed from the case. Barnett

had wanted a psychiatrist to examine Leslie. Learning of this, Manson vetoed the idea, and when the psychiatrist appeared at Sybil Brand, Leslie refused to see him. Her request of Barnett's dismissal came immediately after.

Manson's goal: to run the entire defense himself. In court as well as out, Charlie intended to retain complete control of the Family.

Manson wanted to represent himself, he told the court, because "lawyers play with people, and I am a person and I don't want to be played with in this matter." Most lawyers were only interested in one thing, publicity, Manson said. He'd seen quite a few of them lately and felt he knew what he was talking about. Any attorney previously associated with the DA's Office was not acceptable to him, he added. He had learned that two other defendants had court-appointed attorneys who were once deputy DAs (Caballero and Part).

Judge Keene explained that many lawyers engaged in the practice of criminal law first gained experience in the office of the District Attorney, the City Attorney, or the U.S. Attorney. Knowing how the prosecution worked was often a benefit to their clients.

MANSON: "It sounds good from there, but not from here."

"Your Honor," Manson continued, "I am in a difficult position. The news media has already executed and buried me . . . . If anyone is hypnotized, the people are hypnotized by the lies being told to them . . . . There is no attorney in the world who can represent me as a person. I have to do it myself."

Judge Keene had a suggestion. He would arrange for an experienced attorney to confer with him. Unlike other attorneys to whom Manson talked, this attorney would have no interest in representing him. His function would be solely to discuss with him the legal issues, and the possible dangers, of defending himself. Manson accepted the offer and, after court, Keene arranged for Joseph Ball, a former president of the State Bar Association and former senior counsel to the Warren Commission, to meet with Manson.

Manson talked to Ball and found him "a very nice gentleman," he told Judge Keene on the twenty-fourth. "Mr. Ball probably understands maybe everything there is to know about law, but he doesn't understand the generation gap; he doesn't understand free love society; he doesn't understand people who are trying to get out from underneath all of this . . . ."

Ball, in turn, found Manson "an able, intelligent young man, quiet-spoken and mild-mannered . . . ." Although he had attempted to persuade him, without success, that he could benefit from the services of a skilled lawyer, Ball was obviously impressed with Manson. "We went over different problems of law, and I found he had a ready understanding . . . . Remarkable understanding. As a matter of fact, he has a very fine brain. I complimented him on the fact. I think I told you that he had a high IQ. Must have, to be able to converse as he did." Manson "is not resentful against society," Ball said. "And he feels that if he goes to trial and he is able to permit jurors and the Court to hear him and see him, they will realize he is not the kind of man who would perpetrate horrible crimes."

After Ball had finished, Judge Keene questioned Manson for more than an hour about his knowledge of courtroom procedure, and the possible penalties for the crimes with which he was charged, throughout almost begging him to reconsider his decision to defend himself.

MANSON: "For all my life, as long as I can remember, I've taken your advice. Your faces have changed, but it's the same court, the same structure . . . . All my life I've been put in little slots, Your Honor. And I went along with it . . . . I have no alternative but to fight you back any way I know because you and the District Attorney and all the attorneys I have ever met are all on the same side. The police are on the same side and the newspapers are on the same side and it's all pointed against me, personally . . . . No. I haven't changed my mind."

THE COURT: "Mr. Manson, I am imploring you not to take this step; I am imploring you to either name your own attorney, or, if you are unable to do so, to permit the Court to name one for you."

Manson's mind was made up, however, and Judge Keene finally concluded: "It is, in this Court's opinion, a sad and tragic mistake you are making by taking this course of action, but I can't talk you out of it. . . . Mr. Manson, you are your own lawyer."

■ Permission to reprint courtesy of Vincent Bugliosi.

CHAPTER 5
The Unauthorized Practice of Law

CHAPTER OVERVIEW

This chapter covers the concept and application of the unauthorized practice of law. This ethical consideration is especially important for paralegals because paralegals often face situations in which their actions might cross the already hazy line between being an ethical paralegal and engaging in unauthorized legal practice. Additionally, new ways of viewing paralegals and their abilities have created new issues in this area. This chapter will help you identify the ethical dimensions of the unauthorized practice of law and learn how to recognize and resolve problems that you might encounter in the course of your work.

THE CASE OF THE VENGEFUL RAPPER

Jessica is a paralegal at the firm that represented the rap group Noisy Boys in an obscenity case. The firm also handles normal legal problems for the band. After the obscenity charge was dismissed, the attorney handling the case, Debra Jewell, decided to take a long vacation. While Debra was on vacation, the firm's other attorney, Jon Stevens, was out on parental leave. Jessica and the legal secretary, Allison, are the only two people in the office on the Friday following the trial of the obscenity case.

At 4:59 p.m., Jessica gets a telephone call from Nathan Nasty, the leader of the band, who tells Jessica: "I want to sue those !*!***!!s for defamation of character and I want to do it now! Do we have a case? Shouldn't we file suit today? What is the statute of limitations for a defamation action? I want to do something today!" Jessica knows the answers to all Nathan's questions and does not need to consult an attorney, because she has worked on hundreds of defamation cases before.

What should she do?

THE CASE OF THE NEEDY RELATIVE

Paralegal Jonathan has an aunt, Sue, who is quite poor and is married to a horrible husband. Sue and her husband have decided to divorce, but cannot afford the legal fees, although they can afford the filing fees. Jonathan learns from his mother, Sue's sister, about his aunt's predicament.

Jonathan is a senior paralegal with a firm specializing in family law. He drafts almost all the uncontested divorces for the firm. Wanting to help his aunt, Jonathan offers to draft all her divorce papers free. Jonathan tells Aunt Sue to rewrite all the papers in her handwriting so the judge will not suspect that someone has done the legal work for her.

Has Jonathan done anything wrong?

5.1 THE UNAUTHORIZED PRACTICE OF LAW: AN INTRODUCTION

The one ethical consideration that most directly affects paralegals is the prohibition against the unauthorized practice of law. Through the unauthorized practice doctrine, nonlawyers are prohibited from practicing law; this doctrine also applies to disbarred or suspended lawyers. The issue of unauthorized practice also arises when paralegals fail to disclose themselves as nonlawyers. Paralegals should be sure to advise those with whom they are communicating that they are not attorneys. Lawyers also have the obligation to designate which of their staff are attorneys and which are not. Those who violate this doctrine may thereby commit criminal violations, leaving themselves open to fines and imprisonment, and may be held in contempt of court.

Although the doctrine of unauthorized practice seems self-serving, guaranteeing lawyers a monopoly on legal business, it nonetheless prevents the incompetent and the unscrupulous from taking advantage of the public. Because attorneys are authorized to practice law, the authorizing agency can monitor and discipline attorneys, and prohibit activities that are not in the public interest. Another reason for this legal doctrine concerns the protection of clients against uninsured legal practitioners. Most attorneys and firms carry malpractice insurance; thus, if they have not properly handled a client's case, the client may be compensated by suing the lawyer and attempting to recover damages from the insurance carrier. If a paralegal, especially an independent paralegal, were not covered by firm malpractice insurance, clients injured by paralegal negligence would be left with very little recourse.

Those who oppose authorizing only attorneys to practice law believe that there are many activities, such as preparing wills, divorces, or real estate transactions, that need not be reserved for attorneys, because they are relatively simple and standardized. They claim that reserving these activities for attorneys artificially raises the price of legal services and also estranges those who cannot afford legal services from the legal process. They also assert that when it comes to legal services, consumers should be able to hire whomever they please. These two views are argued in the guest editorials later in this chapter.

Nonlawyers have not always been prohibited from practicing the law. From the colonial period through the nineteenth century, several states allowed nonlawyers to practice. Since the first unauthorized practice committee in 1914, however, bar associations have developed doctrine prohibiting the unauthorized practice of law. The American Bar Association's Special Committee on Unauthorized Practice, founded in 1930, was highly active through the 1950s in developing standards and disciplining violators of the unauthorized practice doctrine. After a relatively quiet period from 1960 to 1980, the 1980s saw increased challenges to and development of this doctrine for many reasons, the most significant being the legal system's inability to serve the lower and middle classes. The entrepreneurial spirit of the early 1980s also encouraged individuals to pursue success aggressively. In the legal profession, this sometimes meant challenging the established power structures. Difficult issues arose when the challenger was motivated not by greed or power but by a concern for providing legal services to those who could least afford them.

Perhaps the most famous challenge was that by Rosemary Furman. Furman did business as Northside Secretarial Service, through which she helped her clients prepare pleadings for divorces and adoptions. Furman had the clients prepare "intake sheets," which sometimes were left incomplete because the clients did not understand what to do; she then interviewed the clients so that they could complete the forms, and instructed them how to represent themselves in the courts. Furman charged $50 or less for her services and was motivated by the desire to help poor or uneducated people, who were estranged from the legal process and could not afford a lawyer, gain the benefits of the law. Furman defied Florida's guidelines at the time, which permitted a nonlawyer to sell and type legal forms, but not to advise, assist, or communicate with the clients concerning the forms. Her clients were too poor or uneducated to comply with those restrictions—so she challenged those restrictions. In *Florida Bar v. Furman,* 376 So. 2d 378 (Fla. 1979), Furman was found to have engaged in the unauthorized practice of law, but the court also directed the Florida Bar to study the problem of lack of access to the legal system. In a highly unusual move, the Florida Supreme Court amended its rules regulating the Florida Bar as follows:

> It shall not constitute the unlicensed practice of law for non-lawyers to engage in limited oral communications to assist individuals in the completion of legal forms approved by the Supreme Court of Florida. Oral communications by non-lawyers are restricted to those communications reasonably necessary to elicit factual information to complete the form(s) and inform the individual how to file such forms.

In re Amendment to Rules Regulating the Florida Bar, 510 So. 2d 596, 597 (Fla. 1987). Rosemary Furman made her point, at least in Florida.

Unauthorized practice issues are so significant for paralegals because paralegals are nonlawyers who have often gained the skills and knowledge to perform certain legal functions. Some procedures are so standardized that they arguably require only the administration of the law, not the practice of the law. Additionally, because of their contact with clients, paralegals frequently receive requests for action or information that may put them in an ethical dilemma. Although it may seem to be clear what is and what is not practicing law, there are more gray areas in this ethical consideration than in almost any other. To understand the concept of the unauthorized practice of law, think of paralegals as nurses and attorneys as doctors. A nurse may know how to diagnose and treat a particular ailment for a patient, but the nurse is prohibited from doing so. The nurse's job, just like the paralegal's, is to assist the licensed professional. Similarly, the paralegal may know what the particular "legal ailment" of a client is and how to "cure" the ailment; however, like the nurse, the paralegal is precluded from "treating" the client. Only doctors and attorneys are permitted to diagnose and treat ailments for clients; they are the only ones permitted to effect a "cure." If in your work you believe or feel that you are making a judgment call as to what step or procedure a client should take in a case, you are probably entering the twilight zone of practicing law. Going back to our nurse/doctor analogy, if you think you are diagnosing or analyzing a client's legal ailment, or recommending a legal cure or solution, you are probably engaging in the unauthorized practice of law.

THE CASE OF THE ADVISING ASSISTANT

Paralegal Deanna is working late, organizing her files for the next day's trial. She receives a call from the receptionist, who asks for Deanna's help in handling a prospective client who has just walked into the office. The client, Ms. Walsh, has come to the firm because she knows that the firm specializes in handicap discrimination suits; the receptionist called Deanna because both lawyers specializing in handicap discrimination are gone for the day, and Deanna is the only other member of the handicap discrimination team.

Ms. Walsh alleges that she was fired from her job because she has narcolepsy, which causes her to fall asleep on the job. Deanna asks for basic information, such as her name, address, telephone number, and the name and address of the former employer. Deanna then asks Ms. Walsh to elaborate on her former employment and on specific situations that Deanna believes could be used to establish discrimination by the former employer. After taking this information, Deanna tells her the standard procedures for a discrimination claim. Deanna goes on to explain that the state follows an employment-at-will rule, and therefore these cases are very difficult to prove. To assure Ms. Walsh that she may in fact have a cause of action under federal law, Deanna explains the legal standards set forth in the U.S. Code. Deanna then tells Ms. Walsh that she is a paralegal and cannot accept her case on behalf of the firm, but believes that the attorneys will not hesitate to accept the case.

Examine Deanna's actions and evaluate which were authorized and which were impermissible.

5.2 WHAT IS PRACTICING LAW?

Practicing law involves applying the law to the facts of a particular case. Advising a client what action to take or what action is best in a particular case is practicing law. However, telling a client when a divorce will become final, or that an answer to a complaint is due within 20 days after service, is not practicing law. Think of it this way—a lawyer makes the blueprints and the paralegal reads them. *Creating* the blueprints is the exercise of professional judgment and therefore practicing law, but *applying* the blueprints to practical use is not practicing law.

There is no single definition for the unauthorized practice of law, and the reluctance of the courts to define what constitutes unauthorized legal practice makes this an ethical grey area. There are, however, certain activities that only lawyers are authorized to perform, and a nonlawyer's performing them would constitute unauthorized practice. The four areas most commonly reserved for attorneys are:

1. Appearing in court or at a legal proceeding, including depositions, to represent a client
2. Preparing legal documents, although the paralegal may draft documents
3. Giving legal advice
4. Accepting or declining representation.

If your work involves one of these four areas and you are not an attorney, it is probably an ethical violation.

In addition to delineating unauthorized activities, courts have evolved numerous tests in an attempt to delineate criteria for determining whether an activity is unauthorized. Some of these tests ask:

Has the activity *traditionally* been performed by attorneys?
Is the activity *commonly understood* to be one performed by an attorney rather than by a legal assistant?
Does the activity involve a *personal relationship* between attorney and client?
Would the *public interest best be served* by requiring that attorneys perform the activity?

These tests are helpful, but they do not provide legal assistants with a bright line that can be easily applied in each situation. Additionally, a state may have defined *practicing law* within its own code or in its case decisions. Connecticut General Statutes § 51-88, for example, prohibits and punishes the unauthorized practice of law:

(a) A person who has not been admitted as an attorney under the provisions of section 51-80 shall not: (1) Practice law or appear as an attorney-at-law for another, in any court of record in this state, (2) make it a business to practice law, or appear as an attorney-at-law for another in any such court, (3) make it a business to solicit employment for an attorney-at-law, (4) hold himself out to the public as being entitled to practice law, (5) assume to be an attorney-at-law, (6) assume, use or advertise the title of lawyer, attorney, and counselor-at-law, attorney-at-law, counselor-at-law, attorney, counselor, attorney and counselor, or an equivalent term, in such manner as to convey the impression that he is a legal practitioner of the law, or (7) advertise that he, either alone or with others, owns, conducts or maintains a law office, or office or place of business of any kind for the practice of law.

(b)   Any person who violates any provision of this section shall be fined not more than two hundred and fifty dollars or imprisoned not more than two months or both.

(c)   Any person who violates any provision of this section shall be deemed in contempt of court, and the superior court shall have jurisdiction in equity upon the petition of any member of the bar of this state in good standing or upon its own motion to restrain such violation.

(d)   The provision of this section shall not be construed (1) as prohibiting a town clerk from preparing or drawing deeds, mortgages, releases, certificates of change of name and trade name certificates which are to be recorded or filed in the town clerk's office in the town in which the town clerk resides or (2) as prohibiting any person from practicing law or pleading at the bar of any court of this state in his own cause.

Another example of an unauthorized practice statute comes from Georgia. Georgia Code Annotated § 15-19-51 provides:

(a)   It shall be unlawful for any person other than a duly licensed attorney at law:

(1)   To practice or appear as an attorney at law for any person other than himself in any court of this state or before any judicial body;

(2)   To make it a business to practice as an attorney at law for any person other than himself in any of such courts;

(3)   To hold himself out to the public or otherwise to any person as being entitled to practice law;

(4)   To render or furnish legal services or advice;

(5)   To furnish attorneys or counsel;

(6)   To render legal services of any kind in actions or proceedings of any nature;

(7)   To assume or use or advertise the title of "lawyer", "attorney", "attorney at law," or equivalent terms in any language in such manner as to convey the impression that he is entitled to practice law or is entitled to furnish legal advice, services, or counsel; or

(8)   To advertise that either alone or together with, by, or through any person, whether a duly and regularly admitted attorney at law or not, he has, owns, conducts, or maintains an office for the practice of law or for furnishing legal advice, services or counsel.

(b)   Unless otherwise provided by law or by rules promulgated by the Supreme Court, it shall be unlawful for any corporation, voluntary association, or company to do or perform any of the acts recited in sub-section (a) of this Code section.

In *State ex rel. Norvell v. Credit Bureau,* 85 N.M. 521, 514 P.2d 40 (1973), the New Mexico Supreme Court offered the following definition, which provides a good framework for understanding the actions frequently considered to constitute the unauthorized practice of law:

> [The] indicia of the practice of law, insofar as court proceedings are concerned, include the following: (1) representation of parties before judicial or administrative bodies, (2) preparation of pleadings and other papers incident to actions and special proceedings, (3) management of such action and proceeding, and non-court related activities such as (4) giving legal advice and counsel, (5) rendering a service that requires the use of legal knowledge or skill, (6) preparing instruments and contracts by which legal rights are secured.

Because each state has developed its own rules for legal professionals, you will need to learn which standard is used in the jurisdiction in which you are working, and you will want to learn how that standard has evolved through the case law. You will thus learn how your jurisdiction has handled unauthorized practice problems and be prepared to make appropriate and ethical decisions as you face these issues in your work.

THE CASE OF THE ASSISTANT'S ALLEGEDLY AUTHORIZED ACTIVITIES

Julian and Harold Livingston are brothers who have created a professional corporation for the practice of law in Olympia, Washington, where they have lived and worked since 1977. Betty Baldwin has been their paralegal since 1982, and the three have worked closely together on many cases as well as many pro bono and community activities.

Betty, who is active in the church, meets twice a week with church officials to help them provide free estate planning information for church parishioners. Harold is aware of Betty's activities and has counseled her on specific issues when requested.

Betty is also proud of her recently completed book, "How to Get Divorced or Start a Corporation—Without a Lawyer." Julian helped her on this project and promised her 25% of the fees for any services he provides from business stimulated by the book. Betty in turn agrees to give Julian 25% of the profits from the book.

Do any of these activities constitute the unauthorized practice of law? Which of the characters, if any, has participated in the unauthorized practice of law?

5.3 WHY SHOULD LEGAL PRACTICE BE AUTHORIZED?

It is important that we now stand back and consider the reasons for making the practice of law a regulated area. One issue to consider is whether the benefits of regulating the practice of law outweigh the dangers of self-regulation, such as the creation of an economic monopoly regulated by its own. The first beneficiary of the regulation of legal practice is the public. Through self-regulation, the bar association or state court can attempt to uphold the quality of legal services, competence, and integrity of those practicing the law. Although no set of guidelines can eliminate deception or incompetence within a professional occupation, guidelines can certainly contribute to the promulgation of ethical, professional legal services. Additionally, bar associations and state courts gain the ability to discipline their members if the profession is regulated. The regulation of legal practice, with the resulting requirement that only attorneys be allowed to perform certain kinds of activities, thus acts as a quality assurance mechanism.

Naturally, there are those, like Rosemary Furman, who oppose reserving certain activities for lawyers. They assert that the rules are self-serving for attorneys; that attorneys reserve for themselves the economic rewards; that lawyers are too expensive for many people; and that the bar has not met the needs of the poor and uneducated for legal services. Challenges to the prohibition of nonlawyers from practicing law have been based on First Amendment grounds, on due process grounds, and on antitrust theories, but the prohibition has withstood challenge as a general concept because of the benefits that regulation provides. Remember, however, that several jurisdictions, most notably California and Florida, have begun to carve out exceptions to this doctrine. In California, for example, under California Code of Civil Procedure § 117.18, paralegals are considered "small claims legal advisors" and may help clients file claims and prepare for trial in small claims court. They cannot, however, represent the litigants in court. Additionally, exceptions exist in areas such as real estate or insurance law. For example, Texas Insurance Code art. 21.07-4, § 1(b)(5) and (6), authorizes insurance

"It says the statute of limitations ran two weeks ago."

adjusters to handle undisputed, uncontested claims arising out of life, health, or accident insurance policies, provided that the adjuster performs only clerical duties.

The reasons for reserving special tasks only for attorneys come from similar arguments used for reserving certain tasks, such as diagnosing illnesses, to doctors. Because both attorneys and doctors are licensed, they have met at least minimal levels of competence. Having at least this minimal level of competence is especially crucial when malpractice has such dire consequences. In the case of a doctor, a patient who is not cared for by an individual with at least minimal skills is more likely to die or suffer permanent bodily damage. In the case of lawyers, clients who are not represented by a professionally educated, trained, and licensed attorney are arguably more likely to be imprisoned or lose their assets.

The debate concerning the unauthorized practice of law doctrine will certainly continue as long as the legal profession exists. The arguments are intellectually stimulating, but it is important to remember that the provision against the unauthorized practice of law does exist, and it is important for you, as a paralegal, to understand that provision so that you can fulfill your professional responsibilities.

THE CASE OF THE WORRIED WOMAN

Melody Weston has been your best friend since childhood. She is a ravishingly beautiful woman who, for better or worse, has had an affair with, and been supported for the last four years by, the United States Senator from your state. The senator, of course, is married, and has kept his relationship with Melody a secret.

Melody needs your advice. She knows that in your career as a paralegal you have worked in both criminal law and domestic relations, and that your supervising attorney is a nationally known expert in those fields. Melody tells you that the senator's wife has finally learned about Melody's relationship with the senator, and she is planning to have Melody arrested and charged with adultery under a little-known and never-before-applied statute from 1916. Melody asks you to discuss the likelihood of her being arrested with your supervising attorney.

You immediately respond that her situation is known in the law as *desuetude,* which means that certain laws are ignored or not applied because they are out of step with the times or public attitudes. Then you tell her, "As far as the law goes, Melody, you don't have a thing to worry about. The law is not valid and it cannot be applied to you."

Is your advice correct? Is it ethical for you to have given Melody this advice? Any advice?

5.4 APPEARING PRO SE

One exception to the unauthorized practice rule concerns self-representation. In this situation, as in other gray areas of unauthorized practice, conflicting rights are at stake. The law sides in favor of the constitutional right of self-representation; therefore, the exception entitles any person to represent himself or herself in any proceeding. Representing oneself in a legal proceeding is known as *appearing pro se.* The right to appear pro se in criminal proceedings is a constitutional right and is not regarded as the unauthorized practice of law. 28 U.S.C. § 1654 is the federal statute that authorizes individuals to represent themselves in federal court proceedings; *Faretta v. California,* 422 U.S. 806 (1975), extended this right to state court proceedings as well.

The key in permitting a person to appear pro se is that the person is representing herself and not a third party. Thus, a legal secretary could go to court in a dispossession hearing and appear on her own behalf, but could not appear on behalf of her mother in a similar proceeding. The appearance of the legal secretary on behalf of her mother is clearly the unauthorized practice of law.

An exception to the general rule that a nonlawyer can always represent himself arises in the area of corporations. Corporations are artificial persons under the law and cannot logically appear pro se, because no one person is responsible for the corporation, as a person is responsible for himself. Pro se representation in the unauthorized-practice-of-law context is easy to understand if you remember that an attorney represents a third party, whereas a person appearing pro se represents only himself.

THE CASE OF THE PROFITS' PRO SE PLEADINGS

Charlotte and Charles Profit, a sister and a brother, lease a house from Melanie Blake. Because the Profits are seven months behind in the rent, Melanie Blake decides to file a dispossessory action against them. When the sheriff arrives to serve the Profits with the dispossessory papers, Charlotte accepts service on behalf of both herself and Charles because, as Charlotte tells the sheriff, "Charles is dumb as a doorknob and couldn't represent himself in court to save his life!" When the hearing is set, Charlotte arrives without Charles and tells the judge that she will argue on behalf of them both. She then presents an affidavit from Charles that grants her permission to represent him.

Should the judge grant her pro se requests?

5.5 RULES AND GUIDELINES CONCERNING UNAUTHORIZED PRACTICE

ABA Model Rules

Rules 5.3 and 5.5(b) of the ABA Model Rules both relate to the lawyer's obligation to prevent the unauthorized practice of law. Rule 5.3, referred to earlier, is the provision that makes lawyers responsible for supervising nonlawyer employees and for ensuring that the nonlawyer's conduct is compatible with the lawyer's professional obligations—one of which is the prevention of unauthorized practice.

RULE 5.3 Responsibilities Regarding Nonlawyer Assistants

With respect to a nonlawyer employed or retained by or associated with a lawyer:

(a) a partner in a law firm shall make reasonable efforts to ensure that the firm has in effect measures giving reasonable assurance that the person's conduct is compatible with the professional obligations of the lawyer;

(b) a lawyer having direct supervisory authority over the nonlawyer shall make reasonable efforts to ensure that the person's conduct is compatible with the professional obligations of the lawyer; and

(c) a lawyer shall be responsible for conduct of such a person that would be a violation of the rules of professional conduct if engaged in by a lawyer if:

(1) the lawyer orders or, with the knowledge of the specific conduct, ratifies the conduct involved ; or

(2) the lawyer is a partner in the law firm in which the person is employed, or has direct supervisory authority over the person, and knows of the conduct at a time when its consequences can be avoided or mitigated but fails to take reasonable remedial action.

The Comment following this rule requires attorneys to give nonlawyer personnel acting as assistants "appropriate instruction and supervision concerning the ethical aspects of their employment."

Rule 5.5(b), like Rule 5.3, requires lawyers to supervise and take responsibility for the work prepared by their nonlawyer employees.

RULE 5.5 Unauthorized Practice of Law

A lawyer shall not:

(a) practice law in a jurisdiction where doing so violates the regulation of the legal profession in that jurisdiction; or

(b) assist a person who is not a member of the bar in the performance of activity that constitutes the unauthorized practice of law.

This rule makes it an ethical violation for the attorney to assist a non-lawyer in performing prohibited activities. The Comments following Rule 5.5 make it clear, however, that attorneys may employ paralegals to assist them; the attorney must, however, supervise their work and take ultimate responsibility for their work. The Comments go on to suggest that this rule does not preclude a lawyer from providing professional advice and instruction to nonlawyers whose job requires a knowledge of the law, such as insurance adjusters and accountants. Further, this rule does not preclude an attorney from counseling a nonlawyer who wishes to appear pro se.

ABA Model Code

Canon 3 of the ABA Model Code provides that "[a] lawyer should assist in preventing the unauthorized practice of law."

DR 3-101 Aiding Unauthorized Practice of Law.

(A) A lawyer shall not aid a non-lawyer in the unauthorized practice of law.

(B) A lawyer shall not practice law in a jurisdiction where to do so would be in violation of regulations of the profession in that jurisdiction.

The Ethical Considerations following this Canon explain the need to prevent the unauthorized practice of law. First, because of the fiduciary relationship between attorneys and clients and the inherent complexity of the legal system, the public can best be assured of responsible and competent representation if the person who represents them is subject to the regulations placed on members of the legal profession (EC 3-1). Second, legal decisions are complex and are best made by those trained in legal processes and bound by ethical commitment (EC 3-2). Third, nonlawyers are not bound by the same ethical standards and regulations as lawyers; therefore, the public is best served and protected by those subject to discipline for unethical conduct (EC 3-3). Fourth, those who seek legal representation may not be in a position to judge whether they are receiving proper professional attention; therefore, the protection of the public demands that no one be permitted to act in the confidential and demanding role of attorney unless she is subject to the regulation of the legal profession (EC 3-4). Fifth, the practice of law is the application of the philosophy of law (exercise of professional judgment) to particular and specific legal problems, which cannot be adequately done by someone who has not received a legal education or achieved competency to practice law (EC 3-5). Sixth, attorneys may delegate tasks to nonlawyers if the attorneys maintain responsibility for the work product. This delegation helps provide more economic and efficient legal service (EC 3-6). Seventh, a lay person retains the right to represent himself (although lawyers should assist the public by explaining why it may be unwise to do so) (EC 3-7). Eighth, a lawyer should not practice law with a nonlawyer or share fees with a nonlawyer. The two exceptions to this rule are that non-lawyers may participate in a firm compensation or pension plan and the lawyer's interest in the firm may be paid to his or her heirs (EC 3-8). Ninth, what constitutes the practice of law varies from state to state; a lawyer must follow each state's rules to practice in that particular state (EC 3-9).

By understanding the reasons behind authorizing the practice of law, you can gain insight into this ethical dimension and increase your awareness about what constitutes unauthorized practice. You will also understand the policy reasons for prohibiting paralegals from doing work that they might be very capable of doing. The Code presents the more traditional view that there should be a clear separation between a lawyer's and a nonlawyer's permissible activities; the more modern Rules do not articulate this position quite as strongly.

The Disciplinary Rules under Canon 3 deal with three specific areas. DR 3-101 precludes an attorney from helping nonlawyers to practice law and from practicing law in a jurisdiction in which the lawyer is not licensed. This Disciplinary Rule is rather straightforward; however, the second provision is not as restrictive as it seems. An important exception to this provision is called *appearing pro hac vice*. Pro hac vice appearances permit an attorney to practice in a jurisdiction in which he is not licensed for one case only. The determination of whether an attorney is permitted to appear pro hac vice in a particular case depends on the civil and criminal procedure rules for various courts. In most cases, the judge assigned to the case decides whether to admit the attorney pro hac vice.

The second area treated in the Disciplinary Rules under Canon 3—the prohibition against sharing legal fees with nonlawyers—includes the two exceptions for compensation or pension plans and heirs contained in EC 3-8. Paralegals, therefore, should not expect to share contingency or referral fees, because this type of fee splitting is prohibited. Paralegals should not under any circumstances initiate any discussion of fee sharing and should refuse to be part of a situation that may violate this rule. However, many firms give paralegals bonuses at the end of the fiscal year depending on the profits of the firm. This type of bonus, or any type of normal increased compensation, such as a bonus, merit raise, salary adjustment, or cost-of-living increase is not prohibited by the Disciplinary Rules. Only when the compensation is tied to a particular case do ethical problems arise.

The third and final area covered by the Disciplinary Rules under Canon 3 is the prohibition against attorneys forming partnerships with non-lawyers for the practice of law.

DR 3-103 Forming a Partnership with a Non-Lawyer.

(A) A lawyer shall not form a partnership with a non-lawyer if any of the activities of the partnership consist of the practice of law.

This rule essentially means that nonlawyers cannot be partners in law firms and are precluded from acting as partners in law firms. The reason behind this prohibition concerns the connection between partner compensation and legal fees; if legal assistants were partners, they would essentially be splitting fees. Some change in this area, however, is appearing on the horizon. In Washington, the only state that does allow nonlawyer partners, a law firm made its accountant a partner in 1990. He is the first nonlawyer partner in a law firm, and other states are watching Washington's experiment to see if this is a desirable development. Washington, D.C., has also adopted a local bar rule that permits nonlawyers to be partners in a firm.

ABA Model Guidelines

Guideline 1 of the ABA Model Guidelines provides that an attorney is responsible for *all* the professional actions of the paralegal. Further, the guideline provides that the supervising lawyer should take reasonable measures to ensure that the paralegal's conduct is consistent with the ABA Rules. The Comments to Guideline 1 emphasize that the supervising attorney should take measures to ensure that the legal assistant is familiar with the profession's ethical obligations and that the paralegal is competent to perform the tasks assigned, based upon experience, education, or training. The responsibility of lawyers for the actions of paralegals is grounded in agency law and makes attorneys ultimately responsible for the work product of the nonlawyers they employ. Interestingly, the Comments to this guideline also elaborate on several states' provisions that require supervising attorneys to be responsible for the conduct of nonlawyers they employ. For example, Illinois Recommendation (A), Kansas Guideline III(a), New Hampshire Rule 35, Sub-Rule 9, and North Carolina Guideline 4 all adopted the language that a supervising attorney is responsible for ensuring that nonlawyers' conduct is compatible with lawyers' professional obligations.

As the Comments also point out, several states have addressed the issue of the attorney's ultimate responsibility for the work of nonlawyers such as legal assistants. Colorado, Kentucky, and Michigan Rules and Guidelines state: "The lawyer remains responsible for the actions of the legal assistant to the same extent as if such representation had been furnished entirely by the lawyer and such actions are those of the lawyer." (Colorado Guideline 1.c; Kentucky Supreme Court Rule 3.7000, Sub Rule 2.C.; Michigan Guideline 1). Connecticut and Rhode Island use even stronger language. In these two states, attorneys are liable for malpractice for the mistakes and omissions of their paralegals (Connecticut Recommendation 2; Rhode Island Guideline III). Think back to the *Goldberg* case in chapter 1; would Goldberg have received more than just a suspension if he had practiced in Connecticut or Rhode Island?

Guideline 2 provides that although a lawyer remains ultimately responsible for the work of a legal assistant, the attorney may delegate to the paralegal any task normally performed by a lawyer except those prohibited to one not licensed to practice law in the state. This guideline emphasizes that delegation of tasks to paralegals is permitted, but only if the work is supervised. The Comments to Guideline 2 define permissible delegation. For example, in South Carolina, paralegals may represent clients in certain administrative proceedings (South Carolina Guideline II). Under the Comment's analysis, proper delegation requires adequate instruction when assigning projects, monitoring projects, and reviewing projects. The Comments cite the case of *Musselman v. Willoughby Corp.,* 230 Va. 337, 337 S.E.2d 724 (1985), in which the court upheld a malpractice action against an attorney partly because of his paralegal's negligence in performing tasks that were properly delegated to her. Finally, the Comments specify that "proper" delegation also means that the delegated work loses its individual source and is "merged" into the work product of the attorney (Florida EC 3-6, 327 So. 2d at 16).

The Model Guidelines mention three specific tasks that may be performed by paralegals with attorney supervision: factual investigation and research, legal research, and preparation of legal documents. State rules delineate even more specific tasks in their guidelines, such as attending client conferences, corresponding with and obtaining information from clients, handling a witness's execution of documents, and maintaining estate or guardianship trust accounts. As the Comments warn, some tasks permitted in one jurisdiction may be impermissible in another. Will executions, real estate closings, and estate planning are three areas where jurisdictions differ as to the role of the paralegal.

It is the attorney's duty to inform clients and others of the status of her assistants. This duty is suggested by the Rules and the Code and is made explicit in Guideline 4 of the ABA Model Guidelines, the Comment to which states:

> While requiring the legal assistant to make such disclosure is one way in which the attorney's responsibility to third parties may be discharged, the Standing Committee is of the view that it is desirable to emphasize the lawyer's responsibility for the disclosure and to leave to the lawyer the discretion to decide whether the lawyer will discharge that responsibility by direct communications with the client, by requiring the legal assistant to make the disclosure, by a written memorandum, or by some other means. Although in most initial engagements by a client it may be prudent to discharge this responsibility with a writing, the Guidelines require only that the lawyer recognize the responsibility and ensure that it is discharged.

NALA

The importance of the ethical concept of the unauthorized practice of law is shown by the fact that six of the twelve canons of NALA's Code of Ethics and Professional Responsibility deal specifically with the unauthorized practice of law. Further, these are the first six canons set forth in the

Code, and they establish the parameters for unauthorized practice from the perspective of the legal assistant.

> Canon 1.   A legal assistant shall not perform any of the duties that lawyers only may perform nor do things that lawyers themselves may not do.
>
> Canon 2.   A legal assistant may perform any task delegated and supervised by a lawyer so long as the lawyer is responsible to the client, maintains a relationship with the client, and assumes full professional responsibility for the work product.
>
> Canon 3.   A legal assistant shall not engage in the practice of law by giving legal advice, appearing in court, setting fees, or accepting cases.
>
> Canon 4.   A legal assistant shall not act in matters involving professional legal judgment as the services of a lawyer are essential in the public interest whenever the exercise of such judgment is required.
>
> Canon 5.   A legal assistant must act prudently in determining the extent to which a client may be assisted without the presence of a lawyer.
>
> Canon 6.   A legal assistant shall not engage in the unauthorized practice of law and shall assist in preventing the unauthorized practice of law.

As you can see, the Canons of NALA's Code almost directly parallel the standards set forth in the ABA Model Code. However, one fundamental difference between the two is that the NALA Code, unlike the ABA Model Code, gives the paralegal, rather than the attorney, the responsibility for determining when the paralegal's actions are crossing the line into the area of unauthorized practice. The reason for this difference is clear. The ABA has no authority to regulate paralegal conduct, just as NALA has no authority to regulate attorney conduct. However, the result of this difference is that the paralegal must, like the attorney, do her part to ensure that she is not intruding over into areas of the legal process specifically reserved for licensed attorneys.

NFPA

Unlike NALA's Canons, NFPA's Affirmation of Professional Responsibility has only one provision governing the unauthorized practice of law. The wording of this provision is very broad and seems to attempt to cover all aspects of the unauthorized practice of law. The NFPA Affirmation focuses on the criminal statutes in each state forbidding the unauthorized practice of law and encourages its members not to violate these statutes. Further, the Affirmation, unlike NALA's Canons, seemingly attempt to expand those activities in which a paralegal may engage without violating unauthorized-practice-of-law statutes. Thus, the NFPA Affirmation takes a broader view of the unauthorized practice of law than do the NALA Canons.

The NFPA provision reads:

> I.   Professional Responsibility—A paralegal shall demonstrate initiative in performing and expanding the paralegal role in the delivery of

legal services within the parameters for the unauthorized practice of law statutes.

DISCUSSION—Recognizing the professional and legal responsibility to abide by the unauthorized practice of law statutes, the Federation supports and encourages new interpretations as to what constitutes the practice of law.

5.6 THE UNAUTHORIZED PRACTICE OF LAW AND THE PARALEGAL

As previously discussed in this chapter, the ethical concept of the unauthorized practice of law is especially important for paralegals, because they are the ones most likely to be confronted with such accusations. Since legal assistants have almost daily contact with clients, who sometimes know the paralegal better than their own attorney, it is very common for paralegals to have to make judgment calls about what information they can and cannot give clients. If you do commit the offense of practicing law without authorization, you subject not only yourself, but also your supervising attorney and firm, to liability; therefore, it is essential that your behavior always conform to this ethical standard.

Further complicating this murky area is the emergence of paralegals who work as independent contractors. These paralegals, rather than working as full-time employees for a law firm, work as needed on particular cases or projects. This can be very attractive for both the law firm and the paralegal. For the firm, it means that they can hire an experienced and competent paralegal without adding a full-time employee who might require training and benefits, and who may not want to leave the firm when the need for his services has been met. For the paralegal, being an independent contractor gives freedom and independence, as the paralegal is in a sense working for himself, and it also enables the paralegal to work in a variety of settings on different cases and projects.

Paralegals who work as independent contractors are frequently called *freelance paralegals;* freelancing is specifically permitted by Rule 5.3. Because a lawyer who hires a freelance paralegal has the same obligations of supervision and responsibility as she does for a paralegal who is a full-time employee of the firm, freelance paralegals do not violate any ethical standards.

It is important to distinguish freelance paralegals from independent paralegals. Independent paralegals, unlike freelance paralegals, do not work under the supervision of an attorney, but instead offer their services directly to the public. This constitutes an unauthorized practice violation unless the paralegal is being supervised by an attorney or the state has created an exception for that particular activity. Generally, nonlawyers will offer unauthorized services in areas such as divorce, bankruptcy, and real estate, areas where there are procedures that paralegals frequently know as well as (or even better than) attorneys. They are also less easily caught, because they may well be able to perform these types of services competently and more cheaply than an attorney. The surest way to get caught is to do something that causes a client to call the bar association, because the bar will move quickly to shut down an unauthorized practice. If unauthorized practice is a criminal violation in that jurisdiction as well, criminal prosecution will surely follow.

Sometimes individuals perform legal work under the guise of a secretarial service. If they are caught, they contend that their activities did not constitute the unauthorized practice of law because they were only doing "secretarial" work. This may or may not be the case in actuality; each case must be analyzed on its own merits. Additionally, each jurisdiction has rules regarding these activities; as previously mentioned, states such as Florida and California have adopted more liberal rules, which allow nonlawyers to perform more activities than in other jurisdictions.

Some people, like Rosemary Furman, engage in this gray area because they truly want to bring affordable legal services to people who can least afford them; others are not so altruistic, being motivated by power or greed. Although these differing motivations are interesting, they do not change the fact that certain activities are unethical to pursue because they represent the unauthorized practice of law as defined by that jurisdiction. However, because individuals have the right to pursue a legal occupation or business, as well as a First Amendment right to speak and print their ideas, courts have attempted to define activities that are permissible for the nonlawyer to pursue. As they have grappled with this issue, courts have allowed nonlawyers to provide information about legal issues, sell printed materials explaining legal practices and procedures, type forms for clients who wish to appear pro se, sell legal forms, and provide notary services. Courts have prohibited activities that resemble counseling rather than secretarial assistance. These prohibited activities include giving legal advice, advising clients as to available remedies, advising clients how to fill out or file forms, correcting errors or omissions on the forms, and advising how best to present evidence at a court hearing.

In most states, independent paralegals violate the unauthorized practice of law doctrine. However, the fact that some paralegals can perform certain kinds of legal work competently and less expensively than lawyers is leading some states, such as California and Florida, to consider allowing independent paralegals to perform limited activities. It will be interesting to watch jurisdictions attempt to balance the need for authorized legal practice with the reality that, in some cases, paralegals can perform legal functions competently, thus increasing public access to legal services.

When it comes to issues of unauthorized practice, no matter what your status as a legal assistant, the best practice is to refuse to say or do anything that you even suspect is improper. Also, do not fall into the common trap of believing that by saying, "Well, I am not an attorney and cannot give legal advice, but as a paralegal I would . . ." you are protected from any accusations of unauthorized practice. The following list, although not intended to be exhaustive, should help you avoid unauthorized practice allegations.

1. Never tell a potential client that the attorney will or will not accept a case. Even if you know the firm does not do a certain type of legal work, leave it up to your supervising lawyer to give the client that news.

2. Always identify yourself to everyone—in person, in writing, on your business cards, and on the telephone—as a legal assistant or paralegal.

3. Never send anything out of the office without the permission of your supervising attorney.

4. Never tell a client what strategy he or she should take with a particular legal problem.

5. Never quote a client a fee without prior authorization from your supervising attorney.

6. Most importantly, when in doubt, *say nothing.*

Related to the unauthorized practice doctrine, and of great significance for the paralegal, are the rules concerning disclosure of a legal assistant's status. Because legal assistants interact professionally with many people, it is essential that all of these people understand that the legal assistant is not a lawyer. This will prevent others from being deceived as to the paralegal's status and it will prevent the paralegal from being approached as an attorney.

Disclosure issues, and therefore unauthorized practice issues, are also implicated by business cards, letterheads, and other communications from a law office that employs legal assistants. The rules today generally follow the rules concerning advertising (which are covered in chapter 6, on advertising and solicitation), which generally allow truthful, nondeceptive communications. Therefore, it is generally permitted for legal assistants to sign documents, have business cards, and have their names appear on law firm letterheads so long as the information is truthful and will not mislead the public. In practice, most law firms provide their paralegals with business cards and memo pads that designate their status. As to letterheads, it is still unusual to see paralegals listed on the firm stationary, but if paralegals do appear, it is likely to be in small or medium-sized law firms. The letterhead from Melvin Belli's law firm, shown in figure 5-1, is an example of firm stationery listing paralegals.

THE CASE OF MRS. CARDIAC'S REQUESTS

Trevor, the newest paralegal in the personal injury law firm of Hit & Run, has been working on a wrongful death case with the attorney assigned to the case, Ann. The case involves a Cola Whiz delivery truck that ran head-on into a Mercedes driven by Dr. Cardiac. The doctor died after an extended hospital stay. Dr. Cardiac was a wealthy 36-year-old cardiologist who had recently developed a new heart valve procedure that completely revolutionized heart surgery. The Cola Whiz employee, Tom Tonic, who was driving the delivery truck, was a habitual violator who had been convicted seven times for driving under the influence and was allegedly intoxicated when the accident occurred. Cola Whiz normally obtained the driving records of all prospective truck drivers to ensure that they were good drivers.

Ann asked Trevor to set up the depositions of Tom Tonic, the director of employment for Cola Whiz, the only eyewitness, and the police officer who investigated the accident. Dr. Cardiac's wife, Mrs. Cardiac, wants to attend the depositions. Mrs. Cardiac calls the office and asks to speak to Trevor, as Ann is in court on another matter. Mrs. Cardiac asks him several questions because Ann has told her that Trevor is assisting with the case: "Isn't a paralegal just like a lawyer? Why are we taking the deposition of the police officer? Is it necessary? What happens at a deposition? What are depositions used for? Do you think that I should settle the case for $2 million? Don't you think I could get more money if we went to trial? Since your name is on the letterhead, you should be able to answer all of my questions."

How should Trevor respond to these questions?

LAW OFFICES OF
BELLI, BELLI, BROWN, MONZIONE, FABBRO & ZAKARIA
The Belli Building
722 Montgomery Street
San Francisco, CA 94133
(415) 981-1849
Telefax: (415) 989-0250
(Temporary Earthquake Address: 574 Pacific Avenue, San Francisco, CA 94133)

MELVIN M. BELLI
MELVIN CAESAR BELLI
    (also Washington, D.C. Bar)
RICHARD E. BROWN
PAUL M. MONZIONE
    (also Massachusetts Bar)
STEVEN A. FABBRO
SHAMOON ZAKARIA
    (also Pakistan and
    Michigan Bar)
KEVIN R. McCLEAN
    (also New York and
    Massachusetts Bar)
RANDALL H. SCARLETT
JACK P. DOUGHERTY
CAROL A. MOOR
CARLOS L. FOURNIER
PARALEGALS
VALERIE J. LAMBERTSON
SHARON M. COHN
JEAN BELLI, R.N.
MICHAEL STANTON
KIMBERLY J. MADGETT

BEVERLY HILLS, CA 90212
(213) 550-6777
9465 WILSHIRE BOULEVARD
SUITE 616
Telefax: (213) 550-7693
SACRAMENTO, CA 95814
(916) 448-9188
1001 SECOND STREET
Telefax: (916) 441-3874
CARMEL MONTEREY
(408) 628-1849
SAN DIEGO, CA
(619) 239-5269
ORANGE CO., CA
(714) 754-1849
STOCKTON, CA
(209) 942-1849
WASHINGTON, D.C.
(301) 881-7800
BELLI, WEIL, & GROZBEAN
11300 ROCKVILLE PIKE
ROCKVILLE, MD 20852
Telefax: (301) 984-0667

FIGURE 5-1
An example of paralegals listed on a firm's letterhead. Reprinted with permission of Melvin Belli.

The following two guest editorials present divergent points of view on the issue of the unauthorized practice of law.

RULES OF PROFESSIONAL CONDUCT AND THE PRACTICE OF LAW BY LEGAL ASSISTANTS

by Dennis A. Rendleman

Gerald Auerbach, in his 1976 book *Unequal Justice*, attributes a speech given by Teddy Roosevelt at Harvard in 1905 attacking corporate lawyers for helping clients evade new regulatory legislation as the catalyst for the development of the first ABA Canons of Professional Ethics, which were adopted in 1908. The Canons were based largely upon George Sharwood's "Essay on Professional Ethics" published in 1854 and upon the first ethical code adopted in Alabama in 1887.

The first canons were a combination of Victorian quaintness, idealistic aspirations, and prohibited behavior.

By the end of the 1950s there were nearly 50 different canons and great dissatisfaction, such that the ABA began in 1964 the process which led to the adoption of the 1969 ABA Model Code of Professional Responsibility. The Code tried to separate aspiration from "thou shalt nots" by creating three tiers—the Canons, of which there were nine general statements; the Ethical Considerations, the behavioral goal toward which all attorneys were to aspire; and the Disciplinary Rules, standards of conduct below which no attorney was to fall.

A little over a decade later, the ABA jettisoned the Code and adopted the present 1983 ABA Model Rules of Professional Conduct. The focus is more clearly now on the black letter prohibitions of misconduct—but still with some aspirational goals interspersed . . . .

At a time when de-regulation has been the political cry which leads us to chaos in the airline industry and the S&L debacles, for example, the contrary trend in the legal profession has been for increased regulation.

Viewed in the longer perspective, the regulation of the legal profession has been a benefit to consumers. In many ways the licensing of lawyers to practice law—

or put another way, the prohibition on non-attorneys from practicing law—is the original consumer protection legislation.

It started with the requirement that one be admitted to the bar before one could practice. The testing began as an oral exam at the beginning of the 1800s and is today, in Illinois, a two day essay and multi-state, multiple choice experience. Along the way, law schools developed, ultimately replacing the "reading of the law," that is, the apprenticeship system.

Mandatory Continuing Legal Education exists in approximately 30 states and is just beginning in California; legal certification and specialization is moving from *de facto* to *de jure* status.

In just the last twenty years, the legal profession has transformed attorney discipline—in Illinois under the Supreme Court's Attorney Registration and Disciplinary Commission—into a professional prosecutorial exercise.

Ironically, at the same time the legal profession has become more institutionally responsible to the consumers and the need for legal services by the consumer has increased, the ability to deliver legal services to the consumer has suffered—at least on the civil side—from court backlog, attorney expense, and a lack of an efficient system for matching attorney to client.

Which brings me to the issue of licensing legal technicians for the unsupervised practice of law encompassed in SB 776. This issue reminds one of the apocryphal story told about President Calvin Coolidge, who is perhaps best remembered for not only his practice of saying very little, but using very few words to do it. He returned from attending church alone one Sunday and his wife asked what the sermon was about. Coolidge said: "Sin."

His wife asked: "What did the pastor say about it?" Coolidge: "He's agin it."

As far as the practice of law by non-attorneys goes, I'm agin it.

While I could go through the drafting and legal problems with SB 776, I prefer to concentrate on the philosophical issues raised by the bill.

SB 776 seeks to make as public policy the state sanctioned practice of law by non-attorneys. It would create a legal subculture—a "mini-bar"—not controlled by or answerable to the courts in which it is to function.

There is no question that there are some clients who need only limited legal services which might be called "simple." There is no question that there are many non-attorney legal assistants who have the skill to perform many legal services. And there is no question that the legal system needs to provide legal services more economically to more people. None of these facts, however, add up to SB 776 as an answer.

First and foremost, it is practically unworkable. How do you define what it is that a legal technician may and may not do? SB 776 fails to draw the line or give guidance as to how the line is to be drawn.

What is a "simple" divorce or a "simple" real estate closing? Is it a divorce with no assets and no kids, or a few assets, or a few kids? We are not talking about a "ten-minute lube and oil change" where the service to be performed is the same for every customer, even if the individual cars are different. We may know a simple divorce or closing when we see it after the fact, but one can never be sure of its simplicity before it happens.

And, if the lines ever can be drawn as to what a legal technician is authorized to do, who decides whether the individual cases fit in the "simple" category or the "complex" category? Since the unspoken premise of SB 776 is that people will go to the legal technician instead of going to a lawyer, that means that the lesser qualified individual—the non-attorney legal technician—is the gatekeeper making the initial analysis of whether a specific individual's matter is "simple" and thus within the non-attorney's scope of authority. The likelihood is that, in most cases, by golly, every case will be simple—either because the non-attorney legal technician wants the case or, more seriously, because the customer doesn't want to pay for anything more, regardless of how inappropriate the "simple" process may be for the individual legal

situation. This is rather like going to the nurse for the diagnosis, but telling the nurse in advance to make sure whatever it is can be cured by aspirin.

Second, the state, by the creation of the "mini-bar," is adopting as a matter of public policy a philosophy that not everyone is entitled to the same level of services or consumer protection. In other words, the cheaper, simple cars are designed by non-engineers and are not made to the same safety standards as the more expensive, complicated cars. Were there some method of triage within the court system to legitimately separate the less complicated case from the more complicated, an argument could be made for an increased role for the legal assistant. But that is not what SB 776 is about.

Finally, why upset the present positive, expanding relationship between the lawyer and the legal assistant? While I recognize the entrepreneurial urge that is a part of the American spirit which gives everyone the desire to be their own boss, why settle for half a loaf? With the experience and skill already possessed, legal assistants can go to law school, be admitted to the bar and have the whole loaf. I have known many successful attorneys who began their careers as legal assistants.

There is a greater threat to the legal profession—both lawyer and legal assistant—than SB 776. I don't know how many of you have seen various cable television advertisements by Al what-ever-his-name-is and others purporting to provide anyone who calls and pays the information to set themselves up as independent legal technicians. Similarly, checkout lane weeklies, as well as some legitimate publications, contain grossly misleading advertisements scamming people into "living or loving" trusts to "avoid probate and legal fees."

These and other modern day medicine shows and snake-oil salesmen prey upon consumers who are afraid of the legal system and fill the vacuum that we as legal professionals have allowed to exist by failing to deliver legal services and a judicial system that is as economical and efficient as it can be. SB 776 is not the answer, but part of the answer has proven to be the development of the legal assistant who, working under the supervision of the attorney, does increase the efficiency of the lawyers.

Let me close with a traditional Arabic story: There was once a man who announced himself a prophet on arrival in a strange village. The townspeople asked, "What are the proofs of your being a prophet?" And he said, "The proof I offer is to tell you exactly what is in your minds." The townspeople said eagerly, "Tell us, then, what do you see in our minds?" And the prophet replied: "You are thinking that I am a liar and not a prophet at all."

■ Dennis A. Rendleman is General Counsel of the Illinois Bar Association. This article is reprinted with permission from the author and the Illinois Paralegal Association *Outlook,* vol. 24, (Winter 1992).

GUEST EDITORIAL

DEFINING THE UNAUTHORIZED PRACTICE OF LAW: SOME NEW WAYS OF LOOKING AT AN OLD QUESTION

by Alan Morrison

It is my thesis today that we need to reexamine the definition of what constitutes the practice of law. The traditional inquiry into what activities constitute the unauthorized practice of law is largely, if not wholly, misguided. What is needed is a whole new mode of analysis. Because we are asking the wrong questions, we are getting answers unacceptable to the way our society operates today. . . .

Now let me turn to the area of the giving of legal advice. Before I do that, let me raise another question, which arises most frequently in this part of the definition of the practice of law. Do you have to be paid for what you have done in order to be guilty of the unauthorized practice of law? While the element of compensation is present in most other areas, it is most prominent in the giving of legal advice. Compensation alone is not enough to trigger guilt, as the selling of legal forms in the five and dime store demonstrates. Of course, there is an old adage that there is no such thing as a free lunch and that is true in the giving of legal advice. Yet, if compensation is an element, it is often very hard to prove and would pose inordinate burdens in many cases. For this reason, in most jurisdictions, the fact that compensation is given or not given is legally irrelevant. It obviates problems of proof, and, I must confess, it is consistent with the notion that we are protecting the person from getting bad advice, not saving the profession from competition.

Yet I have an uneasy feeling that there is an element of overkill here. What the rules of unauthorized practice of law are primarily trying to prohibit is the charlatan who is preying upon innocent people, not the neighbor who simply wants to give you some friendly advice. The compensation problem seems to me to be further proof of the irrational rigidity of the present rules.

Returning to the question of what is legal advice, one finds that it is rather like a question of what is a legal document. It's too broad. So the question has been refined somewhat. Legal advice is advice as to the legal consequences of a course of action on which the recipient relies to determine his or her course of conduct. Now I suppose one could say that when law professors, or perhaps bar review teachers, are giving advice as to what constitutes the law, they are giving legal advice too. But no one has suggested that to be a law professor you have to be admitted to the bar of your state. Indeed, I know one esteemed law school in which there are members of the faculty who are not admitted to practice anyplace, even though they are graduate lawyers. And there are some members of the faculty who aren't even law school graduates. So, the general giving of opinions on the state of the law is not sufficient.

What has been deemed unauthorized practice has been giving particular advice about particular legal consequence. To test that approach, let's pose a problem. I am driving down the highway doing 55 mph and there is a large truck in front of me doing 54 mph. I'm riding with my wife, and she says to me, "Pass that truck." I say to her, "I can't, I am now at the legal speed limit." She says to me, "Oh yes you can. You may exceed the speed limit to pass the truck as long as you resume the speed limit once you have passed the truck and gone back into your lane." Is she practicing law? After all, she has given me particularized advice as to the legal consequences of a transaction on which I am relying to determine my conduct and for which I may go to jail or lose my driver's license if she is wrong.

Or take a comparable situation in the medical area. I go home at Thanksgiving to visit my parents and my Aunt Gertrude is there. I feel just rotten. My Aunt Gertrude says to me, "What you need to do is to go to bed and take lots of fruit juice and aspirin, and sleep it off." If my doctor would tell me exactly the same thing, does that mean my Aunt Gertrude is practicing medicine without a license? And is that any different from my wife practicing law without a license in the other case, and if so, why?

Take a look at the tax area, and I don't mean simply filling in income tax returns. I'm talking about tax advice and planning. Accountants give tax advice. Life insurance agents give tax advice. Stock brokers advise you on the tax ramifications of transactions. Your banker may tell you the tax consequences of certain transactions. Surely, the vast industry of pension advisers is giving lots of tax advice. What they are telling you is, if you do it this way you get the benefits of the law, and if you do it that way, you don't get the benefits. Are these people practicing law without a license? Well, maybe yes and maybe no.

Take the *Rosemary Furman* case, for instance. Leaving aside the question of whether Ms. Furman, in typing divorce papers, was preparing legal documents, let's just take the easier situation before she types anything where people come into her office, and say to her, "I would like a dissolution of my marriage." The first question she asks, and the first question on the form she now uses is, "How long have you been a resident of Florida?" Now, does she give a legal opinion when she decides what constitutes residence and is that the same as domicile? Is she giving legal advice when she tells someone she or he may or may not get a divorce at that time?

I suggest to you that when we're trying to ask questions about what constitutes legal advice under these circumstances, we cannot come up with any sensible answers. We tried, in Ms. Furman's case, to get the court to back off a little bit from where it had come from in the past. We made a constitutional argument which, both in the original brief, and on rehearing, the court decided by refusing to respond at all. We argued that for indigents and others who cannot afford lawyers, for a dissolution of marriage which is a state controlled monopoly, the decisions in *Boddie v. Connecticut* (saying you can't require filing fees for divorces), and *Johnson v. Avery* (the prisoner unauthorized practice case), do not permit a state to require an unaffordable lawyer instead of an affordable legal secretary. In our view the state can no more preclude Rosemary Furman and others from providing that legal assistance than it can preclude prisoners from providing writ writing assistance to their fellow inmates. We lost that case, and we are now going to take it on to the Supreme Court.

Last, let me suggest one other area where legal advice is given all the time. Ann Landers has a column. Undoubtedly you have seen it. She probably practices medicine but on this occasion she was in the legal business. She received a letter in which the writer said, "My husband and I fly around together a lot on airplanes. We don't have a will. We got to thinking the other day when we got in the middle of a bad windstorm, what would happen if the plane went down and we were both killed? Are the godparents of our child legally responsible for bringing her up? And if they aren't, what would happen?" Ann Landers replied "No, the godparents are not legally responsible. If you die intestate, the child will probably be brought up by relatives. But you ought to have a will." Is she giving legal advice? She has certainly told people what she thinks the law is. Is she practicing law without a license? And if so, in what jurisdiction? Well, the problem lies not with the answers but with the questions. What we need are new questions that relate to the reasons that we license attorneys in the first place.

Consider the electrician who comes to your home. Do we require an electrician to change a light bulb? No. Do we require an electrician to do the somewhat more complicated operation of changing a fuse? No. How about if you want to put a new fixture in your dining room? Do we require an electrician to do that? No. How about if you want to rewire your house? The answer is, in most cases, that you cannot do it yourself. The state says that's against the law. No matter how much you want to, you cannot do it, and that rule plainly overrides your free choice and your economic considerations. It overrides it because there is an implicit judgment in it, that the risks of harm, in terms of a major fire, are so great, and the likelihood of success by most lay persons is so small, that cost and free choice are simply no longer relevant.

Take my Aunt Gertrude again. [Suppose] instead of prescribing rest, chicken soup, aspirin and fruit juice, she said, "What you need is open heart surgery performed by me." We would all recoil because the likelihood of her succeeding is so small and the risk of harm to me is so great, that my free choice in that case, even if I consented before everyone in the world, is irrelevant. The state would say no, Aunt Gertrude may not perform that operation on me.

Now even these questions, of course, eliminate the important element of cost. Cost is related to, but in a way different from, questions of free choice. For instance, driving across the country, you are surely more likely to arrive safely in a 1979 Rolls Royce than you would in a 1940 Studebaker. Yet no one has suggested that everyone has to have a Rolls Royce to drive across the country. Even if lawyers are the equivalent of Rolls Royces (and I think most people think they are more equivalent to Studebakers), there are some situations in which society should let people drive Studebakers. In my view, an individual should be able to choose secretaries, real estate brokers, accountants or whatever, instead of having to use lawyers, unless there is a very good reason why free choice and added cost must be imposed for the protection of the individual.

This question of when to limit free choice and when to impose additional cost on individuals is, I think, a rather subjective question. It involves a policy orientated question that is very heavily value laden. It is not the kind of question which courts normally address by applying the law to the facts, and it surely is not a legal question in the sense of interpreting the meaning of a statute, contract or other document. It is the type of judgment which is typically made by legislatures and not by courts. Leaving aside the question of whether the legislature in a particular state has the power to change the rules defining the practice of law, I suggest to you that the judgment is much more legislative than judicial in nature. In fact, the legislatures do this kind of judging in a number of areas involving the legal profession, but it generally has been

to add to those areas which are the exclusive province of the lawyer. The problem, of course, is that the legislature cannot, or will not, look at these problems on a unified and widespread basis.

What is needed, I suggest, is a quasi legislative agency, and in fact, the courts may now be acting as such. I think this is what the Supreme Court of Florida did in the *Brumbaugh* case when it drew the lines in the area of assisting persons seeking to attain dissolution of marriage in the form of allowing written but not oral communications between clients and secretaries trying to help them.

The problem is that these issues are arising with increasing frequency and are imposing great burdens upon the courts. Judges are by and large not selected because they are representative of broad spectrums of interest, or because they are trained or otherwise qualified to make policy judgments. The courts are, moreover, not set up to issue rules that have wide ranging effects, in part because there is little public input into the process. Indeed, in the *Brumbaugh* case the Florida Bar never had an opportunity to really address the issue, because Ms. Brumbaugh was appearing *pro se* and yet, in that very narrow context, the court issued an extremely broad rule that affected virtually everybody in Florida.

As I indicated earlier, the bar plainly cannot take on this task because of its own conflicts of interest and economic self-interest in the area. What we need, I suggest, is a new body, established by the legislature, which has as its component parts three separate institutional interests. One is the interest of the bar, which has a major role to play; second, is the interest of consumers of legal services, who have a very important say in the matter; and third, is a group that I broadly refer to as competitors—title insurance companies, real estate brokers, accountants—who would be performing alternative services, if allowed, in competition with services offered by the bar. This mini-legislature would, I suggest, be able to take into account all of the relevant factors, and to issue rules which would ultimately be subject to judicial review. It would be directed to balance the competing interests under a general standard that would call for a balancing of the risk of harm and the likelihood of success on one hand, against the right of free choice and the added cost on the other. This question is ultimately a practical or policy question, not a "legal" one that the courts are readily able to handle. Moreover, what is needed is flexibility and not rigidity, a further reason for taking this function away from courts who rely so heavily on precedent.

On first thought the answers to the questions in particular cases will not be easy. They will not be automatic simply because we are asking the right questions of an appropriate constitutional body. On the other hand, we will never come up with sensible answers, until at least we start asking sensible questions.

■ Alan Morrison is the Director of the Public Citizen Litigation Group. This article was first presented at the Conference on Public Interest Practice in Florida in November 1979. This article is reprinted with permission of the author and the *Nova Law Journal.*

5.7 CASE LAW INTERPRETING THE UNAUTHORIZED PRACTICE OF LAW

The following cases will help you understand how courts have applied the unauthorized practice doctrine. The *Martin* case is a good overview of the activities which constitute the unauthorized practice of law.

THE FLORIDA BAR, Complainant
v.
Reynold MARTIN, Respondent

Supreme Court of Florida
432 So. 2d 54 (Fla. 1983)

PER CURIAM.

This disciplinary proceeding by The Florida Bar against Reynold Martin is presently before us on Petition Against Unauthorized Practice of Law and report of referee. Pursuant to article XI, Rule 11.06(9)(b) of the Integration Rule of The Florida Bar, the referee's report and record were duly filed with this Court.

The referee entered the following order on March 3, 1983:

THIS CAUSE came before the Court upon the stipulation of the parties and the court having considered said stipulation and being

otherwise fully advised in the premises, it is hereby
ORDERED AND ADJUDGED as follows:

1. The provisions of the foregoing joint motion and stipulation are approved and confirmed.
2. The following activities constitute the unauthorized practice of law and may not be carried out or conducted in Florida by the respondent, who is perpetually restrained and enjoined from:

(a) printing, or having printed on his behalf, stationery identifying respondent as "Reynold Martin, J.D.";

(b) corresponding, or causing an employee or business associate to correspond, with parties or the attorneys of parties as the representative of a client relative to legal matters;

(c) holding himself out to the community as being able to render assistance with legal problems.

3. The respondent now understands that his actions, as enumerated in the petition against the unauthorized practice of law filed herein . . . constituted the unauthorized practice of law.

4. Having considered the pleadings and evidence, we order the respondent be permanently enjoined from engaging in the acts set forth herein in paragraph 2 above and from otherwise engaging in the practice of law in the State of Florida, unless and until respondent is admitted to the membership of The Florida Bar, and licensed to practice law in the State of Florida, and that, in the event that respondent engages in any of the conduct enjoined herein, and has not been duly licensed to practice law in this state, he will be found in indirect criminal contempt of the Supreme Court of the State of Florida for the unauthorized practice of law in this state.

5. In addition, the respondent is ordered to pay the costs of this proceeding to petitioner. The amount of such costs shall be determined by this court upon the filing of a statement of costs by petitioner.

6. The joint motion and stipulation is APPROVED. The proposed order and injunction are adopted as an order of and an injunction by this court.

The referee recommends that respondent be found guilty of the unauthorized practice of law and be permanently enjoined from engaging in the practice of law in the State of Florida, unless and until respondent is admitted to the membership of The Florida Bar, and licensed to practice law in the State of Florida.

Having carefully reviewed the record and stipulation, we approve the findings and recommendations of the referee.

Costs in the amount of $119.80 are hereby taxed against respondent.

It is so ordered.

ADKINS, Acting C.J., and BOYD, OVERTON, McDONALD and EHRLICH, JJ., concur.

CASE QUESTIONS

1. Why are the letters *J.D.* after Martin's name misleading?
2. What is the effect of the court's injunction?
3. In what ways did Martin violate the unauthorized practice of law doctrine?
4. Did Martin's admission of guilt affect his punishment?

The *Alexander* case, which remains a minority view, shows how one state's appellate court supports the use of legal assistants to help in case management as long as the assistant's activities are ministerial rather than advisory.

PEOPLE of the State of Illinois, Plaintiff-Appellee
v.
Walton ALEXANDER, Defendant-Appellant

Appellate Court of Illinois
First District, Fourth Division
202 N.E.2d 841 (Ill. App. Ct. 1964)

DRUCKER, Justice.

This is an appeal from a judgment order adjudging defendant guilty of contempt of court for unauthorized practice of law. The Supreme Court transferred this case to our court and it is to be considered here as a direct contempt.

Defendant is a clerk employed by a firm of attorneys and is not licensed as a lawyer, although he is studying to be an attorney. On October 19, 1962, defendant was present in court when the case of *Ryan v. Monson* was called. Thereafter, he prepared an order spreading of record the fact that after a trial of the case of *Ryan v. Monson* the jury had disagreed and continuing the case until October 22. The trial judge added to that order "a mistrial declared."

Before entering the contempt order, the court issued a rule to show cause and a hearing was held at which only defendant testified. He was examined by his attorney, cross-examined and also interrogated by the judge. A summary of part of this testimony is incorporated into the trial judge's opinion.

In his testimony defendant stated that after the case was called on October 19, he and plaintiff's attorney in the *Ryan v. Monson* case stepped up; that the judge inquired whether they knew of the disagreement by the jury; that the court requested that an order be prepared spreading the mistrial of record; that both defendant and plaintiff's lawyer sat down at a counsel's table and defendant wrote the order which they then presented to the judge in chambers.

An order of court reciting the verdict of a jury or setting out its failure to agree on a verdict is the responsibility of the court and the court clerk is usually ordered by the court to enter an order showing the result of a jury's deliberations. . . .

The preparation of an order, in the instant case, with the collaboration of opposing counsel was a ministerial act for the benefit of the court and a mere recordation of what had transpired. We cannot hold that this conduct of defendant constituted the unauthorized practice of law.

The opinion of the trial court also states as a basis for contempt that on October 22 the judge inquired of defendant whether the case of *Ryan v. Monson* was settled and that defendant answered in the negative. It appears that on that date the court held the case for trial. Defendant testified that he advised the court that the trial attorney was actually engaged in a trial in the Federal Court. The court held that the appearance of defendant constituted the unauthorized practice of law.

Plaintiff contends that any appearance by a non-lawyer before a court for the purpose of apprising the court of an engagement of counsel or transmitting to the court information supplied by the attorney in the case regarding the availability of counsel or the status of the case is the unauthorized practice of law.

The trial judge cites *People v. Securities Discount Corporation*, 361 Ill. 551, 198 N.E. 681 (where the court held a corporation collection agency in contempt for practicing law) and *People ex rel. Chicago Bar Ass'n v. Barasch,* 406 Ill. 253, 94 N.E.2d 148 (where a disbarred lawyer was held in contempt for practicing law) as a basis for its finding. Plaintiff also cites other cases in which non-lawyers directly represented clients in court or performed legal services for clients. In the case of *People ex rel. Illinois State Bar Ass'n v. People's Stock Yards State Bank,* 344 Ill. 462, at page 476, 176 N.E. 901, at page 907, wherein a bank was prosecuted for the unauthorized practice of law, the following quotation is relied upon:

> According to the generally understood definition of the practice of law in this country, it embraces the preparation of pleadings, and other papers incident to actions and special proceedings, and the management of such action and proceedings on behalf of clients before judges and courts . . . .

Since this statement relates to the appearance and management of proceedings in court on behalf of a client, we do not believe it can be applied to a situation where a clerk hired by a law firm presents information to the court on behalf of his employer.

We agree with the trial judge that clerks should not be permitted to make motions or participate in other proceedings which can be considered as "managing" the litigation. However, if apprising the court of an employer's engagement or inability to be present constitutes the making of a motion, we must hold that clerks may make such motions for continuances without being guilty of unauthorized practice of law. Certainly with the large volume of cases appearing on the trial calls these days, it is imperative that this practice be followed.

In *Toth v. Samuel Phillipson & Co.,* 250 Ill. App. 247 (1928) the court said at page 250:

> It is well known in this county where numerous trial courts are sitting at the same time the exigencies of such a situation require that trial attorneys be represented by their clerical force to respond to some of the calls, and that the court acts upon their response the same as if the attorneys of record themselves appeared in person.

After that opinion was handed down, the number of judges was substantially increased in the former Circuit and Superior Courts and the problem of answering court calls has at least doubled. We cannot add to the heavy burden of lawyers who in addition to responding to trial calls must answer pre-trial calls and motion calls—all held in the morning—by insisting that a lawyer must personally appear to present to a court a motion for a continuance on grounds of engagement or inability to appear because of illness or other unexpected circumstances. To reduce the backlog, trial lawyers should be kept busy actually trying lawsuits and not answering court calls.

The judgment order of the Superior Court is reversed.

Reversed.

CASE QUESTIONS

1. What specific acts did the defendant perform?
2. Do you agree with the court's decision?
3. How does this court view the role of the nonlawyer assistant—expansively or restrictively?
4. In this case the clerk was studying to be a lawyer. Would it have made a difference if the clerk had been a legal assistant who was not going to law school?

In the *Pascual* case you will see how a paralegal's actions transcended the ministerial to constitute the unauthorized practice of law.

THE FLORIDA BAR, Petitioner
v.
Julio A. PASCUAL, Respondent

No. 61239
Supreme Court of Florida
Dec. 22, 1982. 424 So. 2d 757 (Fla. 1982)

PER CURIAM.

We review the findings and recommendations of the referee relating to The Florida Bar's petition against Julio A. Pascual's unauthorized practice of law.

The Florida Bar, by petition, seeks to have Pascual held in contempt and enjoined from the unauthorized practice of law. The petition alleged:

Respondent has engaged in the unauthorized practice of law in Dade County, Florida by one or more of the following acts:

1. Andres Herrada retained the services of the employer of the respondent, Leonard J. Kalish, a certified Florida attorney in the purchase of a restaurant.

Respondent, as a paralegal and President of Atlantic Title Corporation, which occupied the same suite of offices as attorney Kalish, represented Herrada in the purchase and at the closing of a restaurant from Carlos Torres without the supervision of attorney Kalish.

2. Respondent gave legal advice to Andres and Pedro Herrada in the presence of Carlos

Torres and Torres's attorney, Vello Veski, without attorney Kalish being present.

3. Respondent corresponded with attorney Vello Veski on attorney Kalish's stationary and signed "For the Firm" without disclaimer of his non-attorney status.

The referee finds, and we agree, that Pascual engaged in the unauthorized practice of law and should be permanently enjoined from engaging in the unauthorized practice of law in this state.

Accordingly, Pascual is permanently enjoined from engaging in the practice of law in this state. In the event that he engages in any of the conduct enjoined, he will be found in direct criminal contempt of this Court for the unauthorized practice of law in this state. He is also ordered to pay the costs of this proceeding.

It is so ordered.

ALDERMAN, C.J., and ADKINS, OVERTON, McDONALD and EHRLICH, JJ., concur.

BOYD, J., dissents.

CASE QUESTIONS

1. Does this punishment strike you as ineffectual? What punishment do you think is more appropriate?

2. Does the order mean that if Pascual graduates from law school and passes the bar, he cannot practice in Florida?

5.8 RECOGNIZING AND RESOLVING UNAUTHORIZED PRACTICE OF LAW PROBLEMS

Case law and ethical rules indicate that paralegals may draft legal documents, interview witnesses and take statements, assemble data, and do legal research so long as an attorney retains responsibility and directs their work. Clearly, the things a paralegal can do outnumber the things paralegals are precluded from doing under ethical standards. Therefore, it is difficult to list those tasks that are not regarded as the unauthorized practice of law, but somewhat easier to prepare guidelines of items that will be deemed the unauthorized practice of law under ethical standards. The following list is not exhaustive, but is a guideline of types of work that constitute the unauthorized practice of law and should not be engaged in by paralegals.

Activities Constituting the Practice of Law

1. Representing clients in judicial proceedings; however, in some cases, a paralegal may represent a client in administrative hearings. Check each state's and agency's rules to see if it is permitted.
2. Representing clients in depositions.
3. Giving legal advice, such as telling clients they need to file a lawsuit, incorporate, file bankruptcy, or take any particular legal action.
4. Setting fees for legal services.
5. Accepting or declining cases.

To resolve ethical dilemmas relating to whether a particular practice is authorized or not, first examine the particular activity involved. Apply the criteria and vocabulary discussed earlier to the activity in question. Naturally, it is best to ask your supervisor or an attorney if you have questions about a particular activity; remember that the supervising attorney is ultimately responsible for your work.

This ethical issue usually arises in one of two ways for paralegals. First, it arises when a paralegal's activities are prohibited as the unauthorized practice of law. Second, it arises when paralegals misrepresent their status. Once you identify which type of ethical dilemma you face, you can resolve it by applying the principles set forth in this chapter. The first way in which the question of unauthorized practice arises can be obviated if you are aware of the five areas previously listed and use these guidelines in your practice. By following these guidelines, you will most certainly be assured that your conduct does not constitute unauthorized practice. The second way in which the question of unauthorized practice arises—when paralegals misrepresent their status—can be avoided if you consistently do two things. First, whenever you are addressing a client, opposing counsel, or court personnel, be sure to identify yourself as a legal assistant. Second, every letter you sign should designate (under your signature) you as a legal assistant. These two steps will ensure that you will never misrepresent yourself and so be faced with an unauthorized practice of law allegation.

5.9 THE PARALEGAL, THE LAWYER, AND THE UNAUTHORIZED PRACTICE OF LAW: A SUMMARY

Unlike most ethical standards, the unauthorized practice of law directly affects and should be a concern for every paralegal. Not only are these standards set forth in NALA's Code and NFPA's Affirmation, but criminal statutes also forbid the unauthorized practice of law. Under the ABA standards, an attorney is ultimately responsible for a paralegal who engages in the unauthorized practice of law, but the paralegal must conform to these standards because of the possibility of criminal sanctions. Paralegals are an asset to the legal community and are becoming vital to the legal process; however, paralegals must remember that their role is distinct from that of the attorney. Just as nurses are indispensable to the medical community, paralegals are necessary for the legal process to become more efficient and economical. This role will erode if paralegals start trying to turn themselves into lawyers. Medicine could not exist without both doctors and nurses, just as the legal process could not exist without both lawyers and paralegals. The role of each is similar but distinct, and ignoring the difference between lawyers and paralegals is known as the unauthorized practice of law.

REVIEW QUESTIONS

1. What major arguments support authorizing the practice of law?
2. Do unauthorized practice of law statutes inhibit the growth of the paralegal profession?
3. What are independent paralegals and freelance paralegals?
4. How is disclosure of status related to the unauthorized practice of law?

QUESTIONS FOR THOUGHT AND DISCUSSION

1. Your brother, who has been arrested for drunk driving, asks you, a paralegal knowledgeable about drunk-driving litigation, to represent him in traffic court. Can you do this?
2. Your supervising attorney asks you, a paralegal, to interview new clients, find out their problems, and explain the process of commencing legal action. Is this permissible?
3. Can a paralegal write his own will?
4. Upon meeting new clients, you, a legal assistant who will probably be working on the case, say, "Hi, I'm Gail Fletcher. I am looking forward to working with you." Any problems?
5. Your supervising attorney asks you to present an order to the judge on the case. You go to the courthouse and the judge asks you substantive questions about the case. What should you do?

6. Attorney Khahn Nguyen is in the process of litigating a huge tax fraud case that has received a great deal of publicity. You are a freelance paralegal working on this case for attorney Nguyen. At a meeting this morning, you were introduced to Mike McCall who, you were told, is an attorney who will be working on this case as well.

   As soon as you met McCall, you recognized him, but you could not put your finger on where you knew him from. Later in the morning it hit you: you had read about him in the Fulton County *Daily Report* because he had been suspended from the practice of law for three years. What should you do?

LAW, LITERATURE, AND ETHICS

From **Death of a Salesman**
By Arthur Miller

BIFF: Where'd you go this time, Dad? Gee, we were lonesome for you.

WILLY: *(pleased, puts an arm around each boy and they come down to the apron):* Lonesome, heh?

BIFF: Missed you every minute.

WILLY: Don't say? Tell you a secret, boys. Don't breathe it to a soul. Someday I'll have my own business, and I'll never have to leave home any more.

HAPPY: Like Uncle Charley, heh?

WILLY: Bigger than Uncle Charley! Because Charley is not liked. He's liked, but he's not well-liked.

BIFF: Where'd you go this time, Dad?

WILLY: Well, I got on the road, and I went north to Providence. Met the Mayor.

BIFF: The Mayor of Providence!

WILLY: He was sitting in the hotel lobby.

BIFF: What'd he say?

WILLY: He said, "Morning!" And I said, "You got a fine city here, Mayor." And then he had coffee with me. And then I went to Waterbury. Waterbury is a fine city. Big clock city, the famous Waterbury clock. Sold a nice bill there. And then Boston—Boston is the cradle of the Revolution. A fine city. And a couple of other towns in Mass., and on to Portland and Bangor and straight home!

BIFF: Gee, I'd love to go with you sometime, Dad.

WILLY: Soon as summer comes.

HAPPY: Promise?

WILLY: You and Hap and I, and I'll show you all the towns. America is full of beautiful towns and fine, upstanding people. And they know me, boys, they know me up and down New England. And when I bring you fellas up, there'll be open sesame for all

of us, 'cause one thing, boys: I have friends. I can park my car in any street in New England, and the cops protect it like their own. This summer, heh?

BIFF and HAPPY *(together):*   Yeah! You bet!

WILLY: We'll take our bathing suits.

HAPPY: We'll carry your bags, Pop!

WILLY: Oh, won't that be something! Me comin' into the Boston stores with you boys carryin' my bags. What a sensation!

(Biff is prancing around, practicing passing the ball.)

WILLY: You nervous, Biff, about the game?

BIFF: Not if you're gonna be there.

WILLY: What do they say about you in school, now that they made you captain?

HAPPY: There's a crowd of girls behind him everytime the classes change.

BIFF *(taking Willy's hand):*   This Saturday, Pop, this Saturday—just for you, I'm going to break through for a touchdown.

HAPPY: You're supposed to pass.

BIFF: I'm takin' one play for Pop. You watch me, Pop, and when I take off my helmet, that means I'm breakin' out. Then you watch me crash through that line!

WILLY *(kisses Biff):*   Oh, wait'll I tell this in Boston!

(Bernard enters in knickers. He is younger than Biff, earnest and loyal, a worried boy.)

BERNARD: Biff, where are you? You are supposed to study with me today.

WILLY: Hey, looka Bernard. What're you lookin' so anemic about, Bernard?

BERNARD: He's gotta study, Uncle Willy. He's got Regents next week.

HAPPY *(tauntingly, spinning Bernard around):* Let's box, Bernard!

BERNARD: Biff! *(He gets away from Happy.)* Listen, Biff, I heard Mr. Birnbaum say that if you don't start studyin' math he's gonna flunk you, and you won't graduate. I heard him!

WILLY: You better study with him, Biff. Go ahead now.

BERNARD: I heard him!

BIFF: Oh, Pop, you didn't see my sneakers! *(He holds up a foot for Willy to look at.)*

WILLY: Hey, that's a beautiful job of printing!

BERNARD *(wiping his glasses):* Just because he printed University of Virginia on his sneakers doesn't mean they've got to graduate him, Uncle Willy!

WILLY *(angrily):* What're you talking about? With scholarships to three universities, they're gonna flunk him?

BERNARD: But I heard Mr. Birnbaum say—

WILLY: Don't be a pest, Bernard! *(To his boys):* What an anemic!

BERNARD: Okay, I'm waiting for you in my house, Biff.

(Bernard goes off. The Lomans laugh.)

WILLY: Bernard is not well-liked, is he?

BIFF: He's liked, but he's not well-liked.

HAPPY: That's right, Pop.

WILLY: That's just what I mean. Bernard can get the best marks in school, y'understand, but when he gets out in the business world, y'understand, you are going to be five times ahead of him. That's why I thank Almighty God you're both built like Adonises. Because the man who makes an appearance in the business world, the man who creates personal interest, is the man who gets ahead. Be liked and you will never want. Take me, for instance. I never have to wait in line to see a buyer. "Willy Loman is here!" That's all they have to know, and I go right through.

■ From *DEATH OF A SALESMAN* by Arthur Miller. Copyright 1949, renewed © 1977 by Arthur Miller. Used by permission of Viking Penguin, a division of Penguin Books USA Inc.

CHAPTER 6
Advertising and Solicitation

CHAPTER OVERVIEW

In this chapter, you will learn about the ethical issues that may arise from marketing legal services. Although the legal profession is permitted to advertise, certain ethical considerations affect advertising for the legal profession. Further, ethical considerations strictly limit activities that are regarded not as advertising but as solicitation; therefore, this chapter will help you to distinguish between these two

187

forms of marketing legal services. You will also consider how the issues of advertising and solicitation affect the work of the legal assistant.

THE CASE OF THE PUBLIC RELATIONS PARALEGAL

Jan, a former account manager for a New York public relations firm, grew tired of the stress and competitive environment of public relations. After having her second child, Jan decided she would return to school and obtain her degree in paralegal studies, which she had read was a recession-proof career. Jan graduated with honors and was soon employed with a general practice firm.

Even though the career of a legal assistant was supposedly recession-proof, Jan discovered that this was not necessarily the case when one worked with a small general practice. The firm had thousands of dollars of outstanding receivables but had a cash-flow problem. Being the go-getter that she was, Jan approached her boss, Tom Butler, and asked if she could use her public relations skills to try to drum up some more business. Tom readily consented; he was impressed by Jan's initiative.

Jan worked overtime developing an advertising campaign that would ensure that Butler & Associates was the premier small firm in New York. Her campaign inundated the populace of New York with information and freebies; if members of the public had a legal problem, or even contemplated a legal course of action, they would certainly have the name of Butler & Associates on the tip of the tongue. All new clients were given a free do-it-yourself will guaranteed to be enforceable in all 50 states. Although the clients would be given the form and instructions on how to fill it out, they would not be given personalized estate planning from an attorney—that was extra. Further, all available billboards in New York and New Jersey were covered with a picture of all the employees of Butler & Associates and the following message: "We guarantee to get you the biggest award or the best settlement for the lowest price or double your money back! No competitor beats our prices—Call Butler & Associates 555-1212. We specialize in EVERYTHING!"

Needless to say, Jan's campaign has alleviated the cash-flow problems at Butler & Associates, but will the firm, and Jan, be guilty of ethical violations stemming from her advertising campaign?

THE CASE OF THE PARALEGAL WITH A HUNDRED CONNECTIONS

Jerry's mother is an influential state senator. Through his mother, Jerry knows everybody, as well as everybody's brother and sister. Whenever he is at a political gathering or social event, Jerry hands out his business card. The card has the firm's name, address, telephone number, fax number, and

Jerry's name on it, but does not designate Jerry as a paralegal. Jerry then urges people to contact him should they ever need any legal assistance. On Derby Day, Jerry meets Troy O'Malley who, unbeknownst to Jerry, is the director of the state bar. Jerry gives O'Malley a business card and urges him to call. Will the director be calling Jerry?

6.1 ADVERTISING AND SOLICITATION: AN INTRODUCTION

The issues of advertising and soliciting for legal services have changed significantly over the past decades. Originally, lawyers were permitted to advertise. However, from the late 1940s until the 1970s, the bar advocated a virtual prohibition against advertising. During this 30-year period, advertising was limited primarily to lawyer referral lists sanctioned by the various bar associations. These referral lists were considered appropriate not only because they were "advertising" from the official organ of the bar, but also because there was no possibility of improper solicitation, as those individuals requiring legal assistance contacted a third party (the bar) for referrals. Even though most lawyers on the lists had to pay some sort of fee to be recommended by the bar, the theory was that this type of advertising, like physician referrals, was dignified.

Television, newspaper, and billboard ads were nonexistent. The rationale behind this ban was that advertising would detract from an attorney's image as a professional, lower the quality of legal services, and humiliate the legal profession. (You can judge from your own reactions to lawyer advertisements on television whether the bar's view was accurate.) This earlier era saw the lawyer as a gentleman and a respected member of the community, who achieved success and gained clients through his reputation.

In the 1970s, several decisions from the United States Supreme Court reopened the door to lawyers' advertising and established the ethical parameters for modern lawyer advertising. These decisions, as well as antitrust lawsuits, pressure from consumer groups, and the evolution of the legal profession itself, encouraged attorneys to advertise. The "lawyer as gentleman" paradigm began to give way, not only because of the increased presence of women in the legal profession, but also because of the changed perception of the legal profession. Practicing law came to be seen as just another business, rather than as the elite occupation of a group offering their expertise to those who could afford to pay. The economics of practicing law when there is economic competition for legal services also served as an impetus to the profession's acceptance of advertising.

Advertising and solicitation are ethical issues for attorneys because of the perception that advertising is unprofessional and makes practicing law seem too commercial; advertising also invites deception and overreaching. Advertising, according to the rationale of the traditional bar, diminishes a lawyer's reputation in the community. Thus, advertising became analogous to undignified conduct. This rationale springs from the history of attorneys as members of a very elite club—the bar.

6.2 CASES DEFINING ETHICS IN ADVERTISING

A series of cases decided by the Supreme Court challenged the older views and provides a natural starting point for an understanding of ethics in lawyer advertising. Remember that prior to these cases, advertising by lawyers was basically not allowed. In *Bates v. State Bar,* 433 U.S. 350, 97 S. Ct. 2691, 53 L. Ed. 2d 810 (1977), two attorneys in Arizona were prosecuted for listing the types of legal services they provided and for stating that these services were offered at "reasonable rates." The Supreme Court held that the First Amendment protects truthful newspaper advertising as to the availability of and fees for legal services. However, the Court also held that the states' regulation of advertising by attorneys did not violate the antitrust provisions of the Sherman Anti-Trust Act. Thus, as a result of the *Bates* decision, states were permitted to subject such advertising to time, place, and manner restrictions, and also to prohibit false or misleading advertising. In response to the *Bates* decision, the ABA redrafted its rules and attempted to specify the information that an attorney could ethically list in advertising. These revised rules are discussed in depth in § 6.5.

Following *Bates,* the Court heard the case of *In re R.M.J.,* 455 U.S. 191, 102 S. Ct. 929, 71 L. Ed. 2d 64 (1982). This case involved an attorney

"Honey, can I add 'for a great lawyer ... Call him at 555-1212' to our 'Just Married' sign?"

in Missouri who advertised that he specialized in real estate and contracts and was a member of the bar of the Supreme Court of the United States. In Missouri, attorneys were permitted to advertise their specialties; however, RMJ did not list his specialty in conformance with the specialties recognized by the bar. For example, he listed "real estate" as a specialty when the bar recognized "property." He listed "contracts" when the bar did not recognize such a specialty. The Supreme Court held that, because Missouri could not show that the lawyer's advertisement was deceptive or misleading, or that the state's restrictions promoted any substantial interests, the limitations were unconstitutional. In its opinion, the Court concluded:

> Thus, the Court has made clear in *Bates* and subsequent cases that regulation and imposition of discipline are permissible where the particular advertising is inherently likely to deceive or where the record indicates that a particular form or method of advertising has in fact been deceptive. . . . Misleading advertising may be prohibited entirely. But the states may not place an absolute prohibition on certain types of potentially misleading information, e.g., a listing of areas of practice, if the information also may be presented in a way that is not deceptive. Thus, the Court in *Bates* suggested that the remedy in the first instance is not necessarily a prohibition but preferably a requirement of disclaimer or explanation. . . . Restrictions upon such advertising [of professional services] may be no broader than necessary to prevent the deception.
>
> Even when a communication is not misleading the state retains some authority to regulate. But the state must assert a substantial interest and the interference with speech must be in proportion to the interest served . . . Restrictions must be narrowly drawn, and the state lawfully may regulate only to the extent regulation furthers the state's substantial interest.

455 U.S. at 202–03.

The Court's approach to lawyer advertising in these cases reflects its general approach to the First Amendment and commercial speech doctrines thereunder. Although commercial speech can be regulated and limited, the thrust of the First Amendment is preservation of the right to free speech. When it comes to commercial, as opposed to private, speech, less protection is afforded, but it is nonetheless protected.

We can see the application of this approach in the Court's handling of the *Zauderer* case. *Zauderer v. Office of Disciplinary Counsel,* 471 U.S. 626, 105 S. Ct. 2265, 85 L. Ed. 2d 652 (1985). In that case, Philip Zauderer, an attorney practicing in Columbus, Ohio, was disciplined for two of his actions involving advertising. First, he advertised that he would represent clients in drunk-driving cases and would refund all their legal fees if they were convicted. What he failed to mention was that he could plea-bargain the charges down to a lesser offense in most cases and still collect his fee. After being contacted by the disciplinary branch of the Ohio Supreme Court, he withdrew the ad and agreed not to represent anyone who responded to the ad. Second, he solicited, via newspaper ads, clients who might have claims against the manufacturer of the Dalkon Shield. (The Dalkon Shield was an intrauterine birth-control device that was found to cause severe injuries to the women who used it.) In his ad, Zauderer also did a very "unlawyerly" thing: his ad showed a picture of the device. He also claimed in that ad that the client would pay no fees; the truth was that they would pay no attorney fees (because Zauderer worked on a contingency basis) but they would have to pay court costs and other expenses. The Court upheld Zauderer's sanction on the deceptive claim as to expenses, but reversed discipline stemming from use of the picture, applying the commercial speech doctrine of the First Amendment:

> Because the illustration for which appellant was disciplined is an accurate representation of the Dalkon Shield and has no features that are likely to deceive, mislead or confuse the reader, the burden is on the State to present a substantial governmental interest justifying the restriction as applied to appellant and to demonstrate that the restriction vindicates that interest through the least restrictive means.

471 U.S. 626 at 647.

In *Zauderer*, Justice White also addressed those who want to ensure that legal advertisements possess the correct amount of "dignity." In so doing, he brought legal advertising into line with other forms of commercial advertising:

> Although the state undoubtedly has a substantial interest in ensuring that attorneys behave with dignity and decorum in the courtroom, we are unsure that the State's desire that attorneys maintain their dignity in their communications with the public is an interest substantial enough to justify the abridgement of their First Amendment rights . . . . The mere possibility that some members of the population might find advertising embarrassing or offensive cannot justify suppressing it. The same might hold true for advertising that some members of the bar find beneath their dignity.

Id. at 647-48. As you can see, the Court has come a long way from the earlier restrictions on advertising, and is now willing to consider legal advertising as commercial speech. This trend continued when the Court decided *Shapero v. Kentucky Bar Association,* 486 U.S. 466, 108 S. Ct. 1916, 100 L. Ed. 2d 475 (1988). In that case, the attorney sent direct-mail advertisements to persons who were known to have a specific legal problem: the impending foreclosure of their homes. The following is excerpted from the letter which the Court quoted in its opinion:

> It has come to my attention that your home is being foreclosed on. If this is true, you may be about to lose your home. Federal law may allow you to keep your home by ORDERING your creditor [sic] to STOP and give you more time to pay them.
>
> You may call my office anytime from 8:30 a.m. to 5:00 p.m. for FREE information on how you can keep your home.

> Call NOW, don't wait. It may surprise you what I may be able to do for you. Just call and tell me that you got this letter. Remember it is FREE, there is NO charge for calling.

108 S. Ct. at 1916.

The lower court did not find Shapero's advertising false or misleading, but sanctioned him because of the complete prohibition in Kentucky against direct-mail advertising. In 1988, more than half the states, including Kentucky, banned direct-mail, targeted advertising, but the Supreme Court held that this is just another form of commercial advertising and that a ban was an unnecessarily and impermissibly broad restriction. In its opinion, the Court held that "the State may not constitutionally ban a particular letter on the theory that to mail it only to those whom it would interest is somehow inherently objectionable." *Id.* at 473-74. Although the state and others argued that this type of advertising was analogous to solicitation, the Court held that the form of communication makes all the difference, and the fact that the advertising was written rather than a face-to-face conversation took it out of the definition of impermissible solicitation.

Although these cases led to the acceptance of legal advertising, legal advertising is still subject to restraints. Since the Supreme Court classified advertising for attorneys as commercial speech, it is subject to more restraint than other types of speech protected by the Bill of Rights. Charles W. Wofram, in his book *Modern Legal Ethics* (West 1986), defines the Supreme Court's interpretation of the states' regulatory power over attorney advertising as follows:

> 1. The state must demonstrate that the advertising is in conflict with a state interest;
>
> 2. If this interest is substantial, such as preventing fraudulent advertising, then the regulation is per se necessary without any further showing;
>
> 3. If the interest is arguable, such as preventing consumers from being misled as to the definition of simple will, then the state must show that the advertising violates a specific rule, violates a substantial state interest, and that the regulation is no broader than necessary to carry out the state's interest.

Id. at 781.

The Supreme Court delineated the constitutional parameters for lawyer advertising, and both the Code of Professional Responsibility and the Rules of Professional Conduct have attempted to specify the types of advertising permissible for attorneys. The following are types of information permissible for an attorney to advertise:

- Specialization
- States where licensed
- Fees
- Firm names, as long as trade names are not used
- Addresses, telephone numbers, telefacsimile numbers, etc.
- Office hours

However, these may be modified depending on the jurisdiction. For example, some jurisdictions prohibit all broadcast media advertising, such as commercials on television and radio. Naturally, your conduct in marketing will be regulated by the jurisdiction in which you are employed, so you will need to learn your state's regulations to comply with its requirements and restrictions.

Letterheads and business cards also fall into the area of lawyer advertising. Until recently, attorneys were severely restricted concerning the information they could include, but the case of *Peel v. Attorney Registration & Disciplinary Commission,* 110 S. Ct. 2281 (1990) limited the ability of states to regulate the information on letterheads or other similar documents. In that case, attorney Gary Peel truthfully designated himself a "Certified Civil Trial Specialist By the National Board of Trial Advocacy." The use of the words "certified" and "specialist" was prohibited under the Illinois Code of Professional Responsibility, so Peel received a public censure. The Supreme Court reversed the censure, however, finding that Peel's First Amendment rights substantially outweighed the possibility of deception that might arise from disclosure of that information. Because of this case, state restrictions on truthful information on letterheads must survive constitutional scrutiny if they are to be upheld, and many existing restrictions may be unconstitutional based on *Peel.*

6.3 SOLICITATION

A specific activity related to advertising that must be understood by those practicing in the legal profession is solicitation. *Solicitation* occurs when a lawyer actively seeks out prospective clients. Unlike advertising, solicitation is either absolutely prohibited or, at the least, severely regulated. Although some states permit closely regulated solicitation, historically it has been absolutely prohibited.

There are two types of solicitation. The simplest form of solicitation occurs when an attorney directly confronts a potential client face-to-face; this creates the possibility of fraud, undue influence, intimidation, or overreaching. Solicitation also occurs when a lawyer attempts to obtain a client referral from a third party. Both situations arguably inhibit the free choice of clients in retaining counsel. These concerns do not come into play in media advertising, for there the consumer has a freedom of choice and action that may not be preserved in an in-person solicitation. When a live interaction takes place, psychological factors may make the potential client feel pressured and unable to make an independent choice. It is these pitfalls that the rules against solicitation attempt to avoid.

Recall the *Shapero* case discussed in § 6.2, in which one of the prosecution's (unsuccessful) arguments was that the attorney's direct-mail advertising rose to the level of solicitation and was thus prohibited. Do you agree with the Supreme Court's decision in this case? Are individuals in dire circumstances, such as those facing foreclosure or criminal charges, pressured by a letter such as the one Shapero sent his potential clients? You will be forced to make these same types of decisions as a practicing paralegal.

Imagine, for example, that an attorney allies himself with an ambulance driver or a nurse in an emergency room, by paying the nurse or driver to refer those with potential legal claims to the paying attorney. This arrangement clearly constitutes the second type of prohibited solicitation, even though the ambulance driver and nurse have their own free-speech interests, because it presents all the dangers that characterize solicitation.

In Nevada, an attorney paid taxi drivers to bring prospective divorce clients directly to his office from the airport. *State Bar v. Raffetto,* 64 Nev. 390, 183 P.2d 621 (1947). This, naturally, was a clearly prohibited form of solicitation.

In Connecticut, statutory law makes it a crime for anyone to solicit clients for an attorney. The statute says:

> (a)   Any person who (1) pays, remunerates or rewards any other person with something of value to solicit or obtain a cause of action or client for an attorney-at-law or (2) employs an agent, runner or other person to solicit or obtain a cause of action or a client for an attorney-at-law or (3) pays, remunerates or rewards any other person with something of value for soliciting or bringing a cause of action or a client to any attorney-at-law or (4) pays, remunerates or rewards with something of value a police officer, court officer, correctional institution officer or employee, a physician, any hospital attaché or employee, an automobile repairman, tower or wrecker, funeral director or any other person who induces any person to seek the services of any attorney or (5) pays, remunerates or rewards any other person with something of value to induce him to bring a cause of action to, or to come to, an attorney or to seek his professional services shall be fined not more than one thousand dollars or imprisoned not more than three years or both. This subsection shall not apply to an attorney's engaging other or additional attorneys for professional assistance or to an attorney's referring a case to another attorney.
>
>   (b)   Any person who knowingly receives or accepts any payment, remuneration or reward of value for referring or bringing a cause of action or prospective client to an attorney-at-law, or for inducing or influencing any other person to seek the professional advice or services of an attorney, shall be fined not more than one thousand dollars or imprisoned not more than three years or both. This subsection shall not apply to the referral by an attorney-at-law of causes of action or clients or other persons to another attorney-at-law.

Conn. Gen. Stat. § 51-87.

Although the majority of states absolutely prohibit solicitation, some jurisdictions, such as Illinois and Washington D.C., regulate rather than prohibit it. The more restrictive view toward solicitation comes from the perception that advertising is information, but solicitation is coercion. The bar has always believed that recommending oneself for employment not only was unprofessional and demeaning to the bar, but also applied undue pressure on an individual to select the person recommending himself as the attorney.

"Call us anytime."

Several Supreme Court cases held that advertising and solicitation do not merit equal constitutional protection. In *Ohralik v. Ohio State Bar Association,* 436 U.S. 447, 98 S. Ct. 1912, 56 L. Ed. 2d 444 (1978), the Supreme Court held that a state may discipline an attorney who solicits business in person when such a situation is likely to create undue pressure on the prospective client. In that case, the Court upheld a blanket prohibition of in-person solicitation—just the kind of pervasive prohibition that was disallowed when it came to advertising. Ohralik met with an accident victim in the hospital. It is easy to understand why, in this situation, the Court found that in-person meetings between an attorney and a prospective client could result in undue pressure being exerted on the client. Also, the lawyer was motivated by financial gain.

In another case that same year, an American Civil Liberties Union (ACLU) lawyer was reprimanded by the state for offering free legal services to a woman allegedly deprived of her civil rights. *In re Primus,* 436 U.S. 412, 98 S. Ct. 1893, 56 L. Ed. 2d 417 (1978). The *Primus* decision held that certain types of solicitation are entitled to the free speech and association protections of the First Amendment. Because the type of solicitation that occurred in *Primus* was not motivated by individual financial gain, but rather by political belief and the desire to provide free legal services to those who might not otherwise get those services, it was permitted.

The types of solicitation protected by the First Amendment are those in which coercion is unlikely to exist. For example, a lawyer may accept employment from a close friend or relative because the attorney gave this person unsolicited legal advice. Other examples are solicitation of a former client, work arising from a lawyer's participation in educational activities sponsored by qualified legal organizations, and employment resulting from an attorney's educational endeavors (such as a writing or speaking engagement), but only if the attorney does not use this forum to brag about his or her legal qualifications. Other exceptions to the ban against solicitation:

1. A lawyer may recommend that she be employed by a friend, relative or former client.

2. An attorney may solicit legal business from other lawyers.

3. A lawyer may solicit when employed by a qualified legal organization such as the ACLU.

4. An attorney may solicit a person who has been designated as a member of a certified class action, such as in the advertising in the *Zauderer* case, which asked prospective clients to contact attorneys during the Dalkon Shield litigation.

Although these actions may technically be solicitation, they are still permitted because, unlike typical solicitation situations, there is no potential to invade a person's privacy, overreach, or exert undue influence.

These permissible types of solicitation do protect prospective clients. Either a third party is protecting the potential client from the solicitation of the attorney, so that the client can make an informed choice, or the lawyer has had a previous relationship with the person, so that the relationship in itself protects against coercion.

THE CASE OF THE PART-TIME LAWYER

Greg and Michelle met when he was a law clerk for the summer at the law firm of Kadish & Scott; Michelle was a paralegal in the estate planning department. They married after Greg graduated from law school, and they decided to move to the North Georgia mountains to enjoy the peace and tranquillity of the country.

Because they lived in a small town, there was not enough legal business for full-time work, so Greg got a position as an officer at the town bank and Michelle became a loan advisor at the bank. They arranged to use the bank offices after closing to operate a law firm. There is no evidence that they directly solicited law clients in their capacity as bank employees, but some of their law clients were customers of the bank.

Does their arrangement constitute unethical advertising or solicitation?

6.4 PROVIDING LEGAL SERVICES

There is also interest in solicitation as a means of providing legal services when individuals, because of culture or situation, are too unfamiliar with the legal process to use it effectively. In Bhopal, India, when a catastrophic accident occurred at the Dow Chemical plant in the mid-1980s, American attorneys were quick to find plaintiffs. As Deborah Rhode reported in "Solicitation," 36 *Journal of Legal Education* 317 (1986):

> Working through local counsel and free of the brooding presence of bar disciplinary committees, United States lawyers completed retainer agreements with few of the customary preliminaries. One of the more industrious lawyers signed over 7,000 individual claimants in less than a week; according to reporters' calculations, that totaled about one victim per 60 seconds. . . .
>
> By all accounts, the circumstances under which such professional relationships were consummated scarcely made for informed dialogue. Most retainer contracts were printed on English forms, and observers recounted that relatively little effort was made to ensure that clients understood the nature of their agreements or that lawyers understood the nature of their clients' injuries. Some local counsel were offering between 50 and 1,000 rupees (roughly 4 to 85 American dollars) per signature, and under such inducements, some victims lost count of the number of agreements they signed. Many were unaware that they were granting multiple powers of attorney or that they were relinquishing one-third of their potential recoveries.

Although solicitation surely invites misrepresentation and overreaching, especially in a situation where the claimants do not speak English, it is also important to note that in some cases solicitation offers legal services to those who might otherwise go unrepresented. A number of commentators, including Professor Rhode, believe that the general prohibition against in-person contact should give way to a more flexible, case-by-case approach; in this way, regulators could focus on those attorneys who are coercive or harassing, or whose greed causes them to underrepresent clients because of the size of their caseloads. It is certainly true that some solicitation leads to attorneys exploiting clients, but it is also true that innocent people can be exploited by a system that does not offer them representation. Because of this ethical complexity, the legal profession will continue to grapple with the issues arising from the processes by which lawyers get clients.

6.5 RULES AND GUIDELINES CONCERNING ADVERTISING AND SOLICITATION

ABA Model Rules

As the newer of the two sets of ethical rules promulgated by the ABA, the Model Rules are not as restrictive as the Code in the area of lawyer advertising. The Rules take a more positive view of advertising and do not restrict it as much as the Code does. This less restrictive, more general approach seems to be the standard evolving in relation to advertising by attorneys.

Rules 7.1 and 7.2 provide the principles of the rules on lawyer advertising. Rule 7.1 concerns all communications from a lawyer, including advertising, and prohibits the communication of false or misleading information.

INFORMATION ABOUT LEGAL SERVICES
RULE 7.1   Communications Concerning a Lawyer's Services

A lawyer shall not make a false or misleading communication about the lawyer or the lawyer's services. A communication is false or misleading if it:

(a)   contains a material misrepresentation of fact or law, or omits a fact necessary to make the statement considered as a whole not materially misleading;

(b)   is likely to create an unjustified expectation about results the lawyer can achieve, or states or implies that the lawyer can achieve results by means that violate the rules of professional conduct or other law; or

(c)   compares the lawyer's services with other lawyers' services, unless the comparison can be factually substantiated.

Rule 7.1 suggests (but does not mandate) that testimonials by clients are improper; although many states still prohibit testimonials because they can be misleading or self-serving, some states, such as California, New York, and Pennsylvania, permit testimonials that meet certain guidelines. Additionally, Rule 7.1 contains no requirement that ads be "dignified," as was required by the Code. This follows Justice White's reasoning in *Zauderer.*

Rule 7.2 permits advertising in media such as telephone books, telephone directories, or legal directories.

RULE 7.2   Advertising

(a)   Subject to the requirements of Rule 7.1, a lawyer may advertise services through public media, such as a telephone directory, legal directory, newspaper or other periodical, outdoor, radio or television, or through written communication not involving solicitation as defined in Rule 7.3.

(b)   A copy or recording of an advertisement or written communication shall be kept for two years after its last dissemination along with a record of when and where it was used.

(c)   A lawyer shall not give anything of value to a person for recommending the lawyer's services, except that a lawyer may pay the reasonable cost of advertising or written communication permitted by this rule and may pay the usual charges of a not-for-profit lawyer referral service or other legal service organization.

(d) Any communication made pursuant to this rule shall include the name of at least one lawyer responsible for its content.

The Comments to this Rule recognize that permitting lawyers to make their services known, through both their reputation and organized information campaigns, helps the public obtain legal services. The Comments further state that the need to educate members of the public, especially those of moderate means unfamiliar with the legal process, is an interest which should prevail. The Rules thereby encourage attorney advertising, unlike the traditional view. The Comment to Rule 7.2 also recognizes that television advertising is tremendously important. Prohibiting legal advertising on television would impede the flow of information about legal services to those of low and moderate income. The present rule reflects the Court's decision in the *Shapero* case. As you can see, the Rules have a much more contemporary outlook on the role of lawyer advertising than does the Code. The Code essentially takes the more traditional view of not encouraging advertising.

Likewise, the Rules and Code differ significantly on solicitation. Rule 7.3, while recognizing its dangers, does not advocate a prohibition on all solicitation.

RULE 7.3 Direct Contact with Prospective Clients

A lawyer may not solicit professional employment from a prospective client with whom the lawyer has no family or prior professional relationship, by mail, in-person or otherwise, when a significant motive for the lawyer's doing so is the lawyer's pecuniary gain. The term "solicit" includes contact in person, by telephone or telegraph, by letter or other writing, or by other communication directed to a specific recipient, but does not include letters addressed or advertising circulars distributed generally to persons not known to need legal services of the kind provided by the lawyer in a particular matter, but who are so situated that they might in general find such services useful.

However, the Comments to Rule 7.3 suggest that, in lieu of solicitation, the same information could be given to potential clients via advertising. Advertising, according to the Comment, informs without the undue influence or coercion usually inherent in direct solicitations. Advertising is also open to more than just one party and is subject to the scrutiny of the entire general population, whereas solicitation does not receive such scrutiny. Rule 7.3 specifically prohibits solicitation only when a significant motive is pecuniary gain, and allows general mailings to organizations seeking a supplier of legal services. The Comment to Rule 7.3 suggests that general mail advertising campaigns do not pose the same potential for abuse as targeted mailings, because they *are* general and are not tailored to individuals who are likely to be especially vulnerable. Thus, according to the Rules, at-torneys should not send direct-mail advertising to individuals known to have a specific legal problem.

Rule 7.4 allows lawyers to communicate their field of practice but prohibits, with the exception of patent or admiralty law, a lawyer from de-scribing himself as a "specialist," because it is misleading.

RULE 7.4 Communication of Fields of Practice

A lawyer may communicate the fact that the lawyer does or does not practice in particular fields of law. A lawyer shall not state or imply that the lawyer is a specialist except as follows:

(a) a lawyer admitted to engage in patent practice before the United States Patent and Trademark Office may use the designation "patent attorney" or a substantially similar designation;

(b) a lawyer engaged in admiralty practice may use the designation "admiralty," "proctor in admiralty" or a substan-tially similar designation; and

(c) (provisions on designation of specialization of the particular state).

According to the Comment to Rule 7.4, the terms "specialist," "lim-ited to," or "concentrated in" in attorney advertising mean, to the general public, that the attorney has formal recognition as a specialist. Therefore, the use of these terms could obviously be misleading. As for "patent" and "admiralty," these two legal areas have long been recognized as specialties, and the designation helps the public find such "super" specialists when their legal problem demands it. This rule, however, may not survive the *Peel* decision.

Rule 7.5 concerns firm names and letterheads.

RULE 7.5 Firm Names and Letterheads

(a) A lawyer shall not use a firm name, letterhead or other profes-sional designation that violates Rule 7.1. A trade name may be used by a lawyer in private practice if it does not imply a connection with a government agency or with a public or charitable legal services organi-zation and is not otherwise in violation of Rule 7.1.

(b) A law firm with offices in more than one jurisdiction may use the same name in each jurisdiction, but identification of the lawyers in an office of the firm shall indicate the jurisdictional limitations on those not licensed to practice in the jurisdiction where the office is located.

(c) The name of a lawyer holding a public office shall not be used in the name of a law firm, or in communications on its behalf, during any substantial period in which the lawyer is not actively and regularly practicing with the firm.

(d) Lawyers may state or imply that they practice in a partnership or other organization only when that is the fact.

Although substantially similar to the Code, it does eliminate the Code's requirement that these forms of communication be "dignified."

ABA Model Code

Canon 2 of the Code of Professional Responsibility contains the ABA's guidelines on lawyer advertising. Specifically, Canon 2 states that "A Lawyer Should Assist the Legal Profession in Fulfilling Its Duty to Make Legal Counsel Available." The Ethical Considerations under Canon 2 deal with the restraints on lawyer advertising. These Considerations state that an attorney, when advertising, should be certain that the information contained in the advertising is accurate, reliable, useful, meaningful, and relevant. As an example of a deceptive information, EC 2-9 tells of an attorney stating that his or her ingenuity or prior record, rather than justice, would be the principal factor determining the result of a legal problem or claim. EC 2-10 emphasizes that advertising should be relevant and disseminated in a useful and understandable manner. ECs 2-11 and 2-12 deal with the impropriety of using a trade name for a legal practice and emphasize that only the names of persons practicing in the firm (or deceased or retired members still in the firm) may be used. Attorneys may not call the firm something like "The Cheap Legal Clinic" or "The Best Award Plaintiff's Firm," nor use slogans such as "A Reasonable Doubt for a Reasonable Fee." However, they may use the names of members of the firm; if the two authors of this book decided to form a firm, the name "Lynton and Lyndall, Attorneys at Law" would be acceptable because it contains truthful, nondeceptive information. *Note:* Many firms and individuals use the initials *P.C.* after the name. This indicates that the firm or individual has been incorporated as a professional corporation, a status that confers some tax advantages. This is a permissible designation.

EC 2-14 emphasizes that attorneys cannot classify themselves as specialists except in the areas of admiralty, trademark, or patent law, unless the jurisdiction in which the attorney practices has other certified specialties. So, for example, a lawyer could not advertise (unless the jurisdiction permits it) that she specializes in bankruptcy or personal injury cases. The reason for excepting admiralty, trademark, and patent law is that these areas are extraordinarily specialized. A patent attorney must have some technical background, such as mechanical engineering, and must pass an additional test in order to be certified as such. This provision, however, like Rule 7.4, may be unconstitutional following the *Peel* decision.

Unlike other disciplinary rules, the rules governing advertising are quite explicit about what conduct does or does not violate the ethical standards of the bar. The type of information permitted in advertising is the type that would generally be helpful to an individual who is contemplating employing an attorney. For example, an immigrant from the former Soviet Union would find the information that an attorney specializes in immigration and speaks Russian to be invaluable; a person wishing to file a patent for a chemical process would need the assistance of a lawyer with a specialty in patents and a background in chemistry. As we have previously discussed, a violation of these rules could subject the violator to disbarment, professional discipline, or civil or criminal penalties.

DR 2-101(B) delineates the information permitted in print or broadcast media advertisements and requires the ads to be "dignified," thus injecting a potentially problematic subjective element into the analysis of attorney advertisements.

DR 2-101 Publicity. [as amended in 1974, 1975, 1977, and 1978]

(A) A lawyer shall not, on behalf of himself, his partner, associate or any other lawyer affiliated with him or his firm, use or participate in the use of any form of public communication containing a false, fraudulent, misleading, deceptive, self-laudatory or unfair statement or claim.

(B) In order to facilitate the process of informed selection of a lawyer by potential consumers of legal services, a lawyer may publish or broadcast, subject to DR 2-103, the following information in print media distributed or over television or radio broadcast in the geographic area or areas in which the lawyer resides or maintains offices or in which a significant part of the lawyer's clientele resides, provided that the information disclosed by the lawyer in such publication or broadcast complies with DR 2-101(A), and is presented in a dignified manner:

(1) Name, including name of law firm and names of professional associates; addresses and telephone numbers;

(2) One or more fields of law in which the lawyer or law firm practices, a statement that practice is limited to one or more fields of law, or a statement that the lawyer or law firm specializes in a particular field of law practice, to the extent authorized under DR 2-105;

(3) Date and place of birth;

(4) Date and place of admission to the bar of state and federal courts;

(5) Schools attended, with dates of graduation, degrees and other scholastic distinctions;

(6) Public or quasi-public offices;

(7) Military service;

(8) Legal authorships;

(9) Legal teaching positions;

(10) Memberships, offices, and committee assignments, in bar associations;

(11) Membership and offices in legal fraternities and legal societies;

(12) Technical and professional licenses;

(13) Memberships in scientific, technical and professional associations and societies;

(14) Foreign language ability;

(15) Names and addresses of bank references;

(16) With their written consent, names of clients regularly represented;

(17) Prepaid or group legal services programs in which the lawyer participates;

(18) Whether credit cards or other credit arrangements are accepted;

(19) Office and telephone answering service hours;

(20) Fee for an initial consultation;

(21) Availability upon request of a written schedule of fees and/or an estimate of the fee to be charged for specific services;

(22) Contingent fee rates subject to DR 2-106(C), provided that the statement discloses whether percentages are computed before or after deduction of costs;

(23) Range of fees for services, provided that the statement discloses that the specific fee within the range which will be charged will vary depending upon the particular matter to be handled for each client and the client is entitled without obligation to an estimate of the fee within the range likely to be charged. In print size equivalent to the largest print used in setting forth the fee information;

(24) Hourly rate, provided that the statement discloses that the total fee charged will depend upon the number of hours which must be devoted to the particular matter to be handled for each client and the client is entitled to without obligation an estimate of the fee likely to be charged, in print size at least equivalent to the largest print used in setting forth the fee information;

(25) Fixed fees for specific legal services, the description of which would not be misunderstood or be deceptive, provided that the statement discloses that the quoted fee will be available only to clients whose matters fall into the services described and that the client is entitled without obligation to a specific estimate of the fee likely to be charged in print size at least equivalent to the largest print used in setting forth the fee information.

(C) Any person desiring to expand the information authorized for disclosure in DR 2-101(B), or to provide for its dissemination through other forums may apply to [the agency having jurisdiction under state law]. Any such application shall be served upon [the agencies having jurisdiction under state law over the regulation of the legal profession and consumer matters] who shall be heard, together with the applicant, on the issue of whether the proposal is necessary in light of the existing provisions of the Code, accords with standards of accuracy, reliability and truthfulness, and would facilitate the process of informed selection of lawyers by potential consumers of legal services. The relief granted in response to any such application shall be promulgated as an amendment to DR 2-101(B), universally applicable to all lawyers.

(D) If the advertisement is communicated to the public over television or radio, it shall be prerecorded, approved for broadcast by the lawyer, and a recording of the actual transmission shall be retained by the lawyer.

(E)   If a lawyer advertises a fee for a service, the lawyer must render that service for no more than the fee advertised.

(F)   Unless otherwise specified in the advertisement if a lawyer publishes any fee information authorized under DR 2-101(B) in a publication that is published more frequently than one time per month, the lawyer shall be bound by any representation made therein for a period of not less than 30 days after such publication. If a lawyer publishes any fee information authorized under DR 2-101(B) in a publication that is published once a month or less frequently, he shall be bound by any representation made therein until the publication of the succeeding issue. If a lawyer publishes any fee information authorized under DR 2-101(B) in a publication which has no fixed date for publication of a succeeding issue, the lawyer shall be bound by any representation made therein for a reasonable period of time after publication but in no event less than one year.

(G)   Unless otherwise specified, if a lawyer broadcasts any fee information authorized under DR 2-101(B), the lawyer shall be bound by any representation made therein for a period of not less than 30 days after such broadcast.

(H)   This rule does not prohibit limited and dignified identification of a lawyer as a lawyer as well as by name:

(1)   In political advertisements when his professional status is germane to the political campaign or to a political issue.

(2)   In public notices when the name and profession of a lawyer are required or authorized by law or are reasonably pertinent for a purpose other than the attraction of potential clients.

(3)   In routine reports and announcements of a bona fide business, civic, professional, or political organization in which he serves as a director or officer.

(4)   In and on legal documents prepared by him.

(5)   In and on legal textbooks, treatises, and other legal publications, and in dignified advertisements thereof.

(I)   A lawyer shall not compensate or give any thing of value to representatives of the press, radio, television, or other communication medium in anticipation of or in return for professional publicity in a news item.

DR 2-102 designates permissible information for business cards, letterheads, and other firm announcements. However, these restrictions may not be constitutional following the *Peel* decision.

DR 2-102   Professional Notices, Letterheads and Offices.

(A)   A lawyer or law firm shall not use or participate in the use of professional cards, professional announcement cards, office signs, letterheads, or similar professional notices or devices, except that the following may be used if they are in dignified form:

(1) A professional card of a lawyer identifying him by name and as a lawyer, and giving his addresses, telephone numbers, the name of his law firm, and any information permitted under DR 2-105. A professional card of a law firm may also give the names of members and associates. Such cards may be used for identification.

(2) A brief professional announcement card stating new or changed associations or addresses, change of firm name, or similar matters pertaining to the professional offices of a lawyer or law firm, which may be mailed to lawyers, clients, former clients, personal friends, and relatives. It shall not state biographical data except to the extent reasonably necessary to identify the lawyer or to explain the change in his association, but it may state the immediate past position of the lawyer. It may give the names and dates of predecessor firms in a continuing line of succession. It shall not state the nature of the practice except as permitted under DR 2-105.

(3) A sign on or near the door of the office and in the building directory identifying the law office. The sign shall not state the nature of the practice, except as permitted under DR 2-105.

(4) A letter head of a lawyer identifying him by name and as a lawyer, and giving his addresses, telephone numbers, the name of his law firm, associates and any information permitted under DR 2-105. A letterhead of a law firm may also give the names of members and associates, and names and dates relating to deceased and retired members. A lawyer may be designated "Of Counsel" on a letterhead if he has a continuing relationship with a lawyer or law firm, other than as a partner or associate. A lawyer or law firm may be designated as "General Counsel" or by similar professional reference on stationary of a client if he or the firm devotes a substantial amount of professional time in the representation of that client. The letterhead of a law firm may give the names and dates of predecessor firms in a continuing line of succession.

(B) A lawyer in private practice shall not practice under a trade name, a name that is misleading as to the identity of the lawyer or lawyers practicing under such name, or a firm name containing names other than those of one or more of the lawyers in the firm, except that the name of a professional corporation or professional association may contain "P.C." or "P.A." or similar symbols indicating the nature of the organization, and if otherwise lawful a firm may use as, or continue to include in, its name the name or names of one or more deceased or retired members of the firm or of a predecessor firm in a continuing line of succession. A lawyer who assumes a judicial, legislative, or public executive or administrative post or office shall not permit his name to remain in the name of a law firm or to be used in professional notices of the firm during any significant period in which he is not actively and regularly practicing law as a member of the firm, and during such period other members of the firm shall not use his name in the firm name or in professional notices of the firm.

(C) A lawyer shall not hold himself out as having a partnership with one or more other lawyers or professional corporations unless they are in fact partners.

(D) A partnership shall not be formed or continued between or among lawyers licensed in different jurisdictions unless all enumerations of the members and associates of the firm on its letterhead and in other permissible listings make clear the jurisdictional limitations on those members and associates of the firm not licensed to practice in all listed jurisdictions; however, the same firm name may be used in each jurisdiction.

(E) Nothing contained herein shall prohibit a lawyer from using or permitting the use of, in connection with his name, an earned degree or title derived therefrom indicating his training in the law.

As to solicitation, the Code is also very specific and restrictive. DR 2-103 disallows most solicitation. It does not distinguish solicitation for pecuniary gain from solicitation to provide legal services for no pecuniary gain. The Code does provide that an attorney may approach a lawyer referral agency or other specific organization, but the thrust of the Code is to retain the prohibition against solicitation. It does not reflect the Supreme Court's more recent rulings on solicitation, as do the Rules.

DR 2-103 Recommendation of Professional Employment.

(A) A lawyer shall not, except as authorized in DR 2-101(B), recommend employment as a private practitioner, of himself, his partner, or associate to a layperson who has not sought his advice regarding employment of a lawyer.

(B) A lawyer shall not compensate or give anything of value to a person or organization to recommend or secure his employment by a client, or as a reward for having made a recommendation resulting in his employment by a client, except that he may pay the usual and reasonable fees or dues charged by any of the organizations listed in DR 2-103(D).

(C) A lawyer shall not request a person or organization to recommend or promote the use of his services or those of his partner or associate, or any other lawyer affiliated with him or his firm, as a private practitioner, except as authorized in DR 2-101, and except that

(1) He may request referrals from a lawyer referral service operated, sponsored, or approved by a bar association and may pay its fees incident thereto.

(2) He may cooperate with the legal service activities of any of the offices or organizations enumerated in DR 2-103(D)(1) through (4) and may perform legal services for those to whom he was recommended by it to do such work if:

(a) The person to whom the recommendation is made is a member or beneficiary of such office or organization; and

(b)   The lawyer remains free to exercise his independent professional judgment on behalf of his client.

(D)   A lawyer or his partner or associate or any other lawyer affiliated with him or his firm may be recommended, employed or paid by, or may cooperate with, one of the following offices or organizations that promote the use of his services or those of his partner or associate or any other lawyer affiliated with him or his firm if there is no interference with the exercise of independent professional judgment in behalf of his client:

(1)   A legal aid office or public defender office:

(a)   Operated or sponsored by a duly accredited law school.

(b)   Operated or sponsored by a bona fide non-profit community organization.

(c)   Operated or sponsored by a governmental agency.

(d)   Operated, sponsored, or approved by a bar association.

(2)   A military legal assistance office.

(3)   A lawyer referral service operated, sponsored, or approved by a bar association.

(4)   Any bona fide organization that recommends, furnishes or pays for legal services to its members or beneficiaries provided the following conditions are satisfied:

(a)   Such organization, including any affiliate, is so organized and operated that no profit is derived by it from the rendition of legal services by lawyers, and that, if the organization is organized for profit, the legal services are not rendered by lawyers employed, directed, supervised or selected by it except in connection with matters where such organization bears ultimate liability of its member or beneficiary.

(b)   Neither the lawyer, nor his partner, nor associate, nor any other lawyer affiliated with him or his firm, nor any non-lawyer, shall have initiated or promoted such organization for the primary purpose of providing financial or other benefit to such lawyer, partner, associate or affiliated lawyer.

(c)   Such organization is not operated for the purpose of procuring legal work or financial benefit for any lawyer as a private practitioner outside of the legal services program of the organization.

(d)   The member or beneficiary to whom the legal services are furnished, and not such organization, is recognized as the client of the lawyer in the matter.

(e)   Any member or beneficiary who is entitled to have legal services furnished or paid for by the organization may, if such member or beneficiary so desires, select counsel other than that furnished, selected or approved by the organization for the particular matter involved; and the legal service plan of such organization provides appropriate relief for any member or beneficiary who asserts a claim that representation by counsel furnished, selected or approved would be unethical, improper or inadequate under the circumstances of the matter involved and the plan provides an appropriate procedure for seeking such relief.

(f)   The lawyer does not know or have cause to know that such organization is in violation of applicable laws, rules of court and other legal requirements that govern its legal service operations.

(g)   Such organization has filed with the appropriate disciplinary authority at least annually a report with respect to its legal service plan, if any, showing its terms, its schedule of benefits, its subscription charges, agreements with counsel, and financial results of its legal service activities or, if it has failed to do so, the lawyer does not know or have cause to know of such failure.

(E)   A lawyer shall not accept employment when he knows or it is obvious that the person who seeks his services does so as a result of conduct prohibited under this Disciplinary Rule.

DR 2-104   Suggestion of Need of Legal Services.

(A)   A lawyer who has given in-person unsolicited advice to a layperson that he should obtain counsel or take legal action shall not accept employment resulting from that advice, except that:

(1)   A lawyer may accept employment by a close friend, relative, former client (if the advice is germane to the former employment), or one whom the lawyer reasonably believes to be a client.

(2)   A lawyer may accept employment that results from his participation in activities designed to educate laypersons to recognize legal problems, to make intelligent selection of counsel, or to utilize available legal services if such activities are conducted or sponsored by a qualified legal assistance organization.

(3)   A lawyer who is recommended, furnished or paid by a qualified legal assistance organization enumerated in DR 2-103(D)(1) through (4) may represent a member or beneficiary thereof, to the extent and under the conditions prescribed therein.

(4)   Without affecting his right to accept employment, a lawyer may speak publicly or write for publication on legal topics so long as he does not emphasize his own professional experience or reputation and does not undertake to give individual advice.

> (5) If success in asserting rights or defenses of his client in litigation in the nature of a class action is dependent upon the joinder of others, a lawyer may accept, but shall not seek, employment from those contacted for the purpose of obtaining their joinder.

Both the Rules and the Code forbid solicitation, to permit individuals to make decisions about legal matters, especially their own, without the influence of those who might benefit, professionally or financially, from their representation. By forbidding attorneys to pressure prospective clients, the Rules and Code attempt to let consumers gain information about legal services just as they would about other professional or commercial services, while being protected from intimidation, harassment, or undue influence in their choice of legal representation. However, the Rules are more tolerant of solicitation than is the Code, suggesting that there do exist situations in which solicitation may not be a great evil that must be avoided at all costs.

ABA Model Guidelines

Guidelines 4 and 5 relate to advertising and solicitation insofar as they concern communications to clients. Guideline 4, which relates to the unauthorized practice of law as well, imposes a duty on lawyers to make all third parties aware of the status of legal assistants they employ. Guideline 5 permits lawyers to identify legal assistants by name and title on the firm letterhead and business cards. Some states, such as Kansas, New Mexico, and North Carolina, do not permit the letterhead to carry the names of legal assistants, but that restriction may have been eroded by *Peel*. Business cards for legal assistants are approved by nearly every state, but some states, such as Iowa and Texas, require that the card contain a clear designation of status and not be used in a deceptive way. New Hampshire's Supreme Court Rule 7 prohibits the use of business cards by legal assistants for unethical solicitation, recognizing that the very action of handing out a business card might be deceptive.

NALA and NFPA Provisions

None of the provisions of the two paralegal codes of ethics deal directly with advertising and solicitation. This is probably because legal assistants are ethically prevented from practicing law, including accepting and declining employment. The older view is that, because a paralegal cannot accept or decline employment, the issues of advertising and solicitation should not arise.

However, in today's competitive legal environment, paralegals and legal assistants may be significant in the business development of a law firm.

Many paralegals are involved in their firm's marketing efforts; this involvement requires paralegals to become keenly aware of the provisions concerning advertising and solicitation. In today's law firms, legal assistants may be marketing committee members and perform activities, both within and without the firm, that contribute to the firm's development as a business entity.

In addition, more and more paralegals work as freelance or independent legal assistants who must market themselves. It is interesting to speculate what type of restrictions might be placed on freelance and independent paralegals. Would it make a difference if the legal assistant's advertising and marketing campaign were targeted to lawyers rather than the general public? The probable answer to that question is yes. The fears of overreaching and vulnerability to deception would arguably not exist if the advertising were aimed only at lawyers. To ensure that any advertising campaign you may set up as a freelance or independent paralegal conforms to ethical requirements, it would be prudent to check with the local bar association. Conform your advertising to the restrictions imposed on attorneys in the jurisdiction.

By understanding the general rules concerning advertising and solicitation, and by becoming aware of a particular jurisdiction's ethical standards, paralegals can participate effectively in a firm's business development efforts, while knowing that their actions comply with the ethical restrictions in these two areas.

THE CASE OF ANNABELLE'S ADVERTISING ANTICS

Annabelle Arapoglu has worked for the firm of Baumgold & Waterman for the past four years, but in all those years, the firm has never faced an economic crisis like the present one. Unless the firm can get some new business, it looks like the firm will not be able to survive. Annabelle loves working at Baumgold & Waterman; actually, the two partners and Annabelle are old tennis buddies, each having played collegiate tennis, and she just cannot imagine working in a different office. So she decides to use some ingenuity to come up with new approaches to finding new business for the firm.

Annabelle thinks up the following ideas: (1) putting a note in her class's section of the *Alumni Bulletin* that says, "I'm working in litigation in Chicago—let me help any of you who need good representation"; (2) playing in a tennis benefit for the victims of drunk drivers, so that later, at the reception, she can hand out business cards that show Baumgold & Waterman's specialty to be personal injury litigation; (3) sending the firm's brochure to her Kappa Alpha Omega sorority sisters; (4) handing out a coupon good for $50 in court costs to anyone who hires Baumgold & Waterman; (5) sending a letter and a sample letter of engagement to all patients of

Dr. H.I.V., a dentist who negligently infected several patients with the HIV virus.

What ethical issues are implicated by these advertising ideas?

6.6 ADVERTISING, SOLICITATION, AND THE PARALEGAL

The ethical aspects of advertising and solicitation for lawyers are also relevant to the paralegal, for several reasons. First, many paralegals handle marketing duties within their firms. Second, as the competition for legal business increases, more and more firms will be advertising their services. Third, paralegals are constantly in contact with clients and others who are potential sources of work for the firm; approaching these individuals must be done in an ethical manner. Fourth, paralegals are often the first individuals from a firm with whom a client comes into contact; therefore, the paralegal must be certain that client recruitment at this stage be done ethically.

Advertising and solicitation issues are also implicated for paralegals when they introduce themselves to others, when they sign letters or legal documents, or when they hand out business cards. Paralegals and legal assistants must identify themselves as nonlawyers in any communication with clients, the general public, the judiciary, and other members of the legal community. Although it is not necessary for you to answer your telephone "Jim Farrell, Paralegal," you should be certain that those with whom you deal, either personally, on the telephone, or through correspondence, understand that you are a legal assistant, not a lawyer.

The paralegal consultant faces a unique advertising dilemma. Most legal assistants who venture into contract work must advertise to secure employment. The question of advertising then becomes twofold. First, what restricts the advertising and solicitation that a paralegal directs at attorneys? As long as the advertising is truthful, can you see any other restrictions that might apply? Would the bar regard direct solicitation of attorneys as falling within the exceptions set forth by the ethical rules for lawyers? Second, what restrictions should be placed on advertising and solicitation to the general public? As legal assistants are absolutely prohibited from practicing law, would there be an absolute prohibition against advertising and solicitation for the paralegal consultant?

If you decide to become a consultant, it would be advisable to check with local bar officials to find out what restrictions, if any, the jurisdiction applies to paralegal advertising. If none exist, the general ethical principles that you have learned should guide you as to the acceptability of any advertising or solicitation you devise. Ethical decisions in this area must also consider the effect of advertising on other ethical principles, including confidentiality, conflict of interest, zealous representation, and handling client funds. All of these areas of ethics should be reviewed to ensure that any solicitation or advertising you do as a freelance paralegal complies with the ethical rules for both your professional organization and the jurisdiction in which you practice.

Finally, your résumé may be regarded as advertising and arguably may be bound by certain ethical considerations. You obviously have a professional obligation to be honest on your résumé; however, other ethical considerations may also arise. These include the duty of preserving client confidences and secrets. It is important for paralegals to consider whether anything on the résumé could be construed as revealing such information. For example, if you worked on a complicated antitrust suit, could you say on your résumé that you participated in settlement negotiations and helped the lawyer obtain a $5 million judgment for the client, even though the client agreed to settle for $1 million? Although this information might show a prospective employer that you have a significant amount of experience, it probably violates your duty of confidentiality to the former client. Another frequent problem with résumés in general is in listing references. Many individuals list references without first checking to ensure that the person is willing to give one. This can be a deadly mistake; both common courtesy and common sense dictate that references be contacted before they are put on one's résumé.

THE CASE OF THE PERPLEXED PARALEGAL

Paralegal Pam has just come out of a marketing meeting in which her firm discussed several methods to bring in new business. She has been assigned the task of placing several advertisements in various forums. Her first task is to place an ad in the Yellow Pages, and she does that, knowing that advertising in the Yellow Pages is an ethically permissible form of advertising. Her second task is to place an ad in the "Talking Yellow Pages," which allows inquiring individuals to receive names of those providing a particular service. Knowing that her firm's goal is to advertise according to the highest ethical standards, Pam has cause to pause. On the one hand, she believes the Talking Yellow Pages to be a form of advertising rather than solicitation, but on the other, she remembers the general rule that telephone solicitation is considered to be in-person solicitation.

Perplexed, Pam calls you, an old friend from paralegal school, to get your advice. Can you cure her confusion?

Scott Myren's guest editorial describes one state's approach to the regulation of lawyer advertising.

GUEST EDITORIAL

PROFESSIONAL RESPONSIBILITY: LAWYER ADVERTISING

by Scott P. Myren

LAWYER ADVERTISING MUST BE PREDOMINANTLY INFORMATIONAL; THE USE OF DRAWINGS, ANIMATIONS, DRAMATIZATION, MUSIC OR LYRICS IS PROHIBITED IN TELEVISION ADVERTISING, AND NO ADVERTISEMENTS MAY RELY UPON THE SHOCK VALUE OF ABSURD PORTRAYALS WHOLLY IRRELEVANT TO THE SELECTION OF COUNSEL. *In re Felmeister & Isaacs,* 104 N.J. 515, 518 A.2d 188 (1986).

Lawyer advertising in America was not always the subject of disdain. Throughout the eighteenth century there were few, if any, prohibitions on lawyer advertising. Recent demands by the public and by the legal profession for greater professionalism have led to a dramatic change in attitude.

In 1948, the New Jersey Supreme Court adopted the *Canons of Professional Responsibility* which condemned lawyer advertising. These Canons were replaced by the *Code of Professional Responsibility.* The Code standards were amended in the wake of the landmark case, *Bates v. State Bar of Arizona,* the first case to bring lawyer advertising within the purview of commercial free speech protection. Subsequent Supreme Court decisions have forced the amendment or abandonment of the various standards of professional conduct, while simultaneously limiting the parameters of lawyer advertising. The end result is that certain lawyer advertising is deemed permissible because it is protected by the right to free speech.

In *In re Felmeister & Isaacs,* the New Jersey Supreme Court reformulated the lawyer advertising standards which governed professional conduct in the state since 1984. The new standards established by the *Felmeister & Isaacs* court provide that: (1) attorney advertising be predominantly informational, (2) the use of "drawings, animations, dramatization, music or lyrics" is prohibited in television advertising, and (3) all advertisements which rely in any way on "shock or amusement value of absurd portrayals

wholly irrelevant to the selection of counsel" are prohibited. In addition, the court established a Committee on Attorney Advertising to continue study in the fledgling area of American lawyer advertising. The court has acted responsibly and thoughtfully in an effort to guide the potentially harmful area through its infancy.

Since the Supreme Court's decision in *Bates,* it is clear that a state cannot completely ban lawyer advertising. However, it is also clear that the state can protect substantial state interests by restricting limited areas of advertising. Since the *Bates* decision, endless debate has focused on where the line should be drawn. This uncertainty has resulted in the battles evident in later decisions.

The New Jersey Supreme Court's responsible approach to the development of lawyer advertising, in all cases, is aimed at fairness. The court has attempted at all phases of development to avoid the difficulties and inequities of line-drawing.

Realizing that the haphazard case-by-case development that has predominated in the area of lawyer advertising results in little more than uncertainty, the court set out to establish a new rule which would serve as the model for resolving this issue. The decision to draft a new rule was based on the realization that attorney advertising is here to stay. Courts may continue to avoid dealing with the issue or approach it responsibly and develop restraints which may survive the test of time.

The *Felmeister & Isaacs* opinion demonstrates an attempt at one such rule. The court's desire to establish a durable rule is evidenced by its attempt to subject each aspect of the new rule to constitutional scrutiny.

The court's constitutional analysis signals that the rule will likely withstand constitutional challenge. Thus, the new rule may effectively end the persistent battle—at least in New Jersey. Furthermore, in yet another demonstration of judicial responsibility, the

Felmeister & Isaacs court established a special agency charged with nothing more than the examination of the new rule's progress. The agency's power to offer advisory opinions to practitioners suggests the certainty of application so vital to an effective rule. Moreover, the agency's authorization to offer suggestions to the Supreme Court reinforces the foundation of adaptability upon which this new rule is formulated.

In *Felmeister & Isaacs* the New Jersey Supreme Court acted responsibly in establishing a new rule governing attorney advertising. Significant to the rule's effectiveness is the built-in flexibility of the rule and the certainty of its language. Moreover, the rule's significance is buttressed by the creation of a special agency charged with the implementation, interpretation, and development of its provisions. Consistent application of the new rule should help alleviate the uncertainties engendered by the case-by-case approach that has dominated the issue of attorney advertising.

■ Scott P. Myren is a practicing attorney. This article was reprinted with permission of the *Rutgers Law Journal.*

6.7 CASE LAW CONCERNING ADVERTISING AND SOLICITATION

The following cases will give you insight into how courts have looked at advertising and solicitation. The *Peel* case illustrates the Supreme Court's contemporary view toward lawyer advertising.

Gary E. PEEL
v.
ATTORNEY REGISTRATION AND DISCIPLINARY COMMISSION OF ILLINOIS
110 S. Ct. 2281 (1990)

Petitioner practices law in Edwardsville, Illinois. He was licensed to practice in Illinois in 1968, in Arizona in 1979, and in Missouri in 1981. He has served as president of the Madison County Bar Association, and has been active in both national and state bar association work. He has tried to verdict over 100 jury trials and over 300 nonjury trials, and has participated in hundreds of other litigated matters that were settled. NBTA issued petitioner a "Certificate in Civil Trial Advocacy" in 1981, renewed it in 1986, and listed him in its 1985 Directory of "Certified Specialists and Board Members."

Since 1983 petitioner's professional letterhead has contained a statement referring to his NBTA certification and to the three States in which he is licensed. It appears as follows:

"Gary E. Peel
Certified Civil Trial Specialist By the National Board of Trial Advocacy
Licensed: Illinois, Missouri, Arizona"

In 1987, the Administrator of the Attorney Registration and Disciplinary Commission of Illinois (Commission) filed a complaint alleging that petitioner, by use of this letterhead, was publicly holding himself out as a certified legal specialist in violation of Rule 2-105(a)(3) of the Illinois Code of Professional Responsibility. That Rule provides:

> "A lawyer or law firm may specify or designate any area or field of law in which he or its partners concentrates or limits his or its practice. Except as set forth in Rule 2-105(a), no lawyer may hold himself out as 'certified' or a 'specialist.' "

The complaint also alleged violations of Rule 2-101(b), which requires that a lawyer's public "communication shall contain all information necessary to make the communication not misleading and shall not contain any false or misleading statement or otherwise operate to deceive," and of Rule 1-102(a)(1), which generally subjects a lawyer to discipline for violation of any Rule of the Code of Professional Responsibility. Disciplinary Rule 2-101(b), 1-102(a)(1) (1988).

In this case we must consider whether petitioner's statement was misleading and, even if it was not, whether the potentially misleading character of such statements creates a state interest sufficiently substantial to justify a categorical ban on their use.

The facts stated on petitioner's letterhead are true and verifiable. It is undisputed that NBTA has certified petitioner as a civil trial specialist and that three States have licensed him to practice law. There is no contention that any potential client or person was actually misled or deceived by petitioner's stationery. Neither the Commission nor the State Supreme Court made any factual finding of actual deception or misunderstanding, but rather concluded, as a matter of law, that petitioner's claims of being "certified" as a

"specialist" were necessarily misleading absent an official state certification program. Notably, although petitioner was originally charged with a violation of Disciplinary Rule 2-101(b), which aims at misleading statements by an attorney, his letterhead was not found to violate this rule.

In evaluating petitioner's claim of certification, the Illinois Supreme Court focused not on its facial accuracy, but on its implied claim "as to the quality of [petitioner's] legal services," and concluded that such a qualitative claim " 'might be so likely to mislead as to warrant restriction.' " This analysis confuses the distinction between statements of opinion or quality and statements of objective facts that may support an inference of quality. A lawyer's certification by NBTA is a verifiable fact, as are the predicate requirements for that certification. Measures of trial experience and hours of continuing education, like information about what schools the lawyer attended or his or her bar activities, are facts about a lawyer's training and practice. A claim of certification is not an unverifiable opinion of the ultimate quality of a lawyer's work or a promise of success, but is simply a fact, albeit one with multiple predicates, from which a consumer may or may not draw an inference of the likely quality of an attorney's work in a given area of practice.

. . . Even if petitioner's letterhead is not actually misleading, the Commission defends Illinois'[s] categorical prohibition against lawyers' claims of being "certified" or a "specialist" on the assertion that these statements are potentially misleading. In the Commission's view, the State's interest in avoiding any possibility of misleading some consumers with such communications is so substantial that it outweighs the cost of providing other consumers with relevant information about lawyers who are certified as specialists.

We may assume that statements of "certification" as a "specialist," even though truthful, may not be understood fully by some readers. However, such statements pose no greater potential of misleading consumers than advertising admission to "Practice before: The United States Supreme Court," *In re R.M.J.,* 455 U.S. 191, 102 S. Ct. 929, 71 L. Ed. 2d 64 (1982), of exploiting the audience of a targeted letter, *Shapero v. Kentucky Bar Assn.,* 486 U.S. 466, 108 S. Ct. 1916, 100 L. Ed. 2d at 475 (1988), or of confusing a reader with an accurate illustration, *Zauderer v. Office of Disciplinary Counsel,* 471 U.S. 626, 105 S. Ct. 2265, 85 L. Ed. 2d 652 (1985). In this case, as in those, we conclude that the particular State rule restricting lawyers' advertising is " 'broader than reasonably necessary to prevent the' perceived evil." The need for a complete prophylactic against any claim of specialty is undermined by the fact that use of titles such as "Registered Patent Attorney" and "Proctor in Admiralty," which are permitted under Rule 2-105(a)'s exceptions, produces the same risk of deception.

. . . "If the naivete of the public will cause advertising by attorneys to be misleading then it is the bar's role to assure that the populace is sufficiently informed as to enable it to place advertising in its proper perspective." *Bates,* 433 U.S., at 375, 97 S. Ct., at 2705. To the extent that potentially misleading statements of private certification or specialization could confuse consumers, a State might consider screening certifying organizations or requiring a disclaimer about the certifying organization or the standards of a specialty. *In re R.M.J.,* 455 U.S., at 201-203, 102 S. Ct., at 936-938. A State may not, however, completely ban statements that are not actually or inherently misleading, such as certification as a specialist by bona fide organizations such as NBTA. Information about certification and specialties facilitates the consumer's access to legal services and thus better serves the administration of justice.

Petitioner's letterhead was neither actually nor inherently misleading. There is no dispute about the bona fides and the relevance of the NBTA certification. The Commission's concern about the possibility of deception in hypothetical cases is not sufficient to rebut the constitutional presumption favoring disclosure over concealment. Disclosure of information such as that on petitioner's letterhead both serves the public interest and encourages the development and utilization of meritorious certification programs for attorneys. As the public censure of petitioner for violating Rule 2-105(a)(3) violates the First Amendment, the judgment of the Illinois Supreme Court is reversed and the case is remanded for proceedings not inconsistent with this opinion.

It is so ordered.

Justice MARSHALL, with whom Justice BRENNAN joins, concurring in the judgment.

Petitioner's letterhead is neither actually nor inherently misleading. I therefore concur in the plurality's holding that Illinois may not prohibit petitioner from holding himself out as a civil trial specialist certified by the National Board of Trial Advocacy. I believe, though, that petitioner's letterhead statement is potentially misleading. Accordingly, I would hold that Illinois may enact regulations other than a total ban to ensure that the public is not misled by such representations. Because Illinois'[s] present regulation is unconstitutional as applied to petitioner, however, the judgment of the Illinois Supreme Court must be reversed and the case remanded for further proceedings.

Justice O'CONNOR, with whom Chief Justice REHNQUIST and Justice SCALIA join, dissenting.

This case provides yet another example of the difficulties raised by rote application of the commercial speech doctrine in the context of state regulation of professional standards for attorneys. Nothing in our prior cases in this area mandates that we strike down the state regulation at issue here, which is designed to ensure a reliable and ethical profession. Failure to accord States considerable latitude in this area embroils this Court in the micromanagement of the State's inherent authority to police the ethical standards of the profession within its borders.

Petitioner argues for the first time before this Court that the statement on his letterhead that he is a certified trial specialist is not commercial speech. I agree with the Court that we need not reach this issue in this case. *Ante,* at 2287. We generally do not "decide federal constitutional issues raised here for the first time on review of state court decisions."

We recently summarized our standards for commercial speech by attorneys in *Zauderer v. Office of Disciplinary Counsel of Supreme Court of Ohio,* 471 U.S. 626, 105 S. Ct. 2265, 85 L. Ed. 2d 652 (1985):

> "The States and the Federal Government are free to prevent the dissemination of commercial speech that is false, deceptive, misleading, see Friedman v. Rogers, 440 U.S. 1 [99 S. Ct. 887, 59 L. Ed. 2d 100] (1979). . . . Commercial speech that is not false or deceptive and does not concern unlawful activities . . . may be restricted only in the service of a substantial governmental interest, and only through means that directly advance that interest." Id., 471 U.S., at 638, 105 S. Ct., at 2275.

In my view, application of this standard requires us to affirm the Illinois Supreme Court's decision that Rule 2-105(a)(3) of the Illinois Code of Professional Responsibility is a valid measure to control misleading and deceptive speech. "The public's comparative lack of knowledge, the limited ability of the professions to police themselves, and the absence of any standardization in the 'product' renders [attorney commercial speech] especially susceptible to abuses that the States have a legitimate interest in controlling." Although certifying organizations, such as the National Board of Trial Advocacy (NBTA), may provide a valuable service to the legal profession and the public, I would permit the States broad latitude to ensure that consumers are not misled or deceived by claims of certification.

CASE QUESTIONS

1. Do you agree with the majority's decision?
2. How might Peel's statement mislead a potential client?
3. Why is the Court taking a less restrictive view towards attorney advertising?

The *Budish* case gives you a chance to see how the Supreme Court of Florida handled a situation in which an attorney placed false and misleading advertisements in the newspaper.

THE FLORIDA BAR, Complainant
v.
Robert P. BUDISH, Respondent

Supreme Court of Florida
421 So. 2d 501 (Fla. 1982)

PER CURIAM.

We have for review the report and recommendation of the referee. Jurisdiction is pursuant to article V, section 15, Florida Constitution.

The report of the referee included the following findings:

As to Count I

1. Based on instructions of Respondent or his agent, the October 10, 1979 edition of the Miami *Herald* carried an advertisement indicating that Respondent's legal clinic would charge $75.00 plus costs to perfect a change of name.

2. After reading the advertisement, Ms. Florence Valentino telephoned Respondent's office and made an appointment for an office conference.

3. On October 23, 1979, Ms. Valentino went to Respondent's office at the appointed time. Respondent told Ms. Valentino that it would cost her $100.00 in attorney's fees and $44.00 for costs to perfect a change of name. Ms. Valentino immediately issued a check to Respondent for $144.00.

As to Count II

4. Based on instructions of Respondent or his agent, between April 23, 1979 and May 23, 1979, the Hollywood *Sun Tattler* carried an advertisement indicating that Respondent's legal clinic would not charge for an initial consultation.

5. After reading the advertisement, Mrs. Wilma Knapp telephoned Respondent's office and made an appointment for a consultation.

6. On May 23, 1979, Mrs. Knapp went to Respondent's office at the appointed time and spoke with Respondent regarding her dissolution of marriage proceedings.

7. At the conclusion of the five (5) minute consultation, Respondent or his agent requested payment of $35.00. Mrs. Knapp immediately issued a check to Respondent for $35.00.

8. Respondent performed no additional work for Mrs. Knapp and has refused to refund the $35.00 payment.

As to Count III

9. Respondent had been doing business under the name of Citizens Legal Services of Hollywood, Inc.

10. Citizens Legal Services of Hollywood, Inc. employed Stewart Doe as its president. Stewart Doe is not an attorney.

The referee recommended that respondent be found guilty as to all counts, and that he receive a private reprimand and be placed on probation with the following conditions:

1. that respondent be placed on probation for a period of three (3) years;

2. that, during the probationary period, respondent's work be supervised by a member of The Florida Bar, who is approved by The Florida Bar and respondent;

3. that respondent submit monthly reports to The Florida Bar designating the cases he is handling, and the status of said cases;

4. that respondent take and pass the ethics portion of The Florida Bar examination

within one year from the date of the Supreme Court's order; and

5. that respondent submit to psychiatric treatment if deemed necessary during his probationary period.

The referee further recommended that respondent make restitution to Ms. Valentino concerning Count I, and to Mrs. Knapp in the amount of $35.00 concerning Count II.

We do not believe that the referee's recommendation of a private reprimand is appropriate in this case. Although the referee properly considered respondent's drug problem and his subsequent rehabilitation as mitigating circumstances in making his recommendation, in view of the nature of respondent's misconduct, a public reprimand is appropriate.

The public should be able to rely on and have confidence in the truthfulness of an attorney's advertisement to the public. In this case, two clients were misled by respondent's false and misleading advertisements. False and deceptive advertising has a great potential for harm, and when an attorney publicly misleads or deceives the public, the public is entitled to be properly informed that such conduct is in violation of this Court's advertising rules and regulations, and that the offending attorney has in fact been disciplined. A private reprimand does not adequately apprise the public of these matters. Only through a public reprimand are the interests of the public protected.

With respect to the referee's recommendation of probation and conditions of probation, we find that these recommendations are unrelated to respondent's misconduct and unnecessary for his rehabilitation or the protection of public interest. Respondent is not charged with rendering incompetent legal services. Rather, he is charged with the advertisement of false and misleading statements in violation of Disciplinary Rules 1-102(A)(4),

2-101(A), 2-101(B)(3) and (6) and the employment of a non-lawyer as president of his legal clinic in violation of Disciplinary Rules 2-102(B), 5-107(C) and Florida Bar Integration Rule, article II, section 7. Given the nature of these violations, we do not feel that the placement of respondent on supervised probation for a period of three years would assist in his rehabilitation, or promote the public's interest. Also, concerning the recommendation that respondent submit to psychiatric treatment if deemed necessary, we believe that this requirement is unnecessary inasmuch as the referee indicated in his recommendation that a psychiatrist had previously determined that respondent was not in need of psychiatric treatment.

For the foregoing reasons, we do not accept all of the referee's recommendation for disciplinary action, and instead find that the appropriate remedy in this case is for respondent to make restitution and be given a public reprimand without probation or additional disciplinary action, and that he shall take and pass the ethics portion of The Florida Bar examination within one year from the date of this order.

Costs in the amount of $751.25 are assessed against respondent.

It is so ordered.

ALDERMAN, C.J., and ADKINS, OVERTON, McDONALD and EHRLICH, JJ., concur.

BOYD, J., concurs in part and dissents in part with an opinion.

BOYD, Justice, concurring in part and dissenting in part.

I concur in the public reprimand and the imposition of costs of this proceeding against respondent. I would adopt the referee's findings that respondent violated the Code of Professional Conduct. I do not feel that the placement of respondent on supervised probation for a period of three years would assist in his rehabilitation, or promote the public's interest. Similarly, except for any punitive effect, I fail to see how the referee's recommendation that respondent take and pass the ethics portion of the Florida Bar Examination would be beneficial to either the public or respondent. Finally, concerning the recommen-dation that respondent submit to psychiatric treatment if deemed necessary, I believe that this requirement is unnecessary inasmuch as the referee indicated in his recommendation that a psychiatrist had previously determined that respondent was not in need of psychiatric treatment.

CASE QUESTIONS

1. What was misleading or deceptive about Budish's advertisement?
2. Would it be correct to say that the advertising was permissible but that Budish's actions were not? Explain.
3. Do you agree that a public reprimand is the appropriate punishment, or should the punishment be more lenient (or stricter)?

The *Caenen* case shows how a court analyzed the behavior of an attorney who allegedly solicited business impermissibly. It also shows how ineffective communication and poor handling of funds combined with other ethical violations to present a disturbing picture of an attorney's behavior.

STATE of Kansas, Petitioner

v.

Thomas J. CAENEN, Respondent

Supreme Court of Kansas
681 P.2d 639 (Kan. 1984)

PER CURIAM:

This is an original proceeding in discipline filed by the Board for Discipline of Attorneys (the Board) by Arno Windscheffel, Disciplinary Administrator, pursuant to Supreme Court Rule 212 (232 Kan. clxvii). A panel of the Board, after a hearing, determined that respondent neglected a legal matter entrusted to him and had violated DR 2-103(A) and (B) (232 Kan. clxxix) and DR 9-102(B) (232 Kan. cxcii), and had failed to cooperate with the Disciplinary Administrator in violation of Rule 207 (232 Kan. clxiv), and recommended the respondent be indefinitely suspended from the practice of law. Respondent filed exceptions to the report of the disciplinary panel.

In November, 1981, the respondent, Thomas J. Caenen, had a collection agency. Caenen employed an individual by the name of Evans. Evans was hired to visit the officers of certain professions and solicit their delinquent accounts for the respondent to attempt collection. Caenen paid Mr. Evans $100.00 per week plus a 20% commission on the gross amount of receipts generated on new collection accounts above his $100.00 a week draw.

About November 11, 1981, Evans and Lisa Smith, nonlawyer employees of Caenen, contacted the office of Eugene McGill, D.D.S., a dentist practicing in the Kansas City area. Neither McGill nor any member of his staff had had prior contact with the respondent or anyone affiliated with him.

Either Smith or Evans, or both, represented themselves to be "account service representatives" for Caenen. They presented the respondent's business card with their own names and the title "Account Service Repr." handwritten on the card. They spoke with Dr. McGill's office manager in an attempt to secure the referral of collection accounts to Caenen's office. Smith and Evans represented that the respondent's fee for the services contemplated would be 40% of any amount collected within one year and 50% of any amount collected after one year. These terms were written on the back of the business card provided Dr. McGill's office.

Dr. McGill's office manager agreed to refer one account to respondent for collection. The account was that of Terry Eason who owed an outstanding balance of $228.00 to Dr. McGill. By a letter dated November 16, 1981, Caenen acknowledged his employment and confirmed the terms as previously represented.

On December 2, 1981, Dr. McGill's receptionist phoned Evans at respondent's office to inquire as to the status of the collection account. Evans informed the receptionist that Eason had promised to be in that Friday with a $50.00 check. On January 5, 1982, the receptionist again contacted Mr. Evans. Mr. Evans informed her that $50.00 had been received.

The only record apparently kept by respondent, and the only record produced by the respondent at the evidentiary hearing on this complaint, was a balance sheet reflecting Mr. Eason's name and the amount of the outstanding balance ($228.00) referred for collection. That sheet contains a handwritten note "12-5 Pd. 50.00." Caenen admitted on cross-examination that the records he maintained reflected that there was a payment of $50.00, and that he acknowledged to Dr. McGill or his office staff that he had a record of payment.

No money was forthcoming from the respondent. Thereafter Dr. McGill's office repeatedly contacted the respondent's office by phone, making inquiry as to the funds collected. On a number of occasions Caenen could not be reached. Messages were left but Caenen did not return the calls. Dr. McGill's office manager spoke to Caenen personally on March 9, 1982, and March 23, 1982. On both occasions he assured her that the amount due would be mailed immediately. The funds were not remitted.

On April 23, 1982, Dr. McGill spoke personally with Caenen by phone. During this conversation, Caenen told McGill his records regarding Mr. Eason's account indicated that he had received one payment of $50.00. Caenen acknowledged that the payment was overdue and said he would remit the amount immediately.

The payment was not remitted as respondent promised. Consequently, Dr. McGill complained to the office of the Disciplinary Administrator by letter dated May 7, 1982. . . .

[The opinion details the fact that Caenen did not respond to communications from the Disciplinary Administrator, Arno Windscheffel, between May 7, 1982 and August 31, 1982.]

. . . Caenen communicated with Dr. McGill after the complaint was filed. On August 5, 1982, Dr. McGill received a phone call from a person representing herself to be Caenen's office manager. McGill explained the situation and the person calling promised payment would be forthcoming in the mail. Payment was not received. On August 25, 1982, Dr. McGill spoke personally with Caenen by phone. During the conversation, respondent implied that his records were not in order and that he would get back to McGill the next day. Caenen did not call Dr. McGill as promised. On September 1, 1982, Dr. McGill again spoke to Caenen. Caenen again attempted to put Dr. McGill off saying his records were not in order. An argument ensued when Caenen implied that the $50.00 payment must have been paid directly to Dr. McGill's office, therefore Dr. McGill owed Caenen $20.00. McGill had no further contact with Caenen.

Mr. Windscheffel testified that Caenen never answered or in any manner responded to the allegations in Dr. McGill's letter of complaint. Consequently, on January 26, 1983, the complaint was referred for consideration to a review committee pursuant to Supreme Court Rule 210(c) (232 Kan. clxvi). Caenen failed to reply to the committee. The committee referred the complaint for formal prosecution. The formal complaint against the respondent was filed on February 14, 1983.

On February 23, 1983, Dr. McGill was contacted by Stephen McAllister, an employee of Caenen. McAllister asked McGill if there was anything that could be done to get the complaint dropped. McGill replied all that he ever wanted from the beginning was payment of the amount owed, which Caenen had acknowledged receiving. The following afternoon a money order was left at McGill's office in the amount of $30.00, fourteen months after the money had been received by Caenen.

Due to the fact that the respondent has practiced law for a number of years and the number and nature of the violations, the panel recommended that the respondent be suspended from the practice of law by the Supreme Court of the State of Kansas.

The respondent contends he did not violate DR 2-103(A) and (C) (232 Kan. clxxix), which provide:

"(A) A lawyer shall not, except as authorized in DR 2-101(B) recommend employment as a private practitioner, of himself, his partner, or associate to a layperson who has not sought his advice regarding employment of a lawyer.

* * *

"(C) A lawyer shall not request a person or organization to recommend or promote the use of his services or those of his partner or associate, or any other lawyer affiliated with him or his firm, as a private practitioner, except as authorized in DR 2-101, and except that:

"(1) He may request referrals from a lawyer referral service operated, sponsored, or approved by a bar association and may pay its fees incident thereto.

"(2) He may cooperate with the legal service activities of any of the offices or organizations enumerated in DR 1-103(D)(1) through (4) and may perform legal services for those to whom he was recommended by it to do such work if:

"(a) The person to whom the recommendation is made is a member or beneficiary of such office or organization; and

"(b) The lawyer remains free to exercise his independent professional judgment on behalf of his client."

The direct solicitation of a stranger by an attorney or his agent for employment for a particular legal matter violates the Code of

Professional Responsibility, DR 2-103, and is subject to discipline as provided by the rules of this court. . . .

Misconduct by the respondent has been clearly and convincingly established. We have given careful consideration as to the nature and extent of the punishment or discipline that should be imposed upon the respondent for his breach of professional responsibility. Due to the numerous violations of professional conduct in this matter and previous violations of professional conduct, we accept the recommendation of the Disciplinary Panel.

IT IS THEREFORE ORDERED AND ADJUDGED that Thomas J. Caenen be and he is hereby indefinitely suspended from the practice of law in the State of Kansas. The costs herein are assessed to the respondent.

IT IS FURTHER ORDERED AND ADJUDGED that respondent shall forthwith comply with Supreme Court Rule 218 (232 Kan. clxx).

This suspension becomes effective when this opinion is filed with the Clerk of the Supreme Court.

CASE QUESTIONS

1. Would Caenen's solicitation have been viewed differently under the Model Rules?
2. What punishment did Caenen receive? Was this punishment appropriate?

6.8 RECOGNIZING AND RESOLVING ADVERTISING AND SOLICITATION PROBLEMS

You may think that merely ensuring that you are not practicing law without a license will prevent you from having to deal with advertising and solicitation problems, but that is not so. Consider, for example, the very real dilemma you would have to face if you were responsible for ordering stationery and letterhead, issuing a press release, or developing a firm résumé. All of these tasks raise ethical issues. Additionally, many paralegals are freelance individuals who must advertise to secure employment. As previously discussed, the advertising or solicitation that freelance or independent paralegals do should meet or exceed the restrictions placed on attorney advertising in the jurisdiction. Additionally, whether the advertising or solicitation is targeted to attorneys or the general public may affect the restrictions on your marketing campaign. Finally, you must advertise yourself in the form of your résumé, and it is best to see a résumé as a form of advertisement which should conform to ethical standards.

Advertising or solicitation problems come from communications which have as their purpose—whether express or implied—the obtaining of employment. It is important to recognize the wide range of activities that might constitute marketing or business development. It may not strike you as "marketing" if you and your supervising attorney were to teach a course in real estate transactions through a community education program, but because business might be generated from that interaction, ethical considerations on advertising and solicitation would apply. For example, if you passed out a "handout" in class describing how much money you saved each of your past clients, that would be unethical advertising. If you required a visit to your office as a prerequisite to passing the course, that would be unethical solicitation. Take a broad view of the activities that might be construed as advertising or solicitation.

Once you have identified that a communication with possible business ramifications exists, it is best to consider it advertising or solicitation. If it is the former, it is presumed valid, as long as the advertisement is truthful and complies with relevant content requirements. If it is solicitation, in contrast, remember that ethical guidelines are much more stringent and that in-person solicitation for financial gain is generally disfavored.

Finally, as with all the ethical provisions discussed in this text, the recognition of this kind of problem really begins with an internal, personal commitment to maintaining the highest ethical standards in your work. Internalize ethics as the background against which actions are chosen; you will then be able to ask the right questions and pursue ethical choices.

6.9 ADVERTISING AND SOLICITATION: A SUMMARY

Although the legal assistant is prohibited from accepting or declining clients, the issues of advertising and solicitation affect the everyday work of the paralegal. Many communications and actions can be regarded as solicitations; therefore, as with every other action within the legal environment, it is best to think before you speak or act. Follow the general guidelines in this chapter, and remember that any action should conform to advertising guidelines set forth by the jurisdiction in which you practice.

REVIEW QUESTIONS

1. What is the difference between advertising and solicitation?

2. How do the Rules and the Code differ on the issues of advertising and solicitation?

3. How is disclosure of nonlawyer status related to advertising and solicitation?

QUESTIONS FOR THOUGHT AND DISCUSSION

1. Do you believe that legal advertising should be regulated?

2. Are there any reasons that solicitation should not be prohibited or regulated? What are these reasons?

3. Renée Knowles is completing her final year of paralegal studies. Like most students, Renée is eager to earn any extra cash she can. Her neighbor, Randy Street, a lawyer, suggests that Renée go to the police department every Monday and get the names and addresses of individuals who were arrested the past weekend for drunk driving. Randy tells Renée to contact these individuals, recommend him to them, and give them his business card. For every person who hires Randy, he will pay Renée $50. Is this a good way for a future paralegal to get legal experience and earn some extra money?

4. Consider this advertisement:

    Ann Greensprings
    Attorney-at-Law
    Specializing in Tax Appeals
    As a former IRS agent, I can use my influence and expertise to get the best settlement.
    Call 555-1212

    Are there any problems with this ad? Would the Rules find this advertisement acceptable? How about the Code? If there are problems, how can the ad be modified to comply with ethical guidelines?

LAW, LITERATURE, AND ETHICS

From **My Life on Trial**
By Melvin Belli

The San Francisco cops seemed to have the goods on Gertrude Jenkins, an engaging madam who ran a pleasure palace out on Broadway during the 1940's. They had her charged with procuring an abortion for one of her girls, but in order to do so they'd violated about seven of the ten freedoms guaranteed in the Bill of Rights. I could have fought the case on any or all of these counts. But the San Francisco courts weren't buying this kind of defense in the mid-forties and I didn't want to take a client through a lot of appeals if I could avoid it. I countered the law's lawlessness with a glorious flimflam of my own.

I knew that Gertrude Jenkins would have been a terrific witness—against herself—and even if she had survived my questioning, she would have caved in under the Deputy D.A.'s cross-examination. On the other hand, I couldn't let her sit there and refuse to testify. At that time in California, the judge could tell jurors they might infer a person's guilt from his or her failure to take the stand. A judge can't do that anymore. Back then, I jumped the gun for justice. I hit upon a compromise.

After I presented my case, I stood up in court and said, "The defense rests, your Honor. Mrs. Jenkins will not take the stand." I had spent the previous night coaching the woman on her next move. And now in the courtroom, she came across as a real Sarah Bernhardt.

"Wait a minute," she cried, jumping to her feet. "Wait a minute. I want to take the stand. I'm innocent."

"Gert," I said softly (but not so softly the jury couldn't hear me). "We *know* you're innocent. You don't *have* to testify."

Of course, the judge gave his instructions to the jurors that they could infer what they wished about the woman's refusal to take the stand. But the jury had heard the woman say, "I'm innocent." And the

jury had heard me say, "We know you're innocent." And though neither Gertrude nor I was under oath, that's what the jury chose to believe. They found her not guilty. (This is not the procedure I recommend while lecturing to law students when they ask me, "Should the defendant always take the stand in a criminal case?")

Gertrude Jenkins had gotten in trouble with the law in the first place because she'd said too much when the cops arrested her. I wanted to make sure that Molly Regan, a madam who ran a very respectable whorehouse on Green Street not far from Gertrude's place, didn't make the same mistake when she was called before a county grand jury. "Molly," I told her, "you can't say a thing without incriminating yourself. Fortunately, according to the Bill of Rights, you can remain silent."

"Bill Wright?" she said. "Who's Bill Wright? And what kind of pull does he have with the grand jury?" Poor Molly. She was one of the best madams in the City and she knew a lot of people (and the "pull" they could exercise) but she knew very little about the foundations of our freedoms. I tried to explain to her about the Fifth Amendment, the embodiment of an ancient legal principle that no one could accuse himself. "You mean they can't make me talk?" she said.

"Right."

"So I just dummy up?"

"Right."

She couldn't understand that. "Then what's the point of my going before the grand jury?"

"They have a job to do down there. They've got to ask you all the questions." She gave me an uncomprehending look. "Look," I said, "I'll make it simple."

The next day, she appeared before the grand jury with copies of three pamphlets I had given her: the Declaration of Independence, the Constitution, and, for show, the Gettysburg Address. Molly dummied up real good. Each time the Deputy District Attorney asked her a question, she pointed to the three pamphlets and held up five fingers. "You're taking the Fifth?" said the startled young prosecutor. She nodded. Never uttered a word. And was never indicted.

. . . I could never summon up much laughter, however, when I saw an innocent man or woman maimed or crippled by a surgeon's scalpel or a motorist's machine—and then spurned by some thieving insurance company or offered a mere pittance to compensate them for a life of pain ever after. And so, whenever I got the upper hand on an insurance company, I squeezed them—hard. And hang the fine ethical distinctions.

In the case of Irene Kincaid, in the early 1950's, I squeezed so hard the insurance company couldn't get out fast enough. As it turned out, they were a bit too fast for their own good. Mrs. Kincaid had been paralyzed by the maladministration of a spinal anesthetic during childbirth. No trouble proving medical malpractice, and so, in pursuing the suit against Stanford Hospital, I didn't even bother getting a medical expert of my own.

I told the lawyers for the hospital they could give Irene Kincaid every test and examination they thought they needed to verify the facts. Then I took depositions from all of them and found enough discrepancies in their stories to make a good case against each person. I subpoenaed a complete set of the medical records from the hospital, made photostats, added them to the deposition and bound the whole thing into a brochure six inches thick. "Trial by brochure," lawyers call it now.

On the eve of the trial, the case pretty well spoke for itself, and so the defense lawyers offered a settlement of $128,000. They made the offer the very night that Irene Kincaid told me she felt a "tingling" in her right foot. To me, that meant sensation was coming back again; maybe she wouldn't be paralyzed for the rest of her life.

Ethically, what was I to do? Tell the other side that she was on the road to recovery? Not exactly. What I did was tell them that now was the time to get their last and final examination. The defense lawyers imagined that I intended to demonstrate an even more serious injury so I could ask for more money. In this case, my reputation really helped. "No thanks," they said. "We don't want any more examinations. We're satisfied. The point is, are you satisfied with the amount of the settlement?" I certainly was. I took the $128,000, and Irene Kincaid did walk again, though haltingly. For her, $128,000 was not too much—though I'm sure the insurance company would have said it was if they'd known about the "tingling" in her foot—that I offered to let them find out for themselves.

CHAPTER 7
Zealous Representation

CHAPTER OVERVIEW

In this chapter you will learn about the concept of zealous representation of clients by legal professionals. This ethical consideration, although primarily relevant to attorneys, also has important ramifications for the paralegal. This chapter will help you define the limits of zealous representation and determine how to resolve problems involving zealous representation that specifically affect the paralegal.

THE CASE OF THE PRESSURED RENTERS

Sharon is an experienced legal assistant with a firm specializing in real estate litigation. A former real estate agent, Sharon has not only the legal training but also the practical experience to assist her in dealing with problems relating to real estate. Because of her extensive background in real estate and her friendship with the real estate agency that is the firm's primary client, Sharon's supervising attorney, Jan Dawn, lets her have more freedom to work the files than other paralegals in the firm. Sharon is also attending law school in the evenings and has made the highest grade in her class for property.

A client of the firm, Eugene Bodner, contacts Sharon one Friday afternoon and asks for her assistance in a landlord-tenant case. Sharon had drafted, and attorney Dawn had reviewed, the lease that Mr. Bodner used when he leased the property at 323 Plantation Avenue to the Rowans. The lease was for 12 months ending in July of the next year. The Rowans signed the lease only two weeks before Mr. Bodner contacted Sharon again.

According to Mr. Bodner, the Rowans informed him that they were buying a house; they wanted to get out of the lease by the end of the next week. The Rowans agreed to pay for the advertising and legal expenses necessary to secure a new tenant. Mr. Bodner advertised and found new tenants who wanted to move in the following week; however, the Rowans refused to move by that date. The new tenants, Carla and Sophie, have agreed to pay Bodner $500 extra per month for the house. Sharon advises Bodner that, as a paralegal, she cannot give legal advice, but that she will let attorney Dawn know of the problem as soon as she comes back from court.

Once Jan Dawn returns from court, Sharon advises her of the situation. Eugene Bodner is one of the biggest clients for the firm, and Jan knows that if she handles the matter quickly and efficiently, she will get "brownie points" from the partners. Jan tells Sharon to immediately draft a letter to the Rowans, telling them that if they do not move out of the property by midnight of the Monday of the following week, she will have the police arrest them for trespassing. Sharon knows from her extensive experience in real estate that having someone arrested for being on property that they have legitimately leased is not possible. Although Sharon believes that attorney Dawn will be successful in getting the Rowans to move out quickly, she also knows that Jan Dawn's threat of arrest is not a proper remedy for Mr. Bodner's situation.

Has Jan Dawn gone beyond the ethical bounds of zealously representing her client? How about Sharon, if she sends the letter? What would you advise Sharon to do?

THE CASE OF THE QUESTIONABLE RESEARCH

Jane is a legal assistant with a small firm specializing in domestic relations cases. On average, she assists her attorney with approximately 200 divorces a year. Jane has been working on a particularly nasty divorce between Elizabeth and Frank Hansen. Jane's firm represents Elizabeth Hansen.

Elizabeth's husband, Frank Hansen, is represented by Brooke Sendele, an excellent divorce attorney who has been successful in obtaining temporary custody of the Hansen's two children for Frank. A final decree will be entered next week, and it appears that Frank will retain custody of the children and will receive the bulk of the marital assets.

Jane's attorney calls her in and asks her to research which countries of South America do not extradite people for kidnapping. She tells Jane to bill the time to the Hansen case.

Has Jane's attorney gone beyond the bounds of zealous representation? Has Jane committed an ethical violation if she performs the research without questioning its propriety?

7.1 ZEALOUS REPRESENTATION: AN INTRODUCTION

We have all seen it on television, if not in reality: the young, ambitious lawyer who does everything in his or her power to represent the client effectively. The attorney wants to be the best and serve the client's interest as fully and completely as possible. In the attempt to achieve these goals, the attorney may or may not cross the line from the robust, yet ethical, representation of a client to the performance of unethical or illegal acts.

The concept of fervently representing a client's interest is known as *zealous representation*. In fact, the entire adversarial system of law is built upon the idea that if each side is zealously represented, the adversarial process will cause the truth to emerge. Doing everything allowed is a cornerstone of effective (and therefore) ethical representation. However, doing everything allowed is not the same as doing anything and everything you can think of. Even though lawyers are charged with representing their clients zealously, "zealousness" does have limits. The area of ethics concerned with zealous representation articulates those limits.

The essential purpose of limiting what can be done in the name of zealous representation is to eliminate illegal activity and activity which, if not illegal, is unfair and contrary to public policy. Ethical standards require attorneys to represent their clients within the bounds of the law. Traditionally, this has meant that an attorney should not:

1. Advise a client to commit an illegal act
2. File a claim on behalf of a client which the attorney knows to be without merit
3. Conceal that which the attorney is required by law to reveal

4. Knowingly make a false statement of law or fact
5. Knowingly use perjured testimony
6. Fail to reveal contrary authority
7. Knowingly engage in conduct that is contrary to a disciplinary rule
8. Settle a legal claim on behalf of a client without first obtaining proper authorization.

The ethical considerations affecting a client's representation attempt to ensure that not only illegal actions, but also unfair actions will not corrupt the process of justice. These considerations limit, among other things, communications with those holding adverse interests; threatening criminal prosecution; conduct at trial or conduct concerning trial publicity; and communications with jurors, witnesses, or court officials. The court's concern is that all the participants in the legal process be playing on a level field. To be sure, lawyers compete on this field, and they compete to win. Sometimes they try very hard yet remain within proper ethical bounds. Sometimes, in the effort to do whatever it takes to have a client win, they go beyond the bounds of what is acceptable to the legal profession.

THE CASE OF THE TEMPTING SETTLEMENT

Attorney Vicki and her legal assistant Marcy have worked together for 20 years, representing plaintiffs in personal injury and worker's compensation cases. They are also friends who care deeply about each other.

They await the arrival of client Michelle, who will be informed that the insurance company they are suing is offering a settlement of $60,000 in her case. Marcy knows that Vicki is under a great deal of financial pressure at the present time and could really use her share of the settlement right now, if only Michelle would decide to settle. She also knows that it would take a year or two to go to trial, but that the trial award could well be closer to $200,000. Waiting in their offices for the client to arrive, Vicki reminds Marcy of the need for some immediate income, and tells Marcy that she will give Marcy a $1,000 bonus if she helps Michelle decide to settle.

When Michelle comes into the office, she learns of the proposed settlement offer. When Michelle asks Marcy what she thinks, Marcy tells her that $60,000 is a lot of money and that it would be hard to get that much at trial. She also tells Michelle that it would be great to have the whole thing over with.

Have Vicki and Marcy acted unethically?

A metaphor that fairly well illustrates the idea of zealous representation is that the attorney need not show his entire hand of cards, but must make sure he has not marked the deck. Although an attorney is like a film director in many respects, unlike the director, the lawyer cannot create new dialogue or change the set on a whim. Although winning is important, the greater goal is that justice be served, and justice cannot be served if one of the parties is not playing fairly.

THE CASE OF TOMMY TESTOSTERONE

Attorney Tommy Testosterone is a dashing, eligible bachelor in Dallas who is known as the keenest defender of father's rights in divorce cases. His client, Donald Plump, wants Tommy to get whatever information he can from Irene Plump, his ex-to-be, so that Donald will get custody of their children. Donald also tells Tommy that Irene loves cocaine.

Tommy goes to his contact on the police force and gets some cocaine from the "confiscated materials" department. He visits Irene, and she enjoys both the cocaine and Tommy. In the course of their intimacy, Irene reveals some details which are very damaging to her credibility as a mother. Tommy figures he can use those later if he needs them. After he leaves, he tips his police pal as to the whereabouts of Irene's cocaine, so she gets arrested for possession. That should help Donald get custody of the kids!

Has Tommy been too zealous? If so, what punishment should he receive?

7.2 ZEALOUSNESS AND FRIVOLOUSNESS

Two important safeguards against the proliferation of frivolous law-suits are the tort of *malicious prosecution,* also called *abusive litigation,* and Rule 11 of the Federal Rules of Civil Procedure. These two mechanisms attempt to ensure that litigation is initiated in good faith and for an ethical purpose.

The tort of malicious prosecution (abusive litigation) provides a cause of action against those who use the legal system to harass, intimidate, or injure another. As you are aware, legal proceedings are stressful and expensive; in some instances, a person or organization might try to win by misusing the legal system and initiating unnecessary litigation. This type of activity crosses the line from zealous behavior to tortious behavior.

Rule 11 of the Federal Rules of Civil Procedure, and analogous state rules, state that when an attorney signs a pleading, he is indicating that the pleading is being filed in good faith to legally assist his case, not merely to harass or annoy the opposing party. For example, filing a complaint against a neighbor to convince her to move, knowing there is no legal basis for the action, is a violation of this rule. Violation of this rule is grounds for attorney discipline, either through a contempt of court citation, a fine, or an order to pay the opposing party's legal fees.

"Oh, no! I forgot to tell Investigator Graves to intimidate Juror No. 4!"

These two causes of action function as ethical assurances that a lawsuit will be based on an authentic dispute; they safeguard the legal system from being used oppressively, as a means of intimidation and harassment, rather than as a means of enforcing the law and achieving justice.

7.3 RULES AND GUIDELINES CONCERNING ZEALOUS REPRESENTATION

ABA Model Rules

The guidelines for advocacy and zealous representation of clients are defined in several sections of Rule 3 in the Model Rules.

DR 2-109 Acceptance of Employment.

(A)   A lawyer shall not accept employment on behalf of a person if he knows or it is obvious that such person wishes to:

(1)   Bring a legal action, conduct a defense, or assert a position in litigation, or otherwise have steps taken for him, merely for the purpose of harassing or maliciously injuring any person.

(2)   Present a claim or defense in litigation that is not warranted under existing law, unless it can be supported by good faith argument for an extension, modification, or reversal of existing law.

Rule 3.1 requires that the attorney bring only meritorious claims that are not frivolous.

RULE 3.1 Meritorious Claims and Contentions

A lawyer shall not bring or defend a proceeding, or assert or controvert an issue therein, unless there is a basis for doing so that is not frivolous, which includes a good faith argument for an extension, modification or reversal of existing law. A lawyer for the defendant in a criminal proceeding, or the respondent in a proceeding that could result in incarceration, may nevertheless so defend the proceeding as to require that every element of the case be established.

The Comments following this Rule emphasize that legal proceedings are to be used to assist the client to the fullest extent possible, but not to abuse the process. Further, the Comments elaborate on what is and is not frivolous litigation. For example, a claim is not frivolous merely because the facts have not been fully developed or substantiated before filing the complaint. Nor is a case frivolous if the attorney is fairly certain that the client is unlikely to prevail. Rather, frivolous actions are those filed primarily to harass or maliciously injure the opposing party; it is also frivolous to file a claim for which the attorney cannot make a good faith argument on the merits of the action or an argument to extend, modify, or reverse existing law on the issue.

Rule 3.2 prohibits dilatory practices by attorneys, requiring them to move forward with litigation as expeditiously as possible.

RULE 3.2 Expediting Litigation

A lawyer shall make reasonable efforts to expedite litigation consistent with the interests of the client.

The Comments to Rule 3.2 explain that delaying proceedings to result in financial or other benefit is not legitimate. Thus, delay should not be requested for the convenience of the lawyers or to frustrate the opposing party's attempt to obtain rightful redress or repose. Therefore, delaying proceedings must be for some substantial purpose and must be in good faith.

Rule 3.3 defines the lawyer's duty of candor to the tribunal. It prohibits making false statements of material facts or law, failing to disclose a material fact relevant to a criminal or fraudulent act, failing to reveal contrary authority, and presenting evidence known to be false.

RULE 3.3 Candor Toward the Tribunal

(a) A lawyer shall not knowingly:
   (1) make a false statement of material fact or law to a tribunal;

(2) fail to disclose a material fact to a tribunal when disclosure is necessary to avoid assisting a criminal or fraudulent act by the client;

(3) fail to disclose to the tribunal legal authority in the controlling jurisdiction known to the lawyer to be directly adverse to the position of the client and not disclosed by opposing counsel; or

(4) offer evidence that the lawyer knows to be false. If a lawyer has offered material evidence and comes to know of its falsity, the lawyer shall take reasonable remedial measures.

(b) The duties stated in paragraph (a) continue to the conclusion of the proceeding, and apply even if compliance requires disclosure of information otherwise protected by Rule 1.6.

(c) A lawyer may refuse to offer evidence that the lawyer reasonably believes is false.

(d) In an ex parte proceeding, a lawyer shall inform the tribunal of all material facts known to the lawyer which will enable the tribunal to make an informed decision, whether or not the facts are adverse.

Comments following Rule 3.3 state that an advocate's duty to be persuasive must be tempered by the duty to maintain candor toward the tribunal, even when a client's confidences are involved. Thus, if a client tells the attorney she is going to commit perjury, the lawyer, under this rule, would have a duty to offer the client's testimony into the record and may even have a duty to reveal the intended perjury to the tribunal.

Rule 3.4 defines permissible behaviors toward opposing parties or counsel.

RULE 3.4 Fairness to Opposing Party and Counsel

A lawyer shall not:

(a) unlawfully obstruct another party's access to evidence or unlawfully alter, destroy or conceal a document or other material having potential evidentiary value. A lawyer shall not counsel or assist another person to do any such act;

(b) falsify evidence, counsel or assist a witness to testify falsely, or offer an inducement to a witness that is prohibited by law;

(c) knowingly disobey an obligation under the rules of a tribunal except for an open refusal based on an assertion that no valid obligation exists;

(d) in pretrial procedure, make a frivolous discovery request or fail to make reasonably diligent effort to comply with a legally proper discovery request by an opposing party;

(e) in trial, allude to any matter that the lawyer does not reasonably believe is relevant or that will not be supported by admissible evidence, assert personal knowledge of facts in issue except when testifying as a witness, or state a personal opinion as to the justness of a cause, the credibility of a witness, the culpability of a civil litigant or the guilt or innocence of an accused; or

(f) request a person other than a client to refrain from voluntarily giving relevant information to another party unless:

(1) the person is a relative or an employee or other agent of a client; and

(2) the lawyer reasonably believes that the person's interests will not be adversely affected by refraining from giving such information.

Comments to Rule 3.4 provide that fair competition in the adversarial process does not mean that one may destroy or conceal evidence, improperly influence witnesses, or use destructive tactics in the discovery process.

Rule 3.5 prohibits improper or disruptive behavior in a courtroom.

RULE 3.5 Impartiality and Decorum of the Tribunal

A lawyer shall not:

(a) seek to influence a judge, juror, prospective juror or other official by means prohibited by law;

(b) communicate ex parte with such a person except as permitted by law; or

(c) engage in conduct intended to disrupt a tribunal.

Because an advocate's job is to present evidence and argument in court, the advocate must refrain from offensive and abusive conduct.

THE CASE OF THE EXCITED UTTERANCE

Attorney Lara and her legal assistant Leif are representing attorney Roxanne Watson, who is suing the law firm of Lynch & McCall for sexual discrimination. At trial, Lara calls Keith McCall, the managing partner of the law firm.

"Isn't it true that you consider your own wife a second-class citizen, verbally and physically abusing her to the point that she attempted suicide?" Lara queries, even though she knows this allegation to be unprovable.

"Objection!" cries the defense. "We call for a mistrial, Your Honor."

"This whole thing is a mistrial," screams Lara. The jurors perk up at this heated exchange. "The judge is a notorious sexist, and he knows it's true that all the defense witnesses are in collusion to prevent my client from advancing because she is a woman!"

Has Lara gone beyond the bounds of zealous representation? What if Lara's allegations were true?

Finally, Rule 3.6, concerning trial publicity, defines the types of extrajudicial statements which are and are not appropriate for counsel to make.

Those statements which the Comments to the Rule designate as appropriate are those intended to protect the public and general public concerns. Publicity for its own sake is not condoned. However, the Comments recognize that certain confidentiality and closed proceedings may be necessary in juvenile, domestic, and mental disability proceedings.

RULE 3.6 Trial Publicity

(a) A lawyer shall not make an extrajudicial statement that a reasonable person would expect to be disseminated by means of public communication if the lawyer knows or reasonably should know that it will have a substantial likelihood of materially prejudicing an adjudicative proceeding.

(b) A statement referred to in paragraph (a) ordinarily is likely to have such an effect when it refers to a civil matter triable to a jury, a criminal matter, or any other proceeding that could result in incarceration, and the statement relates to:

(1) the character, credibility, reputation or criminal record of a party, suspect in a criminal investigation or witness, or the identity of a witness, or the expected testimony of a party or witness;

(2) in a criminal case or proceeding that could result in incarceration, the possibility of a plea of guilty to the offense or the existence or contents of any confession, admission, or statement given by a defendant or suspect or that person's refusal or failure to make a statement;

(3) the performance or results of any examination or test or the refusal or failure of a person to submit to an examination or test, or the identity or nature of physical evidence expected to be presented;

(4) any opinion as to the guilt or innocence of a defendant or suspect in a criminal case or proceeding that could result in incarceration;

(5) information the lawyer knows or reasonably should know is likely to be inadmissible as evidence in a trial and would if disclosed create a substantial risk of prejudicing an impartial trial; or

(6) the fact that a defendant has been charged with a crime, unless there is included therein a statement explaining that the charge is merely an accusation and that the defendant is presumed innocent until and unless proven guilty.

(c) Notwithstanding paragraph (a) and (b)(1-5), a lawyer involved in the investigation or litigation of a matter may state without elaboration:

(1) the general nature of the claim or defense;

(2) the information contained in a public record.

(3) that an investigation of the matter is in progress, including the general scope of the investigation, the offense or claim or defense involved and, except when prohibited by law, the identity of the persons involved;

(4) the scheduling or result of any step in litigation;

(5)   a request for assistance in obtaining evidence and information necessary thereto;

(6)   a warning of danger concerning the behavior of a person involved, when there is reason to believe that there exists the likelihood of substantial harm to an individual or to the public interest; and

(7)   in a criminal case:

(i)   the identity, residence, occupation and family status of the accused;

(ii)   if the accused has not been apprehended, information necessary to aid in apprehension of that person;

(iii)   the fact, time and place of arrest; and

(iv)   the identity of investigating and arresting officers or agencies and the length of the investigation.

RULE 4.1   Truthfulness in Statements to Others

In the course of representing a client a lawyer shall not knowingly:

(a)   make a false statement of material fact or law to a third person; or

(b)   fail to disclose a material fact to a third person when disclosure is necessary to avoid assisting a criminal or fraudulent act by a client, unless disclosure is prohibited by Rule 1.6.

RULE 4.2   Communication with Person Represented by Counsel

In representing a client, a lawyer shall not communicate about the subject of the representation with a party the lawyer knows to be represented by another lawyer in the matter, unless the lawyer has the consent of the other lawyer or is authorized by law to do so.

RULE 4.3   Dealing with Unrepresented Person

In dealing on behalf of a client with a person who is not represented by counsel, a lawyer shall not state or imply that the lawyer is disinterested. When the lawyer knows or reasonably should know that the unrepresented person misunderstands the lawyer's role in the matter, the lawyer shall make reasonable efforts to correct the misunderstanding.

RULE 4.4   Respect for Rights of Third Persons

In representing a client, a lawyer shall not use means that have no substantial purpose other than to embarrass, delay, or burden a third person, or use methods of obtaining evidence that violate the legal rights of such a person.

ABA Model Code

The Model Rules concerning zealous representation do not represent a major departure from the Code of Professional Responsibility. Canon 7 of the Code states unequivocally that "A Lawyer Should Represent a Client Zealously Within the Bounds of the Law." Naturally, this statement might be interpreted differently by different people, so the Disciplinary Rules following that Canon deal with specific conduct that goes beyond the realm of zealous representation. Specifically, DR 7-101 precludes an attorney from:

1. Failing to seek the lawful objectives of a client through reasonably available means, but the attorney shall accede to reasonable requests of opposing counsel, be punctual in fulfilling all professional commitments, avoid offensive tactics, and treat others with courtesy

2. Failing to carry out the employment contract with the client unless the attorney properly withdraws

3. Prejudicing or damaging the client during the course of the professional relationship.

DR 7-101   Representing a Client Zealously.

(A)   A lawyer shall not intentionally:

(1)   Fail to seek the lawful objectives of his client through reasonably available means permitted by law and the Disciplinary Rules, except as provided by DR 7-101(B). A lawyer does not violate this Disciplinary Rule, however, by acceding to reasonable requests of opposing counsel which do not prejudice the rights of his client, by being punctual in fulfilling all professional commitments, by avoiding offensive tactics, or by treating with courtesy and consideration all persons involved in the legal process.

(2)   Fail to carry out a contract of employment entered into with a client for professional services, but he may withdraw as permitted under DR 2-110, DR 5-102, and DR 5-105.

(3)   Prejudice or damage his client during the course of the professional relationship except as required under DR 7-102(B).

(B)   In his representation of a client, a lawyer may:

(1)   Where permissible, exercise his professional judgment to waive or fail to assert a right or position of his client.

(2)   Refuse to aid or participate in conduct that he believes to be unlawful, even though there is some support for an argument that the conduct is legal.

However, this Disciplinary Rule does permit an attorney to exercise her professional judgment to waive, or fail to assert, a claim and to refuse to participate in conduct which she believes to be unlawful, even if there is some support for the argument that the conduct is legal.

DR 7-102 specifies the types of representation that are outside the bounds of the law.

DR 7-102 Representing a Client Within the Bounds of the Law.

(A)   In his representation of a client, a lawyer shall not:

(1)   File a suit, assert a position, conduct a defense, delay a trial, or take other action on behalf of his client when he knows or when it is obvious that such action would serve merely to harass or maliciously injure another.

(2)   Knowingly advance a claim or defense that is unwarranted under existing law, except that he may advance such claim or defense it if can be supported by good faith argument for an extension, modification, or reversal of existing law.

(3)   Conceal or knowingly fail to disclose that which he is required by law to reveal.

(4)   Knowingly use perjured testimony or false evidence.

(5)   Knowingly make a false statement of law or fact.

(6)   Participate in the creation or preservation of evidence when he knows or it is obvious that the evidence is false.

(7)   Counsel or assist his client in conduct that the lawyer knows to be illegal or fraudulent.

(8)   Knowingly engage in other illegal conduct or conduct contrary to a Disciplinary Rule.

(B)   A lawyer who receives information clearly establishing that:

(1)   His client has, in the course of the representation, perpetrated a fraud upon a person or tribunal shall promptly call upon his client to rectify the same, and if his client refuses or is unable to do so, he shall reveal the fraud to the affected person or tribunal, except when the information is protected as a privileged communication.

(2)   A person other than his client has perpetrated a fraud upon a tribunal shall promptly reveal the fraud to the tribunal.

Conduct in violation of the Disciplinary Rules includes filing a suit or pursuing a defense merely to harass another party; and knowingly advancing a claim or defense unwarranted under existing law, unless the claim is supported by a good faith argument for an extension or modification of existing law. It is also improper to conceal that which the law requires an attorney to reveal, to knowingly use perjured testimony or evidence, or to knowingly make a false statement of law or fact. An attorney or his agent is also prohibited from creating or preserving evidence which he knows is false. This disciplinary rule precludes a lawyer from counseling her client to commit some fraudulent act or engage in illegal conduct or conduct prohibited by a Disciplinary Rule.

A significant but often abused area is the settling of a claim or dispute without prior authorization from the client. Attorneys often believe that they know what is best for the client and therefore settle claims for sums which the client has not authorized. The best practice is for the attorney to obtain the client's authority to settle in writing before accepting any settlement.

This Disciplinary Rule also requires an attorney to report any fraud that a client or other person may try to effect upon a tribunal. The issue of client perjury is covered by this rule, and it is an extremely complex and important area. In general, if an attorney in a civil case knows that his client is about to commit perjury, he should not call the client as a witness. Some jurisdictions recommend or require withdrawal or disclosure, but most adhere to the general rule. In criminal cases, withdrawal is appropriate because constitutional law grants criminal defendants an absolute right to testify.

 ## THE CASE OF THE NEW LEASE ON LIFE

Paralegal Rita is the head paralegal for Attorney Lanning, who specializes in criminal defense work. Rita, who is half Sioux, has been particularly active in Native American law, and has worked with Lanning on the defense of several Native Americans.

Their newest criminal client is Half Moon River, who has been charged with murder. Rita's preliminary investigation has unearthed the very real possibility that Half Moon is being framed by government officials, but she is concerned that a jury will be swayed against Half Moon by prejudice and by some incriminating, though circumstantial, evidence. As an expert in Native American law, Rita is aware of a little-known provision which will remove Half Moon from that jurisdiction into a tribal jurisdiction, where it is likely that he will be found innocent, as she believes him to be. The requirement for the change in jurisdiction is that Half Moon be a resident of a Native American reservation for 90 days prior to the filing of the indictment—and Rita's friend Kim can rent Half Moon an apartment on an approved reservation and have the lease backdated. This would enable Half Moon to be tried in the more favorable jurisdiction.

Should Rita tell Half Moon to call Kim? Should Rita tell attorney Lanning of her plan?

DR 7-103 applies specifically to prosecuting attorneys and governmental attorneys.

DR 7-103 Performing the Duty of Public Prosecutor or Other Government Lawyer.

(A)   A public prosecutor or other government lawyer shall not institute or cause to be instituted criminal charges when he knows or it is obvious that the charges are not supported by probable cause.

(B) A public prosecutor or other government lawyer in criminal litigation shall make timely disclosure to counsel for the defendant, or to the defendant if he has no counsel, of the existence of evidence, known to the prosecutor or other government lawyer, that tends to negate the guilt of the accused, mitigate the degree of the offense, or reduce the punishment.

Basically, this disciplinary rule forbids a prosecuting attorney from pursuing any criminal charges that the attorney feels lack probable cause. Likewise, DR 7-107 specifies the type of information an attorney may disseminate to the public during the course of a criminal proceeding. This Disciplinary Rule tries to preserve the concept that a criminal defendant is innocent until proven guilty by ensuring that unnecessary and potentially prejudicial information will not be given to the general public via the media.

Of all of the disciplinary rules pertaining to zealous representation, probably the most important is DR 7-104.

DR 7-104 Communicating With One of Adverse Interest.

(A) During the course of his representation of a client a lawyer shall not:

(1) Communicate or cause another to communicate on the subject of the representation with a party he knows to be represented by a lawyer in that matter unless he has the prior consent of the lawyer representing such other party or is authorized by law to do so.

(2) Give advice to a person who is not represented by a lawyer, other than the advice to secure counsel, if the interests of such person are or have a reasonable possibility of being in conflict with the interests of his client.

This disciplinary rule deals with communications with one having an adverse interest. Essentially, this rule prohibits an attorney from speaking to a person having an interest contrary to that of the attorney's client (unless the other party's attorney consents). In some jurisdictions, this prior consent must be in writing. Further, if a party having an adverse interest has no legal counsel, the attorney cannot give that party legal advice except for the advice to seek representation. These rules are designed to give all parties a level playing field, whether represented by counsel or not. If one party is represented and the other not represented by counsel, it would be very easy for an attorney to manipulate the process and take unfair advantage of the unrepresented party.

DR 7-105 complements DR 7-104; it precludes an attorney from threatening criminal charges when the only reason for the threat is to gain an unfair advantage in a civil matter.

DR 7-105 Threatening Criminal Prosecution.

(A) A lawyer shall not present, participate in presenting or threaten to present criminal charges solely to obtain an advantage in a civil matter.

For example, the issue might arise in a domestic relations context. If the attorney represents a client who has custody of minor children, and the opposing spouse comes for visitation but fails to return the children, then the lawyer can probably threaten criminal prosecution for kidnapping. In contrast, in the same domestic relations scenario, an attorney could not threaten the opposing spouse with charges of child molestation just to help his own client obtain custody of the children.

The other Disciplinary Rules in this section deal with zealous representation during trial. DR 7-106 is the primary rule dealing with trial conduct. It specifies conduct during trial that would be regarded as unethical.

DR 7-106 Trial Conduct.

(A) A lawyer shall not disregard or advise his client to disregard a standing rule of a tribunal or a ruling of a tribunal made in the course of a proceeding, but he may take appropriate steps in good faith to test the validity of such rule or ruling.

(B) In presenting a matter to a tribunal, a lawyer shall disclose:

(1) Legal authority in the controlling jurisdiction known to him to be directly adverse to the position of his client and which is not disclosed by opposing counsel.

(2) Unless privileged or irrelevant, the identities of the clients he represents and of the persons who employed him.

(C) In appearing in his professional capacity before a tribunal, a lawyer shall not:

(1) State or allude to any matter that he has no reasonable basis to believe is relevant to the case or that will not be supported by admissible evidence.

(2) Ask any question that he has no reasonable basis to believe is relevant to the case and that is intended to degrade a witness or other person.

(3) Assert his personal knowledge of the facts in issue, except when testifying as a witness.

(4) Assert his personal opinion as to the justness of a cause, as to the credibility of a witness, as to the culpability of a civil litigant, or as to the guilt or innocence of an accused; but he may argue, on his analysis of the evidence, for any position or conclusion with respect to the matters stated herein.

(5) Fail to comply with known local customs of courtesy or practice of the bar or a particular tribunal without giving to opposing counsel timely notice of his intent not to comply.

(6) Engage in undignified or discourteous conduct which is degrading to a tribunal.

(7) Intentionally or habitually violate any established rule of procedure or of evidence.

The rules in this section recognize that an attorney not only is responsible to her client and to the general public, but also is an officer of the court. As an officer of the court, the attorney must follow certain established guidelines to ensure that justice is maintained.

DR 7-107 deals specifically with communicating to the media during the investigation of a criminal matter. It is especially applicable to the prosecutor.

DR 7-107 Trial Publicity.

(A) A lawyer participating in or associated with the investigation of a criminal matter shall not make or participate in making an extrajudicial statement that a reasonable person would expect to be disseminated by means of public communication and that does more than state without elaboration:

(1) Information contained in a public record.

(2) That the investigation is in progress.

(3) The general scope of the investigation including a description of the offense and, if permitted by law, the identity of the victim.

(4) A request for assistance in apprehending a suspect or assistance in other matters and the information necessary thereto.

(5) A warning to the public of any dangers.

(B) A lawyer or law firm associated with the prosecution or defense of a criminal matter shall not, from the time of the filing of a complaint, information, or indictment, the issuance of an arrest warrant, or arrest until the commencement of the trial or disposition without trial, make or participate in making an extrajudicial statement that a reasonable person would expect to be disseminated by means of public communication and that relates to:

(1) The character, reputation, or prior criminal record (including arrests, indictments, or other charges of crime) of the accused.

(2) The possibility of a plea of guilty to the offense charged or to a lesser offense.

(3) The existence or contents of any confession, admission, or statement given by the accused or his refusal or failure to make a statement.

(4) The performance or results of any examinations or tests or the refusal or failure of the accused to submit to examination or tests.

(5) The identity, testimony, or credibility of a prospective witness.

(6) Any opinion as to the guilt or innocence of the accused, the evidence, or the merits of the case.

(C) DR 7-107(B) does not preclude a lawyer during such period from announcing:

(1) The name, age, residence, occupation, and family status of the accused.

(2) If the accused has not been apprehended, any information necessary to aid in his apprehension or to warn the public of any dangers he may present.

(3) A request for assistance in obtaining evidence.

(4) The identity of the victim of the crime.

(5) The fact, time, and place of arrest, resistance, pursuit, and use of weapons.

(6) The identity of investigating and arresting officers or agencies and the length of the investigation.

(7) At the time of seizure, a description of the physical evidence seized, other than a confession, admission, or statement.

(8) The nature, substance, or text of the charge.

(9) Quotations from or references to public records of the court in the case.

(10) The scheduling or result of any step in the judicial proceedings.

(11) That the accused denies the charges made against him.

(D) During the selection of a jury or the trial of a criminal matter, a lawyer or law firm associated with the prosecution or defense of a criminal matter shall not make or participate in making an extra-judicial statement that a reasonable person would expect to be disseminated by means of public communication and that relates to the trial, parties, or issues in the trial or other matters that are reasonably likely to interfere with a fair trial, except that he may quote from or refer without comment to public records of the court in the case.

(E) After the completion of a trial or disposition without trial of a criminal matter and prior to the imposition of sentence, a lawyer or law firm associated with the prosecution or defense shall not make or participate in making an extra-judicial statement that a reasonable person would expect to be disseminated by public communication and that is reasonably likely to affect the imposition of sentence.

(F) The foregoing provisions of DR 7-107 also apply to professional disciplinary proceedings and juvenile disciplinary proceedings when pertinent and consistent with other law applicable to such proceedings.

(G) A lawyer or law firm associated with a civil action shall not during its investigation or litigation make or participate in making an extra-judicial statement, other than a quotation from or reference to public records, that a reasonable person would expect to be disseminated by means of public communication and that relates to:

(1) Evidence regarding the occurrence or transaction involved.

(2) The character, credibility, or criminal record of a party, witness, or prospective witness.

(3) The performance or results of any examinations or tests or the refusal or failure of a party to submit to such.

(4) His opinion as to the merits of the claims or defenses of a party, except as required by law or administrative rule.

(5) Any other matter reasonably likely to interfere with a fair trial of the action.

(H) During the pendency of an administrative proceeding, a lawyer or law firm associated therewith shall not make or participate in making a statement, other than a quotation from or reference to public records, that a reasonable person would expect to be disseminated by means of public communication if it is made outside the official course of the proceeding and relates to:

(1) Evidence regarding the occurrence or transaction involved.

(2) The character, credibility, or criminal record of a party, witness, or prospective witness.

(3) Physical evidence or the performance or results of any examinations or tests or the refusal or failure of a party to submit to such.

(4) His opinion as to the merits of the claims, defenses, or positions of an interested person.

(5) Any other matter reasonably likely to interfere with a fair hearing.

(I) The foregoing provisions of DR 7-107 do not preclude a lawyer from replying to charges of misconduct publicly made against him or from participating in the proceedings of legislative, administrative, or other investigative bodies.

(J) A lawyer shall exercise reasonable care to prevent his employees and associates from making an extra-judicial statement that he would be prohibited from making under DR 7-107.

The rule prohibits an attorney from providing any information to the media except: information contained in the public record (i.e., the indictment); that an investigation is in progress; the general scope of the investigation and the specific crime; the identity of the victim, if permitted by law (most jurisdictions forbid the identification of a rape victim—however, recall the William Kennedy Smith trial!); request for assistance in apprehending the suspect; and a warning to the public of any dangers. As you can see, this Disciplinary Rule helps maintain the basic premise of American criminal law: that the accused is innocent until proven guilty. Section (B) specifies what information an attorney can release from the point of the issuance of an arrest warrant or arrest until the commencement of the trial or disposition without trial. Section (G) of DR 7-107 deals with civil litigation conduct and defines the statements that attorneys in civil matters are prohibited from making.

Section (H) of DR 7-107 specifies forbidden conduct in an administrative setting. Paralegals should be aware that Section (J) of DR 7-107 applies to them directly. This section reads: "A lawyer shall exercise reasonable care to prevent his employees and associates from making an extrajudicial statement that he would be prohibited from making under DR 7-107." The attorney cannot use paralegals to do something which the attorney is ethically precluded from doing. Thus, an attorney cannot ask a paralegal to talk to a potential juror when he himself cannot. Think about this obligation; what would you do if an employer asked you to do something you knew was prohibited? By considering now what your response might be, you will be better able to handle such a difficult situation if it happens in reality.

DR 7-108, dealing with jurors, and DR 7-110, dealing with officials, are written to prevent an attorney from unduly influencing either.

DR 7-108 Communication with or Investigation of Jurors.

(A) Before the trial of a case a lawyer connected therewith shall not communicate with or cause another to communicate with anyone he knows to be a member of the venire from which the jury will be selected for the trial of the case.

(B) During the trial of a case:

(1) A lawyer connected therewith shall not communicate with or cause another to communicate with any member of the jury.

(2) A lawyer who is not connected therewith shall not communicate with or cause another to communicate with a juror concerning the case.

(C) DR 7-108(A) and (B) do not prohibit a lawyer from communicating with veniremen or jurors in the course of official proceedings.

(D) After discharge of the jury from further consideration of a case with which the lawyer was connected, the lawyer shall not ask questions of or make comments to a member of that jury that are calculated merely to harass or embarrass the juror or to influence his actions in future jury service.

(E) A lawyer shall not conduct or cause, by financial support or otherwise, another to conduct a vexatious or harassing investigation of either a venireman or a juror.

(F) All restrictions imposed by DR 7-108 upon a lawyer also apply to communications with or investigations of members of a family of a venireman or a juror.

(G) A lawyer shall reveal promptly to the court improper conduct by a venireman or a juror, or by another toward a venireman or a juror or a member of his family, of which the lawyer has knowledge.

DR 7-110 Contact with Officials.

(A) A lawyer shall not give or lend any thing of value to a judge, official, or employee of a tribunal, except as permitted by Section C(4) of Canon 5 of the Code of Judicial Conduct, but a lawyer may make a contribution to the campaign fund of a candidate for judicial office in conformity with Section B(2) under Canon 7 of the Code of Judicial Conduct.

(B) In an adversary proceeding, a lawyer shall not communicate, or cause another to communicate, as to the merits of the cause with a judge or an official before whom the proceeding is pending, except:

(1) In the course of official proceedings in the cause.

(2) In writing if he promptly delivers a copy of the writing to opposing counsel or to the adverse party if he is not represented by a lawyer.

(3) Orally upon adequate notice to opposing counsel or to the adverse party if he is not represented by a lawyer.

(4) As otherwise authorized by law, or by Section A(4) under Canon 3 of the Code of Judicial Conduct.

For example, the lawyer cannot bribe either the juror or the official to obtain an unfair advantage.

The best rules for the paralegal to follow to comply with these ethical provisions are:

1. *Never* talk to a juror, except in certain limited circumstances at the end of a trial.
2. *Never* talk to an official, such as a judge, about the merits of a case except when asked in the course of official proceedings, such as a trial.

DR 7-109 deals with witnesses.

DR 7-109 Contact with Witnesses.

(A) A lawyer shall not suppress any evidence that he or his client has a legal obligation to reveal or produce.

(B) A lawyer shall not advise or cause a person to secrete himself or to leave the jurisdiction of a tribunal for the purpose of making him unavailable as a witness therein.

(C) A lawyer shall not pay, offer to pay, or acquiesce in the payment of compensation to a witness contingent upon the content of his testimony or the outcome of the case. But a lawyer may advance, guarantee, or acquiesce in the payment of:

(1) Expenses reasonably incurred by a witness in attending or testifying.

(2) Reasonable compensation to a witness for his loss of time in attending or testifying.

(3) A reasonable fee for the professional services of an expert witness.

It is especially important for the paralegal to understand this rule, because many times legal assistants are involved in interviewing witnesses for a case. The basic principle is to avoid influencing a witness and avoid putting words into the witness's mouth. The practical way to avoid such situations is to let the witness tell the story before you start asking questions.

NALA and NFPA

None of the provisions of either the NALA's Code of Ethics or the NFPA's Affirmation of Professional Responsibility deals directly with zealous representation. However, as previously discussed, both the Code and the Affirmation require the legal assistant to uphold ethical principles such as those contained in the Code of Professional Responsibility for Attorneys.

THE CASE OF THE DEFENSE TEAM'S DILEMMA

Attorney Klauber and paralegal Maartens are representing the Riverdale Corporation in a shareholder's derivative suit. Lasalla Lamberton, the CEO of the corporation, tells the attorney that when he met with the stockholders, contrary to their allegations, they told him to sell the successful subsidiary in question. Lasalla tells Klauber and Maartens that Tom Stanback, the senior vice president, was present during this meeting and heard the shareholders demand that the subsidiary be sold. In fact, Stanback was not present at the meeting, a fact that attorney Klauber later learned.

Stanback tells Klauber that he was at the meeting, with his buddies Moose Mignocchi and "Quick" John Kao, and that he should interview his friends and bring them to court to testify. Klauber is suspicious of this possible testimony and sends Maartens to investigate. Maartens learns that Mignocchi and Kao are planning to lie at the trial—they had not really been with Stanback at the meeting. When she reports this information to Klauber, Klauber decides not to call Mignocchi and Kao at trial, over the protest of his client. Klauber also does not make a motion to withdraw as counsel.

Lasalla is found liable. Lasalla files an appeal of the jury verdict, alleging that he was denied zealous representation because Klauber did not call the corroborating witnesses. Lasalla argues that the jury should have been allowed to decide whether the witnesses were lying, and that his lawyer had the obligation of at least bringing the witnesses forward.

Was Klauber's decision not to call the witnesses the correct ethical choice, or did he betray the client by refusing to represent him as zealously as possible?

7.4 ZEALOUS REPRESENTATION AND THE PARALEGAL

The issues concerning zealous representation affect the paralegal in numerous ways, because paralegals perform many activities on behalf of clients, some of which require interaction with opposing counsel or witnesses. Additionally, the paralegal usually interacts extensively with clients, speaking to them and informing them of the status of their cases. In some firms, paralegals are the first individuals to whom a potential client speaks; therefore, it is of the utmost importance for legal assistants to realize how far legal representation can go. Even though legal assistants do not actually legally represent clients, they serve the attorney in that representation. Also, many paralegals are responsible for interviewing clients prior to trial, and so must be aware how much can be said to a potential witness. Saying or doing the wrong thing with a potential witness can lead to accusations of tampering with evidence.

Every paralegal, whether involved in litigation, real estate, or another legal area, must constantly contact individuals who have interests contrary to the client's interests. Hence, it is vital that the legal assistant know how to protect the client's interests and obtain information without jeopardizing any advantages the client may have. Because of these many and varied opportunities for application of the doctrine of zealous representation, the concept applies to legal assistants just as much as it does to the attorney.

One particularly important application of the doctrine of zealous representation for paralegals concerns abuses of the discovery process. Discovery is an integral part of litigation and is intended to help both the plaintiffs and the defendants gather the facts relevant and necessary to present an effective case. Sometimes this process is abused. Discovery is an expensive process; sometimes issuing excessive discovery requests can cause a party to settle a case because it is financially unable to respond to discovery. Only discovery that is necessary and tailored to the facts of the case should be propounded. Discovery should not be used as "excessive ammunition" to coerce a party to settle. Think of the case in which an indigent plaintiff is suing a huge corporation with unlimited legal resources. The corporation could easily schedule multitudes of depositions of experts to cause the plaintiff to settle the case prematurely or even to dismiss the case. Further, attorneys can manipulate the discovery process to take tactical advantage of the opposing party. Serving "form" interrogatories, requests for production of documents, and requests for admissions with the complaint may be means for the attorney to gain a tactical advantage, because failure to respond to these discovery requests can result in the imposition of sanctions (such as attorney fees or court costs). By serving these discovery requests with the initial complaint, the attorney can pressure the defendants to answer before they are truly ready. DR 7-102(A) prevents abusive discovery practices, but Rule 3.4(d) is more specific; it provides that making frivolous discovery requests and failing to comply with proper discovery requests is improper. Discovery should be used to find relevant facts about a case or claim, not as a tactical tool for coercing the opposing party to take certain actions.

THE CASE OF THE 10 MILLION DEPOSITIONS

Paralegal Nick works for the Sewanee Sloppers (a professional baseball team) in their legal department. Recently, the team has been sued by Soul Proprietor, a Sewanee businessman who alleges improper collusion, price-fixing, and fraud in the contracts for concessions in the ballpark. Over and above the merits of the case, the negative publicity generated by the case will surely cause a decrease in fan attendance and profits for the team.

Attorney Aparacio calls his paralegal into his office to discuss the team's approach to the case. Basically the management and head lawyers have decided that the best approach is to pursue extensive discovery for the purpose of "encouraging" Soul Proprietor to settle because he cannot afford the legal fees that would be occasioned by extensive pretrial work. "I don't care if it takes 10 million years or we attend 10 million depositions; let's get this little guy to go away," Aparacio tells Nick.

Is paralegal Nick faced with an ethical dilemma? If so, what should he do?

7.5   CASE LAW INTERPRETING ZEALOUS REPRESENTATION

The following cases examine the way the courts have looked at the issue of zealous representation. The *Crumpacker* case shows how an attorney crossed the line from appropriately zealous representation to inappropriate behavior by making unethical extrajudicial statements and outrageous personal attacks on adversaries.

In the Matter of Owen W. CRUMPACKER

Supreme Court of Indiana
383 N.E.2d 36 (Ind. 1978)

. . . We have examined all matters submitted in this cause and now find that during the Klaas litigation a motion was filed to strike the Respondent's appearance. On June 10, 1974, Respondent filed a one hundred page brief in support of his objections directed toward the Motion to Strike and sent a copy of such brief to over 80 attorneys and judges not associated with the Klaas case. The following matters, which are indicative of the contents of the brief, have been taken from its table of contents: [At this point, the opinion quotes at length from the brief.]

. . . The above findings establish that the statements contained in the brief were extrajudicial and that such extrajudicial matters were intentionally directed by the Respondent to members of the Bench and Bar, who had no relationship to the pending litigation.

It appears that Respondent's intent was to have such matter communicated generally among the Bench and Bar. Sending such a document to over 80 individuals reasonably suggests an intent for public dissemination and we conclude that these extrajudicial statements were made in such a manner that a reasonable person would expect them to be disseminated by means of public communication.

Accordingly, this Court holds that Respondent made extrajudicial statements in a pending civil case concerning evidence regarding the occurrence or transaction involved, the character or credibility of parties, witnesses and prospective witnesses, his opinion as to the merits of claims and concerning matters reasonably likely to interfere with a fair trial. In so doing Respondent violated the Disciplinary Rules 7-107(G)(1), (2), (4), and (5), 1-102(A)(1), (5), and (6).

In the Klaas litigation, as noted before, Judge Moody struck Respondent's appearance by reason of a conflict of interest. The Respondent thereafter wrote two letters excoriating Judge Moody. His letter of July 1, 1974, to Judge Moody forms the basis of Count XII; the one of August 8, 1974, to Richard Grabham, Count XIII. Both letters were released to the press. Together with the general charges of misconduct under Disciplinary Rule 1-102(A)(1) and (6), the Respondent is specifically charged with violating Disciplinary Rule 8-102(B) which provides:

"A lawyer shall not knowingly make false accusations against a judge or other adjudicatory officer."

After reviewing all matters submitted herein, we now find that on June 24, 1974, Judge Moody, as Special Judge in the Klaas case, entered an order finding that the Respondent was engaged in a conflict of interest by attempting to represent the Plaintiffs (Connellys) in this litigation; Judge Moody ordered Crumpacker's appearance stricken. The judge did not release a copy of his order to the press; however, the press obtained the order and published such findings. On July 1, 1974, Respondent wrote Judge Moody a letter in which the Respondent accused Judge Moody of deliberately covering up gross

fraud and publishing the order, among other accusations. Respondent then petitioned for Judge Moody to be joined in the disciplinary proceeding against the Respondent. Judge Moody replied with a 10 page response. The Respondent countered with a 17 page letter to Richard Grabham, then Executive Secretary of the Disciplinary Commission, generally suggesting that Judge Moody was engaged in the conspiracy taking place, that he lived under a rock, was somehow associated with the Watergate scandal, was in Reed's vest pocket, and was otherwise a corrupt public official. Respondent made attempts but wholly failed to prove any of the acts of impropriety alleged in his letters. The Respondent furnished copies of his correspondence to the news media in both instances.

In light of the above facts we find that after receiving an unfavorable ruling from Judge Moody, the Respondent launched an unmitigated assault on Judge Moody's character and integrity. The accusations contained in his letters are totally unreasonable and false. The Respondent should have known and probably did know such accusations were false. Thus, we conclude that Respondent engaged in the misconduct charged under Counts XII and XIII and violated Disciplinary Rules 8-102(B) and 1-102(A)(1) and (6). . . .

In Count IX the Respondent is charged with directing discourteous and derogatory remarks toward opposing counsel and the Plaintiff during the course of a hearing before Judge Pinkerton. As under Count VIII, the Respondent is charged with violating Disciplinary Rules 1-102(A)(1), (5), and (6) and 7-106(C)(6).

This Court following a review of all matters submitted in this cause now finds that on March 24, 1974, before Judge Pinkerton, during a hearing on a protective order, the Respondent directed the following remarks and others toward opposing counsel, Johnson, and/or the Plaintiff, Winslow Van Horne: (Toward Johnson): "Now if your Honor isn't going to cover him up, fine, kiss him off, send him back to the country club, let him get up on a bar stool and continue. ... there he could find better people to argue with as your Honor is aware"; (Toward Johnson): ". . . a young man who leaves the bar stool out of the men's grill. . . ." (Toward Johnson): ". . . this little pipsqueak who couldn't make a living except for Nipsco"; (Toward Johnson): ". . . he couldn't make a living if Don Mitchell gave him a pocket full of cash."; (Toward Van Horne): ". . . better get back over and sober up."; (Toward Van Horne): "Van Horne, you go back to Auburn and get drunk and get your god damned liver. . . ."

These remarks were improper, but more than that these were direct, personal, insulting references directed toward opposing counsel and the Plaintiff, who happened to be an attorney. Standing alone, this one incident probably would not be sufficient to warrant serious discipline. However, this one Count does not stand alone; Respondent's behavior in the case noted under this count appears to be indicative of his method of operation. When reviewing this record, it is evident that in many instances the Respondent browbeats, shouts at and attempts to intimidate his opponents. His tirades are, at times, irrational and his rage appears to be uncontrolled. Ethical Consideration 7-37 has application in the present circumstances:

> EC 7-37 In adversary proceedings, clients are litigants and though ill feeling may exist between clients, such ill feeling should not influence a lawyer in his conduct, attitude, and demeanor towards opposing lawyers. A lawyer should not make unfair or derogatory personal reference to opposing counsel. Haranguing and offensive tactics by lawyers

interfere with the orderly administration of justice and have no proper place in our legal system.

In light of the above considerations, we now conclude that the Respondent violated Disciplinary Rules 7-106(C)(6) and 1-102(A)(1), (5), and (6), as charged under Count IX of the amended complaint.

Count X charges the Respondent with making insulting remarks toward opposing counsel, John Patrick McQuillan, and the witness during the taking of a deposition. Respondent is charged with the same violation of the Code as under Counts VIII and IX, i.e., violation of Disciplinary Rules 7-106(C)(6) and 1-102(A)(1), (5), and (6).

We now find that the incident involved in this Count was the deposition of Henry Herschbach, an 82 year old man. During such deposition, which lasted eleven days, the Respondent shouted at the witness, pointed his finger in the witness'[s] face and verbally abused the opposing counsel and the witness. The Respondent frequently accused opposing counsel of corruption, "hanky-panky," scheming to convert and steal funds and documents, falsification of records, swindling, compounding a felony, dishonesty and evasive conduct. On the final day, during the course of the deposition and in the presence of the deponent, the deponent's wife, the plaintiff, and others, Respondent told opposing counsel, John P. McQuillan, on three occasions, that Respondent was going to stick or put McQuillan's head in a "toilet bowl." During the course of the said deposition the Respondent also accused the deponent of dishonesty, lying, corruption, conversion, embezzlement, and other crimes. A number of these accusations were accompanied by Respondent pointing at the eighty-two year old witness, shaking his hands and fingers at the witness, and shouting at the witness.

In light of the above findings, this Court now concludes that the Respondent engaged in conduct which adversely reflects on his fitness to practice law and which was prejudicial to the administration of justice. . . . [A]n orderly process of dispute resolution is not possible unless there is respect for the procedures and an attempt to work within an established framework. Discourteous and undignified behavior detracts from the orderly process of dispute resolution and clearly falls outside an acceptable level of attorney conduct. It appears insignificant whether such conduct occurs during the taking of a deposition or during the examination of a witness at trial. Both instances require an orderly process and mandate customary courtesies.

. . . It now becomes the duty of this Court to impose an appropriate disciplinary sanction by reason of the above-cited acts of misconduct. As this Court has noted on several previous occasions, in reaching such decision many factors are considered, such as the nature of the violation, the specific acts of misconduct, this Court's responsibility to preserve the integrity of the Bar, and the risk, if any, to which we will subject the public by permitting the Respondent to continue in the profession or be reinstated at some future date.

In the present case, the evidence presents a particular course of conduct totally contrary to the effective administration of justice and all standards of professional conduct. The acts set out under the various counts wherein this Court has found misconduct create a picture of a vicious, sinister person, tunnel-visioned by personal pique, and willing to forego all professional responsibilities which conflict with acts of preconceived vengeance on personal enemies. The Respondent's wrath has no bounds and his ire affixes to any and all persons who oppose him, even if such opposition is in a professional capacity. The Respondent verbally insults his adversaries at a personal level. Professional advocacy is totally submerged into vitriolic obloquy and all of the Respondent's adversaries, professional or personal, immediately become part and parcel of a grand fraud or conspiracy being perpetrated on some party for whom the Respondent asserts representation.

The course of conduct demonstrated by the Respondent has no place within the contemporary practice of law. A lawyer owes an obligation to his client to provide the best representation possible, an obligation to the legal profession to strive for justice, and an obligation to himself to meet the demands of his profession. When a lawyer loses sight of his purpose and uses the legal system for personal vengeance, he fails in his obligations to his client, profession, and self. In the present cause the Respondent used information gained in the course of professional services to form the basis of a suit against his former client; he employed the legal system as a vehicle for personal vengeance; and in the end the Respondent abandoned any standard of professional behavior. This conduct, unfortunately, represents a total failure of all obligations.

In light of the above considerations, this Court is forced to conclude that the strongest sanction available under the Constitution of the State of Indiana must be imposed to preserve the integrity of the legal profession and to protect the public from future acts of misconduct as found in this case. It is therefore ordered that by reasons of the misconduct found in this cause the Respondent be, and he hereby is, disbarred as an attorney in the State of Indiana.

CASE QUESTIONS

1. Which of Crumpacker's specific actions caused him to be disciplined?
2. Is disbarment an appropriate punishment? Would suspension and required counseling be a more effective punishment?

In the *Crane* case, an attorney is alleged to have violated ethical rules concerning dishonesty and improper communication with adverse parties.

Fred R. CRANE, Petitioner
v.
The STATE BAR OF CALIFORNIA, Respondent

Supreme Court of California, En Banc
635 P.2d 163 (Cal. 1981)

BY THE COURT:

We review a recommendation of the State Bar Court that petitioner, Fred R. Crane, be suspended from the practice of law for one year, but that the suspension be stayed on conditions of one year's probation, passage of the Professional Responsibility Examination, and compliance with rule 9565 of the Rules of Court in the event petitioner does not pass that examination within one year of the effective date of his suspension. Petitioner contends that the findings of the State Bar Court are not supported by the evidence, and that the discipline recommended is excessive. We conclude that properly supported findings fully warrant the recommendations.

Petitioner was admitted to practice law in California in the summer of 1972 and has no prior discipline. Before his admission, petitioner had been a real estate salesman since 1961 and a real estate broker since 1964. His legal practice has been largely confined to real estate matters.

On December 18, 1979, formal proceedings were instituted against petitioner by a notice to show cause charging him with violation of his oath and duties as an attorney (Bus. & Prof. Code, section 6103), commission of acts involving moral turpitude and dishonesty (*id.*, section 6106) and wilful violation of rules 7-103 and 7-104 of the Rules of Professional Conduct of the State Bar of California. Those charges arose from two unrelated matters.

1. *The Mercury Case*

Representing sellers of a residence, in April 1978 petitioner sought and obtained from Mercury Savings and Loan Association (Mercury), the beneficiary under a first trust deed, a beneficiary statement describing the status and indebtedness of the underlying loan. Without either the consent or knowledge of Mercury, he then "crossed out" certain printed material included in the statement by Mercury. The deleted language gave notice that Mercury intended to enforce an acceleration clause in the note and deed of trust unless it received an assumption agreement executed by any purchaser of the premises. Petitioner subsequently forwarded the altered statement to the escrow company handling the sale, describing it as "the Beneficiary Statement from the . . . lender on your escrow," and without notifying the company that the deletions were made by him and were wholly unauthorized.

The State Bar Court found petitioner's conduct in this regard to be wilful, improper and a dishonest act under the statute.

2. *The Robinson Case*

In December 1978 petitioner communicated with counsel for Mr. and Mrs. Robinson both by telephone and by mail in connection with the unrecorded claim of petitioner's client to real property which was subject to a trust deed then being foreclosed by the Robinsons. Both orally and in writing, the Robinsons' attorney specifically advised petitioner that he represented the Robinsons. Thereafter, petitioner's office sent two letters directly to the Robinsons without notifying their lawyer. The first—which apparently was a "follow-up" to a still earlier letter sent to the Robinsons before petitioner had been contacted by their lawyer—repeated a request for a beneficiary statement on their trust deed and offered to "waive" the $100 statutory penalty if it was received promptly. The second, sent seven days later, demanded that the Robinsons forward "forthwith" the $100 and the beneficiary statement. It stated further that if the statement was not received within five days, an action would be commenced against the Robinsons to recover both damages and the forfeiture, and that "the Department of Savings and Loan and the Attorney General's office will be requested to assist us

in solution." A notation on the last letter indicated that copies were being sent to a named commissioner of the Department of Savings and Loan and to a named deputy attorney general. The letters were on petitioner's legal stationery and purported to be signed by him.

The State Bar Court found that petitioner's direct communication with the Robinsons despite his knowledge that they were represented by an attorney was a clear violation of rule 7-103 of the Rules of Professional Conduct, and that his final letter to them constituted an impermissible threat in violation of rule 7-104.

DISCUSSION

With respect to the Mercury matter, petitioner admits both his unauthorized alteration of the beneficiary statement and his failure to advise the escrow company that the deletion was his, and not that of the beneficiary or trustee under the trust deed. He denies, however, that he was "dishonest" arguing that he had no intent to deceive the escrow company, but merely sought to prevent Mercury from improperly interfering with the prospective sale by asserting demands which Mercury had no right to make in the beneficiary statement.

We reject petitioner's disavowal of any dishonest intent. Even if we assume for purposes of argument that Mercury endangered the successful closing of escrow by asserting a right which it did not have, any such risk could be removed or minimized *only* if the reader of the statement believed the acceleration language was deleted by Mercury itself. The circumstances of petitioner's unauthorized unilateral alteration were deceptive and known by him to be so.

In the Robinson matter, petitioner also admitted in a stipulation of facts filed with the State Bar Court his "technical violation" of rule 7-103 of the Rules of Professional Conduct by communicating directly with the

Robinsons despite his awareness that they were represented by counsel. He now contends, however, that the letters to the Robinsons requesting, and then demanding, the beneficiary statement and statutory penalty, and threatening suit and action by state officials, were not "upon a subject of controversy" and that his client and the Robinsons were not "adverse parties" within the meaning of that rule.

There was substantial evidence to the contrary, however, including testimony of the Robinsons' lawyer that he had discussed with petitioner the adverse interest of the parties in connection with the foreclosure of the trust deed, and beyond that evidence, the contents of the letters themselves belie petitioner's claims.

We similarly reject petitioner's asserted excuse that any violation of rule 7-103 was inadvertent and precipitated by members of his staff. Acknowledging negligence in failing properly to prevent direct contact with represented parties by correspondence on his letterhead and over his purported signature, petitioner contends that the discipline proposed for that negligence is unduly severe. Petitioner's attempt to avoid the blame for his violation of the Rules of Professional Conduct is unconvincing. An attorney is responsible for the work product of his employees which is performed pursuant to his direction

and authority. The legal onus for the violation of rule 7-103 rests upon petitioner alone. . . .

Finally, petitioner challenges the recommended discipline as too severe. While we have the ultimate responsibility for determining appropriate discipline, the burden rests upon petitioner to demonstrate the impropriety of the discipline recommended by the State Bar for the protection of the public, the courts and the legal profession itself. In our view petitioner has failed to carry that burden. His actions clearly violated the statutes and State Bar Rules. His attempt to deceive the escrow agent by his falsification of the Mercury beneficiary statement was a dishonest act involving moral turpitude (Bus. & Prof. Code, section 6106) and his wilful and direct communications with the Robinsons violated the State Bar's Rules of Professional Conduct. (Rules 7-103, 7-104.) Comparable discipline has been imposed in similar cases. While it is arguable that the penalty imposed is actually lenient, we adopt the recommendations of the State Bar Court.

Accordingly, it is ordered that Fred R. Crane be suspended from the practice of law in this state for a period of one year, but that such suspension be stayed and petitioner placed on probation for one year on condition that he pass the Professional Responsibility Examination during that period. This order is effective 30 days after the filing of this opinion.

CASE QUESTIONS

1. Which specific provisions of the Code did Crane violate?
2. Look at §§ 3.3 and 3.4 of the Rules. Do these rules apply to Crane's actions?
3. Crane contended that his violation is a "technical" one, implying that it was not serious. Do you agree?

7.6 RECOGNIZING AND RESOLVING ZEALOUS REPRESENTATION PROBLEMS

If you keep in mind that the purpose of the rules prohibiting certain conduct is to balance the principle of zealous representation with the fact that zealous representation does not mean unfair or prejudicial representation, then you will likely avoid problems in this area. If your conduct gives your client an unfair advantage, it is probably unethical. The following guidelines will help you avoid improprieties relative to the issue of zealous representation:

1. Never help a client do anything illegal.
2. Never say anything to an opposing party except that he or she needs representation.
3. If you must talk to the opposing party (for example, to set up a deposition), always get permission from opposing counsel, preferably in writing, that such communication is authorized.
4. Never talk to a juror, except in certain limited circumstances after completion of a trial.
5. Never talk to a judge except to give essential information or when asked a question.
6. Never talk to the media.
7. Consider everything you have heard in the firm pertaining to business as confidential.
8. When interviewing witnesses, let them tell their side of the story before asking any questions. Do not try to get them to say something that they do not know, and always tell them that the important thing, when being a witness, is to tell the absolute truth.

By following these eight general guidelines, you will gain a sensitivity to this ethical provision, enabling you to maintain acceptable behavior in your quest to represent your client effectively.

In his guest editorial, Bennett Gershman describes various things that prosecutors do which straddle the line between zealous representation and unethical conduct.

GUEST EDITORIAL

TRICKS PROSECUTORS PLAY

by Bennett L. Gershman

Criminal defense lawyers must recognize and challenge prosecutorial misconduct whenever it occurs. In my opinion, prosecutors today wield greater power, engage in more egregious misconduct, and are less subject to judicial or bar association oversight than ever before. Few defense lawyers or commentators would disagree with these conclusions. Indeed, some types of prosecutorial misconduct have become almost "normative to the system."

This is not to say, of course, that private attorneys do not engage in similar misconduct. They do. There are, however, important differences between prosecutors and defense attorneys that make prosecutorial violations much more insidious.

Prosecutors are generally perceived by juries as prestigious and honorable "champions of justice." They have powerful strategic and financial resources that usually give them distinct advantages over their adversaries. And prosecutors operate under higher ethical standards than other lawyers—i.e., a special obligation "to seek justice." Despite or because of these differences, prosecutorial misconduct is all too often overlooked, condoned, or found to be harmless.

Prosecutors function in a variety of contexts in the criminal justice system. They enjoy vast decision-making powers in areas such as charging crimes, plea bargaining, granting immunity, summoning witnesses to grand juries, and determining sentences. Prosecutorial domination over the "awful instruments of the criminal law," to use Justice Felix Frankfurter's apt terminology, is largely uncontrolled by the courts. Indeed, unfettered prosecutorial discretion may be the most terrifying and the most insoluble problem in the administration of criminal justice.

That problem, however, is beyond the scope of this article. The focus here is on prosecutorial misconduct at trial that results in depriving the defendant of a fair and reliable determination of guilt. While the incidence of misconduct is increasing, judges' willingness to impose remedies such as reversal of convictions or dismissal of charges is decreasing. This is not an anomaly. There is a direct correlation between this laissez faire judicial attitude and the escalation of prosecutorial misconduct.

Just as the threat of penal sanctions is thought to deter illegal behavior by criminals, the prospect of judicial sanctions such as reversals, dismissals, or contempt citations would be expected to deter errant behavior by rational prosecutors. However, since "winning the war on crime" is a major political preoccupation today, the procedural safeguards and prohibitions set up to ensure that defendants get fair trials may be seen by some as retarding progress toward that goal.

It is therefore not surprising that to affirm convictions despite prosecutorial misconduct, appellate courts increasingly invoke a variety of questionable procedures. These include broadening use of harmless-error review, overlooking misconduct that was allegedly "invited" by defense counsel, ignoring misconduct to which defense counsel failed to object, or indulging in the fiction that so-called "curative instructions" by the trial judge actually mitigate the harm.

By the same token, access to collateral review through the writ of habeas corpus is generally being eroded through doctrinal and procedural bars. Examples of these barriers include exhaustion, default, waiver, and the need to show prejudice.

This is not to say that trial or appellate courts are completely insensitive to prosecutorial excesses. Some trial judges monitor prosecutors quite closely—particularly those with track records of behaving overzealously. Some appellate courts also keep watch on the prosecutors. And some bar association officials bring disciplinary charges against prosecutors for egregious trial behavior.

Having said this, I will now turn to a discussion of some of the more egregious "trial tricks" that prosecutors sometimes play.

ASSASSINATING DEFENDANT'S CHARACTER

Attacking a defendant's character makes a conviction more likely. The devastating impact on a jury of a defendant's prior criminal or sordid acts is clear and has been empirically proven. Consider the William Kennedy Smith rape trial in Florida. Had the prosecution been able to place before the jury evidence that Smith had engaged in three prior episodes of sexual misconduct, the verdict might have been different.

Prosecutors have portrayed defendants as dangerous, sinister, and undesirable characters who are therefore more likely to have committed the crime charged, and convictions occasionally are reversed because of such misconduct. Attempting to insinuate that a defendant was guilty by showing that he had associated with, was related to, or was in the company of criminals is improper. So is stigmatizing defendants either directly (through cross-examination) or indirectly (through extrinsic proof) by intimating that the defendant has a criminal record and therefore is more likely to have committed the crime charged.

INTRODUCING IMPROPER EVIDENCE

Presenting false, misleading, or inadmissible evidence is unethical and potentially violates due process. Examples of this practice include using perjured testimony and introducing physical or other evidence that deceives the jury about a material fact. It is also unethical for prosecutors to seek to make a false impression on the jury by loading questions with innuendos when no supporting evidence exists. Suggesting without any factual basis that defendant's wife left him because of his drug transactions is an example of such a bad-faith question.

Similarly, referring to polygraph tests, withdrawn guilty pleas, or guilty pleas of co-conspirators may be an improper tactic deliberately designed to distort the fact-finding process against the defendant. Forcing a defendant or defense witness under cross-examination to characterize the testimony of a prosecution witness as "lies" is a frequently used tactic that invites appellate censure.

INFLAMING JUROR PREJUDICE

Prosecutors know that appeals to the jury's passions and prejudices, although improper, may skew the jury's evaluation of the proof toward conviction. To that end, prosecutors have displayed inflammatory and inadmissible physical evidence before juries; offered gruesome and irrelevant photographs of the victim; elicited inflammatory testimony; and injected gratuitous, inflammatory rhetoric into the proceedings.

Summation gives the prosecutor a unique opportunity to prejudice the defendant. Common examples of inflammatory argument include exhorting juries to win the war on crime; inciting them to vengeance; using insulting and abusive epithets and invective to describe the defendant; appealing to racial, ethnic, national, or religious prejudice; appealing to wealth and class bias; and imputing to the defendant violence and threats against witnesses.

VIOLATING THE PRIVILEGE AGAINST SELF-INCRIMINATION

It is improper for a prosecutor to encourage the jury to infer guilt from the defendant's silence at trial or failure to explain his conduct to the police after arrest. This tactic has been used to impeach a defendant's testimony at trial and to argue that if the defendant was innocent, he would have testified, but because he has not, he is guilty.

Appellate reversal is more likely when the prosecutor's comments refer directly to the defendant's failure to testify. Prosecutors therefore try to make the point more subtly, through oblique references to the government's proof being "uncontradicted," "unrefuted," or "undenied." Although the prosecutor's intent here is clear, such references often escape appellate sanction.

Comments about the defendant's failure to call witnesses should also be closely scrutinized to determine whether they involve a prohibited comment on the privilege against self-incrimination.

DENIGRATING DEFENSE COUNSEL

Attacks on defense counsel are not unusual. By belittling defense counsel, prosecutors may believe that they can gain an advantage before the jury. Some prosecutors disparage the defense by suggesting that defense counsel's objections were made in bad faith. Another tactic is to insinuate that defense counsel does not believe the client's testimony or has no confidence in the case.

Personal attacks on defense counsel's ethics and integrity are not uncommon. Prosecutors have insinuated that defense counsel presented "contrived testimony," "fabricated a defense," or engaged in illegal conduct.

Some jurisdictions allow prosecutors to make an opening summation and then a rebuttal summation. Some courts have recognized a phenomenon known as "sandbagging," where the prosecutor makes new arguments and raises new theories for the first time during rebuttal summation. Courts look with disfavor on this practice when it unfairly takes defense counsel by surprise.

EXPLOITING PROSECUTORIAL PRESTIGE

It is unethical for prosecutors to manipulate the jury's evaluation of the evidence by stressing their own personal integrity and the prestige of their office. Prosecutors disregard this rule when they try to enhance a witness's credibility by expressing their own faith in the witness's truthfulness or the defendant's guilt. This personal vouching makes the prosecutor an unsworn witness.

Insinuating that information outside the record verifies the witness's truthfulness is another form of improper vouching. So is suggesting that cooperation agreements with witnesses show that the prosecutor knows what the truth is and that by entering into such an agreement with the witness, the prosecutor is ensuring that the truth will be revealed.

MISREPRESENTING THE RECORD

It is improper for prosecutors to refer to matters outside the record; to point to exhibits or testimony that have not been entered into evidence, implying they are incriminating; to misrepresent the record; or to insinuate that issues of fact have already been decided. Prosecutors have also been rebuked for going outside the record and commenting on the consequences that might result from the jury's verdict. These comments are intended to lessen the jurors' sense of responsibility and recognition of the seriousness of their verdict. Impermissible remarks include references to the possibility of mitigation of punishment by the judge, the availability of pardon or executive clemency, and the availability of appellate review.

FINDING REMEDIES

Sanctions for prosecutorial misconduct are infrequent. Appellate reversal is seen as too costly to society. Judge Learned Hand's argument is endorsed by most courts. Referring to a prosecutor's misconduct, Judge Hand wrote, "That was plainly an improper remark, and if reversal would do more than show our disapproval, we might reverse. Unhappily, it would accomplish little towards punishing the offender, and would upset the conviction of a plainly guilty man. . . . It seems to us that reversal would be an immoderate penalty."

Civil damage actions against prosecutors are generally unsuccessful because of the doctrine of prosecutorial immunity. Contempt sanctions are rarely employed, and professional discipline is even more rarely utilized.

In such a climate of opinion, effectively challenging prosecutorial misconduct at the trial level becomes more important all the time. It requires, first, a thorough understanding of the substantive rules governing the parameters of prosecutorial behavior; second, an alertness to conduct that violates those rules; and third, the ability to make a record through timely objection or by other means. Valid claims are frequently lost through the failure of trial counsel to register a timely protest.

Knowing from the outset that prosecutorial misconduct may occur allows defense counsel to make an advance motion such as a motion in limine to prevent such misconduct before it occurs. These motions have been made when defense counsel knows that a particular prosecutor has a track record of engaging in specific types of misbehavior—for example, asking questions without any evidentiary foundation, eliciting inadmissible and inflammatory evidence such as prior bad acts by the defendant, or using particularly inflammatory language in argument to the jury.

Many defense lawyers are reluctant to antagonize prosecutors with whom they have to deal on a regular basis. However, making a formal complaint with a state or local bar association or with the U.S. Department of Justice's Office of Professional Responsibility may be not only an appropriate and effective course, but the best when prosecutorial misconduct occurs.

■ Bennett L. Gershman, former Assistant District Attorney of New York County, is a Professor of Law at Pace College of Law. This article was reprinted with permission of *TRIAL* (April, 1992). © The Association of Trial Lawyers of America.

7.7   THE PARALEGAL, THE LAWYER, AND ZEALOUS REPRESENTATION: A SUMMARY

At the heart of the legal process is the notion of adversarial competition. On one hand, the law is about justice, but on the other, and in a very real way, the law is about winning for your client. To preserve the rights of the client, ethical rules and constitutional interpretation of the right to counsel require that an attorney represent her client fully and completely, and that she leave no stone unturned in her quest to help her client. However, that requirement of full, complete, zealous representation has limits; ethical guidelines delineate the boundary between permissible zealous representation and actions that cannot be condoned because they are unfair and subversive of the legal system. Some behaviors, such as performing an illegal act, clearly go beyond that which is allowed. Others, such as communicating with individuals having interests adverse to those of your client, straddle the ethical line. By understanding that the requirement of zealous representation is tempered by ethical boundaries, the legal professional can gauge the propriety of actions in providing zealous (but not too zealous) representation of clients.

REVIEW QUESTIONS

1. Why should lawyers represent their clients zealously?
2. Where is the line drawn between zealous representation and unethical conduct?
3. What kind of unethical activities constitute abuse of the discovery process?
4. What should you do if your client says he is going to lie on the witness stand?

QUESTIONS FOR THOUGHT AND DISCUSSION

1. Is preparing a witness before trial an appropriately zealous or an unethical activity?
2. Laurinda is drafting responses to interrogatories in the *Brown University* case. In the most recent set, Laurinda must give the names and most recent addresses of all witnesses. She knows that the only witness whose testimony could hurt her firm's client will be moving to Ireland next week. Laurinda realizes that she could finish her responses now, but that if she gets an extension to answer, the defendant will not have an opportunity to interview the witness. Should she request an extension?

3. You overhear Charles Johnson, your supervising attorney, say, "If you don't give my client custody of the children, I'll make sure everyone knows you're a homosexual!" Is this zealous representation?

4. Kyle is a legal assistant working for an insurance defense firm. Julie claims to be paralyzed, but Kyle suspects she is not telling the truth. Unfortunately, Lorenzo the private investigator has been unable to get any pictures of Julie walking. Kyle suggests that they put a hidden video camera in Julie's bathroom to get to the truth. Is this an ethical suggestion, or is it overly zealous?

LAW, LITERATURE, AND ETHICS

From Intruder in the Dust
By William Faulkner

And that was when they saw Lucas crossing the Square, probably at the same time—the cocked hat and the thin fierce glint of the tilted gold toothpick and he said,

'Where do you suppose it was all the time? I never did see it. Surely he had it with him that afternoon, a Saturday when he was not only wearing that black suit but he even had the pistol? Surely he never left home without the toothpick too.'

'Didn't I tell you?' his uncle said. That was the first thing he did when Mr. Hampton walked into Skipworth's house where Skipworth had Lucas handcuffed to the bedpost—gave Hampton the toothpick and told him to keep it until he called for it.'

'Oh,' he said. 'He's coming up here.'

'Yes,' his uncle said. 'To gloat. Oh,' he said quickly, 'he's a gentleman; he wont remind me to my face that I was wrong; he's just going to ask me how much he owes me as his lawyer.'

Then in his chair beside the water cooler and his uncle once more behind the table thay heard the long airy rumble and creek of the stairs then Lucas' feet steadily though with no haste and Lucas came tieless and even collarless this time except for the button but with an old-time white waistcoat not soilcd so much as stained undcr the black coat and the worn gold loop of the watchchain—the same face which he had seen for the first time when he climbed dripping up out of the icy creek that morning four years ago, unchanged, to which nothing had happened since not even age—in the act of putting the toothpick into one of the upper waistcoat pockets as he came through the door, saying generally,

'Gentle-men,' and then to him: 'Young man—' courteous and intractable, more than bland: downright cheerful almost, removing the raked swagger of the hat: 'You aint fell in no more creeks lately, have you?'

'That's right,' he said. 'I'm saving that until you get some more ice on yours.'

'You'll be welcome without waiting for a freeze,' Lucas said.

'Have a seat Lucas,' his uncle said but he had already begun to, taking the same hard chair beside the door which nobody else but Miss Habersham had ever chosen, a little akimbo as though he were posing for a camera, the hat laid crownup back across his forearm, looking at both of them still and saying again,

'Gentle-men.'

'You didn't come here for me to tell you what to do so I'm going to tell you anyway,' his uncle said.

Lucas blinked rapidly once. He looked at his uncle. 'I cant say I did.' Then he said cheerily: 'But I'm always ready to listen to good advice.'

'Go and see Miss Habersham,' his uncle said.

Lucas looked at his uncle. He blinked twice this time. I aint much of a visiting man,' he said.

'You were not much of a hanging man either,' his uncle said. But you dont need me to tell you how close you came.'

'No,' Lucas said. 'I dont reckon I do. What do you want me to tell her?'

'You cant,' his uncle said. 'You dont know how to say thank you. I've got that fixed too. Take her some flowers.'

'Flowers?' Lucas said. 'I aint had no flowers to speak of since Molly died.'

'And that too,' his uncle said. 'I'll telephone home. My sister'll have a bunch ready. Chick'll drive you up in my car to get them and then take you out to Miss Habersham's gate.'

'Nemmine that. Once I got the flowers I can walk.'

'And you can throw the flowers away too,' his uncle said. 'But I know you wont do one and I dont think you'll do the other in the car with Chick.'

'Well,' Lucas said. 'If wont nothing else satisfy you—' (And when he got back to town and finally found a place three blocks away to park the car and mounted the stairs again his uncle was striking the match, holding it to the pipe and speaking through with into the smoke: 'You and Booker T. Washington, no that's wrong, you and Miss Habersham and Aleck Sander and Sheriff Hampton, and Booker T. Washington because he did only what everybody expected of him so there was no real reason why he should have while you all did not only what nobody expected you to but all Jefferson and Yoknapawpha County would have risen in active concord for once to prevent you if they had known in time and even a year from now some (when and if they do at all) will remember with disapproval and distaste not that you were ghouls nor that you defied your color because they would have passed either singly but that you violated a white grave to save a nigger so you had every reason why you should have. Just dont stop:' and he:

'You dont think that just because its Saturday afternoon again somebody is hiding behind Miss Habersham's jasmine bush with a pistol aimed at her waiting for Lucas to walk up the front steps. Besides Lucas didn't have his pistol today and besides that Crawford Gowrie—' and his uncle:

'Why not, what's out yonder in the ground at Caledonia Church was Crawford Gowrie for only a second or two last Saturday and Lucas Beauchamp will be carrying his pigment into ten thousand situations a wiser man would have avoided and a lighter escaped ten thousand times after what was Lucas Beauchamp for a second or so last Saturday is in the ground at his Caledonia Church too, because that Yoknapatawpha County which would have stopped you and Aleck Sander and Miss Habersham last Sunday night are right actually, Lucas' life the breathing and eating and sleeping is of no importance just like yours and mine are not but his unchallengable right to it in peace and security and in fact this earth would be much more comfortable with a good deal fewer Beauchamps and Stevenses and Malisons of all colors in it if there was only some painless way to efface not only the clumsy room-devouring carcasses which can be done but the memory which cannot—that inevictible immortal memory awareness of having once been alive which

exists forever still ten thousand years afterward in ten thousand recollections of injustice and suffering, too many of us not because of the room we take up but because we are willing to sell liberty short at any tawdry price for the sake of what we call our own which is a constitutional statutory license to pursue each his private postulate of happiness and contentment regardless of grief and cost even to the cruxfiction of someone whose nose or pigment we dont like and even these can be coped with provided that few of others who believe that a human life is valuable simply because it has a right to keep on breathing no matter what pigment its lungs distend or nose inhales the air and are willing to defend that right at any price, it doesnt take many three were enough last Sunday night even on ecan be enough and with enough ones willing to be more than grieved and shamed Lucas will no longer run the risk of needing without warning to be saved:' and he:

'Maybe not three the other night. One and two halves would be nearer right:' and his uncle:

'I said it's all right to be proud. It's all right even to boast. Just dont stop.')—and came to the table and laid the hat on it and took from the inside coat pocket a leather snap- purse patina-ed like old silver and almost as big as Miss Habersham's handbag and said,

'I believe you got a little bill against me.'

'What for?' his uncle said.

'For representing my case,' Lucas said. 'Name whatever your fee is within reason. I want to pay it.'

'Not me,' his uncle said. 'I didn't do anything.'

'I sent for you,' Lucas said. 'I authorized you. How much do I owe you?'

'Nothing,' his uncle said. 'Because I didn't believe you. That boy there is the reason you're walking around today.'

Now Lucas looked at him, holding the purse in one hand poised to unsnap it—the same face to which it was not that nothing had happened but which had simply refused to accept it; now he opened the purse. 'All right. I'll pay him.'

'And I'll have you both arrested,' his uncle said, 'you for corrupting a minor and him for practising law without a license.'

Lucas looked back to his uncle; he watched them staring at one another. Then once more Lucas blinked twice. 'All right,' he said. 'I'll pay the expenses then. Name your expenses at anything within reason and let's get this thing settled.'

'Expenses?' his uncle said. 'Yes, I had an expense sitting here last Tuesday trying to write down all the different things you finally told me in such a way that Mr Hampton could get enough sense out of it to discharge you from the jail and so the more I tried it the worse it got and the worse it got the worse I got until when I came to again my fountain pen was sticking up on its point in the floor down here like an arrow. Of course the paper belongs to the county but the fountain pen was mine and it cost me two dollars to have a new point put in. You owe me two dollars.'

'Two dollars?' Lucas said. He blinked twice again. Then he blinked twice again. 'Just two dollars?' Now he just blinked once, then he did something with his breath: not a sigh, simply a discharge of it, putting his first two fingers into the purse: 'That dont sound like much to me but then I'm a farming man and you're a lawing man and whether you know your business or not I reckon it aint none of my red wagon as the music box says to try to learn you different:' and drew from the purse a worn bill crumpled into a ball not much larger than a shriveled olive and opened it enough to read it then opened it out and laid it on the desk and from the purse took a half dollar and laid it on the desk then counted onto the desk from the purse one by one four dimes and two nickles and then counted them again with his forefinger, moving them one by one about half an inch, his lips moving under the moustache, the purse still open in the other hand, then he picked up two of the dimes and a nickle and put them into the hand holding the open purse and took from the open purse a quarter and put it on the desk and looked down at the coins for a rapid second then put the two dimes and the nickle back on the desk and took up the half dollar and put it back into the purse.

'That aint but six bits,' his uncle said.

'Nemmine that,' Lucas said and took up the quarter and dropped it back into the purse and closed it and watching Lucas he realized that the purse had at least two different compartments and maybe more, a second almost elbow-deep section opening beneath Lucas' fingers and for a time Lucas stood looking down into it exactly as you would look down at your reflection in a well then took from that compartment a knotted soiled cloth tobacco sack bulging and solid looking which struck on the desk top with a dull thick chink.

'That makes it out,' he said. 'Four bits in pennies. I was aiming to take them to the bank but you can save me the trip. You want to count um?'

'Yes,' his uncle said. So Lucas unknotted the sack and dumped the pennies out on the desk and counted them one by one moving each one with his forefinger into the first small mass of dimes and nickles, counting aloud, then snapped the purse shut and put it back inside his coat and with the other hand shoved the whole mass of coins and the crumpled bill across the table until the desk blotter stopped tham and took a bandana handkerchief from the side pocket of the coat and wiped his hands and put the handkerchief back and stood again intractable and calm and not looking at either of them now while the fixed blaring of the radios and the blatting creep of the automobile horns and all the rest of the whole County's Saturday uproar came up on the bright afternoon.

'Now what?' his uncle said. 'What are you waiting for now?'

'My receipt,' Lucas said.

CHAPTER 8
Client Funds and Other Money Matters

CHAPTER OVERVIEW

In this chapter you will learn about the importance of handling client funds with extreme care. The standards of ethics have very strict guidelines for legal professionals, outlining specifically how client funds are to be administered. As a legal assistant, you may have the task of drawing up client checks, balancing client retainers, and handling other situations requiring an understanding of the ethical considerations surrounding the handling of client funds. You will also learn about other ethical concerns arising out of the issue of fees for legal services.

THE CASE OF THE ASSISTANT'S AWKWARD ACCOUNTING

Elizabeth Nagrom is a paralegal with the small firm of Hurt, Payne, and Suphering, which specializes in plaintiffs' personal injury litigation. Because of her attention to detail, Elizabeth is assigned to deposit settlement checks and distribute funds to the proper parties, as well as to ensure that the settlement papers are properly signed and notarized. Additionally, because the firm's office manager is on personal leave for several months, Elizabeth is also assigned to handle other accounts for the firm.

Hurt, Payne, and Suphering has three bank accounts: general operating, payroll, and escrow. Elizabeth has been depositing the settlement checks in the general operating account of the firm, putting enough money to cover the clients' portions of settlements in the escrow account, and writing checks to clients from the escrow account (covering the client's portion of the settlement).

Do you see any problems with this practice? If so, how would you suggest that Elizabeth handle the settlement checks?

THE CASE OF THE BORROWED BOUQUET

Willie Klein is a paralegal with a small firm in Lutherville, Maryland. He is a hard-working legal assistant; because this is his first position out of paralegal school, he has been careful to act ethically and professionally in all circumstances. Willie assists his supervising attorney primarily in divorces and real estate closings, and he maintains the books and accounts and trains new paralegals.

Willie, who is in love with Gloria, plans to ask her to marry him on Valentine's day, just two days away. Unfortunately, Willie is broke, and he cannot afford the bouquet he wanted to buy to present to Gloria when he pops the question. He then has a brainstorm: He can borrow $100 from the client escrow account and pay it back in eight days, when he gets paid out of the general operating expenses account. Willie gets excited when he realizes that his activity probably would not be noticed by any of the attorneys, but he hesitates at the thought of doing something that he would have to hide from the attorneys.

Should Willie borrow the money from the client escrow account?

___

8.1 HANDLING CLIENT FUNDS: AN INTRODUCTION

Ethical considerations for the practice of law pertaining to client funds and monies in general relating to the practice of law can be divided into the following categories:

1. Fees for legal services
2. Division of fees among lawyers
3. Division of fees with a nonlawyer
4. Preservation of the identity of funds and property of a client.

Although problems with accounting and client funds are responsible for some of the most severe punishments from bar associations, the ethical aspects of legal accounting can easily be complied with by using proper accounting procedures. Proper accounting systems include setting up a separate escrow account for client funds, distributing retainers only after the work has been completed, setting up a general operating account, and ensuring that there is a paper trail for all monetary transactions. Naturally, proper use of these procedures must come from your ethical commitment to handling money properly—it certainly seems greed can cause even the most ethical people to gamble with their careers and lives. In all likelihood, you will deal with large sums of money at some point in your career; you must therefore learn how to handle this responsibility ethically and professionally.

8.2 FEES FOR LEGAL SERVICES

Ethical standards preclude an attorney from charging clients excessively for legal work. Because the prices of certain legal services, unlike the price of a product, are not readily available to the legal consumer, ethical considerations have been promulgated to keep unscrupulous lawyers from taking advantage of uninformed clients. Essentially, legal fees must be reasonable under the circumstances.

There are many types of fee arrangements. There are flat fees, hourly fees, contingency fees, and sliding-scale contingency fees. *Flat fees,* also called *fixed fees,* are generally charged when the matter is routine, such as an uncontested divorce or a will. In a flat-fee arrangement, the attorney handles the matter for an agreed-upon amount, no matter how long it takes to complete the case. *Hourly fees* require the client to pay an agreed-upon amount for each hour or part of an hour that the attorney works on the case. *Contingency fee* arrangements pay the attorney out of the settlement of a case; the ethical considerations governing contingency cases permit an attorney to handle a case not for a set fee, but rather for a percentage of the settlement (minus expenses such as filing costs and discovery expenses).

Regardless of the type of arrangement, the fee must not be excessive. An example of an excessive fee might be in a case being handled on a contingency basis. Usually, contingency fees are set at one-fourth for cases that do not go to trial and one-third for those that do, with a greater percentage if the case is subsequently appealed. This is known as a *sliding-scale contingency fee;* it reflects the reality that more time must be spent on a case if it goes to trial and then is appealed. It also reflects the fact that, at each level, the attorney's risk of receiving no compensation at all greatly increases; therefore, the attorney's share of the settlement is increased to compensate for the increased risk. The amount of the contingency depends on the attorney's skill and experience and the complexity of the matter. It would be unethical, however, for an attorney to take 75 percent of a settlement amount—that would be excessive. It is also unethical to work on a contingency fee in a criminal case. Contingency fees are prohibited in divorce cases if the fee is contingent on obtaining the divorce, alimony, or child support. Sometimes an attorney will accept a case on a contingency basis but will not state the percentage, hoping that an uninformed and perhaps intimidated client will not balk at a high percentage. The best procedure is to have the essentials of the lawyer-client relationship reduced to writing before any actual work is begun. (See figure 8-1.) Remember that in contingency cases, expenses such as filing fees, witness fees, copying, postage, and other administrative fees will be deducted from the settlement. This is required because in most jurisdictions attorneys are not permitted to have a stake in the litigation or to finance their clients' cases.

Fees are frequently paid through a retainer. A *retainer* is an amount of money paid to the attorney at the beginning of the representation; this assures the client that the lawyer will be working for the client and assures the attorney that he will get paid. A *refundable retainer* requires the attorney to bill actual hours against the retainer and return any unused funds. For example, if a client paid a $2,500 retainer, and the lawyer billed 20 hours at $100 an hour, the client would be refunded $500. If a retainer is nonrefundable, part of the retainer is charged to hourly rates but is paid to the attorney to guarantee her representation. This might be done if the attorney, by taking one client, thereby precludes himself from taking other legal work. If a client paid an attorney a $20,000 retainer, with $5,000 of it nonrefundable, then the attorney would be entitled to immediately use the $5,000, but would have to bill her time at the hourly rate for the remaining $15,000. Thus, if she billed 100 hours at $100 per hour, she would be entitled to keep $10,000 plus the $5,000 nonrefundable portion of the retainer, but $5,000 would be refunded to the client. Remember also that expenses such as filing fees, courier fees, facsimile charges, postage, copying, and court reporter fees are also deducted from the retainer before any money is refunded to the client.

Some fees are based on the type of work done, such as writing a will or a security deed. Fixed fees are assessed based on the complexity of the matter, how unusual it is, the location in which an attorney practices, and the reputation and experience of the attorney handling the matter. For instance, a will distributing several million dollars through many trusts set up in New York City would cost more than a simple will distributing two savings and checking accounts in Cherokee, Iowa. Likewise, retaining F. Lee Bailey to represent you would cost much more than retaining A. New Attorney, who has little or no experience.

MAXINE FARLEY
ATTORNEY AT LAW
3131 PINE CONE CIRCLE
BUCKHEAD, GEORGIA 30333
TELEPHONE: (404) 555-1212

July 7, 1992

<u>By Hand Delivery</u>

Mr. Lawrence Arabia
1516 Hamm Court
Allison, Georgia 31111

RE: State vs. Lawrence Arabia
DUI Charges, Polk County
Citation No. 433-18-19-B

Dear Mr. Arabia:

You have asked me to represent you in connection with the above-captioned matter. I am pleased to have this opportunity to assist you, and want to acquaint you with the manner in which I will be representing you.

Representation: I will represent you up to, including, and throughout the conclusion of the above-referenced matters.

Keeping You Informed: I will keep you informed of the status of your case and will send to you copies of all documents which I initiate here and copies of documents I receive from others. Usually, you will have to take no action upon receipt of this information, but you should read it to be aware of what is taking place. I suggest you maintain a file to hold these copies.

Authority: You empower me, as your attorney, to dispose of the matter and to file such documents as I deem advisable. However, it is understood and agreed that neither client nor attorney shall dispose of the legal matter without first having advised the other party and obtaining the other party's consent thereto.

Fees: Pursuant to our conversation on today's date, you agree to pay the following fees, as indicated, for my legal services:

(a) $1,000.00 payable in three installments over the next sixty (60) days. Receipt of a $50.00 nonrefundable retainer is hereby acknowledged.

FIGURE 8-1
Sample engagement
letter

(b)   This contract of employment does not cover or include appellate work or services unless so stated specifically.

You agree to be liable for all costs and expenses (i.e., court costs, witness fees, photocopying, depositions, long-distance telephone calls, etc.) necessary to handle this matter and to reimburse the attorney within ten (10) days for any costs or expenses paid on the client's behalf. It is further understood and agreed that costs may be billed, or the attorney may require the client, and the client agrees, to deposit funds, in advance, sufficient to pay estimated expenses.

In the event any statement from me to you is not paid when due, unless other arrangements are made in advance, or in the event that you cannot be located, I may, at my professional discretion,withdraw from this matter and discontinue legal services by contacting you by letter at the following address:

Further, should I withdraw, all legal documents, files, evidence, or materials shall remain in my possession until your account is paid in full.

You understand and agree that any statement not paid within thirty (30) days from the date of billing will be charged interest at the rate of 1.5% per month on the unpaid balance, pursuant to O.C.G.A. Section 7-14-16 and you agree to pay all interest charged until the account is paid in full.

I agree to devote my best professional abilities to this matter, but you acknowledge that I have made NO PROMISES or GUARANTEES regarding the outcome of this matter.

Your Acceptance. If the foregoing terms and conditions accurately summarize and confirm your understanding of our attorney-client relationship, please indicate your approval and acceptance by dating and signing this letter. I have signed a copy of this letter of agreement and enclose it for your file.

Sincerely,

Maxine Farley

Approved and Accepted this the
_____ day of _____ , 1992.

_____
[Client's signature]

FIGURE 8-1
(Continued)

When considering reasonableness of fees, all the relevant factors in a particular case must be examined in light of usual legal practices. For example, in *In re Kutner,* 78 Ill. 2d 157, 399 N.E.2d 963 (1979), an attorney charged $5,000 for about 10 hours' work on a routine case involving a guilty plea in a simple battery defense case. The court found that fee excessive.

In the corporate context, large fees have been found reasonable, especially when the hiring corporation is represented by its own attorneys in setting the fee. In *Brobeck, Phleger & Harrison v. Telex Corp.,* 602 F.2d 866

(9th Cir.), cert. denied, 444 U.S. 981, 100 S. Ct. 483, L. Ed. 2d 407 (1979), a corporation, represented by its own counsel during fee setting, hired a nationally prominent expert in antitrust law to assist in the preparation of its petition for certiorari to the United States Supreme Court. The expert's fee was $1 million—and the court upheld the fee as reasonable under the circumstances.

Although large fees are not per se unreasonable, they may become unreasonable if the law firm charges for services it does not perform. In *Arens & Alexander v. Committee on Professional Conduct,* 307 Ark. 308, 820 S.W.2d 263 (1991), the attorneys were paid a $60,000 retainer, in part because the case required a great deal of immediate attention. The attorneys, upon being discharged, billed for over 1,100 hours of legal services, though they had actually performed minimal legal services. Among other things, the attorneys attributed between 500 and 600 hours to the research and preparation of a federal complaint that was ultimately dismissed. In affirming the sanction imposed by the bar association, the Arkansas Supreme Court asserted that the sanction was based not on the amount of the retainer but rather on the attorneys' being paid for services they did not provide.

Additionally, it is inherently unreasonable for an attorney to charge more than the fee upon which the attorney and client have agreed. Even if a case turns out to be more difficult and complex than anticipated, the attorney may not charge more than the agreed-upon price unless he renegotiates with the client. Deliberate acts that result in the attorney making more money than agreed upon are naturally unethical, and it is amazing to read the case law and see the many ways in which attorneys have deliberately violated ethical standards concerning client funds. The McGrew hypothetical case is based on some of those real-life instances.

THE CASE OF GREED E. McGREW

Greed E. McGrew (Greedy) is at the end of another long day at the law office. As is his custom, he gives his accounts receivable to his new legal assistant, Reid Coleman. Reid is very familiar with legal billing practices, as he had that responsibility while working for a large firm, but he has never done billing for Greedy before now. As Reid peruses the bills, he first notices a $1,200 bill for a real estate closing, though the contract specified a fixed fee of $500. Reid remembers sending the engagement letter, but has no recollection of any fee renegotiation. He then looks at the Bates account, which is being handled on a contingency basis, and notices that certain items have been double-charged, increasing the contingency amount. In the Jesse James file, Reid finds a signed agreement for a contingency fee to be paid for McGrew's work on the armed robbery charge against James; the fee will be adjusted according to the severity of the punishment imposed on James. Finally, he looks at the file in the Hunter case. Ms. Hunter gave

Greedy a retainer of $1,000 at the initial interview, but then called and discharged him. When Reid tried to return the retainer to Ms. Hunter, he found that it had been deposited into Greedy's personal account. "What in the world is going on here?" wonders Reid. And then he remembers: he is a legal assistant to the one and only Greed E. McGrew.

Statutory Fees

One additional type of fee is the *statutory fee.* In this instance, a statute provides that the legal bill be paid by the opposing party. In the American legal system, attorney fees are generally paid by the client who hires the attorney; in England, the source of much American law, and some European countries, lawyer fees are paid by the losing party. When a statute's remedy includes attorney fees, part of the award for a prevailing litigant is compensation for attorney fees. As you can imagine, this can come to a tremendous amount of money.

Statutory fees are significant for legal assistants who work in litigation which provides for statutory fee cases. In *Missouri v. Jenkins,* 491 U.S. 274 (1989) (excerpted in § 3.10), the United States Supreme Court confronted the issues of whether paralegal fees were part of statutory fees and, if so, whether they were payable at cost or at market rate. This decision was critically important and positive for the paralegal profession; the Court upheld the payment of paralegal fees—and at market rates, which include profits to the firm, not merely the cost for the paralegal service. This decision solidified the position of the legal assistant within the legal profession, because the Supreme Court officially recognized what many in the legal profession had already realized: that paralegals help contain costs for litigants and should be compensated as valuable contributors to the legal team.

Despite the *Missouri* decision, courts continue to scrutinize fee requests in statutory cases to make sure that the fees charged are reasonable. In *In re Continental Securities Litigation* 750 F. Supp. 868 (N.D. Ill. 1990), three law firms requested an average hourly rate of $65 for paralegal and law clerk services. (Under *Missouri v. Jenkins,* market rates, rather than costs, are allowed.) The firms initially offered no justification for the rate, and further investigation showed that hourly rates for the paralegals working on the case ranged from $10 to $21.50, with most at the lower end of the scale. The court took the highest paralegal fee of $21.50, added 40 percent for profit (which it stated was reasonable), and concluded that the proper hourly rate for paralegal services was $44.10, not $65. This case shows that although paralegals are accepted within the profession enough to be paid market rates in statutory fee cases, firms must bill for paralegal and law clerk services at reasonable rates.

Division of Fees among Lawyers

Ethical rules prevent an attorney from dividing a fee for legal services with a lawyer who is not a partner or associate of the law firm except under three limited circumstances: when the client consents to the employment of the other attorney, after full disclosure; when the division of fees is in accordance with the percentage of work performed; and when the total fee of the two lawyers is not excessive. This ethical standard has been criticized by many who believe that the prohibition against fee-splitting with an attorney from another firm is an impetus for lawyers not to seek co-counsel, causing attorneys to take on cases that they may not be competent to handle.

You may wonder why there are ethical standards regarding the division of fees among lawyers. This rule buttresses the provisions against solicitation and the unauthorized practice of law. If lawyers were ethically permitted to split fees with nonlawyers, unethical lawyers could circumvent the rules prohibiting solicitation and nonlawyers arguably could practice law. The fiduciary relationship between the attorney and client might also be undermined if an attorney split the fee with someone else. The lawyer owes an absolute duty of loyalty to the client and must always act in the best interests of that client. Hypothetically, if a lawyer has a financial obligation to another who is not a client, the client being represented may not be zealously represented. By keeping in mind that any conflicting obligations owed by the attorney may undermine effective representation, you can understand why the ethical rules prohibit fee-splitting with nonlawyers.

THE CASE OF THE REDUCED FEE

Attorney Felix is a solo practitioner; paralegal Sheila is his trusted assistant. Attorney Felix recently handled Sheila's divorce for a reduced fee of $200. Today, Sheila is asked to write a letter to Ms. Jerri von Micks, informing Ms. Micks that attorney Felix has waived his fee in her divorce case. Sheila is personally annoyed that she did not get a full fee waiver, and she also tells Felix that ethical rules prohibit a lawyer from engaging in price discrimination.

Has Felix done anything unethical?

Dividing Fees with a Nonlawyer

The ethical considerations are significantly stricter regarding the division of fees with nonlawyers. This principle is especially important for the paralegal to learn and understand. Basically, the rule is that a lawyer should never share a fee with a nonlawyer. However, like all other ethical considerations, there are some exceptions to this general rule.

RULE 5.4 Professional Independence of a Lawyer

(a) A lawyer or law firm shall not share legal fees with a nonlawyer, except that:

(1) an agreement by a lawyer with the lawyer's firm, partner, or associate may provide for the payment of money, over a reasonable period of time after the lawyer's death, to the lawyer's estate or to one or more specified persons;

(2) a lawyer who undertakes to complete unfinished legal business of a deceased lawyer may pay to the estate of the deceased lawyer that proportion of the total compensation which fairly represents the services rendered by the deceased lawyer; and

(3) a lawyer or law firm may include nonlawyer employees in a compensation or retirement plan, even though the plan is based in whole or in part on a profit-sharing arrangement.

(b) A lawyer shall not form a partnership with a nonlawyer if any of the activities of the partnership consist of the practice of law.

(c) A lawyer shall not permit a person who recommends, employs, or pays the lawyer to render legal services for another to direct or regulate the lawyer's professional judgment in rendering such legal services.

(d) A lawyer shall not practice with or in the form of a professional corporation or association authorized to practice law for a profit, if:

(1) a nonlawyer owns any interest therein, except that a fiduciary representative of the estate of a lawyer may hold the stock or interest of the lawyer for a reasonable time during administration;

(2) a nonlawyer is a corporate director or officer thereof; or

(3) a nonlawyer has the right to direct or control the professional judgment of a lawyer.

The rules preclude splitting fees with nonlawyers so that attorneys cannot bypass the prohibitions against solicitation by using nonlawyers on staff to solicit business for the attorney. By not permitting fee-splitting, the incidence of nonlawyers soliciting business on behalf of lawyers theoretically is greatly reduced, because nonlawyers thus have less incentive to solicit cases. It is less likely that a legal assistant will take the time and effort to solicit a case if there is no financial reward for doing so. A percentage of the judgment, however, might be a very attractive motivation for a legal assistant to solicit business; because this arrangement might encourage unethical marketing practices, it is impermissible.

In addition to responding to concerns about improper solicitation, the ethical considerations precluding fee-splitting with nonlawyers also support the prohibition against the unauthorized practice of law. When soliciting, a legal assistant could easily be put in a situation of having to give advice or assurance of representation (which might constitute unauthorized legal practice).

The exceptions to this rule cover situations in which these circumstances are not likely. First, an attorney may make an agreement with his partner or firm to pay his estate or other specified persons. Second, the lawyer may complete the unfinished business of a deceased lawyer and pay the deceased lawyer's estate for the services rendered by the deceased lawyer. Third, the lawyer or law firm may include nonlawyers in a retirement plan, even if the plan is based on profit sharing. In all these exceptions, the attorney's duty to the client is not jeopardized; therefore, the rules except these situations that technically would amount to an unethical splitting of legal fees and compensation.

THE CASE OF THE CONNECTED CHIROPRACTOR

Sharon Avey is an excellent chiropractor with a large practice in Detroit. Her twin brothers, Robert and Richard, recently graduated from law school and opened their own firm, also in Detroit, specializing in personal injury and worker's compensation. They realize that their sister Sharon might be an excellent source of referrals, so they make a deal with Sharon: for every client she sends them, they will pay her a "referral fee" of 15 percent of their earned legal fees on the case.

Is there anything unethical about this arrangement?

8.3 PRESERVING CLIENT FUNDS

The most significant ethical rule pertaining to legal accounting concerns the preservation of clients' funds. This is a principle that many paralegals face daily and most have to deal with routinely. The ethical standards governing client funds are as follows:

1. An attorney should *never* commingle personal funds with clients' funds.
2. An attorney should promptly notify the client when she receives property for the client.
3. When a client has paid a retainer, the attorney should withdraw only that amount earned to date.

Following these three principles will help the persons responsible for client monies avoid problems involving client funds. As for the commingling of funds, all settlements, retainers, or other client funds which the attorney holds must be deposited in an escrow account. The escrow account should be separate from the general operating account that the attorney uses to pay rent, salaries, and other expenses.

When the attorney receives settlement funds on behalf of the client, the client should be notified. Frequently, this involves billing the client. If fees owed are to be paid out of this settlement, the attorney should conform to the agreement in deducting fees and expenses from the settlement. For example, in cases taken on a contingency basis, the attorney receives a certain percentage of the settlement amount. In such a situation, the attorney should deposit the settlement check in his escrow account and then cut separate checks for the client, his attorney fees, and any reimbursable expenses accrued during the course of representation. This procedure provides the best documentation, for ethical reasons as well as tax purposes. The attorney should then send the check to the client with a copy of the agreement and a letter documenting all of the expenses deducted. This simple procedure eliminates most accounting problems.

If a client pays a retainer to a lawyer, both attorney and client should execute a contract specifying the billing arrangements. Further, the contract, sometimes known as a *letter of representation* or an *engagement letter,* should designate whether the retainer is refundable and how the retainer will be used (e.g., taken on a monthly basis at a particular hourly rate or taken in a certain amount per month). Sums paid by clients for retainers should be placed in the lawyer's escrow account. The attorney should bill the client for the work done and then pay herself with a check from the escrow account.

"This goes into the general operating account, this goes into escrow, this . . ."

8.4 MISAPPROPRIATION OF CLIENT FUNDS

Commingling of client funds is but one way in which an attorney can misappropriate client monies. An attorney may, with all good intentions, "borrow" money from one account to pay bills on another, or may deliberately embezzle money from clients. Poor accounting practices, ineffective office systems and procedures, and general carelessness also lead to misappropriation of client funds. Misuse of client funds takes many forms and can occur at many stages during client representation. It is a clear and, unfortunately, not uncommon, type of unethical behavior by attorneys.

Although the attorney's intent does affect the severity of the punishment, even unintentional misappropriation is cause for the bar to discipline the attorney. In general, unintentional misappropriation results in suspension, while intentional misappropriation results in the most severe form of attorney discipline—disbarment. For example, carelessness in accounting generally will not lead to disbarment, but intentional use of client funds, acts to conceal improper use, and willful unauthorized use would be cause for disbarment. Although courts look at the facts of each case in a disbarment proceeding, do not expect courts to be lenient with those who act unethically with client funds. As an example of the courts' harshness towards intentional misappropriation, consider *Disciplinary Board v. Kim,* 583 P.2d 333 (Haw. 1978). Attorney Kim had in fact misappropriated almost all of his client's $55,000 trust fund account; he did, however, repay the full amount. Testimony also indicated that he was fit to practice law but had been in poor health at the time of the misappropriation, a fact that might explain his unethical conduct. Nonetheless, the Hawaii Supreme Court sustained Kim's disbarment from the practice of law.

When an attorney has converted client or firm funds, most jurisdictions, like Hawaii, will not consider mitigating factors and will move to disbar the attorney. As the court stated in *In re Salinger,* 88 A.D.2d 133 (N.Y. 1st Dep't 1982), in which a young attorney converted cash fees and had checks made out to him rather than the law firm, "Any attorney who converts funds entrusted to his custody is, presumptively, unfit to be a member of the Bar." Clearly, legal professionals who handle client funds must take great care in establishing systems and procedures which ensure that their actions conform to the ethical standards of the legal profession. If those ethical standards are violated, severe penalties will follow.

8.5 RULES AND GUIDELINES CONCERNING FUNDS

ABA Model Rules

Rule 1.5 of the Model Rules concerns fees. It is a relatively straightforward provision.

RULE 1.5 Fees

(a) A lawyer's fee shall be reasonable. The factors to be considered in determining the reasonableness of a fee include the following:

(1) the time and labor required, the novelty and difficulty of the questions involved, and the skill requisite to perform the legal service properly;

(2) the likelihood, if apparent to the client, that the acceptance of the particular employment will preclude other employment by the lawyer;

(3) the fee customarily charged in the locality for similar legal services;

(4) the amount involved and the results obtained;

(5) the time limitations imposed by the client or by the circumstances;

(6) the nature and length of the professional relationship with the client;

(7) the experience, reputation, and ability of the lawyer or lawyers performing the services; and

(8) whether the fee is fixed or contingent.

(b) When the lawyer has not regularly represented the client, the basis or rate of the fee shall be communicated to the client, preferably in writing, before or within a reasonable time after commencing the representation.

(c) A fee may be contingent on the outcome of the matter for which the service is rendered, except in a matter in which a contingent fee is prohibited by paragraph (d) or other law. A contingent fee agreement shall be in writing and shall state the method by which the fee is to be determined, including the percentage or percentages that shall accrue to the lawyer in the event of settlement, trial or appeal, litigation and other expenses to be deducted from the recovery, and whether such expenses are to be deducted before or after the contingent fee is calculated. Upon conclusion of a contingent fee matter, the lawyer shall provide the client with a written statement stating the outcome of the matter and, if there is a recovery, showing the remittance to the client and the method of its determination.

(d) A lawyer shall not enter into an arrangement for, charge, or collect:

(1) any fee in a domestic relations matter, the payment or amount of which is contingent upon the securing of a divorce or upon the amount of alimony or support, or property settlement in lieu thereof; or

(2) a contingent fee for representing a defendant in a criminal case.

(e) A division of fee between lawyers who are not in the same firm may be made only if:

(1) the division is in proportion to the services performed by each lawyer or, by written agreement with the client, each lawyer assumes joint responsibility for the representation;

(2) the client is advised of and does not object to the participation of all the lawyers involved; and

(3) the total fee is reasonable.

Section 1.5(a) requires that the fee be reasonable and lists the factors to be considered in evaluating the reasonableness of the fee. Section 1.5(b) requires that a lawyer tell the client the fee structure within a reasonable time after commencing representation, preferably in writing. Section 1.5(c) concerns contingent fee arrangements, requiring that they be in writing and specify how the fee will be determined. Note that, under the Rules, contingent fee arrangements are required to be in writing, although other fee agreements need not be. Section 1.5(d) prohibits contingency fees in criminal or domestic relations cases. Finally, section 1.5(e) allows lawyers not in the same firm to share fees if the division is proportional or a written agreement assures the client that each lawyer assumes joint responsibility for the case, the client agrees, and the total fee is reasonable. The Comments following this Rule emphasize that the fee arrangement should be discussed and agreed upon early in the attorney-client relationship. It is completely ethical for a lawyer to accept as compensation property or an ownership interest in an enterprise as long as the attorney's interest does not amount to a proprietary interest in the cause of action or subject matter of the litigation—such an interest is contrary to Rule 1.8(j). Further, the value of the property should be commensurate with the value of the attorney's services. The Comments also forbid a fee arrangement that would induce the lawyer to improperly curtail services for the client. For example, the advocate should not enter into an agreement specifying that services will be provided only up to a stated amount if the matter might foreseeably require more extensive services. In fee-splitting arrangements with other lawyers, it is not necessary, according to the Comments following Rule 1.6, that the client be made aware of each attorney's percentage.

Rule 1.15 deals with the safekeeping of client property.

RULE 1.15 Safekeeping Property

(a) A lawyer shall hold property of clients or third persons that is in a lawyer's possession in connection with a representation separate from the lawyer's own property. Funds shall be kept in a separate account maintained in the state where the lawyer's office is situated, or elsewhere with the consent of the client or third person. Other property shall be identified as such and appropriately safeguarded. Complete records of such account funds and other property shall be kept by the lawyer and shall be preserved for a period of [five years] after termination of the representation.

(b) Upon receiving funds or other property in which a client or third person has an interest, a lawyer shall promptly notify the client or third person. Except as stated in this Rule or otherwise permitted by law or by agreement with the client, a lawyer shall promptly deliver to the client or third person any funds or other property that the client or third person is entitled to receive and, upon request by the client or third person, shall promptly render a full accounting regarding such property.

(c)   When in the course of representation a lawyer is in possession of property in which both the lawyer and another person claim interests, the property shall be kept separate by the lawyer until there is an accounting and severance of their interests. If a dispute arises concerning their respective interests, the portion in dispute shall be kept separate by the lawyer until the dispute is resolved.

Essentially, the Rule requires that attorneys hold clients' property with the same care required of professional fiduciaries. Thus, lawyers should handle clients' money as it would be handled by a trust department or a bank. This Rule emphasizes that client property should be kept separate from that of the attorney. If a lawyer obtains, from a third party, money from which his fee is to be paid, the attorney may retain that portion due to him for attorney fees. This situation often occurs when a lawyer settles a case with an insurance company on behalf of the client. If the client disputes the amount of money owed the attorney, the disputed amount should be held in escrow until the dispute is resolved. However, this is unlikely to occur if the lawyer and client have an engagement letter with the fee arrangement in it. Finally, if a third party has a right to a portion of the funds, such as in a garnishment action, the attorney may turn the money over to the client's creditor. In this situation, the lawyer has a duty to prevent the client from interfering in the disbursement of the funds to the third party.

As to pro bono work, ABA Rule 6.1 suggests that performing public service work is an ethical duty of the legal professional. (See § 3.9.) The Rules acknowledge and accept the basic responsibility of a lawyer to provide legal services in the public interest.

RULE 6.1   Pro Bono Publico Service

A lawyer should render public interest legal service. A lawyer may discharge this responsibility by providing professional services at no fee or a reduced fee to persons of limited means or to public service or charitable groups or organizations, by service in activities for improving the law, the legal system or the legal profession, and by financial support for organizations that provide legal services to persons of limited means.

The Comment to this Rule encourages "every lawyer, regardless of professional prominence or professional workload, [to] . . . find time to participate in or otherwise support the provision of free legal services to the disadvantaged." The Rules make the provision of legal services to the disadvantaged a greater ethical obligation than did the Code.

ABA Model Code

Disciplinary Rule 2-106 provides that attorneys may not charge excessive fees. The Disciplinary Rules delineate the factors to be taken into consideration when determining fees.

DR 2-106 Fees for Legal Services.

(A) A lawyer shall not enter into an agreement for, charge, or collect an illegal or clearly excessive fee.

(B) A fee is clearly excessive when, after a review of the facts, a lawyer of ordinary prudence would be left with a definite and firm conviction that the fee is in excess of a reasonable fee. Factors to be considered as guides in determining the reasonableness of a fee include the following:

(1) The time and labor required, the novelty and difficulty of the questions involved, and the skill requisite to perform the legal service properly.

(2) The likelihood, if apparent to the client, that the acceptance of the particular employment will preclude other employment by the lawyer.

(3) The fee customarily charged in the locality for similar legal services.

(4) The amount involved and the results obtained.

(5) The time limitations imposed by the client or by the circumstances.

(6) The nature and length of the professional relationship with the client.

(7) The experience, reputation, and ability of the lawyer or lawyers performing the services.

(8) Whether the fee is fixed or contingent.

(C) A lawyer shall not enter into an arrangement for, charge, or collect a contingent fee for representing a defendant in a criminal case.

DR 2-107 precludes attorneys from dividing fees when one is not the partner or associate of the other.

DR 2-107 Division of Fees Among Lawyers.

(A) A lawyer shall not divide a fee for legal services with another lawyer who is not a partner in or associate of his law firm or law office, unless:

(1) The client consents to employment of the other lawyer after a full disclosure that a division of fees will be made.

(2) The division is made in proportion to the services performed and responsibility assumed by each.

(3) The total fee of the lawyers does not clearly exceed reasonable compensation for all legal services they rendered the client.

(B)   This Disciplinary Rule does not prohibit payment to a former partner or associate pursuant to a separation or retirement agreement.

The Rule specifies that the fee may be split if the client consents after being informed of the fee-splitting arrangement, the division is made in proportion to the amount of work each attorney does, and the total fee of the attorneys is not excessive. This rule is inapplicable when a partner or associate is leaving the firm or retiring.

Disciplinary Rule 3-102 prevents attorneys from splitting fees with nonlawyers.

DR 3-102   Dividing Legal Fees with a Non-Lawyer.

(A)   A lawyer or law firm shall not share legal fees with a nonlawyer, except that:

(1)   An agreement by a lawyer with his firm, partner, or associate may provide for the payment of money, over a reasonable period of time after his death, to his estate or to one or more specified persons.

(2)   A lawyer who undertakes to complete unfinished legal business of a deceased lawyer may pay to the estate of the deceased lawyer that proportion of the total compensation which fairly represents the services rendered by the deceased lawyer.

(3)   A lawyer or law firm may include non-lawyer employees in a compensation or retirement plan, even though the plan is based in whole or in part on a profit-sharing arrangement providing such plan does not circumvent another disciplinary rule.

As previously discussed, this prevents attorneys from bypassing the ethical considerations surrounding advertising and solicitation by promising nonlawyers who refer clients to them a share in the fee from such cases. The Rule excepts cases in which the firm pays the estate of a partner or associate and instances when a firm includes nonlawyer employees in retirement plans, even though the plans may be based in whole or in part on profit sharing. These exceptions clearly do not fly in the face of the intent of the rule, which is to prevent circumvention of the prohibitions against solicitation or any unauthorized practice of the law.

The most extensive provision regarding clients funds is the requirement that such funds must be preserved and not commingled. *Commingling* occurs when client funds and attorney funds are not distinct; "commingling is committed when a client's money is intermingled with that of his attorney and its separate identity lost so that it may be used for the attorney's personal expenses or subjected to claims of his creditors." *Black v. State Bar,* 368 P.2d 118 (Cal. 1962). DR 9-102 sets forth the ethical standards for handling client funds.

DR 9-102   Preserving Identity of Funds and Property of a Client.

(A)   All funds of clients paid to a lawyer or law firm, other than advances for costs and expenses, shall be deposited in one or more identifiable bank accounts maintained in the state in which the law office is situated and no funds belonging to the lawyer or law firm shall be deposited therein except as follows:

(1)   Funds reasonably sufficient to pay bank charges may be deposited therein.

(2)   Funds belonging in part to a client and in part presently or potentially to the lawyer or law firm must be deposited therein, but the portion belonging to the lawyer or law firm may be withdrawn when due unless the right of the lawyer or law firm to receive it is disputed by the client, in which event the disputed portion shall not be withdrawn until the dispute is finally resolved.

(B)   A lawyer shall:

(1)   Promptly notify a client of the receipt of his funds, securities, or other properties.

(2)   Identify and label securities and properties of a client promptly upon receipt and place them in a safe deposit box or other place of safekeeping as soon as practicable.

(3)   Maintain complete records of all funds, securities, and other properties of a client coming into the possession of the lawyer and render appropriate accounts to his client regarding them.

(4)   Promptly pay or deliver to the client as requested by a client the funds, securities, or other properties in the possession of the lawyer which the client is entitled to receive.

The Disciplinary Rule states four principles that, if followed, will undoubtedly ensure that the prohibition against commingling funds will not be violated. First, lawyers have a duty to promptly notify the client of the receipt of funds, securities, or other properties. Second, the property of clients must be separately identified. Third, the attorney must maintain complete records. Fourth, the attorney must promptly pay any final settlement given to him as an attorney.

As for pro bono work, the Code has no provision comparable to that of Rule 6.1. The Code does provide, in EC 2-25, that each lawyer is responsible for providing legal services to those who cannot afford to pay for such services. EC 8-9, which encourages lawyers to advance the legal system, could be construed to motivate lawyers to accept pro bono cases. Although there is no affirmative obligation under the Code to handle pro bono cases, EC 8-3 states: "Those persons unable to pay for legal services should be provided needed services." Thus, the Code does not assert the need to handle pro bono cases as affirmatively or aggressively as do the Rules. (See § 3.9.)

NALA and NFPA

Because paralegals are precluded from accepting or declining representation, neither NALA nor NFPA sets forth any standards specific to this subject. However, the reality is that in many cases paralegals are responsible for properly depositing and accounting for client monies. Even though paralegals may not perform activities that might constitute the unauthorized practice of law, there is no limitation on paralegals doing accounting. Therefore, it is absolutely necessary that you understand the ethical considerations surrounding the handling of client funds, as this is one area in which the legal assistant can truly help the attorney manage the law practice.

Both NALA and NFPA state, in different ways, that pro bono work is encouraged. (See § 3.9.) Canon 10 of the NALA Code of Ethics and Professional Responsibility provides that: "A legal assistant shall strive for perfection through education in order to better assist the legal profession in fulfilling its duty of making legal services available to clients and the public." NFPA's Affirmation of Responsibility has two sections that could be construed to encourage pro bono work. NFPA states that: "The paralegal is dedicated to the development of the paralegal profession and endeavors to expand the responsibilities and the scope of paralegal work." The Discussion following section V., Protection of Public Interest, clearly encourages pro bono work: "The paralegal upholds the responsibility of protecting public interests by contributing to the delivery of quality legal services and by maintaining a sensitivity to public needs."

Finally, the fact that paralegals are choosing to freelance or become independent paralegals may raise issues concerning the ethical handling of funds. Therefore, even though NALA and NFPA do not have ethical guidelines for the paralegal who handles client funds, those contemplating freelance or independent paralegal work must understand and apply the standards and requirements of the local bar associations.

ABA Model Guidelines

Guideline 8 states: "A lawyer may include a charge for the work performed by a legal assistant in setting a charge for legal services." The Comment to this Guideline tracks the Supreme Court's decision in *Missouri v. Jenkins,* which recognized that an attorney, as part of reasonable attorney fees, may include a fee for legal assistants at market rates rather than at the attorney's actual cost for the paralegals. However, this Comment goes on to emphasize that the Court's decision in *Missouri v. Jenkins* should not abrogate an attorney's duty to set a reasonable fee for legal services.

Guideline 9 prohibits attorneys from splitting fees with a legal assistant, paying a legal assistant for referrals, or compensating the assistant on a contingency basis. This prohibition follows Rule 5.4, DR 3-102(A), and DR 3-103(A) and is found in all state bar association guidelines. Guideline 9 provides: "A lawyer may not split legal fees with a legal assistant nor pay a legal assistant for the referral of legal business. A lawyer may compensate a legal assistant based on the quantity and quality of the legal assistant's work and the value of that work to a law practice, but the legal assistant's compensation may not be contingent, by advance agreement, upon the profitability of the lawyer's practice." The Comment to this Guideline recognizes that there is nothing wrong with an attorney giving a paralegal a bonus during a particularly profitable period; however, the legal assistant's usual compensation should not be tied to the contingencies of particular cases.

Guideline 10 holds: "A lawyer who employs a legal assistant should facilitate the legal assistant's participation in appropriate continuing legal education and pro bono publico activities." Like the Rules, the Model Guidelines affirmatively encourage pro bono work. This Guideline, as its following Comments state, does not appear to have been adopted by any of the state bar associations. The Comments further assert that encouraging the use of paralegals in pro bono cases is consistent with the role of the legal assistant in the delivery of legal services generally. Both paralegals and the public benefit from pro bono work.

8.6 INTEREST EARNED ON CLIENT FUNDS

In all jurisdictions except the state of Indiana, attorneys who handle client funds, such as settlements and nonrefundable retainers, have an obligation to put these funds into a special interest-bearing account. These are known as Interest on Lawyers' Trust Accounts (IOLTA). There are three types of IOLTA: voluntary, mandatory, and opt-out. A voluntary account means that the attorney can choose whether to participate. A mandatory account means that the governing authority requires attorneys to participate if they handle client funds. Opt-out accounts are similar to voluntary accounts, but all attorneys must participate unless they affirmatively declare that they are unwilling to participate in the IOLTA program. The interest from such accounts is forwarded by the bank to the state bar or some other body, to be used by that particular organization or for charitable purposes. Usually, the attorney opening the account must certify that he or she does in fact have this account, uses the account of the firm, or does not handle client funds because he or she works for a governmental agency (such as the district or prosecuting attorney's office). In other jurisdictions, the attorney is able to open an escrow account for client funds, but may keep the interest earned. It is best to check the jurisdiction in which you practice to see if there are any special rules for these accounts. Most jurisdictions have either a voluntary or an opt-out IOLTA system, but some states, such as Georgia, have mandatory IOLTAs.

8.7 CLIENT SECURITY FUNDS

Although the ethical rules prohibit attorneys from taking client funds for their own use, there are many reports of lawyers who have taken their clients' money and used it for themselves. This is perhaps one of the most common breaches of ethical standards. Most bar associations either assess all bar members a special fee, ask for voluntary donations, or take the interest earned from IOLTAs and use this money to compensate individuals whose attorneys have absconded with their money. Legal professionals believe this to be good public relations, not to mention an ethical response to unethical behavior. By creating a fund through which clients damaged by the unscrupulous behavior of their attorneys can recoup their losses, the legal profession can somewhat alleviate the plight of those abused clients.

8.8 ETHICS AND BILLABLE HOURS

We have previously discussed different fee arrangements used by attorneys and clients, such as flat or contingency fees. One common fee arrangement has the law firm bill for the time expended on the client's behalf according to the hourly rate of the person providing the service. Attorneys and paralegals must therefore keep track of the time they spend which can be billed to each client— their *billable hours*.

The most frequently used method of tracking time divides an hour into 10-minute units. It is also common for firms to establish billable hour goals or requirements, for it is through billable hours that the firm generates income. Attorneys in large law firms might have yearly billable hour requirements in the 2,000- to 2,400-hour range; paralegals might fall into the 1,200- to 1,800-hour range. To appreciate how much work that is, realize that a yearly requirement of 2,000 billable hours works out to 40 billable hours per week for 50 weeks of the year; of course, hours you spend at lunch, in office meetings, organizing your form files, and preparing your time sheet are not billable.

The billable hour system obviously implicates several important ethical issues. First, it requires legal professionals to be remarkably exact in accounting for their time. Mistakes and misrepresentations may not be easy to detect, given the quantity of hours lawyers and paralegals bill and the number of timekeepers in a firm. Second, yearly billable hour goals send a "quantity over quality" message to the firm's timekeepers. Finally, the timesheet can change from a quality control device to the actual goal of practice, thereby transforming the legal practice from one of servicing clients to one of increasing billable hours.

To be sure, precise accounting and timekeeping is necessary for an ethical, successful law firm. Accounting and timekeeping enable the firm's clients to see what they have gotten for their legal fees, and they also help law firms assess their own work and productivity. However, the delicate issues involved in the concept of billable hours invite a corruption of the legal process, making it a money-driven, rather than service-driven, profession. The ethical law firm and practitioner must struggle to balance the need for structured accounting and productivity with the need to recognize that money should be the byproduct—not the goal—of practicing law.

THE CASE OF FLORIDA'S POOR ATTORNEY GENERAL

1991 was a tough year for Florida's attorney general when it came to finding inexpensive—or even reasonable—legal help. In March 1991, the New York law firm of Skadden, Arps, Slate, Meagher & Flom billed a state agency more than $5.7 million in an environmental case. Later that year, in November, four firms representing the state in a prison assault case charged $130,529 for a case that settled for $10,000. The inmate's ex-lawyer had originally offered to settle for $30,000; the firms that handled the case billed for a private pilot and hotel movie rental fees. It's tough, at least for the Florida AG, to find a decent fee these days!

8.9 PRO BONO WORK

Any discussion of fees and client funds must mention work that is performed without charging a fee, known as *pro bono work. Pro bono* is the shorthand phrase used by lawyers in place of the full phrase *pro bono publico,* which means "for the good of the public." Pro bono work is one important way the legal community can provide legal services for those who cannot afford to pay an attorney. As previously discussed, both the Rules and the Model Guidelines affirmatively encourage pro bono work. (See § 3.5.) Even the Code, though less obviously, encourages pro bono work.

Lawyers and legal assistants face an inherent conflict of interest in performing pro bono work. On one hand, pro bono work meets a real social need and can be rewarding and satisfying to the legal professional. On the other hand, it takes valuable time, and many legal professionals are already

"I specialize in pro bono work."

pressured by their firm's billable hour requirements and the demands of their existing caseload. Partly because of this conflict, voluntary pro bono efforts, although noble, really have not met the needs of the poor to find adequate legal representation. Some have made efforts to make pro bono work mandatory. Naturally, attorneys have resisted, but the future will see increasing efforts to provide services for the poor. Paralegals can make a significant contribution to providing services in the public interest, because the cost of paralegals is less than that of attorneys. In recognition of this, the NFPA Affirmation of Responsibility encourages the paralegal to "make every effort to educate the public as to the services and tasks the paralegal may render. Such services may be performed within a defined program specifically addressed to the needs of increased legal services to the public, including pro bono work." The future holds increased encouragement for the legal community to work in the public interest, and state legislatures and bar associations will continue to look for ways to increase the participation of professionals in public service work.

In his guest editorial, Ben Kempinen describes an innovative and exciting program using paralegals to help prisoners access the legal system.

GUEST EDITORIAL

PRISONER ACCESS TO JUSTICE AND PARALEGALS:
The Fox Lake Paralegal Program

by Ben Kempinen

A basic premise of our adversary system is that a correct result occurs when equally competent advocates present their claims to an informed and detached decision-maker. Whether this premise is realized depends on persons having meaningful access to legal assistance.

Nowhere is the need for legal assistance greater than in correctional and mental health institutions. The limited abilities of many offenders, inherent misconceptions and suspicions about the legal system, and the fact of confinement combine to make meaningful participation in the legal system difficult at best. Although most jurisdictions provide counsel to indigents in connection with their convictions, offenders experience a range of other legal problems for which legal assistance is both necessary and desirable. Among these are divorce, child support, visitation, consumer credit, traffic, and ordinance problems.

Since 1983, a paralegal program has been in existence at the medium security prison at Fox Lake, Wisconsin. In its current form, two inmate paralegals work in the program as their institutional job assignment. The assignment is initially made for a one-year period. The paralegals are supervised by attorneys from the Legal Assistance to Institutionalized Persons Program (LAIP), a clinical program of the University of Wisconsin Law School in Madison. LAIP helped develop the program and continues to supervise the inmate paralegals. The institution provides the paralegals with an office where they interview other offenders and maintain files and records. At least once every two weeks a supervising attorney from the law school consults with the paralegals about each of their cases.

At present, the program assists convicted offenders with civil and criminal law problems, including postconviction matters, obtaining sentence credits, resolving pending charges, and dealing with family law problems. To avoid conflicts with staff and to focus on other types of inmate problems, assistance is not provided in situations concerning conditions of confinement. Both the types of cases handled and the priorities among them parallel the activities of the LAIP Program, which involves the supervised work of second- and third-year law students. Consistent with LAIP priorities, the paralegal program has emphasized problems for which the offender has no other source of help and which, if resolved, would serve a correctional objective. For example, assisting an offender in resolving a child support problem while confined may enhance his chances of reintegration following release by encouraging a responsible approach to his support obligation.

All paralegal work is reviewed and approved by the supervising attorney. Also, strict controls are maintained over the paralegals' caseloads to ensure prompt and thorough work on each client's case. The program has greatly expanded the extent to which residents at the Fox Lake prison can expect legal help, particularly with civil law problems.

The Fox Lake experience provides an opportunity to examine the potential of paralegals in the delivery of legal service in an adult correctional institution. The experience may also be relevant to the lawyer's general use of paralegals.

A carefully structured and closely supervised paralegal program can be an effective response to the legal service needs of a prison population. The Fox Lake experience is instructive regarding the steps which should be taken in designing and operating such a program.

One threshold task is defining the paralegal's role and making sure that its scope and limits are understood and consistent with both the paralegal's abilities and the population's needs. Thorough attorney supervision of all work is also important to provide adequate guidance to paralegals and avoid unauthorized tender of legal assistance.

The Fox Lake paralegals were most effective when written, verbal and organizational skills, rather than knowledge of substantive and procedural law, were emphasized. A "systems" approach to recurring inmate problems was a helpful way of assuring the thoroughness and quality of work in specific areas. Inmate satisfaction with the paralegals' work was high, reflecting the emphasis on client contact and ensuring informed involvement of the client in all aspects of the case.

The program also provides useful vocational training to the participants, although the limited number of inmates with the ability to effectively perform as paralegals and the need for close attorney supervision of those working in the program prevented involvement by a significant number of inmates.

Finally, the program provided a number of benefits to the institution as a whole, particularly by encouraging a positive and cooperative effort between offenders, attorneys, and prison administrators to achieve common goals. For all of these reasons, the Fox Lake experience suggests a workable option for attorneys and correctional authorities who wish to ensure that offenders have meaningful access to justice.

■ Ben Kempinen is Clinical Associate Professor at the University of Wisconsin School of Law. This article was reprinted with permission of the copyright holder, *The New England Journal on Criminal and Civil Confinement.*

8.10 FUNDS AND THE PARALEGAL

The ethical considerations concerning funds affect legal assistants in many ways. Paralegals are usually involved in the law firm accounting process in one way or another, and some legal assistants are responsible for all of the firm's accounting, especially if it is a smaller firm. Even paralegals who do not have direct responsibility for accounting must be aware of how the process works so that the appropriate accounts will be used for certain tasks, such as depositing settlement checks, paying salaries, and the like. Unlike other businesses, law firms have ethical and legal obligations to place certain types of funds in particular accounts. If you, a paralegal, have primary responsibility for the firm's accounting, you must be sure that it is done correctly and professionally. This means not only ensuring that funds are deposited and withdrawn from the proper accounts, but also that the accounts are balanced each month, deposits and withdrawals are promptly recorded, and checks are not written on accounts with insufficient funds. You should also make yourself aware of any relevant Internal Revenue Service requirements.

Another special area of concern dealing with funds that affects paralegals is billable hours. Most legal assistants, except some in public practice, must keep records of the time they spend performing specific duties for particular clients in each case. Time is the commodity which the legal profession sells to the public; therefore, it is imperative that time recording be done correctly and accurately. There are two basic rules to follow when filling out one's timesheet: do it honestly and do it intelligently.

Honesty means, basically, not charging a client for something that you have not done or charging the client for more time than it took you to perform a particular task. This practice is known as "padding your time." Although in the short run padding your time may make you seem more productive and efficient than you actually are, it can easily catch up with you. If you bill a client for a task that you did not perform, someone will eventually realize that you lied on your timesheet. This undermines your integrity and casts doubt on your general work ethic.

The intelligence aspect of billing time balances awareness of the client's needs against the economics of performing a task in a certain manner. If you are working on a $200,000 personal injury case rather than a $200 collection case, you can probably justify summarizing and digesting depositions. Further, you probably should not use overnight mail for a noncritical document when working on the $200 collection case. Always be aware of your objectives and try to find the most inexpensive way to achieve them, to assist the client effectively. Paying attention to deadlines and not waiting until the last minute to complete important assignments is an excellent way to avoid spending unnecessary funds on a case. Although there are times when using overnight mail and couriers is unavoidable, save those times for when the delay is caused not by your own lack of preparation but by something beyond your control.

The Code, the Rules, and the Model Guidelines prohibit fee splitting between lawyers and nonlawyers. This means that an attorney cannot say that he will compensate you with a certain percentage of any amount he collects on a particular case. However, neither the Code, the Rules, nor the Model Guidelines preclude an attorney from compensating legal assistants with bonuses. Sometimes such a bonus is given at the end of the year, in the form of a Christmas bonus, or when the attorney settles an especially large case and decides that you deserve something extra for your excellent performance. Although the difference between fee splitting and bonuses is somewhat technical, it is nonetheless important to understand. Fee splitting occurs when your compensation is tied to the results in a particular case, whereas bonuses are extra payments that your employer may choose to give you for various reasons, such as doing excellent work or working especially long hours.

Pro bono work, as previously discussed, is legal work that the legal professional provides free of charge. The reasons for getting involved in pro bono work are not always obvious. Besides the general principle that one should help others, there are other, more selfish reasons to do pro bono work. It helps create a positive public image of the legal profession and paralegals. Further, it gives you a chance to work on many interesting cases and may in fact help you develop your skills. Pro bono work is not only interesting, but can also be very challenging. Even though it is not financially lucrative, it can be both personally and professionally rewarding.

Finally, as previously discussed, the Supreme Court decided in *Missouri v. Jenkins* that paralegal time would be compensated based at market rate rather than at the cost of the paralegal to the attorney. Thus, under *Missouri v. Jenkins,* paralegal time provides a profit mechanism for firms. The Supreme Court has recognized what many legal professionals have known for some time: namely, that paralegals are true professionals and should be treated as such.

8.11 CASE LAW CONCERNING FUNDS

The following cases show how courts have handled ethical violations relating to client funds. In the *Powell* case, ethical violations regarding funds, combined with instances of fraud and dishonesty, combined to cause attorney Powell to be disbarred.

LOUISIANA STATE BAR ASSOCIATION
v.
Jerome T. POWELL

Supreme Court of Louisiana
439 So. 2d 415 (La. 1983)

DENNIS, Justice.

This is an attorney disciplinary proceeding. The proceeding arises out of the attorney's handling of two different matters.

The Bates Succession

In 1977 respondent attorney, Jerome T. Powell, was retained by the heirs of Liner Bates to handle Bates' succession. Representing that it was necessary to mortgage some of the succession property to pay succession debts, Powell obtained the heirs' signatures on a promissory note secured by a mortgage on the Bates family home. Powell pledged the note to a mortgage company to secure a loan by it to himself in the amount of $8321.00. Subsequently, the mortgage company foreclosed on the property and demanded rent from the Bates heirs.

The Bates heirs testified that they did not receive any of the loan proceeds, [and] that although their signatures were on the note, they did not remember having signed it. In his defense, Powell testified that the heirs knowingly signed the instruments to enable him to pay the succession debts and that all of the loan proceeds were used for this purpose, for advances to the Bates heirs, or for the payment of expenses for them. Powell produced an itemized statement which purported to describe his expenditures of the loan proceeds. This statement was compiled by Powell in response to a discovery motion filed by an attorney for the Bates heirs in a civil suit and was not a contemporaneous record of the expenditures. The Bates heirs acknowledged that some of the items were valid but specifically denied having received direct or indirect benefit of many of the payments on Powell's list. Powell had never tendered a statement of account to the Bates heirs showing his fees or expenses in connection with the succession.

The Commissioner found clear and convincing evidence that Powell had violated Disciplinary Rule 9-102, "Preserving Identity of Funds and Property of a Client," by his failure to preserve the identity of the funds owed his clients and owed him by his clients, and/or to be disbursed by him on behalf of his clients. The Commissioner's findings are correct because Powell did not keep his client's funds in a separate bank account, notify his clients of the receipt of their funds, securities or other properties, maintain complete records of client funds coming into his possession, render appropriate accounts to his clients regarding them, or promptly pay or deliver to the clients as requested the funds or property in the lawyer's possession which they were entitled to receive. . . .

Although the Commissioner found some evidence that Powell had defrauded his clients by obtaining their signatures by misrepresentation, D.R. 1-102, and had neglected a legal matter entrusted to him, D.R. 6-101(A)(3), he apparently felt that the burden of proof had not been sustained as to these alleged violations and did not recommend any sanction in this regard. For the commingling breach, however, the Commissioner recommended a six-month suspension of membership in the bar.

In its brief in this court the Committee on Professional Responsibility contends that Powell obtained the heirs' consent to the mortgage of their home through fraud and subterfuge and converted all of the funds to his own use. The Committee points out that many of the payments listed on Powell's itemized statement do not relate to succession debts which the loan was designed to retire but to purported personal expenses of the heirs incurred later during Powell's unnecessary and unwarranted retention of the proceeds. Nevertheless, we agree with the Commissioner that the Committee failed to prove a case of fraud in this instance by clear and convincing evidence as required by our jurisprudence. It is undisputed that the Bates' heirs received benefit of a substantial part of the loan proceeds, that they actually signed the note in question, and that they were aware Powell intended to mortgage succession property. While there is abundant evidence of undisciplined commingling of funds, the Committee has not sustained its burden of proof as to actual fraud.

The Brown E. Moore Note

In 1979, Respondent attorney Powell presented to the Pioneer Bank & Trust Company a promissory note signed by his client Brown E. Moore, payable to the order of the bank in the amount of $2000. Powell endorsed the note himself to renew a loan which, according to Mr. Powell, Brown E. Moore had made for Powell's benefit. At the time of this transaction Brown E. Moore was suffering from his last illness and was incapable of having signed the note. A handwriting expert employed by the Committee compared the signature on the note with other specimens of Brown E. Moore's handwriting and testified that the note signature had been forged. In his defense, Powell testified that on an occasion prior to Moore's illness, when Moore was leaving for an extended trip to California, Moore had given Powell the signed note to use in obtaining funds in case Powell was unable to make timely payments on his bank note. However, Powell did not contest the fact that the note was a forgery. He testified that he received the signed note in an envelope from Moore, and he presented no expert handwriting testimony of his own.

The Commissioner and the Committee concur in finding that the respondent breached D.R. . . . 1-102 by engaging in conduct involving dishonesty, fraud, deceit or misrepresentation and D.R. 9-102 by commingling of his client's funds with his own. We agree with the findings of dishonesty and fraud, but the evidence does not support a finding of commingling since Powell obtained credit and not funds by his deceit. The respondent's explanation is weak and unlikely in view of the damning evidence against him.

As a sanction, the Commissioner recommends a three-year suspension and the Committee recommends disbarment.

Conclusion

The purpose of lawyer disciplinary proceedings is not so much to punish the attorney as it is to maintain appropriate standards of professional conduct in order to protect the public and the administration of justice. . . . The discipline to be imposed in a particular case, of course, will depend upon the seriousness and circumstances of the offense, fashioned in light of the purpose of lawyer discipline, taking into account aggravating and mitigating circumstances.

In view of these precepts and our finding that respondent has violated Disciplinary Rules 1-102 and 9-102, we adopt the Committee on Professional Responsibility's recommendation that respondent be disbarred. The misuse of a client's funds by an attorney represents the gravest form of professional misconduct. It strikes at the heart of public confidence in the legal profession. Obtaining credit by fraud at a client's expense is equally grave and reprehensible. Additionally, this is the second time defendant has been found guilty of a serious disciplinary rule violation. See *LSBA v. Powell,* 248 La. 237, 178 So.2d 235 (1965). Under these circumstances, and in the absence of any significant mitigating factors, we conclude that the maintenance of appropriate professional standards, the protection of the public, and the administration of justice require that the respondent be removed from the practice of law.

Accordingly, for the reasons assigned, it is ordered, adjudged, and decreed that the name of Jerome T. Powell, respondent, be stricken from the roll of attorneys and his license to practice law in the State of Louisiana be revoked.

DISBARMENT ORDERED.

CASE QUESTIONS

1. What specific Code provisions and other factors did the court consider in its evaluation of Powell's actions?

2. Do you agree with the Louisiana Supreme Court that disbarment is a better penalty than a three-year suspension?

3. According to the court, which was Powell's gravest violation, fraud or commingling? In your opinion, is one of these violations more serious than the other, or are they equally serious?

In the *Mannis* case, you will see how an attorney receives a public reprimand because his employees commingled funds; although the attorney was disciplined, his relatively lenient punishment was due to his lack of knowledge of the situation, his lack of intent to enrich himself, lack of harm to the client, and good faith efforts to handle funds properly.

In re Complaint as to the CONDUCT OF Richard S. MANNIS, Accused

Supreme Court of Oregon
668 P.2d 1224 (Or. 1983)

PER CURIAM.

The issue framed by the briefs and oral argument is what sanction to impose for violations of DR 9-102(A) of the Code of Professional Responsibility, which provides:

"All funds of clients paid to a lawyer or law firm, including advances for costs and expenses, shall be deposited in one or more identifiable trust accounts maintained in the state in which the law office is situated and no funds belonging to the lawyer or law firm shall be deposited therein except as follows:

"(1) Funds reasonably sufficient to pay account charges may be deposited therein.

"(2) Funds belonging in part to a client and in part presently or potentially to the lawyer or law firm must be deposited therein, but the portion belonging to the lawyer or law firm may be withdrawn when due unless the right of the lawyer or law firm to receive it is disputed by the client, in which event the disputed portion shall not be withdrawn until the dispute is finally resolved."

Simply stated, the record discloses that the accused's clients' funds, on many occasions, were not deposited in an identifiable trust account; rather, they were deposited in the accused's general account.

We find that it has not been established by clear and convincing evidence that the accused was personally aware of the commingling of his clients' funds with his own. We accept the findings of the Trial Board and the Disciplinary Review Board that the accused's employees were responsible for the comminglings and that the accused had spent considerable funds in attempting to establish his banking, bookkeeping and accounting systems on both a businesslike and ethical basis. We further find, as did the Boards, that the commingling was done with no intent of the accused to enrich himself and that no client was harmed by reason of the comminglings.

During oral argument, a member of this court raised the question of whether DR 9-102(A) is a "strict liability" provision and, therefore, a lawyer may be held to have violated the rule upon other than a personal participation basis. The parties, through respective counsel, acknowledged that nowhere in the course of these proceedings had that point been addressed. We are loath to do so without adversarial briefing and argument.

We shall, accordingly, assume for the purpose of disposition of this case that the lawyer is responsible for his employees' acts in commingling his funds with those of his clients.

The Disciplinary Review Board has recommended that this court publicly reprimand the accused. The record discloses that the accused has now instituted bookkeeping procedures to prevent further commingling. In the circumstances, we do not believe that a more serious sanction is justified. Although we stated in *In re Pierson,* 280 Or. 513, 571 P.2d 907 (1977), in general terms, that lawyers who converted their client's funds were to be disbarred, we have implicitly recognized that conversions may differ in kind. Here, although there was technically a conversion of clients' funds in the tort sense, the accused would be guilty of conversion only under the doctrine of respondeat superior.

This opinion will serve as a public reprimand to the accused. The Oregon State Bar is awarded its actual and necessary costs and disbursements.

CASE QUESTIONS

1. What factors did the court consider in disciplining the attorney?
2. Should attorney Mannis have been disbarred?
3. Is a violation under the doctrine of respondeat superior less serious than a direct violation? Is that what the court is implying?

Other sections of the *Caenen* case were featured in chapter 6, on advertising and solicitation, where you learned that Caenen was ultimately disbarred. This excerpt concerns Caenen's ethical violations of the rules concerning client funds. Caenen argued that it was his assistant who committed the violations.

STATE of Kansas, Petitioner

v.

Thomas J. CAENEN, Respondent

Supreme Court of Kansas
681 P.2d 639 (Kan. 1984)

The respondent challenges the panel's determination that he violated Disciplinary Rule 9-102(B)(1), (3) & (4) (232 Kan. cxcii), which provides:

"(B) A lawyer shall:

"(1) Promptly notify a client of the receipt of his funds, securities, or other properties. . . .

"(3) Maintain complete records of all funds, securities, and other properties of a client coming into the possession of the lawyer and render appropriate accounts to his client regarding them.

"(4) Promptly pay or deliver to the client as requested by a client the funds, securities, or other properties in the possession of the lawyer which the client is entitled to receive."

Caenen argues the person responsible for his collections, Mr. Evans, did not keep accurate records, and that the respondent has trouble substantiating that a $50.00 payment was made by Eason to the respondent's office. In *State v. Barrett,* 207 Kan. 178, 184, 483 P.2d 1106 (1971), the court stated:

"It is intimated by respondent that some of the shortcomings set forth in the record may have occurred by reason of the action of his secretaries and other lay persons in the office.

"A lawyer often delegates tasks to clerks, secretaries and other lay persons in his office. Such delegation is proper if the lawyer maintains a direct relationship with his client, supervises the delegated work, and has complete professional responsibility for the work product. [Citation omitted.]

"The work done by secretaries and other lay persons is done as agents of the lawyer employing them. The lawyer must supervise their work and be responsible for their work product or the lack of it. [Citation omitted.]"

Evans' records showed a $50.00 payment had been made by Eason. Caenen admitted his office records indicated the payment was received. Respondent must take responsibility for Evans' records. The hearing panel's conclusion that DR 9-102(B)(1), (3) and (4) were violated is supported by the evidence.

CASE QUESTIONS

1. Why is Caenen responsible if he did not make the mistake?
2. Does the amount of the error matter? Does the fact that the issue is a $50 payment mitigate the violation?
3. In the *Mannis* case, the attorney's lack of effective supervision was treated much more leniently than in this case. Why?

The previous cases excerpted in this section concerned ethical violations stemming from improper handling of funds. The following landmark case, heard by the Supreme Court, addresses the issue of paralegal fees under a fee-shifting statute. This case is significant not only because it focuses on paralegals but also because it holds that paralegal fees, determined at market rate and not at cost, are properly included in a statutory fee case.

MISSOURI, et al., Petitioners
v.
Kalima JENKINS, by her friend, Kamau AGYEI, et al.

109 S. Ct. 2463 (1989)

Justice BRENNAN delivered the opinion of the Court.

This is the attorney's-fee aftermath of major school desegregation litigation in Kansas City, Missouri. We granted certiorari, 488 U.S. __, 109 S.Ct. 218, 102 L.Ed. 2d 209 (1988) to resolve two questions relating to fees litigation under 42 U.S.C. 1988. First, does the Eleventh Amendment prohibit enhancement of a fee award against a State to compensate for delay in payment? Second, should the fee award compensate the work of paralegals and law clerks by applying the market rate for their work?

* * *

III

Missouri's second contention is that the District Court erred in compensating the work of law clerks and paralegals (hereinafter collectively "paralegals") at the market rates for their services, rather than at their cost to the attorney. While Missouri agrees that compensation for the cost of these personnel should be included in the fee award, it suggests that an hourly rate of $15—which it argued below corresponded to their salaries, benefits, and overhead—would be appropriate, rather than the market rates of $35 to $50. According to

Missouri, [42 U.S.C. §] 1988 does not authorize billing paralegals' hours at market rates, and doing so produces a "windfall" for the attorney.

We begin with the language, which provides simply for "a reasonable attorney's fee as part of the costs." 42 U.S.C. [§] 1988. Clearly, a "reasonable attorney's fee" cannot have been meant to compensate only work performed personally by members of the bar. Rather, the term must refer to a reasonable fee for the work product of an attorney. Thus, the fee must take into account the work not only of attorneys, but also of secretaries, messengers, librarians, janitors, and others whose labor contributes to the work product for which an attorney bills her client; and it must also take account of other expenses and profit. The parties have suggested no reason why the work of paralegals should not be similarly compensated, nor can we think of any. We thus take as our starting point the self-evident proposition the "reasonable attorney's fee" provided for by statute should compensate the work of paralegals, as well as that of attorneys. The more difficult question is how the work of paralegals is to be valued in calculating the overall attorney's fee.

The statute specifies a "reasonable" fee for the attorney's work product. In determining how other elements of the attorney's fee are to be calculated, we have consistently looked to the marketplace as our guide to what is "reasonable." In *Blum v. Stenson,* 465 U.S. 886, 104 S.Ct. 1541, 79 L.Ed.2d 891 (1984), for example, we rejected an argument that attorney's fees for nonprofit legal service organizations should be based on cost. We said: "The statute and legislative history establish that 'reasonable fees' under 1988 are to be calculated according to the prevailing market rates in the relevant community. . . ." *Id.,* at 895, 104 S.Ct., at 1547. . . . A reasonable attorney's fee under 1988 is calculated on the basis of rates and practices prevailing in the relevant market, *i.e.,* "in line with those [rates] prevailing in the community for similar services by lawyers of reasonable comparable skill, experience, and reputation," *Blum, supra,* 465 U.S., at 896 n.11, 104 S.Ct., at 1547, n.11, and one that grants the successful civil rights plaintiff a "fully compensatory fee," comparable to what "is traditional with attorneys compensated by a fee-paying client."

If an attorney's fee awarded under 1988 is to yield the same level of compensation that would be available from the market, the "increasingly widespread custom of separately billing for the services of paralegals and law students who serve as clerks," *Ramos v. Lamm,* 713 F.2d 546, 558 (CA10 1983), must be taken into account. All else being equal, the hourly fee charged by an attorney whose rates include paralegal work in her hourly fee, or who bills separately for the work of paralegals at cost, will be higher than the hourly fee charged by an attorney competing in the same market who bills separately for the work of paralegals at "market rates." In other words, the prevailing "market rate" for attorney time is not independent of the manner in which

paralegal time is accounted for. Thus, if the prevailing practice in a given community were to bill paralegal time separately at market rates, fees awarded the attorney at market rates for attorney time would not be fully compensatory if the court refused to compensate hours billed by paralegals or did so only at "cost." Similarly, the fee awarded would be too high if the court accepted separate billing for paralegal hours in a market where that was not the custom.

We reject the argument that compensation for paralegals at rates above "cost" would yield a "windfall" for the prevailing attorney. Neither petitioners nor anyone else, to our knowledge, have ever suggested that the hourly rate applied to the work of an associate attorney in a law firm creates a windfall for the firm's partners or is otherwise improper under 1988, merely because it exceeds the cost of the attorney's services. If the fees are consistent with market rates and practices, the "windfall" argument has no more force with regard to paralegals than it does for associates. And it would hardly accord with Congress' intent to provide a "fully compensatory fee" if the prevailing plaintiff's attorney in a civil rights lawsuit were not permitted to bill separately for paralegals, while the defense attorney in the same litigation was able to take advantage of the prevailing practice and obtain market rates for such work. Yet that is precisely the result sought in this case by the State of Missouri, which appears to have paid its own outside counsel for the work of paralegals at the hourly rate of $35. . . .

Nothing in 1988 requires that the work of paralegals invariably be billed separately. If it is the practice in the relevant market to do so, or to bill the work of paralegals only at cost, that is all that 1988 requires. Where, however, the prevailing practice is to bill paralegal work at market rates, treating civil rights law-yers' fee requests in the same way is not only permitted by 1988, but also makes economic sense. By encouraging the use of lower-cost paralegals rather than attorneys wherever pos-sible, permitting market-rate billing of parale-gal hours "encourages cost-effective delivery of legal services and, by reducing the spiral-ling cost of civil rights litigation, furthers the policies underlying civil rights statutes."

Such separate billing appears to be the practice in most communities today. In the present case, Missouri concedes that "the lo-cal market typically bills separately for para-legal services," . . . and the District Court found that the requested hourly rates of $35 for law clerks, $40 for paralegals, and $50 for recent law graduates were the prevailing rates for such services in the Kansas City area. Un-der these circumstances, the court's decision

to award separate compensation at these rates was fully in accord with 1988.

IV

The courts below correctly granted a fee enhancement to compensate for delay in pay-ment and approved compensation of parale-gals and law clerks at market rates. The judgment of the Court of Appeals is therefore affirmed.

Justice MARSHALL took no part in the consideration or decision of this case.

Justice O'CONNOR, with whom Justice SCALIA joins, and with whom the Chief Jus-tice joins in part, concurring in part and dis-senting in part.

I agree with the Court that 42 U.S.C. 1988 allows compensation for the work of parale-gals and law clerks at market rates, and there-fore join Parts I and III of its opinion.

CASE QUESTIONS

1. What is the Court's view of the paralegal profession?
2. How do you think this case will affect the paralegal profession?
3. Is the Court correct in stating that paralegals should be compensated at market value rather than cost? Why?

8.12 RECOGNIZING AND RESOLVING PROBLEMS WITH CLIENT FUNDS

Ethical problems relating to client funds are easy to detect, for they re-volve around the accounting procedures and structures used by a law firm. To handle client funds ethically, it is only necessary to establish separate ac-counts and follow ethical procedures in the handling of those accounts.

Pro bono issues are also easy to identify: they occur when somebody wants you to work for free! But the decision to perform pro bono work pre-sents more difficult problems, because such work appeals to one's sense of fairness and justice but at the same time requires uncompensated time. Through pro bono work, those who most need, yet can least afford, legal services receive the benefits of your efforts. Nevertheless, providing these services takes personal sacrifice of time and energy, two of your most precious resources.

8.13 HANDLING CLIENT FUNDS: A SUMMARY

In the legal profession, as in many other walks of life, money can present some sticky problems. For legal professionals, who may be faced with handling large amounts of money that are not their own, a professional attitude toward handling money, combined with effective accounting systems and structures, will bring about compliance with the ethical rules in this area. At the outset of your legal career, be aware that one area of your work will involve handling client and firm funds; also be aware that some of the strictest bar punishments are responses to unethical behavior relating to money. The ethical paralegal is characterized by a total commitment to respect the rules concerning client funds and general money matters.

REVIEW QUESTIONS

1. How do you determine if an attorney's fee is reasonable?
2. What kinds of fee arrangements must be in writing? Which should be in writing?
3. What is pro bono work? Should pro bono work be mandatory for lawyers? Legal assistants?
4. What bank accounts are essential for a law office?

QUESTIONS FOR THOUGHT AND DISCUSSION

1. Can all a firm's accounts be at the same bank? Should they be?
2. Your billable hour requirements mandate that you bill 35 hours a week. Because you usually work 10 hours a day, this requirement has not been a problem. Recently, however, you and your spouse have been having problems, and you are finding it difficult to achieve your billable hour goals. What should you do?
3. Your supervising attorney recently settled a personal injury case for $2 million and gave you a $20,000 bonus because you referred the case to him. Is this ethical? What if the bonus was because of your hard work?
4. It has been a very difficult time for the small firm of Make, Jake, and Rake—sometimes there is barely enough for payroll. This week the firm cannot meet its payroll, but the firm has just received a $10,000 nonrefundable retainer from a new client, on whose case it has just begun work. Can the firm put the $10,000 into its payroll account?

5. Ed Leroy is a highly motivated and well-trained legal assistant who has worked with a group of attorneys in a large metropolitan Atlanta firm for nine years. The group for which Ed works has decided to leave the big firm practice and set up their own boutique firm specializing in bond, debenture, and securities work. They have asked Ed to be the office manager and supervising paralegal at their new firm.

Ed readily agrees and gives the current firm two weeks' notice. On one of his lunch breaks during his last two weeks, Ed makes a list of various business-related matters that he must take care of for the new firm. One of these is setting up the bank accounts. What accounts should Ed set up and why? When drafting the office manual for the firm, what should Ed specify as to each account?

Finally, Ed goes to work at the new firm. On the very first day, the City of New Orleans retains the firm to help it handle its new bonds issuances for the construction of Super Dome Two. The attorney for the city has issued a check for $1 million to the firm as a retainer for doing the bond work. Ed is given the check and is told to handle it. Ecstatic that the firm already has $1 million in revenues, Ed deposits the check and orders $750,000 of office equipment and supplies, cash on delivery. Any problems?

Chapter 9 Feature: Competence

LAW, LITERATURE AND ETHICS

From **Fatal Vision**
By Joe McGinniss

In early June, Bernie Segal had written Jeffrey MacDonald a letter.

Dear Jeff:

I am a little concerned about your wardrobe for the trial. The most important matter is for you (1) *not* to convey a "southern California image," (too much sun tan, polyester and beachy colors); (2) that you do not appear to be "too casual" about the whole matter (the world needs to see you looking somber, serious, burdened and even concerned about this trial); and (3) that you *do* appear to be (at least as to your looks) truthful, reliable and responsible. . . .

Segal was also concerned about the jury. At a cost of $15,000, he employed a Duke University psychology professor to assemble a demographic profile of the "ideal juror." The professor's staff made more than nine hundred random phone calls, asking respondents such general questions as whether they believed people in military service were more likely to commit violent crimes than civilians, whether they felt doctors made too much money, and whether they accepted the notion that a person who has an extramarital affair is not necessarily a bad person.

In reference to the MacDonald case specifically, those contacted were asked whether they had heard of it (81 percent had) and whether they had formed an opinion about his guilt (6 percent said he was "certainly guilty"; 29 percent said "probably guilty"; 33 percent said "probably not guilty"; 5 percent said "certainly not guilty" and 27 percent said they did not know).

The respondents were also asked a series of demographic questions pertaining to age, race, marital status, length of residence in the county, educational background, political affiliation, and regularity of church attendance.

A subsequent analysis of the demographic and attitudinal responses disclosed the combinations most closely associated with a predisposition toward belief in innocence. The professor had then weighted each of the factors, much as a horse player will do when analyzing a field of thoroughbreds, and had devised a mathematical formula that would enable Segal to evaluate each prospective juror quickly on the basis of responses to questions asked during the selection process.

The surprising result of the survey, the professor from Duke said, on the Friday before jury selection was to begin, was that the ideal jury would be composed mainly of conservative whites over the age of thirty-five—in most cases, just the kind of jury sought by the prosecution.

"It's true," the professor conceded in the temporary office Segal had acquired in downtown Raleigh. "What we want is the kind of typical 'good citizen' that the government is probably going to go after. They won't be able to figure out what we're doing. In fact, they may think we've gone a little crazy. You know, normally you see an American flag in the lapel, you get rid of the guy. Here, that's just the type we're looking for."

Jeffrey MacDonald, who was at the meeting, shook his head. "I hope you're as good as your reputation," he said, "because everything you're saying goes against my gut feeling."

"I know, I know," the professor said, "and I know that it's your life, not mine. But I'll tell you what," he continued, suddenly smiling. "If I'm wrong, I won't serve any time for you, but I promise I'll work for free on your appeal."

Jeffrey MacDonald glared at the man from Duke. Bernie Segal quickly interceded, employing his most soothing tone. "Jeff, Jeff, relax. There's not going to be any appeal. We're going to pick a jury that will not only acquit you but will come back and award punitive damages."

"I hope you're right," MacDonald said, getting up to leave the office. "Because, frankly, this scares the hell out of me."

Once the client had departed, the professor, who himself could be described as young and liberal, was able to speak with greater candor. "What Jeff doesn't understand," he said, gesturing toward his pile of statistical analysis, "is that it's my friends we want most to get rid of. They all think he's guilty as hell."

■ Reprinted by permission of The Putnam Publishing Group from *FATAL VISION* by Joe McGinnis. Copyright © 1983 by Joe McGinnis.

CHAPTER 9
Achieving Professional Competence

CHAPTER OVERVIEW

In this chapter you will learn about the concept of competence and how it relates to the paralegal profession, and the nexus between competency and communication. This chapter will help you understand the definition of competence *unique to the legal profession. You will learn ways to ensure that you, the legal assistant, always act in a competent manner and maintain your competence by participating in activities designed to develop your abilities as a legal professional.*

THE CASE OF THE SPECIALIZED GENERALIST

Mickey is a litigation paralegal who is politically very active. He enjoys his job as a legal assistant and has no plans to further his legal education through law school. Mickey has been involved in litigation his entire legal career and believes that, even lacking a law degree or certification from the bar, he can handle the job of a legal assistant in even the most complex litigation matters. His legal experiences have been many and varied. Not only was he the team leader for the paralegal group that worked on the firm's biggest case, an antitrust case against the national bar review course, but he has also worked intensively on other technical and complex cases during his 20-year paralegal career.

Mickey recently had his employment review and was given a 5 percent raise, the highest raise possible in the firm. He is already the highest-paid paralegal in the firm, but his salary is still $10,000 less than the lowest-paid attorney in the office. Mickey disagrees with this firm policy and decides that he should look for another position with better compensation.

Mickey signs a contract with the most prestigious headhunter for paralegals in the city. On his résumé, he states that he has had experience in all areas of the law and feels competent in handling any legal situation. Ms. Centre, the principal in the headhunting firm, sees Mickey's résumé and calls him in for an interview. After the interview she sends Mickey's résumé to the firm of Dollar, Quarter, and Dime, a firm specializing in corporate law. Mr. Dollar, the partner in charge of hiring a new paralegal, agrees to interview Mickey.

The next week Mickey interviews with Mr. Dollar. During the interview, Mr. Dollar tells Mickey that the paralegal needed must be intimately familiar with corporate transactions; this person will lead a team of paralegals working on a corporate merger. Mr. Dollar asks Mickey if he feels capable of handling the position. Mickey has found out that most paralegals in the firm of Dollar, Quarter, and Dime make as much as the attorneys, so he says yes and tells Mr. Dollar that he has worked on several cases involving corporate mergers. In truth, Mickey has never worked on any such case. His only real experience with corporations is in litigating cases that involved a corporation, but he does feel competent to perform the work.

Is Mickey headed for trouble? What might the ramifications for the firm be? Is it Mickey's or Mr. Dollar's responsibility to ensure that Mickey is competent to handle the job?

THE CASE OF THE EXTRADITION EXPERT

Roy is a legal assistant with the Danville County district attorney's office in Virginia. Because Danville County has a large international airport serving Washington, D.C., a significant portion of the cases handled by the district attorney's office are drug-related. The district attorney's office in

Danville is understaffed, like most prosecuting attorneys' offices throughout the country. To free the attorneys to handle courtroom duties, Roy has become the expert on extradition in the office. He performs all of the work for the extraditions, from drafting the documents to communicating with the various jurisdictions involved in a particular extradition. The only aspect of the job that Roy does not perform is appearing in court; he knows he cannot because of the ethical prohibition against practicing law without a license. Roy is so well-versed in extraditions that the district attorneys' offices throughout the state often contact him to ask questions about proper procedures.

Roy's most recent case involves a defendant being extradited to the former Soviet Union. Because Roy has handled over 2,000 extraditions to and from numerous foreign countries, has taken all continuing legal education requirements in the area of criminal law, and keeps abreast of world events, Roy feels that this extradition will be business as usual. Because this is a rush extradition, Roy stays late to draft the proper documents. The next morning, Roy hands the documents to the attorney, who is rushing to court. The attorney asks Roy if he has researched the issue of extradition to the former Soviet Union and properly followed any requirements the law or custom may require. Roy responds: "Of course, what do you think I am, incompetent?"

Has Roy in fact been incompetent? How would you have advised Roy to handle the situation? Is the attorney guilty of acting incompetently?

9.1 COMPETENCE: AN INTRODUCTION

Competence in the law is more than doing the job to the best of your ability or being proficient. Because the legal profession is founded on the principle of the fiduciary relationship of legal professionals to their clients, competence in the legal context requires more than giving 100 percent. Ethical considerations for both the attorney and the paralegal require that both be competent in representing the client's interests.

Both attorneys and paralegals begin developing professional competence through education, although in some cases they first gain competence through training or experience. Attorneys must graduate from law school, pass the bar examination, and, in many cases, pass an ethics exam before being admitted to practice. Most law firms have formal and informal training programs to help new attorneys learn to practice ethically and competently. Additionally, attorneys in at least 30 states must complete mandatory continuing legal education (CLE) classes, which ensure that legal practitioners are current in their understanding of the law.

Educational requirements for legal assistants are less standardized than they are for lawyers because legal assistants are not licensed by the state. Legal assistant programs can be found in a wide variety of settings, ranging from universities to community colleges to vocational schools. Paralegal training and education are offered at both public and private institutions. At present, about 30 percent of those programs have been approved by the ABA. ABA approval is voluntary; it signifies that the program has complied with requirements in areas such as curriculum, faculty, library, and school finances. Some legal assistants do not have a degree or certificate but have been trained on the job. Many practicing paralegals started their careers in other positions, such as legal secretary, and were chosen by their firm to be trained as a legal assistant.

Education, complemented by experience and training, is the means by which a professional achieves competence. *Competence* means fundamentally that the legal professional should handle only matters which he or she feels capable, by experience, education, or training, of handling. For instance, a real estate attorney, whose only exposure to criminal law was his law school classes and the criminal law portion of the bar examination, would be acting incompetently if he handled a capital felony case for a client. In addition to handling cases out of one's area of expertise, incompetence would also occur if a legal professional did not adequately prepare to handle a legal matter or neglected a matter entrusted to her.

> Neglect involves indifference and a consistent failure to carry out the obligations which the lawyer has assumed to his client or a conscious disregard for the responsibility owed to the client. The concept of ordinary negligence is different. Neglect usually involves more than a single act or omission. Neglect cannot be found if the acts or omissions complained of were inadvertent, or the result of an error in judgement made in good faith.

ABA Informal Opinion No. 1273 (1973). Although competence is hard to define, certain elements, taken together, might give more specific meaning to the idea of competence. In *Modern Legal Ethics* (West 1986), Charles Wolfram summarizes what he believes to be the elements of competence. These are:

1. Knowledge of the law, the legal process, and legal problems
2. Legal skills, including advising, analyzing, mediating, litigating, communicating, researching, and planning
3. Office management, including the development of an office system that will facilitate effective legal representation
4. Character, to serve clients effectively and ethically
5. Capability, that is, possessing the well-being to run a successful practice.

Although this list was prepared with lawyers in mind, these elements apply to paralegal competence as well (with modifications to the second). For paralegals, add an awareness of the distinctions between paralegals and lawyers; it is, for example, incompetence as well as unauthorized for a paralegal to practice law without a license. For legal assistants, knowing the parameters of their practice is integral to being competent.

As we have noted, the legal profession and the medical profession have a number of similarities. Like medicine, there are many specialties within the broad profession of law. The medical field has specialists on the parts of the body; the legal field has specialists for different legal problems. Within the law, common specialties include real estate, litigation, corporate, international law, bankruptcy, tax, and patent and trademark. Within these specialties, there are sub-specialties; in the area of litigation, one can specialize in commercial, personal injury, or family law litigation. The concept of competency does not mean that the general practitioner, in law or in medicine, can handle only one type of case. Rather, it means that a legal professional should not take a case unless the professional believes that the client's interests will not be harmed by the representation. Take, for example, our hypothetical situation of a real estate attorney handling a capital felony case. The attorney might in fact be competent *if* she does all the research necessary to understand the idiosyncrasies of criminal law. In this way, the client will not pay for the attorney's lack of experience, in the sense of either inadequate representation or financially (by having to pay for the attorney's research time).

Claims of legal malpractice might well arise with allegations of incompetency. As discussed, malpractice is a tort action against a professional filed by a client when the client believes that the professional breached the duty of competence. Thus, an attorney who routinely does real estate closings is not incompetent to handle a particular real estate closing, but might act incompetently by missing a lien on the property.

Although legal malpractice is the most extreme form of incompetence, incompetence can result from other actions not rising to the level of the tort of malpractice or professional negligence. These actions include:

1. Handling a case in an area in which the legal professional is not minimally proficient
2. Failing to advise someone who comes for advice that the case must be filed within the statute of limitations, or failing to advise them to seek counsel
3. Failing to follow accepted standards in the profession, such as docket control and conflict-of-interest checks
4. Failing to act professionally because of alcoholism or drug abuse
5. Failing to keep abreast of new laws, changes in current laws, and new case law
6. Failing to maintain the minimum levels of continuing education required by a particular professional organization, such as the state bar, NALA, or NFPA
7. Overestimating one's abilities
8. Failing to disclose or covering up an ethical problem

9. Failing to maintain contact and communicate effectively with the client.

This list is not all-inclusive, but it does provide a general guide to the kinds of actions that have been construed to be professional incompetence for legal practitioners.

Although malpractice is generally an attorney issue, and although paralegal negligence is usually imputed to the attorney on the basis of respondeat superior, paralegal liability might exist in certain circumstances. Under the doctrine of respondeat superior, the principal (the attorney) is liable for the wrongful acts of his agent (the paralegal) if the wrongful act occurred within the scope of the agent's employment. If, however, the wrongful act occurred outside the paralegal's scope of employment, the attorney is not liable. If a paralegal gave legal advice, contrary to specific instructions not to do so, or accepted or declined a case, contrary to the strict policy of the firm, the paralegal would be acting outside the scope of his employment. Under the doctrine of respondeat superior, the attorney and firm would not be liable to the client, but the paralegal would be. The best approach is for the legal assistant to take personal responsibility for achieving competence; not only will competence help you avoid negative consequences, but it is a cornerstone upon which you can build a professional identity and succeed in your career.

THE CASE OF NO WRONGFUL NATIVITY

Robert Carrie is a legal assistant in a small firm specializing in medical malpractice actions. Carrie works strictly on medical malpractice cases and has found his background as a nurse to be invaluable to both his work and the firm. He knows all the nuances of professional negligence cases and the proper procedures to ensure that clients collect the greatest amount of money possible for their claims. Because of Robert Carrie's medical expertise, he has been made responsible for drafting the initial complaints and ensuring that all of the allegations are properly asserted. His work is checked frequently by his supervising attorney, Ben Bali; however, Ben is confident that Robert does an outstanding job and rarely does more than skim the draft complaints before having the final versions printed. Robert knows that this is Ben's practice and is flattered by this show of confidence.

On Wednesday, after returning from lunch, Robert meets Tricia Allen in the waiting room. She needs to speak to an attorney immediately, for she thinks that the statute of limitations for her complaint will run tomorrow. As there is no attorney in the office, Robert takes down all the necessary information. He knows that ethical rules prohibit him from accepting a client but, because of his experience, he believes that he can get enough relevant information for Ben to decide whether to take the case.

Apparently, Tricia Allen has nine children, and after the ninth decided to have a tubal ligation. Ten months after having the tubal ligation, Tricia delivered a child who was severely retarded. Tricia had heard about a similar case in California in which the mother collected 4 million dollars in a cause of action called "wrongful birth." Tricia asks Robert if he can file such a claim. He responds that he cannot give legal advice, but that he will talk to the lawyer and see.

As Ben is not expected back in the office until later, Robert pulls the California case and discovers that Tricia is correct: there is a cause of action for wrongful birth and the statute of limitations is two years from the date of birth. Robert drafts a complaint and puts it, along with a letter accepting employment, on Ben's desk for his signature. As is his normal practice, Ben signs both without hesitation.

Once the doctor is served with the complaint, his lawyer files an answer and motion to dismiss in which he cites a 1992 statute: "There is no cause of action for wrongful birth in the State of Georgia." Obviously, the case is dismissed.

Did Robert or Ben act incompetently?

9.2 RULES AND REGULATIONS CONCERNING COMPETENCE

ABA Model Rules

A number of provisions of the Rules combine to give a relatively clear picture of the concept of competence for the legal professional. Rule 1.1 asserts that competence requires legal knowledge, skill, thoroughness, and preparation.

RULE 1.1 Competence

A lawyer shall provide competent representation to a client. Competent representation requires the legal knowledge, skill, thoroughness and preparation reasonably necessary for the representation.

The Comments to this Rule specify that competence does not necessarily require special training, or even prior experience, in handling unfamiliar legal problems. Rather, the essential elements of competence are skills such as analyzing precedent, evaluating evidence, legal drafting, and determining the nature of the legal claim.

Rule 1.3 imposes a duty of diligence and promptness on the attorney.

RULE 1.3 Diligence

A lawyer shall act with reasonable diligence and promptness in representing a client.

The Comments to Rule 1.3 show an awareness that procrastination is one of the most widely resented behaviors and can adversely affect a client's interests. Even when procrastination does not substantively affect a client's interest, it may cause needless anxiety and undermine confidence in the legal profession. Further, unless an attorney properly terminates the attorney-client relationship, as provided in Rule 1.16, the lawyer should conclude all matters undertaken for the client. This Comment emphasizes that if the attorney's representation of the client's interest is limited, it is best to clarify that limitation to the client in writing.

Rule 1.4 connects competence and communication by requiring the attorney to keep the client informed and to explain clearly so that the client can make informed decisions. Lacking complete information, the client cannot make intelligent decisions to advance his own interest.

RULE 1.4 Communication

(a) A lawyer shall keep a client reasonably informed about the status of a matter and promptly comply with reasonable requests for information.

(b) A lawyer shall explain a matter to the extent reasonably necessary to permit the client to make informed decisions regarding the representation.

The Comments following Rule 1.4 state, however, that an attorney may withhold information for a limited time if the lawyer believes that the client would react imprudently if told immediately. Likewise, some information, such as the results of a psychiatric evaluation, may be completely withheld if disclosure would harm the client. However, in no case may a lawyer withhold information to further his own interests or for his convenience.

Rule 8.3 extends competence to the reporting of unethical behavior by lawyers or judges. This rule requires a lawyer to report violations that implicate honesty, trustworthiness, or fitness to be a lawyer to the bar; it therefore defines competence as an affirmative duty to report the misconduct of others. Rule 8.4 specifically delineates professional behavior that characterizes misconduct, thus further defining what it means to provide competent representation.

RULE 8.3 Reporting Professional Misconduct

(a) A lawyer having knowledge that another lawyer has committed a violation of the Rules of Professional Conduct that raises a substantial question as to that lawyer's honesty, trustworthiness or fitness as a lawyer in other respects, shall inform the appropriate professional authority.

(b)   A lawyer having knowledge that a judge has committed a violation of applicable rules of judicial conduct that raises a substantial question as to the judge's fitness for office shall inform the appropriate authority.

(c)   This rules does not require disclosure of information otherwise protected by Rule 1.6.

RULE 8.4 Misconduct

It is professional misconduct for a lawyer to:

(a)   violate or attempt to violate the rules of professional conduct, knowingly assist or induce another to do so, or do so through the acts of another;

(b)   commit a criminal act that reflects adversely on the lawyer's honesty, trustworthiness or fitness as a lawyer in other respects;

(c)   engage in conduct involving dishonesty, fraud, deceit or misrepresentation;

(d)   engage in conduct that is prejudicial to the administration of justice;

(e)   state or imply an ability to influence improperly a government agency or official; or

(f)   knowingly assist a judge or judicial officer in conduct that is a violation of applicable rules of judicial conduct or other law.

ABA Model Code

The Code is less specific than the Rules concerning competence. Canon 6 of the Rules of Professional Responsibility provides that an attorney should represent a client competently. DR 6-101(A)(2) requires adequate preparation and DR 6-101(A)(2) prohibits neglecting a matter entrusted to the attorney.

DR 6-101 Failing to Act Competently.

(A)   A lawyer shall not:

(1)   Handle a legal matter which he knows or should know that he is not competent to handle, without associating with him a lawyer who is competent to handle it.

(2)   Handle a legal matter without preparation adequate in the circumstances.

(3)   Neglect a legal matter entrusted to him.

These general directives are made more specific by the Ethical Considerations concerning competency. The considerations direct the attorney to:

1. Remain proficient in the areas of practice and not accept cases that she is not or *does not intend to become* competent to handle (EC 6-1)
2. Maintain competence by keeping abreast of current legal developments and literature (EC 6-2)
3. Accept only cases for which she is competent or expects to become competent, and only if she will not unreasonably delay, or increase the expense to, the client while becoming competent. She may associate with another attorney competent in the matter (EC 6-3)
4. After accepting a case, safeguard the interests of the client (EC 6-4)
5. Seek to maintain competence as a part of professional responsibility, not merely to avoid a penalty (EC 6-5)
6. Limit her potential liability to a client (EC 6-6).

You may wonder why the Code permits an attorney to take a case in which he is not currently competent, but expects to become competent. Think of the newly admitted lawyer; in a real sense, he is not qualified to handle anything when he starts practicing. In this way, the Code attempts to deal with the practical problems associated with practicing law.

Like the Rules, the Code also attempts to define misconduct. This definition is found in DR 1-102, and DR 1-103 explains how to report professional misconduct.

DR 1-102 Misconduct.

(A) A lawyer shall not:
(1) Violate a Disciplinary Rule.
(2) Circumvent a Disciplinary Rule through actions of another.
(3) Engage in illegal conduct involving moral turpitude.
(4) Engage in conduct involving dishonesty, fraud, deceit, or misrepresentation.
(5) Engage in conduct that is prejudicial to the administration of justice.
(6) Engage in any other conduct that adversely reflects on his fitness to practice law.

DR 1-103 Disclosure of Information to Authorities.

(A) A lawyer possessing unprivileged knowledge of a violation of DR 1-102 shall report such knowledge to a tribunal or other authority empowered to investigate or act upon such violation.
(B) A lawyer possessing unprivileged knowledge or evidence concerning another lawyer or a judge shall reveal fully such knowledge or evidence upon proper request of a tribunal or other authority empowered to investigate or act upon the conduct of lawyers or judges.

These two sections are substantially similar to the Rules. DR 1-102 defines misconduct both specifically, as in a rule violation or fraudulent

activity, and generally, such as prohibiting behavior that adversely reflects on an attorney's ability to practice law. This vagueness is appropriate, as no rule can contemplate every possible type of incompetence or misconduct. Like Rule 8.3, DR 1-103 requires lawyers possessing nonprivileged information concerning a lawyer's or judge's violation of DR 1-102 to report that violation to the appropriate tribunal or authority.

NALA and NFPA

Both NALA and NFPA provide that paralegals, like attorneys, have a duty to act competently. The NFPA Affirmation provides that:

> A paralegal shall maintain a high level of competence and shall contribute to the integrity of the legal profession.
> Discussion: The integrity of the paralegal profession is predicated upon individual competence. Professional competence is each paralegal's responsibility and is achieved through continuing education, awareness of developments in the field of law and aspiring to the highest standards of personal performance.

Like NFPA, NALA's ethical rules specify that competence is necessary for the success of the legal assistant.

The specific Canons that relate to competency and the legal assistant are Canon 9, dealing with competence, and Canon 10, dealing with continuing legal education. These Canons provide as follows:

> Canon 9—A legal assistant shall work continually to maintain integrity and a high degree of competency throughout the legal profession.
> Canon 10—A legal assistant shall strive for perfection through education in order to better assist the legal profession in fulfilling its duty of making legal services available to clients and the public.

Although both paralegal associations deal with competence, there is one major difference between NFPA and NALA. As discussed earlier, NALA encourages legal assistants to obtain certification. This certification is intended to designate professional competence. Once a paralegal has successfully completed the exam, she is able to use the initials "CLA" after her name to designate that she is a certified legal assistant. Certification is entirely voluntary.

The program began in 1976. The initial test, which lasts two days, covers both substantive areas of the law and communication and analytical skills. The test covers only federal procedural and substantive law. The substantive areas include litigation, criminal law, bankruptcy, contract, corporate and administrative law, real estate, and probate and estate planning. Proponents of certification argue that regulating paralegals helps ensure competency in the paralegal profession.

In 1982, NALA established a procedure for specialty certification. This is an advanced level of certification available to legal assistants who have successfully completed the initial test. A legal assistant can be certified as a specialist in civil litigation, probate and estate planning, corporate and business law, real estate, or criminal law and procedure. NALA requires that CLAs renew their credentials every five years by attending a specific number of continuing legal education programs. According to NALA, this renewal provision "recognizes the constantly changing nature of the legal profession." NFPA does not advocate certification of paralegals.

Regardless of whether a paralegal pursues NALA certification, there are a number of ways for a legal assistant to increase his skills and knowledge. It is certainly a good idea to take continuing legal education (CLE) classes. These classes, which are usually offered by paralegal or bar associations, cover a wide variety of legal topics and enable participants to stay up-to-date with new developments in the law. A paralegal can also develop competence through individual study; this includes reading recent opinions, newly passed statutes, and amended procedural rules. The competent paralegal should also be a voracious reader of professional trade magazines and law journals. Paralegals should also learn to use newly emerging technologies in legal applications. A final way to maintain and develop professional competence is through membership in national or local organizations. Membership will expose you to new people and ideas, thus helping you develop your professional identity.

THE CASE OF THE COUNSELOR'S COMPETENCE

Attorney Jacobs is frazzled yet ecstatic, having just won a huge sex discrimination suit against the DeKalb Medical Center. Unfortunately, during the long suit, one of his paralegals had a baby and the other broke both legs in a skiing accident. Because both paralegals were out, Jacobs did not receive inquiries from client Shepord and left his calls unreturned. When client Bigelow arrived for an appointment to do his will, Jacobs had his secretary give Bigelow some standardized forms and instructions; Bigelow was told that the materials contained everything he needed to prepare his will. Jacobs's secretary also told him that she had lost the telephone number of witness Blumenkranz, who was to appear on behalf of Jacobs's client at trial next week. Jacobs told her not to worry about it. Finally, an electrical surge knocked out the firm's computers, but because both paralegals were out, no one contacted technical service to bring the system back up. The system contained the firm's docket control. Since the system was down and no one had double-checked the calendar, client Johansen's claim was barred because the filing date for the statute of limitations passed.

Jacobs hires you, a paralegal consultant, to help him with his office administration. He tells you his sad story and asks whether any of the situations rises to the level of incompetence and whether he has anything to worry about. What do you tell him?

"We paralegals gotta stay in shape."

9.3 THE SIXTH AMENDMENT AND THE RIGHT TO COMPETENT COUNSEL

The Sixth Amendment to the Constitution protects criminal defendants by guaranteeing them not merely assistance of counsel, but *effective* assistance of counsel. You might remember this concept from the *Blalock* case in chapter 4, in which the attorney's sexual conflict of interest was held to be ineffective assistance of counsel. The Sixth Amendment therefore acknowledges that it is not just an attorney, but a level of competence that is required to fulfill the Constitution's language. If such assistance is not forthcoming, that defendant may claim a constitutional violation based on the ineffective assistance of counsel. In *Strickland v. Washington,* 466 U.S. 668 (1984), the Supreme Court articulated a two-part test to determine whether a criminal defendant has been represented incompetently:

> A convicted defendant's claim that the counsel's assistance was so defective as to require reversal of a conviction or death sentence has two components. First, the defendant must show that the counsel's performance was deficient. This requires showing that counsel made errors so serious that counsel was not functioning as the "counsel" guaranteed the defendant by the Sixth Amendment. Second, the defendant must show that the deficient performance prejudiced the defense. This requires showing that counsel's errors were so serious as to deprive the defendant of a fair trial, a trial whose result is reliable. Unless a defendant makes both showings, it cannot be said that the conviction or death sentence resulted from a breakdown in the adversary process that renders the result unreliable.

Id. at 687.

In general, the attorney must satisfy an objective standard of reasonableness; the Court has found that failing to conduct pretrial discovery, failing to investigate an alibi defense, and being unfamiliar with trial procedures and examination techniques do constitute ineffective assistance of counsel. The Sixth Amendment, therefore, protects criminal defendants from incompetent representation upon a showing of deficient performance and prejudice to the defendant. Thus, criminal defendants have a constitutional protection against incompetence.

9.4 COMPETENCE, COMMUNICATION, AND THE PARALEGAL

Competence is an issue for all legal professionals. Both NALA's and NFPA's ethical standards require that the legal assistant act in a competent manner. Although these organizations differ on certification, they both support continuing development of knowledge and skills as a prerequisite to developing professional competence.

Every paralegal is responsible for his or her part of a case. Just as in a relay race, where one runner hands the baton to another, the legal assistant, as a member of the legal team, must make sure that her work is professional and competent, so that when the case is handed off to the next individual, he can successfully complete his leg of the race. Although attorneys are ultimately responsible for the work of their legal assistants, the time and money saved by using paralegals will be lost if the attorney must supervise every detail of the legal assistant's work. By doing such simple things as making sure that statutes have not been amended, ascertaining the filing deadlines for various offices, and shepardizing every case, you can ensure that you have competently performed your duties.

Competence does not depend on where you went to school, where you work, or where you grew up; rather, it springs from wanting to excel. Most attorneys will tell you that the key to being a successful legal professional is to pay attention to detail and be careful.

Perhaps the most important way legal assistants can make a difference in client relations and malpractice prevention is in the area of communication with clients. It is amazing to see the number of complaints bar organizations receive because attorneys fail to do simple things, such as return telephone calls from clients. By returning clients' calls, taking complete messages, and relaying the messages to the lawyer, a paralegal can help avoid a significant number of complaints to the bar as well as potential malpractice suits. Even if the legal assistant is so overworked that she cannot follow through with all these steps, simply telling a client that an attorney is unavailable, because she is out of town taking a deposition, may satisfy the client. Effective communication can be a powerful deterrent to malpractice allegations; as the court noted in *Kaiser v. Hanson*, 221 N.W.2d 734, 738 (N.D. 1974), "we do not suggest that either side is without sin in this matter.

If there had been a greater degree of communication between lawyer and client . . . this matter may never have resulted in litigation."

Legal assistants can fill the void that often occurs in communications between lawyer and client not only by returning telephone calls, but also by following several additional standard procedures. First, send the client a copy of *everything* related to his case; this may help the client appreciate the attention that the firm, attorney, and paralegal are giving to that particular case. Second, always meet deadlines promised to clients, or at least explain why the deadline will not be or was not met. Third, do not overestimate the likelihood of success in a client's case. Fourth, explain what is happening in the client's case and what will happen next. Although legal advice, such as whether to file a bankruptcy, must be given by an attorney, once a bankruptcy is filed, a paralegal can certainly explain to the client what a § 341 hearing is and when it is scheduled. Such explanations will significantly reduce the client's anxiety. Fifth, document conversations with clients to eliminate confusion and miscommunication. Finally, realize the pragmatics of practicing law. For example, a client may be willing to spend $2,000 on courier bills in a multimillion-dollar case, but not in a simple, uncontested divorce action.

THE CASE OF THE RINGING TELEPHONE

Tamara Oak is a busy domestic relations attorney. Her right-hand woman is her legal assistant, Joyce Edward, who has practiced in the area of domestic relations for as many years as Tamara. Both Tamara and Joyce know that divorce and child custody matters are highly stressful, are familiar with the idiosyncrasies of the practice, and understand that maintaining client contact is essential to a successful practice.

Tamara has recently been retained by Carol Fleming to represent Carol in her messy divorce from her successful husband, Walter Fleming, a prominent endocrinologist who discovered a cure for diabetes. Carol is a very well-educated and intelligent woman; however, Walter has treated her so horribly that she has become obsessed with her divorce and with keeping custody of her two children, Mary Lynne and Kay. She calls Tamara or Joyce daily; sometimes she calls hourly.

Both Tamara and Joyce are becoming impatient with Carol and dread her telephone calls. Carol calls if Walter is 10 minutes late picking up or returning the children on the visitation schedule. She calls if the heater on her outdoor pool breaks and insists that Joyce or Tamara immediately contact Walter and demand that he have it fixed so Mary Lynne and Kay can go swimming.

After a week of more than 100 calls, with Tamara in court in a month-long trial, Joyce gets fed up with Carol's calls and tells the secretary to tell Carol that she is out of the office. Joyce enjoys her free afternoon so much that she tells the secretary to inform Carol she is out of the office for the month with Tamara.

The calls do not decrease. Carol leaves a message every time, and the office uses seven message books in one week. The messages would say "urgent" every time, but Joyce still does not return the calls, even though Tamara instructed her to handle Carol with kid gloves. After two weeks, Joyce realizes how much easier her job has been without Carol's constant telephone calls, and how much work she has gotten done on the case. In fact, Joyce has completed almost all of the discovery and the case is almost ready to go to court. Joyce has billed 80 hours on Carol's case alone!

That very day, the general counsel for the state bar calls for Tamara. Joyce takes the call. Carol has filed a formal grievance with the state bar and has been calling all this time to say that she hired other counsel because of the failure to return telephone calls.

Has Joyce or Tamara acted incompetently by failing to communicate?

In her guest editorial, Diane Soroko reviews the practical steps a paralegal can take to achieve and maintain professional competence.

GUEST EDITORIAL

PROFESSIONAL COMPETENCY:
A Working Guide For Paralegals

By Diane L. Soroko

Read any code of professional responsibility or canons of ethics and you will find such lofty ideals as integrity and competency, but it remains unclear how to achieve professional competence. Webster's defines *competent* as "having requisite or adequate ability or qualities." No matter how elusive the definition, we all recognize competency when we see it; more importantly, we remember incompetency long after we encounter it.

Like attorneys, paralegals have the professional responsibility to develop and maintain competency in their scope of practice. For both attorneys and paralegals, competency begins with education. Paralegals come from diverse backgrounds, and their educational backgrounds are just as diverse. In the past, this has

been one of the strengths of our developing profession. However, the time has come that, given the caliber of work and responsibilities given to today's paralegals, formal education should be a beginning mechanism for fulfilling the demands of professional responsibility. Although formal education is not by law a prerequisite to becoming a paralegal, it is the foundation of a competent paralegal.

Once the minimum requirements are met, what obligation does the paralegal have to go beyond requisite ability, or is minimum competence enough? That depends on you. In today's legal market, minimum abilities may get you employed, but they are unlikely to keep you employed. As the fastest growing profession of the 1990s, the paralegal profession will be characterized by a high degree of professionalism. Education is an important component of professional competence, and it should not stop with a bachelor's degree or a paralegal certificate. Because the law is a continually changing, continually evolving process, formal education undertaken to provide a foundation for competence must be complemented by continuing legal education (CLE). This continuing education may be comprised of formal seminars or self-education, but it is absolutely necessary to maintain the integrity of the profession and the competence of legal professionals.

CLE can come in many forms. The most basic involves staying current and expanding your knowledge by reading professional journals. Every law library and most law firms have subscriptions to numerous professional journals. Most journals specialize in a given practice area—environmental law, immigration, litigation support, etc. These journals compile, condense, and editorialize the changes and proposed changes in any given area of law. This is an easy and inexpensive beginning to CLE.

The seminars for paralegals offered by professional associations have improved vastly over the past few years, but they still can be expensive, especially when travel is involved. Currently, formal CLE is not a requirement for paralegals; however, many professional associations are raising awareness of its importance by making CLE a membership requirement. The expense of seminars should be balanced against the many benefits, the most prominent of which are participating in excellent educational opportunities focusing on specific practice areas and networking with other paralegals from around the country.

Networking should not be discounted as a social event. Networking is a skill which should be practiced and developed along with legal skills. Legal practices are no longer localized; the contacts made during networking opportunities can often help you find a competent court reporter in Montana or delineate the local practice procedures in Florida. Competent paralegals learn to cultivate contacts and use their expertise and knowledge to accomplish or streamline a job.

Involvement, not just passive membership, in professional organizations will open countless avenues of information and networking opportunities. State, local, and national paralegal associations form a strong communications network and constitute a voice for the profession. These associations strive to increase quality, efficiency, and accessibility in the delivery of legal services and work to develop the profession as an integral partner in the delivery of legal services to the public.

A professional attitude is also intertwined with competency. A professional who focuses on taking initiative, doing a good job every day, and "going the extra mile" realizes that competence is just as much a matter of attitude as it is a matter of skill.

Competence can be built using education, initiative, experience and networking. Paralegals have an obligation as members of the legal profession to go beyond mere competence and strive for excellence. In making competence an important component of their professional responsibility, paralegals can not only assist in the effective representation of their firm's clients but can also lay the foundation for a successful career as a valued member of the legal team.

■ Diane L. Soroko is a practicing paralegal, concentrating in the areas of immigration and nationalization and telecommunications, who has been highly involved with local and national paralegal associations. She was instrumental in the drafting and adoption of a Code of Professional Responsibility for paralegals in Georgia. This article was reprinted by permission of the author.

9.5 CASE LAW INTERPRETING COMPETENCE

The following case excerpts will give you insight into how the courts have looked at the issue of competence for the legal professional. In the

White case, the Michigan appeals court applied the two-part test for ineffective assistance of counsel; also note that the attorney's being paid by the defendant's father created a possible conflict of interest.

PEOPLE of the State of Michigan
v.
John Douglas WHITE

Court of Appeals of Michigan
338 N.W.2d 556 (Mich. Ct. App. 1983)

PER CURIAM.

Defendant was convicted of assault with intent to murder and was sentenced to five to ten years imprisonment. Defendant moved for a new trial alleging ineffective assistance of counsel. That motion was denied by the trial court. Defendant brings this appeal of right.

Defendant contends that he did not receive effective assistance of counsel because of defense counsel's failure to raise an insanity defense. We agree that defendant did not receive effective assistance of counsel, but for slightly different reasons than those advanced by defendant.

At the hearing on the motion for new trial, defense counsel testified that he had originally intended to have an independent psychiatric evaluation of defendant to support his insanity defense. Defense counsel submitted the names of three psychiatrists to defendant's father, who was paying defendant's legal expenses. Defendant's father did not wish to proceed with any of the proffered physicians. Apparently, defendant's father was not willing to pay the cost of their services. Defense counsel approached the father again but was again rebuffed. Finally, counsel concluded that defendant's father did not wish to retain a psychiatrist. Without the testimony of such a physician, defense counsel decided there would be no point in pursuing an insanity

defense. Thus, he did not file a notice of insanity defense.

In evaluating an effective assistance of counsel claim, Michigan courts apply a two-prong test. First, we assess the defense counsel's conduct in light of the standard of performance set forth in *Beasley v. United States,* 491 F.2d 687, 696 (CA6, 1974):

> "Defense counsel must perform at least as well as a lawyer with ordinary training and skill in the criminal law and must conscientiously protect his client's interests, undeflected by conflicting considerations."

We also consider whether counsel made a "serious mistake" and, if so, whether "but for this mistake defendant would have had a reasonably likely chance of acquittal."

In the present case, we find that defense counsel's conduct did not satisfy the *Beasley* standard, for he did not "conscientiously protect his client's interests, undeflected by conflicting considerations."

An attorney is under a duty to represent his client. He shall not permit a person who pays him to render legal services for another to direct or regulate his professional judgment in rendering those services. On the record in this case, defense counsel was more concerned with the desires of defendant's father, who retained him, than with the best interests of his client. Such representation does not meet the *Beasley* standard and constitutes ineffective assistance of counsel. Therefore, we reverse defendant's conviction and remand the case to the circuit court for a new trial.

Reversed and remanded.

CASE QUESTIONS

1. How would you have advised counsel to proceed in this case?
2. Which sections of the Rules and Code deal with an attorney being compensated by a third party?
3. What other ethical principles are implicated when a client is denied effective assistance of counsel?

In the *Orton* case, attorney Orton's lack of action, lack of communication, lack of honesty, and failure to represent his client zealously all combined to create a situation in which the client was not represented in a competent manner.

In the Matter of the Disciplinary Proceedings Against: Jon W. ORTON, An Attorney at Law

Supreme Court of Washington, En Banc
643 P.2d 448 (1982)

BRACHTENBACK, Chief Justice.

This is an attorney discipline matter. Jon W. Orton, admitted to practice on November 10, 1977, maintains his office in Puyallup.

The hearing panel officer found that Orton violated the Code of Professional Responsibility (CPR) DR 1-102(A)(4), (CPR) DR 6-101(A)(3) and (CPR) DR 7-101(A)(2). These provisions prohibit conduct involving fraud or misrepresentation, neglect of a legal matter and failure to carry out contracts of employment respectively. The hearing and panel officer recommended a 30-day suspension with costs to be paid prior to resumption of practice. The Disciplinary Board adopted those findings, conclusions and recommendation.

These charges arise from the following incident. In January 1980, respondent Orton accepted a retainer fee of $150 to represent a woman in a dissolution action against her husband who was serving in the military in another state. Respondent prepared a petition and the client signed it on January 16, 1980. In June, 1980, Orton advised his client that due to her husband's military status a guardian ad litem would have to be appointed; he requested an additional payment of $100, which she paid promptly. In September 1980, Orton advised his client that a guardian ad litem had been appointed.

In March 1981, the client, after consulting another lawyer, learned that not only had no guardian ad litem been appointed, but the dissolution petition had never been filed. The client discharged Orton who refunded $96. Orton retained $154. Since he had incurred no costs this entire amount was attributable to his services.

Orton did not file an answer to the Bar's complaint, did not appear at the hearing and did not file a brief in this court. He did, however, appear at the oral argument. He was questioned by the court, but his only explanation for his violations was that he had "taken on too much work." Orton argues that suspension is too harsh a sanction.

The unchallenged facts show that for a period of 14 months after he was retained, respondent did nothing on this matter except prepare a petition. The hearing panel officer concluded that Orton had neglected a legal matter and intentionally failed to carry out a contract of employment. We agree.

We view delay, procrastination and neglect as a serious matter. This court has suspended attorneys for this conduct. Protection of the public and maintenance of respect for and confidence in the legal profession mandate our concerns.

We find particularly disturbing respondent's representation to his client that the dissolution action had been filed and that a guardian ad litem had been appointed. This was patently false. For 14 months the client justifiably believed that her dissolution action was proceeding when in fact it was not. Being overworked does not justify lying to a client.

There has been no challenge to this finding of misrepresentation; it was not a mere misunderstanding. Respondent's conduct falls squarely within the prohibition of (CPR) DR 1-102(A)(4).

Given the combination of the admitted violations, the recommended 30-day suspension is fully warranted. Respondent is suspended for 30 days. The suspension shall commence 14 days after the filing of this opinion. No exception was filed to the assessment by the Disciplinary Board of costs of $173.58. Consequently, pursuant to DRA 7.3 respondent shall not resume practice until costs have been paid.

ROSELLINI, UTTER, DOLLIVER, WILLIAMS, DORE, DIMMICK and PEARSON, JJ., concur.

STAFFORD, Justice (concurring).

I concur with the recitation of the facts and the law. I feel, however, that respondent's complete failure to represent his client as well as his patently false misrepresentation concerning the status of her case warrants a longer suspension. I would suspend him for no less than 60 days.

CASE QUESTIONS

1. Which sections of the Model Code did Orton violate?
2. How might Orton have communicated effectively with his client so that the client was represented competently?
3. Do you agree with Judge Stafford that a longer suspension is warranted? What should the punishment be in this case?

In the *Leon* case, attorney Leon's indefinite suspension from the practice of law was overturned by the Kansas Supreme Court in favor of a public censure.

STATE of Kansas, Petitioner
v.
Phillip LEON, Respondent

Supreme Court of Kansas
621 P.2d 1016 (Kan. 1981)

PER CURIAM:

This is a disciplinary action against attorney Phillip Leon arising from a complaint initiated by his former client, Carolyn Winn. The disciplinary hearing panel found Leon in violation of DR 7-101 and DR 6-101 and recommended he be indefinitely suspended from the practice of law. The respondent filed exceptions to the report of the hearing panel.

Phillip Leon represented Carolyn Hoyle, now Winn, in a divorce action against Jim W. Hoyle. The Hoyles had no children and amicably agreed to a division of their property and debts. Hoyle waived notice and consented to an immediate hearing of the petition which was filed on July 1, 1977. The divorce was granted the same day on an emergency basis. Hoyle did not appear. There was no controversy. The journal entry ordered the parties to make monthly payments of $56.00 to the court to apply on a note to I.S.C., now Beneficial Finance Co., Augusta, Kansas. The note was signed by both parties and neither party was a creditor of the other.

After the divorce, with Winn's consent, respondent represented Jim Hoyle on various matters including the annulment of Hoyle's subsequent marriage. Respondent also advised Hoyle with regard to his rental property, performed legal work for Hoyle's mother, and counseled Hoyle concerning the potential inheritance of his mother's property. Hoyle met with respondent on the average of twice a month.

On September 24, 1978, Winn contacted respondent concerning her steadily deteriorating financial condition. She had been in the hospital and lost her job due to illness. Respondent advised her to file a bankruptcy action since she owed secured creditors $4204 and unsecured creditors the sum of $5111.38 and had assets of only $2750. Included in the unsecured category was the debt to Beneficial Finance mentioned in the divorce settlement. It was a joint and several obligation of both parties. Winn's obligation to the court on the I.S.C. note was not listed in the bankruptcy proceedings. The bankruptcy action was prepared in September, 1978, but not filed until April 3, 1979. Winn agreed to pay a fee of $150.00. The first meeting of creditors was held April 30, 1979, at which time Winn gave respondent a post-dated check for one-half the attorney fee. Winn had no further contact with the respondent until she received a letter from him dated July 16, 1979, stating he had been retained by Hoyle to pursue a contempt action against her for not having made her part of the payments of the I.S.C. account as ordered by the divorce decree. Respondent also requested the balance of his fee for the bankruptcy action. Winn was discharged in bankruptcy on October 17, 1979.

Respondent did not pursue the threatened contempt action against Winn but the action was subsequently filed by other counsel for Hoyle. On May 6, 1980, the contempt action against Winn was heard by Judge Ron Rogg. The court found Winn's obligation on the I.S.C. debt listed in the divorce decree was still owing and the court ordered Winn to reimburse Hoyle in the amount of $1020.50. The court found Winn not guilty of indirect contempt. Following her receipt of the letter from respondent, Winn filed a complaint with the Wichita Bar Association alleging respondent had violated the Code of Professional Responsibility. A formal complaint was filed by the Disciplinary Administrator and a hearing was held in Wichita on June 9, 1980. The panel found respondent in violation of DR 7-101, "by accepting employment by Jim Hoyle in a matter affecting a different client, Mrs. Winn, from whom respondent first accepted employment," and DR 6-101, "by reason of the failure of Phillip Leon to competently advise client, Mrs. Winn, of the legal effect of an action (bankruptcy) which he was retained and paid to advise Mrs. Winn concerning and to handle." The panel recommended respondent be suspended from the practice of law.

DR 6-101 states:

"(A)   A lawyer shall not:
(1)   Handle a legal matter which he knows or should know that he is not competent to handle, without association with him a lawyer who is competent to handle it.
(2)   Handle a legal matter without preparation adequate in the circumstances.
(3)   Neglect a legal matter entrusted to him."

We find the State failed to prove a violation of DR 6-101 by clear and convincing evidence. Mrs. Winn and Jim Hoyle both executed the note to I.S.C. They were jointly and severally liable for the debt. If, prior to the

discharge in bankruptcy, Hoyle had defaulted, I.S.C. could look to Winn for the entire debt. The bankruptcy proceeding removed her obligation to I.S.C. on that note. Her obligation to the court, however, is enforceable by contempt and cannot be removed by bankruptcy. Respondent correctly omitted Hoyle from the bankruptcy action.

DR 7-101 provides:

"(A)   A lawyer shall not intentionally:
(1)   Fail to seek the lawful objectives of his client through reasonable available means permitted by law and the Disciplinary Rules, except as provided by DR 7-101(B). A lawyer does not violate this Disciplinary Rule, however, by acceding to reasonable requests of opposing counsel which do not prejudice the rights of his client, by being punctual in fulfilling all professional commitments, by avoiding offensive tactics, or by treating with courtesy and consideration all persons involved in the legal process.
(2)   Fail to carry out a contract of employment entered into with a client for professional services, but he may withdraw as permitted under DR 2-110, DR 5-102 and DR 5-105.
(3)   Prejudice or damage his client during the course of the professional relationship, except as required under DR 7-102.
(B)   In his representation of a client, a lawyer may:
(1)   Where permissible, exercise his professional judgement to waive or fail to assert a right or position of his client.
(2)   Refuse to aid or participate in conduct that he believes to be unlawful, even though there is some support for an argument that the conduct is legal."

Respondent admits he wrote the July 16, 1979, letter to Mrs. Winn stating he had been retained by Hoyle to cite her for contempt but claims Hoyle's continual harassment regarding the I.S.C. debt prompted him to warn Winn what could happen if she didn't pay her half of the debt. Respondent asserts that he was not actually retained, he received no fee and he filed nothing on Hoyle's behalf. Respondent places him on the "horns of dilemma." He was either retained as stated in the letter or he made a false statement. Either action is unacceptable conduct for a lawyer and deserves punishment.

The findings and recommendations of the hearing panel or Board are advisory only and are not binding on this court. We have the duty to examine the evidence and determine the judgment to be entered. In determining the discipline to be invoked, it is proper to consider an attorney's past record of professional conduct. Leon has been before this court before on another disciplinary matter. He was found in violation of DR 9-102 because he "commingled child support payments with his personal funds, thus depriving a client of funds to which she was lawfully entitled for an unreasonable time." *In re Leon,* 224 Kan. 613, 584 P.2d 1255 (1978).

We have considered respondent's record of misconduct and find the current violation of DR 7-101 coupled with that record necessitates punishment by public censure.

CASE QUESTIONS

1. Do you agree that Attorney Leon did not violate DR 6-101?
2. Which specific section(s) of DR 7-101 did Leon violate?
3. Was Leon's incompetence caused by a conflict of interest?
4. Is public censure the appropriate punishment in this case? Would you prefer the panel's initial recommended punishment of suspension?
5. What should be the effect of Leon's previous ethical violation? Should a previous violation be considered when an attorney faces disciplinary action?

9.6 RECOGNIZING AND RESOLVING COMPETENCY PROBLEMS

The ethical mandate of achieving and maintaining competence is easy to understand yet difficult to define. If one continues to keep up with the advances in the law, never overestimates one's abilities, and never professes to be capable of handling an unfamiliar legal matter, it would be easy to think that the issue of competency would never arise. However, because of the competitive nature of the legal profession, the constant stress of deadlines, and the very real concerns about billable hours and continuing to operate a profitable business, the issue of competency comes into play almost every day. It is easy to say "I won't shepardize this case or double-check this statute, just this once," but this practice will sooner or later (and often much sooner) get you cited for incompetence.

By never overestimating your abilities, being very concerned with detail, always following good legal practice, and following office systems and procedures, you will be able to perform your work competently. By realizing that learning is a never-ending process, and by continuing to develop your skills, abilities, and areas of expertise, you will be participating in a process of great significance: that of establishing the foundation of competency as a cornerstone of your career.

THE CASE OF GINNY'S GORGEOUS GESTALT

Ginny is an excellent litigation paralegal specializing in insurance defense work. Prior to becoming a paralegal, Ginny was a dancer and a gymnast, and she has continued her involvement with physical fitness by becoming a certified step-aerobics instructor. She leads fitness classes three times a week and, as a result, has a gorgeous, well-toned figure.

Ginny wears classic, professional attire to court, but her suits are usually tight-fitting and her skirts are quite short. Because she is so beautiful and sensual, she is frequently noticed for her appearance in the courtroom. One judge even commented that Ginny was welcome in his courtroom or his chambers at any time.

Does Ginny's appearance constitute an ethical violation if it causes a negative reaction toward her client? How about if Ginny uses her appearance to help her client? Is her competence as a professional connected to her appearance?

9.7 ACHIEVING PROFESSIONAL COMPETENCE: A SUMMARY

Being an ethical and successful legal assistant means more than doing your job or even doing your job well. It means, rather, that you recognize your fiduciary duty, as a legal professional, to represent your client competently. This duty of competence is connected to malpractice allegations, for accusations of negligence mean that the client does not believe he was represented competently. It is also connected to the issue of zealous representation, for it is hard to be zealous when you are still unsure of elementary principles or procedures. Breaches of confidentiality, failures to disclose conflicts of interest, and improper handling of funds are also potential manifestations of incompetence by legal professionals. For this reason, achieving competence and avoiding negligence should be among the highest priorities for all legal professionals.

Achieving competence requires a commitment to continual training and development; as you have already learned, the law is an ever-changing, ever-evolving process. Cases are overturned; new laws are passed; laws are reinterpreted; procedures are reformatted. Achieving competence means developing your skills, abilities, and knowledge through education or experience so that you are able to fulfill your responsibilities to your attorney and to your client. By maintaining your professional competence, you will not only represent your clients effectively, but you will also develop the skills and knowledge which will increase your options and opportunities in your own career.

REVIEW QUESTIONS

1. What characterizes competence for legal professionals?
2. How does the Sixth Amendment ensure competent representation for criminal defendants?
3. How can a paralegal maintain competence in a field where the rules change and evolve?

QUESTIONS FOR THOUGHT AND DISCUSSION

1. Should paralegals be required to attend a specific number of continuing professional education courses per year?
2. Meena is helping prepare a response to a motion for summary judgment. She is asked to shepardize the supporting cases to determine if they are still good law. The brief is due later this morning; it is now 2:00 a.m. The final five cases are all recent opinions, and Meena decides she does not need to shepardize them because she assumes that they are still good law. She leaves a note for the attorney, assuring him that the cases are still good law. Has Meena acted incompetently? What if you knew the cases were all issued within the last two weeks?
3. Should the Sixth Amendment's protection against the ineffective assistance of counsel be extended to include civil cases?
4. Would it be incompetent for a litigation paralegal to assist the tax department during tax season?

LAW, LITERATURE, AND ETHICS

From **Confessions of a Criminal Lawyer**
By Seymour Wishman

The court clerk spun the wooden drum on his desk. It stopped. He turned the key and opened the latch. The clerk placed his hand inside the drum, and, in a moment, withdrew a small pink paper. "Juror number 124," he called out in a voice deeper than normal.

I scanned the jurors remaining in the box. Number 8 looked good. She was a social worker in Newark. She must have seen as many atrocities as I. She could no longer be outraged by crime in the same emotional way as those who hadn't seen what it was like out there. Some social workers were so hardened to violent crime that they could even get angry at victims for putting themselves in the position to be mugged. I have sometimes felt that that kind of impatience with victims myself.

"Juror number 124," the clerk repeated in an even deeper voice.

In the last row a black man dressed in a green polyester suit and a red bow tie shot his hand into the air. He jumped to his feet. 'That's me." He looked as if he had just hit a bingo. He walked forward—white vinyl shoes. I nodded at him. I wanted him, each of them, to think we had a special relationship. I tried for a connection from the moment they stepped into the courtroom. At least I didn't wink at them like Scola. Scola had no shame; he would do anything. I had to watch that guy every second.

One out of four or so nodded back. This guy didn't. If they did, I was more likely to deep them. I did better with women. I was better looking than Scola. No small thing. A kind of flirtation sometimes when on with women jurors, and I was as sure as hell not beneath that. In my last case I had been slightly flirtatious with a juror I thought was gay. . . . But at least I hadn't winked.

I ran down the jury sheet to number 124. He was a mechanical engineer. I liked that. He had to use a slide rule, measuring quantities with precision. Perhaps he would measure the pieces of evidence as if they were bricks and find some shortage. The more disposed he was toward "objectivity," the less room there would be for him to get carried away by the viciousness of the charge against my client. I was a trial lawyer concerned about controlling the events of a trial and their impact on a jury, and it was only natural that I would measure this engineer by the way he might measure the evidence. But I was convinced that the D.A. would knock him off because he was black.

I looked over at the group sitting in the jury box. Not a black face among them. Some defense lawyers figured that black jurors were more likely to convict a black defendant because they were frequently the victims of crime. But I wanted black jurors because I felt they might have some sympathy or loyalty to a "brother", that was why most D.A.'s knocked all blacks off the jury. One thing was clear: for every good reason one had to choose a particular kind of juror, there was an equally compelling reason not to choose him.

The judge asked number 124 all the stock questions. Ever been the victim of a crime? Ever sat on a grand jury? Any relatives in law enforcement? He answered no to all of them. That was good. even better, he answered calmly and confidently. If he were the only holdout for an acquittal, perhaps he would be able to withstand the pressure of the other eleven jurors. A conviction has to be unanimous. On the other hand, of course, if he were for a conviction, he might be able to push the others into it. I looked at the jurors I had left on. They looked strong: an advertising executive, a couple of small businessmen, a high school teacher. They weren't going to be pushed around. All I needed was one holdout—a hung jury with a case like this was a win. I liked the foreman, who, like all jury foremen, had won that distinction by having been called to sit in the first seat of the jury box. He looked weak, and that might mean he wouldn't be able to control the rest of them. Good. The last kind of person I wanted in charge was a tyrant.

If I hung this one, I knew the D.A. would probably give me a better plea bargain, maybe larceny instead of robbery. But with all the evidence against my client, he had been crazy to turn down the D.A.'s offer of four years. With his record, if he was convicted after a trial, the judge could easily give him eight. But there was a chance that if I hung a second jury, the D.A. wouldn't retry, and the indictment would be dismissed. Who could tell? Maybe my guy would be lucky.

The engineer said he worked on poverty projects at his church. Shit. Too good. That plus his blackness was going to be too much for Scola.

"I'll excuse the juror," Scola said.

I jumped to my feet and threw my pencil down on the table, as I had thrown similar pencils in similar situations. "That's the sixth black juror the prosecutor has excused," I said in practiced disgust.

"I'll see you both at side-bar," the judge said.

The D.A. and I walked around the counsel table and marched up to the judge's bench on the side furthest from the jury. The court reporter picked up her machine and carried it around to where we were, placing it between the judge and us.

"Wishman, you know better than that," the judge said with exasperation. "If you have that kind of objection to make, you know you're supposed to make it out of the hearing of the jury."

"I'm sorry, Judge. I guess I lost my head."

"Sure you did," Scola said.

"Lose your head again, and I'll hold you in contempt," the judge said.

"I apologize. In any event, I would like to put my objection on the record."

"Of course," the judge said.

"Your Honor, the prosecutor has systematically excluded all blacks from this jury, and is thereby depriving my black client of his right to a trial by his peers, discriminating against him because of his race in violation of his constitutional rights. The prosecutor's actions are racist. I move for a mistrial."

"Is that all, Mr. Wishman?" the judge asked.

"Yes, sir."

"I'd like to respond to this personal attack against me," Scola said, his face flushed with anger.

"I didn't make a personal attack."

"You did so. You called me a racist."

"I did not. I said that your actions were racist."

"Enough," the judge said. "The United States Supreme Court has dealt with this issue. Each side has ten *peremptory challenges,* and they may be exercised in any manner a party sees fit. We're not talking about the unlimited number of *challenges for cause* each side may use to dismiss jurors when there are legal impediments to their serving. The challenge in question is a peremptory challenge, and no legal justification need be furnished. Your motion, Mr Wishman, is denied."

Scola and I returned to our places at counsel table. I had gotten my point across to the white jurors in the box that the D.A. was playing them for their prejudices. Maybe one of them would be angry at that. Also, I had rattled Scola, and I liked doing that.

The clerk reached into the stomach of the wooden drum. He called another number. A man in the back row stood and came forward. Late fifties, thick glasses, rumpled look in a corduroy jacket with patches.

My client asked me what had gone on at side-bar with the judge. "Nothing," I told him, "Just some maneuvering."

"How are we doing, Mr. Wishman?" my client asked.

"Matthew, nothing's changed since I spoke to you in jail this morning. You've got a tough case. It's going to be very hard to get the jury to believe your word over the victim's."

"Maybe I should have taken the plea," Matthew said, tracing the scar on his cheek with his knuckles.

"Like I told you, that's up to you. It's your life."

■ From *Confessions of a Criminal Lawyer* by Seymour Wishman. Copyright © 1981 by Seymour Wishman. Reprinted by permission of Times Books, a division of Random House, Inc.

CHAPTER 10
Ethical Issues in Specialized Practices

OUTLINE

CHAPTER OVERVIEW
10.1 CRIMINAL LAW
10.2 DOMESTIC RELATIONS
10.3 LITIGATION
10.4 CORPORATE AND REAL ESTATE LAW
10.5 PUBLIC PRACTICE
10.6 THE PARALEGAL AS NOTARY
10.7 CONCLUSION

CHAPTER OVERVIEW

The first two sections of this book described and analyzed the ethical issues and dilemmas facing all paralegals. Issues such as confidentiality, unauthorized practice, and conflict of interest affect all legal assistants, no matter what their area of practice. However, like most other professionals today, paralegals often specialize in one area of the law, and each specialty has ethical dilemmas unique to that area of practice. This chapter helps you understand the ethical issues of the major specializations and suggests ways to avoid problems.

10.1 CRIMINAL LAW

Specializing in criminal law involves different ethical issues depending on the type of criminal law practiced. Criminal law is a type of litigation, and the ethical considerations applicable to litigation also apply to criminal law practice. All criminal law legal assistants work either for the prosecution or for the defense. Paralegals working for the prosecution are usually employed by the government, such as by the district attorney's or prosecuting attorney's office. (Those working for the federal government are employed by the U.S. Attorney's Office.) District attorney's offices usually employ many attorneys to prosecute criminal cases, including some at the appellate level, on behalf of the state, county, or municipality; these prosecutors are known as *assistant district attorneys.* The head of the office, the *district attorney,* is usually either elected in a general election or appointed. Besides the assistant district attorneys, the office usually has numerous investigators and paralegals. Sometimes the investigator and paralegal are one and the same; sometimes offices employ investigators who have specialized training in criminal investigations or who are former police officers.

All employees of the district attorney's office represent the interests of the general public. Their obligation is to ensure prosecution of those who have violated a criminal statute in the state or jurisdiction. These legal professionals have no particular client, as does a legal professional in a private law firm, but rather act to enforce the law and protect the public interest.

If you specialize in criminal law but do not work for the district attorney's office, usually you will be employed by a private criminal defense practice or by a public foundation dealing primarily with criminal defense. Private criminal defense work is similar to other specialties; the attorney defends a client against accusations of criminal violations.

Because many alleged criminals cannot afford to hire attorneys, some foundations and agencies attempt to provide legal assistance for them. The public defender's office, which exists in almost every large city, handles criminal defense. Both state and federal courts have public defender's offices. These offices are usually headed by a public defender who, like the district attorney, is either elected or appointed to the position. Attorneys assisting the public defender are called *assistant public defenders.* Like district attorney's offices, public defender's offices are publicly funded; this funding assures criminal felony defendants of their constitutional right to legal representation regardless of ability to pay. Of course, some criminal defendants retain their own counsel, but those who cannot afford counsel can have counsel appointed for them by the courts. To be represented by a public defender, the defendant must complete and sign a form requesting information on his or her ability to pay. The counsel appointed for these defendants are usually members of the public defender's office. If a conflict of interest exists in the public defender's office for representing many individuals, outside counsel is appointed. Outside counsel is then compensated by the court for representing the accused.

Unlike the district attorney, whose "client" is the public interest, public defenders and other lawyers doing criminal defense work do in fact represent the interests of particular clients. As in civil representation, the attorney representing the criminal defendant owes absolute loyalty to the interests of that client. The defense attorney owes the same obligations to the criminal defendant as an attorney representing a party in a civil suit owes that party.

Because of the power vested in prosecuting attorneys, there exist special responsibilities and limitations to ensure that prosecutors do not abuse their powers. These are set forth in Rule 3.8.

RULE 3.8 Special Responsibilities of a Prosecutor

The prosecutor in a criminal case shall:

(a) refrain from prosecuting a charge that the prosecutor knows is not supported by probable cause;

(b) make reasonable efforts to assure that the accused has been advised of the right to, and the procedure for obtaining, counsel and has been given reasonable opportunity to obtain counsel;

(c) not seek to obtain from an unrepresented accused a waiver of important pretrial rights, such as the right to a preliminary hearing;

(d) make timely disclosure to the defense of all evidence or information known to the prosecutor that tends to negate the guilt of the accused or mitigates the offense, and, in connection with sentencing, disclose to the defense and to the tribunal all unprivileged mitigating information known to the prosecutor, except when the prosecutor is relieved of this responsibility by a protective order of the tribunal; and

(e) exercise reasonable care to prevent investigators, law enforcement personnel, employees or other persons assisting or associated with the prosecutor in a criminal case from making an extrajudicial statement that the prosecutor would be prohibited from making under Rule 3.6.

The parallel Code section, DR 7-103, also places limitations on the prosecuting attorney, but is not as detailed as Rule 3.8.

DR 7-103 Performing the Duty of Public Prosecutor or Other Government Lawyer.

(A) A public prosecutor or other government lawyer shall not institute or cause to be instituted criminal charges when he knows or it is obvious that the charges are not supported by probable cause.

(B) A public prosecutor or other government lawyer in criminal litigation shall make timely disclosure to counsel for the defendant, or to the defendant if he has no counsel, of the existence of evidence, known to the prosecutor or other government lawyer, that tends to negate the guilt of the accused, mitigate the degree of the offense, or reduce the punishment.

Unlike a civil action, in which a person is generally subject to losing money, a home, or something else of monetary value, a criminal defendant faces the possibility of a fine, imprisonment, or both. The possibility of losing one's freedom makes the stakes significantly higher in a criminal action than in a civil action. Because criminal defendants face possible imprisonment, are sometimes embarrassed by the criminal prosecution, and may be willing to do anything to get off, they are more likely not to divulge the complete facts of their situation and to lie. This is especially difficult for the legal professional because, in addition to the duty to the client, legal professionals owe an obligation to the court and tribunal. These sometimes conflicting roles can make it hard to decide what to do when, for example, your client is not telling the truth.

Sometimes politics and the media bring ethical dilemmas to the criminal law arena. The media often publicize accused criminals and criminal acts, making violations of confidentiality more likely. The public may become interested in the case, making it difficult for the defendant to get a fair trial. A defendant's family members and friends are likely to ask the attorney for confidential information, which the attorney is ethically precluded from revealing. Witnesses may be difficult to locate and unwilling to testify, wanting to avoid involvement in a criminal proceeding. Also, because district attorneys and public defenders are often elected officials, they of course want to appear to be zealously protecting the public interest, especially during elections and high-profile cases. Political pressures and the quest for power may contribute to ethical problems in this area.

Another issue for those in criminal law is being accused of ineffective assistance of counsel (discussed in chapter 9, on competence). A criminal defendant may appeal his case on these grounds. This cause of action is a defense to a conviction and a reason to order a new trial, not a civil action, as is malpractice, to sue the attorney for breach of a professional standard. (Remember that ineffective assistance of counsel means that the lawyer did not adequately represent the client within standards generally accepted by the bar.) To successfully claim ineffective assistance of counsel, the defendant must show that the attorney's representation was not minimally competent and that this failure to represent competently was the reason for the defendant's conviction.

As is elaborated in § 10.3, considerations of trial publicity and contact with witnesses affect those practicing criminal law. This area is covered by Rules 3.4 and 3.6 and by DR 7-107 of the Code of Professional Responsibility. These rules prevent anyone participating in, or associated with, a criminal investigation (including paralegals) from making extrajudicial statements that could be publicized. Extrajudicial statements are permitted if they concern information contained in the public record, information about the general scope of the investigation, or the fact that an investigation is in process. Extrajudicial statements are also allowed to request assistance in apprehending a suspect or obtaining additional information for the case, or to issue a warning to the public. These rules are designed to balance free speech rights with the right to a fair trial. Remember the *Crumpacker* case in chapter 7, in which the attorney's conduct and comments caused him to be disbarred. Constraining communication helps protect the impartiality of the judge and jurors. Constraints attempt to ensure that the accused goes to trial with the presumption of innocence and that the burden of proof remains on the prosecution.

THE CASE OF THE BLOODY INQUISITION

Paralegal Steve Kihm is drafting a motion to suppress in the firm's newest criminal case. Just as he finishes dictating, the secretary comes in with a bloodied gun, left for Steve by a woman calling herself Annette Gross. Just as the secretary lays the gun on Steve's desk, Steve's telephone rings and an individual identifying herself as Annette Gross says that she has just murdered the Mayor; she wants Kihm's firm to represent her. She asks Steve: "Can you represent me? I'll come by later with $300,000 that I am going to steal from the First National Bank of Gold, gotta go there's a police car right behind me."

Immediately following that disconnection, the secretary tells Steve that District Attorney Mendl is on the telephone for him. Kihm is a close friend of Mendl's and has been promised the position of chief paralegal and investigator for the district attorney's office if Mendl wins the election. Mendl says: "Have you heard that the Mayor was murdered one block from your office? Did you see anything or know anything about the murder? I thought that since your firm has such an outstanding record in criminal defense, the individual who committed the crime might have come to you for help. Did they come to your office? You know, Steve, if I could just solve this crime, I would be guaranteed to be re-elected."

What ethical issues does paralegal Steve face, and how should he resolve them?

Perhaps the most difficult, and the most personal, ethical dilemma concerns dealing with the accused. As a prosecutor, it is sometimes difficult to remember that the accused is an individual whose case presents a unique situation, because prosecutors see so much criminal (and even despicable) activity that they may lose compassion for people. Also, because prosecutors must zealously protect society against those who break its rules, the possibility of sending the wrong person to jail always exists. As a defense attorney, the most difficult ethical issue is that, unless you are Perry Mason, many of your clients will be guilty—and you will still have to defend someone who has done wrong, sometimes grievous wrong. At those times you need to remember that the professional must sometimes distance herself from her work to fulfill the highest ethical mandate—effectively representing a criminally accused person.

Criminal lawyers often represent unpopular individuals and causes. Although some individuals and causes may directly conflict with your own personal morality, you must put it aside and help represent these individuals and causes to the best of your ability. This is how the issue of zealous representation arises in criminal law. Remember that, unlike civil litigants, criminal defendants are constitutionally guaranteed effective representation. Everyone has an absolute constitutional right to representation in actions involving allegedly felonious acts, and it is a foundation of our legal system that an accused criminal is innocent until proven guilty.

However, the ethical legal professional must keep zealous representation within the bounds of the law. Because of the nature of criminal cases, you may be able to change evidence ever so slightly to benefit your case. Witnesses may be coerced, and they may be more willing to perjure themselves than civil defendants. Although it may make the defense easier, it is absolutely unethical to mislead a witness or the court, or to manufacture, alter, or destroy evidence. A paralegal who alters criminal evidence may face criminal charges for tampering with evidence.

Many times, individuals will confess to a crime. As you are aware from chapter 3's discussion on confidentiality and the attorney-client privilege, you may not reveal that your client confessed to a crime committed in the past. However, neither confidentiality requirements nor the attorney-client privilege protects communications from clients to those representing them and their agents when the clients reveal the intent to commit a future crime. An example would be Annette Gross's conversation with paralegal Kihm. If the attorney-client relationship was in fact present, Kihm could not reveal that Annette Gross had already committed a crime (the murder), but the information that she intended to rob the bank would not be a protected communication, at least under the Code, because it concerned a future crime. Under the Rules, the intended crime would be confidential unless it might result in death or significant bodily injury.

Conflict-of-interest issues most often arise, in the criminal context, when an attorney represents multiple defendants in a criminal action. When several defendants are involved in a crime, as frequently occurs, one party's actions may prevent the other individuals from being criminally prosecuted. For example, if one defendant in an armed robbery case confessed to the crime, his confession might exonerate another defendant who had also been accused of the crime. Further, the prosecuting attorney will often strike a deal with one defendant who agrees, in return for a lighter sentence, to testify against the other defendants. Therefore, it is critical, when representing multiple defendants in a criminal action, that your defense of one does not prejudice your defense of the others. Another conflict of interest in the criminal context arises when an individual "flips sides," i.e., leaves private practice for the district attorney's office or vice versa. You should never work for a new firm on a case that you worked on with your previous employer; likewise, you must never work on the same criminal case on both the prosecution and defense sides. If you do switch sides, everything you learned in the context of your former employment is confidential and subject to the attorney-client privilege. If you are in this position, apply the guidelines for the situation of changing employment discussed in chapter 4, on conflict of interest.

10.2 DOMESTIC RELATIONS

The specialty known as *domestic relations* or *family law* deals with divorces, prenuptial agreements, adoptions, probate, and child custody matters. Although these subspecialties all fall within the general definition of domestic relations, each has its own peculiarities. Divorce law is naturally involved when a married couple want to terminate their marriage. Sometimes the marriage is a traditional one, licensed by the state; other times it is a common-law marriage recognized by the particular jurisdiction. Divorces range from simple uncontested ones to ones involving millions of dollars and nasty child custody matters. Regardless of the type of divorce, this area of the law especially implicates ethics because of the uniqueness of the husband-wife relationship; not only is this relationship valued by society, but it is also a highly confidential relationship. When such a relationship breaks up, many ethical concerns come into play. Additionally, in this area of the law, each case is truly unique and presents its own particular ethical dilemmas, unlike other specialties, in which more standardized principles apply to each case.

A less adversarial approach to divorce than the traditional civil action is divorce mediation. In mediation, the parties to a case go before an impartial, trained, third party to attempt to resolve their dispute. Mediators attempt to diminish the hostilities that frequently accompany divorce and try to have the parties agree on the nature of their marriage's dissolution. For the domestic relations specialist, divorce mediation presents many dilemmas. Successful mediation means the loss of some potentially hefty fees; remember, though, that monetary gain should always be secondary to doing what is truly best for your client. In this area, however, it is sometimes hard to know what really *is* best for the client. With mediation, you must balance the potential benefits of mediation—peace of mind and minimal antagonism—against the financial compromises your client might have to make. Because much at stake in a divorce proceeding is intangible, it is frequently difficult to determine the best course of action.

Prenuptial agreements, also called *antenuptial agreements,* are made before marriage, as attempts by the parties to determine how assets will be distributed if the marriage is later dissolved through divorce. This aspect of domestic relations law can give rise to peculiar ethical issues. First, when the agreement is originally made, it is likely to be the party with more to lose that has his or her attorney draft the agreement. Naturally, the agreement will protect the party who hired the attorney, leaving the other spouse's interests unrepresented. For example, if you were representing the male, and the female called asking your advice as to whether to sign the prenuptial agreement, you should inform her that you are representing the other spouse and that she should seek other counsel. Ethical behavior in forming prenuptial agreements definitely contributes to their being enforced, if necessary, at a later time. A second ethical concern with prenuptial agreements is the status of the attorney who drafted the prenuptial agreement in a later divorce proceeding. That attorney may be precluded from representing either party in the divorce, depending on the particular case.

Adoptions, like divorces, also range from the simple to the very complicated. For example, it is very common for a person to want to adopt a new spouse's children. This can be very straightforward if the other birth parent agrees; it can also be very difficult if the birth parent contests the adoption. Child custody cases can also be stressful and traumatic. When children are involved, you must assess the long-term impact of the case on the child and on the family unit, and this can be difficult to do. (Sometimes the court will appoint a guardian ad litem to ensure that the child's interests are protected.) Also, one parent may try to use children to hurt the other parent. For the attorney or paralegal, these situations can be difficult because you have to balance zealous representation of your client with the interests of children, parents, and prospective adoptive parents. These can also be highly emotional proceedings—and when clients are under pressure concerning fundamental issues in their lives, they might be more concerned with winning than with acting ethically. More than one angry parent has kidnapped and hidden a child from a spouse in the wake of an unwanted legal proceeding involving the family.

These kinds of domestic relations issues probably result in more malpractice and bar complaints than any other area of the law. Thus, you can see why it is especially important to be aware of the ethical situations attendant to this specialty. This specialty gives rise to so many complaints and problems because it is at the very heart of a client's personal life. Many times, normally sane and rational individuals become absolutely unglued when involved in a divorce or child custody matter. The same holds true for distribution of the assets of a family member or friend who has just died. Some persons may be upset that they were not left anything under the will, or may simply be upset over the death. They may act and do things that they would not normally do. A significant number of these clients become dependent on the legal professional and are easily coerced during this very fragile period of their lives. People working in this specialty are more than just legal professionals: they act as parents, friends, counselors, psychologists, and sounding boards. Legal professionals specializing in this area should have excellent interpersonal skills and be very sympathetic to the especially stressful environment clients endure when involved in family law matters. They must also be able to help clients make difficult decisions concerning essential issues in their lives.

Conflict of interest can be a problem in domestic relations. Especially in divorce cases, couples often think that they can resolve the issues themselves and hire only one attorney. This may not be a problem if the divorce does stay amicable; however, the reality is that many divorces become difficult and messy. In many cases it is best for each spouse to have his or her own attorney, so that his or her interests, which probably do not coincide with those of the divorcing spouse, can be adequately represented.

Legal professionals should advise clients, when working with both parties to obtain a divorce, that if the divorce becomes adversarial, the professional cannot represent either party. Further, the trend is for parties to go to divorce mediation before filing actual divorce papers. The mediator is often an attorney or legal assistant specializing in domestic relations. The mediator should never handle or work on a case involving any of the parties to the mediation. This is an absolute conflict of interest and jeopardizes the role of mediation.

Another conflict of interest that might arise is when the "family" attorney is brought in on a divorce action. Often an attorney has been employed by a couple to handle routine legal problems such as writing wills or establishing a trust. When the couple is contemplating divorce, the parties often go to the family lawyer to handle it. The lawyer in this situation must be very careful to ensure that no conflicts of interest exist.

This issue also arises in the context of adoptions. Usually one attorney handles the adoption from the perspective of both the person or persons adopting the child and the child's interests. However, if there is an unusual situation, such as when the child desires not to be adopted, it might be wise to have the child be separately represented. If these situations do arise, the courts will generally appoint an attorney, known as a *guardian ad litem,* to protect and further the best interests of the child.

In general, family law presents ethical conflicts because of clients' frequently emotional reactions to the legal proceedings. Stress causes people to act emotionally and sometimes irrationally, and the legal team in family law must be aware of the sometimes bitter nature of family law conflicts. When in such a hostile environment, clients involved in domestic proceedings sometimes do crazy things, things that may be stupid, illegal, or unethical. Lawyers and legal assistants in this area can also get caught up in the emotion of the situation. By being aware of this aspect of family law practice, you can remember to represent your client zealously without losing the professional distance that helps you make ethical choices.

THE CASE OF THE MELLOW YELLOWS

Sylvia and Harold Yellow have been married for 30 years and are now contemplating divorce. They want to resolve the matter quickly and quietly. Sylvia and Harold were very close throughout most of their marriage and are very close to each other's families. Sylvia, a successful paralegal, specializes in probate law. She suggests that they both go to mediation, work out an agreement themselves, and have someone help them draft the pleadings so that they can file the divorce themselves.

The Yellows go to Jeff Crandell to mediate their case. Crandell is a legal assistant who specializes in domestic cases and is Sylvia's co-worker at her firm. Actually, Jeff previously was an attorney; he represented Harold

Yellow in a divorce action against Sylvia 10 years earlier (the Yellows did divorce but subsequently remarried). Jeff Crandell was disbarred for stealing funds from a client a couple of years after the Yellows' first divorce; therefore, he now practices as a paralegal.

After mediation, the Yellows reach an agreement; however, Harold is concerned with a provision that says he will pay all the financial obligations of the marriage. When Harold asks Jeff about this aspect of the agreement, Jeff tells him not to worry about it, because Sylvia is very ethical and will only make Harold pay his fair portion of the marital debts.

As the Yellows agreed, Jeff Crandell drafts the divorce petition and advises both of them on how to proceed, because it is merely a simple, uncontested case. Two days after the divorce is filed, Harold's mother dies. Sylvia, because of her expertise in probate law, is the executor of Mrs. Yellow's will, so she commences handling the administration of this estate. The will specifically stated: "My executor is my daughter-in-law, Sylvia Yellow, because of her continuing devotion and marriage to my only son, Harold. With her experience in probate law, I know she will be sure to distribute the assets of my estate fairly so that Harold will be taken care of the rest of his life." Sylvia interprets this sentence to mean that she has complete discretion over the funds. She cuts herself a check for $5 million, the amount of the entire estate. She takes $200,000 and sets up an account for Harold. She then files the appropriate papers with the probate court to ensure that the case will be closed.

Identify and analyze all ethical issues arising from this situation.

10.3 LITIGATION

The specialty of litigation and its subspecialties raise issues of conduct during judicial and administrative proceedings and with witnesses and jurors. Litigation also encompasses criminal law and domestic relations, previously discussed. Litigation, as we will now use that term, is the specialty involving the parties in a civil lawsuit of some sort. This area of practice and its ethical considerations are especially important to paralegals, because litigation is the area in which most paralegals work.

Litigation usually entails an appearance in judicial or administrative proceedings in which the issues of candor toward the tribunal, communication with witnesses and jurors, trial publicity, and acquiring an interest in litigation are of extreme importance. Even though legal assistants may not represent clients in official proceedings, they sometimes communicate with the tribunal, either in the course of assisting an attorney or when presenting or delivering documents to the judge or tribunal. Thus, it is important for every litigation paralegal to understand the limits ethically imposed on communications with a judge or tribunal. These are contained in DR 7-110.

DR 7-110 Contact with Officials.

(A)   A lawyer shall not give or lend any thing of value to a judge, official, or employee of a tribunal, except as permitted by Section C(4) of Canon 5 of the Code of Judicial Conduct, but a lawyer may make a contribution to the campaign fund of a candidate for judicial office in conformity with Section B(2) under Canon 7 of the Code of Judicial Conduct.

(B)   In an adversary proceeding, a lawyer shall not communicate, or cause another to communicate, as to the merits of the cause with a judge or an official before whom the proceeding is pending, except:

(1)   In the course of official proceedings in the cause.

(2)   In writing if he promptly delivers a copy of the writing to opposing counsel or to the adverse party if he is not represented by a lawyer.

(3)   Orally upon adequate notice to opposing counsel or to the adverse party if he is not represented by a lawyer.

(4)   As otherwise authorized by law, or by Section A(4) under Canon 3 of the Code of Judicial Conduct.

The ethical considerations surrounding trial publicity are unique to litigation. DR 7-107 provides that a lawyer participating in or associated with a trial shall not make extrajudicial statements (other than those from the public record) if that statement falls within one of the general guidelines regarding information not to be disclosed. The following types of information may not be disclosed by anyone participating in or associated with a trial:

1.   Evidence regarding the occurrence or transaction involved

2.   The character, credibility, or criminal record of a party, witness, or prospective witness

3.   The performance or results of any examinations or tests, or the refusal or failure of a party to submit to such tests

4.   An opinion on the merits of the claims or defenses of a party (except as required by law or administrative rule)

5.   Any other matter reasonably likely to interfere with a fair trial of the action.

Like the provisions of DR 7-107 applicable to criminal cases, this Rule is intended to ensure that cases will be tried according to the rules of evidence, not speculation, conjecture, or emotion. For paralegals, an especially important provision of this Rule states: "A lawyer shall exercise reasonable case to prevent his employees and associates from making an extrajudicial statement that he would be prohibited from making under DR 7-107."

Disciplinary Rule 7-108 specifies the limits concerning communication with or investigation of jurors. Prior to or during a trial, a lawyer shall not communicate with or cause another (such as a legal assistant) to communicate with a juror. Nor is an attorney permitted to conduct a vexatious or harassing investigation of either a juror or potential juror. Again, these provisions are intended to preserve the integrity and impartiality of the proceeding. At the conclusion of the proceeding, a lawyer or his employee may speak to jurors; however, this contact should not be for the purpose of harassing the juror. One acceptable purpose might be to get feedback from jurors on the lawyer's presentation of the case, to improve his or her litigation skills. Although no provision specifically precludes communication with jurors after the proceedings have concluded, many judges and tribunals frown on such conduct. Therefore, it is best to check beforehand if you are assigned to interview jurors at the conclusion of a case.

Disciplinary Rule 7-109 relates to witnesses in judicial and administrative proceedings. Although this Rule applies directly to lawyers, many legal assistants interview witnesses before trial; a paralegal should therefore conform her interviewing techniques to the principles set forth in this Rule.

Another litigation mandate is that legal professionals should not acquire a proprietary interest in the client's cause of action. This means, basically, that those involved in litigation should not finance a client's case. Although contingency fees are permissible, the client must pay all expenses, in addition to any contingency fee; expenses include costs of filing the lawsuit, depositions, copies, and travel expenses of the attorney. The lawyer may advance these fees to the client, thus making litigation possible, but ultimately, no matter what amount is recovered, the client remains responsible for the costs of litigation. This provision appears in DR 5-103 of the Code of Professional Responsibility. However, in jurisdictions that have adopted a rule based on Model Rule 1.8(e)(1) and (2), the attorney may advance court costs, the repayment of which may be contingent on the outcome, and may pay court costs and expenses of litigation for an indigent client.

One important subspecialty of litigation is the area of insurance defense law. Insurance defense is that area of practice in which legal professionals represent insureds for an insurance company. For example, if Denise Schoengold buys an insurance policy for her 1992 Volvo from Willingham Insurance Company and subsequently has an accident that is covered by the policy, Willingham Insurance will hire an attorney to represent Denise under the policy. The ethical considerations of insurance defense are that, although the insurance company pays the attorney's bills, the attorney represents the insured. However, the attorney represents the insured only up to the amount of the policy. Thus, if Denise Schoengold's insurance policy with Willingham is for $100,000, and the plaintiff sues for $150,000, the insurance company has no obligation to pay over the $100,000 limit. Therefore, Denise should hire her own attorney to represent her interests for the additional $50,000. If an insurance defense attorney finds that the insured is likely to be liable for more than the limits of the policy, the attorney should inform the insured of that fact so the insured can hire her own attorney to protect her interests. This principle is set forth in DR 5-107.

In general, the ethical problems unique to litigation of concern to legal assistants involve contact with witnesses, jurors, and tribunals. To avoid any ethical problems when communicating with these individuals, keep in mind the reason for these limitations on your ability to communicate: the desire to have a case decided on its merits by an impartial tribunal and jury. Do not communicate anything—to anyone—that you believe will jeopardize the possibility of a fair trial. Do not try to convince the tribunal or jurors that your client's position is the correct one or coerce them. Rather, make sure your communications relate only those facts and issues that you know are permissibly discussed. For example, in Mary Lynne's hypothetical case, if the juror had asked for directions to the bathroom, would the same ethical problem have arisen? How about if the juror had asked whether Mary Lynne had a good case?

THE CASE OF THE JITTERY JUROR

Mary Lynne Johnson is a litigation paralegal with a large firm representing a corporation in a products liability suit. She has worked on the three-year-old case since it was filed and goes to the trial with her supervising attorney. It takes an entire day for the jury to be chosen. At 5:00 P.M., the judge excuses the jurors and tells them to return at 9:00 the next morning. Mary Lynne leaves ahead of the jurors, to get the van so that she and the attorney can load up all the exhibits. On her way back up the elevator she meets a juror who says: "I was so nervous about coming to court this morning that I forgot my money at home. Could you loan me $5.00 for parking?" Mary Lynne willingly complies.

Any problems?

10.4 CORPORATE AND REAL ESTATE LAW

Corporate law involves the representation of a corporation by in-house counsel or a private firm. Corporate paralegals perform such duties as preparing articles of incorporation and corporate minutes, and handling mergers and acquisitions. The ethical issues unique to corporate law arise because the lawyer represents the corporation—not the officers, chief executive officers, board of directors, or shareholders. These individuals' interests may at times be contrary to those of the corporation. However, if you remember that your client is the corporation as a whole, not individuals or groups within that corporation, you should have no ethical problems concerning conflict of interest. Rule 1.13 specifies that loyalty is owed to the organization rather than to the officers, directors, shareholders, or employees. This same reasoning applies when a lawyer represents a governmental agency.

RULE 1.13 Organization as Client

(a) A lawyer employed or retained by an organization represents the organization acting through its duly authorized constituents.

(b) If a lawyer for an organization knows that an officer, employee or other person associated with the organization is engaged in action, intends to act or refuses to act in a matter related to the representation that is a violation of a legal obligation to the organization, or a violation of law which reasonably might be imputed to the organization, and is likely to result in substantial injury to the organization, the lawyer shall proceed as is reasonably necessary in the best interest of the organization. In determining how to proceed, the lawyer shall give due consideraton to the seriousness of the violation and its consequences, the scope and nature of the lawyer's representation, the responsibility in the organization and the apparent motivation of the person involved, the policies of the organization concerning such matters and any other relevant considerations. Any measures taken shall be designed to minimize disruption of the organization and the risk of revealing information relating to the representation to persons outside the organization. Such measures may include among others:

(1) asking reconsideration of the matter;

(2) advising that a separate legal opinion on the matter be sought for presentation to appropriate authority in the organization; and

(3) referring the matter to higher authority in the organization, including, if warranted by the seriousness of the matter, referral to the highest authority that can act in behalf of the organization as determined by applicable law.

(c) If, despite the lawyer's efforts in accordance with paragraph (b), the highest authority that can act on behalf of the organization insists upon action, or a refusal to act, that is clearly a violation of law and is likely to result in substantial injury to the organization, the lawyer may resign in accordance with Rule 1.16.

(d) In dealing with an organization's directors, officers, employees, members, shareholders or other constituents, a lawyer shall explain the identity of the client when it is apparent that the organization's interests are adverse to those of the constituents with whom the lawyer is dealing.

(e) A lawyer representing an organization may also represent any of its directors, officers, employees, members, shareholders or other constituents, subject to the provisions of Rule 1.7. If the organization's consent to the dual representation is required by Rule 1.7, the consent shall be given by an appropriate official of the organization other than the individual who is to be represented, or by the shareholders.

Insider trading is a particular problem that has received a significant amount of publicity in recent years. Insider trading is not only ethically forbidden but is also a criminal act punishable by fines or imprisonment. As a corporate paralegal, you will no doubt have access to confidential, privileged information that you could use to buy stock at financially advantageous times. The best way to protect against problems is not to own any stock of any corporation with which you work. However, if this is not possible, or if you purchased stock prior to your employment, certainly never use any information you learn while working with the corporation for your own pecuniary benefit. Although not directly on point, DR 5-104 does limit the amount and type of business that lawyers can conduct with clients.

As for real estate paralegals or paralegals representing lending institutions, the important ethical issue is similar to that of the insurance defense paralegal: Who is the client? If you are involved in closing the loan, your client is the bank or lending institution. To be represented, the buyer and seller must retain their own counsel. If buyers or sellers contact you during the loan closing, you must not engage in the unauthorized practice of law; you should also inform them that your firm represents the lending institution, not the buyer or the seller.

Ethical dilemmas in corporate and real estate law center around conflict-of-interest issues. By remembering at all times who your client is and ensuring that your actions are in the best interests of that client, these issues will not be difficult to resolve in your practice. Paralegals in all areas of practice owe a duty of absolute loyalty to their clients; however, these two specialties are different in that determining the identity of the "client" is sometimes difficult.

THE CASE OF THE CAROUSING CEO'S COVERUP

David Waller is a corporate paralegal working in-house with Buzz Beer Company. He attended the last corporate meeting and is now preparing the notes of that meeting for the corporate minute book. The CEO comes into David's office and says: "Could you please note in the corporate minutes that the meeting was at 7:00 P.M. instead of noon? I had a date with my mistress, and my wife wants evidence that I was at the corporate meeting."

What should David do?

10.5 PUBLIC PRACTICE

Public practice, or government work, has its own ethical issues. Unlike other types of practice, the public legal professional does not necessarily represent a person or corporation, but rather represents the interests of the state or a cause. DR 7-103 deals with public lawyers in the criminal context; it provides that prosecuting attorneys shall not institute or cause to be instituted criminal charges that are obviously not supported by probable cause. DR 8-101 sets the parameters of conduct for the lawyer holding a public office; however, these standards apply to any legal professional practicing in the public sector.

DR 8-101 Action as a Public Official.

(A) A lawyer who holds public office shall not:

(1) Use his public position to obtain, or attempt to obtain, a special advantage in legislative matters for himself or for a client under circumstances where he knows or it is obvious that such action is not in the public interest.

(2) Use his public position to influence, or attempt to influence, a tribunal to act in favor of himself or of a client.

(3) Accept any thing of value from any person when the lawyer knows or it is obvious that the offer is for the purpose of influencing his action as a public official.

The public sector lawyer should never use the position to obtain a special advantage for himself or others, use the office to influence others, or accept anything of value which the individual knows is offered for the purpose of influence. The importance of these standards can be understood if one remembers that public sector lawyers include not only prosecutors, but members of attorneys general's offices, federal and state agencies, legislatures, and executive offices. Legal professionals are found throughout government. Although they may not practice law in the traditional sense, they are still bound by the same standards of conduct.

Rule 1.11 is the governmental counterpart to the imputed disqualification rule. This Rule prohibits ex-government employees from exploiting the knowledge and information obtained as public sector employees for the benefit of a private client. This Rule prevents private clients from obtaining an unfair advantage by hiring former government employees who may unethically exploit their former positions.

RULE 1.11 Successive Government and Private Employment

(a) Except as law may otherwise expressly permit, a lawyer shall not represent a private client in connection with a matter in which the lawyer participated personally and substantially as a public officer or employee, unless the appropriate government agency consents after consultation. No lawyer in a firm with which that lawyer is associated may knowingly undertake or continue representation in such a matter unless:

(1) the disqualified lawyer is screened from any participation in the matter and is apportioned no part of the fee therefrom; and

(2) written notice is promptly given to the appropriate government agency to enable it to ascertain compliance with the provisions of this rule.

(b) Except as law may otherwise expressly permit, a lawyer having information that the lawyer knows is confidential government information about a person acquired when the lawyer was a public officer or employee, may not represent a private client whose interests are adverse to that person in a matter in which the information could be used to the material disadvantage of that person. A firm with which that lawyer is associated may undertake or continue representation in the matter only if the disqualified lawyer is screened from any participation in the matter and is apportioned no part of the fee therefrom.

(c)   Except as law may otherwise expressly permit, a lawyer serving as a public officer or employee shall not:

(1)   participate in a matter in which the lawyer participated personally and substantially while in private practice or nongovernmental employment, unless under applicable law no one is, or by lawful delegation may be, authorized to act in the lawyer's stead in the matter; or

(2)   negotiate for private employment with any person who is involved as a party or as attorney for a party in a matter in which the lawyer is participating personally and substantially.

(d)   As used in this Rule, the term "matter" includes:

(1)   any judicial or other proceeding, application, request for a ruling or other determination, contract, claim, controversy, investigation, charge, accusation, arrest or other particular matter involving a specific party or parties; and

(2)   any other matter covered by the conflict of interest rules of the appropriate government agency.

(e)   As used in this Rule, the term "confidential government information" means information which has been obtained under governmental authority and which, at the time this Rule is applied, the government is prohibited by law from disclosing to the public or has a legal privilege not to disclose, and which is not otherwise available to the public.

As a public sector legal professional, being aware that you are a public servant and must act only in the best interests of the public will help you remain ethical. Because of the visibility and responsibility of public sector work, ethical standards are strict; it is best to be overly cautious and avoid even the appearance of impropriety. Because government employees are closely scrutinized, it is wise to maintain the highest ethical standards, both personally and professionally, if you practice in the public sector. As a legal professional working in the public sector, your actions affect not only you and your organization, but the general cause or government you represent.

THE CASE OF THE FREE LUNCH

Jamal Langham is an in-house paralegal for the New Mexico Public Service Commission. He helps prosecute cases involving gas companies that have violated the Commission's pipeline safety standards. Because he handles the same kinds of cases, with the same gas companies, he knows the attorneys and personnel for these companies very well.

One Saturday Jamal and his wife go out for lunch and run into the head lobbyist for the Pueblo Gas Company, who asks them to join him; they do. When the bill comes, the lobbyist pays for the meal and tells Jamal not to worry about it because Pueblo Gas Company has no cases pending before the Commission.

As they are leaving the restaurant, the lobbyist pulls Jamal aside and tells him he has a special favor he wants Jamal to do. He asks Jamal to destroy the citation dated January 7, 1992, which was a response to a pipeline explosion that killed 30 people. He also tells Jamal to destroy any other documentation of the citation.

Should Jamal have accepted the free lunch? How should he respond to the lobbyist's requests?

In his editorial, Professor Dennis Grady explains how the ethical demands of government work go beyond the boundaries established for private practice, reflecting the notion that public sector work must be characterized by the highest level of concern for ethics.

GUEST EDITORIAL

THE COMPLEXITY OF PUBLIC SECTOR ETHICS

By Dennis Grady

In Fawn Hall's testimony before the Iran-Contra Congressional Investigatory Committee she admitted, unapologetically, shredding government documents and secreting other documents out of the National Security Agency's offices in order to protect her boss, Oliver North, from potential prosecution and President Reagan from potential impeachment. While the national press had a field-day speculating on the relationship between the comely Ms. Hall and the handsome Lt. Colonel (nothing untoward was ever revealed), while she was not prosecuted for the destruction and theft of government property (she had been granted prosecutorial immunity for her testimony), and while the general public was sympathetic to Ms. Hall's dilemma, many observers of the proceedings were shocked when she justified her actions by asserting that, "Sometimes you have to break the law for a higher purpose." If adherence to the law is not the basic standard of ethical behavior for public servants, what then determines that standard and how do we hold public servants accountable for actions taken and decisions made on behalf of the public's interest? The answers to those two questions have been a major concern for the past fifty years among those of us who teach future public administrators. The answers are not straightforward.

There are three basic reasons why we hold public sector employees to a different standard of ethics than private sector employees. First, the structure of the public sector divides government among three branches (executive, legislative, judicial) and across three levels (national, state, and local). A public servant's ethical responsibility may vary depending upon which branch and level of government employs her. In the private sector, despite its diversity, an ethical violation in a Denver law firm is not much different than an ethical violation in a Cleveland law firm; nor do the standards vary significantly between real estate law practices or family law firms. While the issues may vary from practice to practice, the general standards are the same. Not so in the public sector. Second, the relationship between the public servant and the client is different than the relationship between a private employee and a client. In the private sector, the relationship is direct and generally contractual. The public servant's relationship to clients is indirect and fiduciary. The private sector operates on a fee for services arrangement. If services are not provided, fees are not forthcoming. The public sector operates on a taxes for services arrangement. If services are not provided, taxes are still collected. Third, the consequences of ethical violations in the public sector are potentially more far-reaching and profound than ethical violations in the private sector. An ethical breach in a private law firm may well harm a client and bring shame to the firm. The same violation in the city attorney's office could well harm hundreds of innocent citizens and threaten the trust and political legitimacy of the entire city government.

In terms of the structural complexity difference, it is important to note that standards of professional conduct do vary from branch to branch. For example, it is the norm for various interest groups to provide entertainment for legislators during legislative sessions. As a paralegal employed on the human resources legislative committee staff, it would not be improper to attend, as committee staff, a reception thrown by the state medical association. In fact, it might be expected that you go if the committee chairman requested your presence in anticipation that she would be responding to questions regarding pending or anticipated legislation affecting the medical community. On the other hand, it would be improper and potentially unethical for your counterpart on the staff of Department of Human Resources (executive branch) to attend the same function. Why? Because the Department of Human Resources manages Medicare, Medicaid, nursing home licensing, and other programs directly affecting the medical community. Attending social functions of groups over which you have some regulatory responsibility could

well be considered a conflict of interest or opening yourself up to charges of influence peddling.

Because the relationship to clients differs between the private sector and public sector, a relatively elaborate set of laws and regulations has emerged over access to information. Freedom of information laws, open meeting laws, and public record access laws exist in all public sector jurisdictions so that citizens may monitor how the fiduciary trust held by public servants is being handled. In the private sector, your firm's information is your firm's. No one has a "right to know" what a private operation is doing except under special situations—contractual agreements with government agencies, subpoena, discovery processes, etc. In the public sector, everyone has a "right to know" except under special situations—personnel records, pending government land transactions, national security issues, and criminal investigations. And even here the line is murky.

For example, in response to a local newspaper reporter's inquiry about the status of the city council's acquisition of land for a landfill, what may you tell her as a paralegal in the city attorney's office?

She asks, "Is there going to be land acquired?"

You respond, "Yes."

She follows with, "Where in the acquisition process is the council?"

You respond, "They are reviewing potential sites."

She probes, "How many sites are they considering?"

Here your answer may vary depending upon estate law or local ordinances. You may be required to state the number, give a range, or refuse to answer.

She asks pointedly, "Are they considering buying Councilmember Smith's acreage in Snowy Gap?"

Now you may well be ethically stuck. You know they are considering Smith's acreage, you know that Smith bought the land in anticipation of making a killing when he sold it to the city as a landfill, and you know that the site has problems in terms of soil density and potential water pollution. The law says you may not release that information. Your moral compass says that Smith is a crooked public official and the community may be harmed irreparably by locating the landfill there. If you tell the truth, you break the law, probably lose your job, protect the community, and get rid of a crooked politician. If you follow the law, you protect your job, shield a crook, and damage the community.

"Sometimes you have to break the law for a higher purpose."

Public servants frequently face issues that are morally and ethically ambiguous. Simple "rules of thumb" get contorted as the public servant moves through different branches of government and different levels of government. Being responsible and accountable to your fellow citizens elevates the consequences of unethical behavior beyond those typically faced by private sector employees. When faced with an ethically ambiguous choice, I tell my students this: Make the choice that in your estimation causes the greatest good for the next generation—you are their voice. You may very well lose your job. But you will be able to face yourself in the mirror the next morning.

■ Dennis Grady is associate professor of political science and public administration at Appalachian State University. This essay was reproduced by permission of the author.

10.6 THE PARALEGAL AS NOTARY

One duty that almost all paralegals have is as an official of the jurisdiction—the office of notary public. Notaries public are responsible for witnessing signatures and signing affidavits that the person who signed a document did in fact sign it in the notary's presence. Thus, notaries attest signatures for affidavits and other legal documents.

Many paralegals are notaries, especially those who work in small firms. It is therefore important for you to understand the guidelines, duties, and regulations for notaries in the jurisdiction in which you practice. Violating these standards can result not only in professional sanctions but also in criminal charges. The most important key to avoiding ethical problems in your notary duties is to be sure that the person who signs the document is in fact the person whose signature line is on the document. You must also watch the person sign the document.

It is a crime to falsely attest an affidavit. In *Johnson v. State,* 238 N.E.2d 651 (Ind. 1968), the court upheld the criminal conviction of a notary public, Eugene Johnson, who signed an application for an absentee voter's ballot as Floyd Mitchell. In truth, Floyd Mitchell, a personal acquaintance of Johnson, had been dead for five months at the time of the purported notarization. The court concluded that "a central factor in determining whether a notary public has the intention to falsely attest an affidavit is whether he has knowledge of the true state of the facts, or a reasonable means of acquiring such knowledge at the time and under the circumstances." *Id.* at 653. In this case, the court upheld the trial court's finding of guilt.

10.7 CONCLUSION

Although the ethical issues of confidentiality, unauthorized practice of law, and conflict of interest affect all paralegals, almost every specialty has its own ethical dilemmas that regularly arise. By ensuring that you understand and practice not only the general ethical principles, but also those unique to your area of specialization, you will develop the knowledge and sensitivity to help you become an ethical and effective legal assistant.

REVIEW QUESTIONS

1. Why do certain legal specialties present unique ethical issues?
2. What are the ethical issues unique to criminal law, family law, litigation, and corporate practices?

LAW, LITERATURE, AND ETHICS

From **The Fall**
By Albert Camus

A few years ago I was a lawyer in Paris and, indeed, a rather well-known lawyer. Of course, I didn't tell you my real name. I had a specialty: noble cases. Widows and orphans, as the saying goes—I don't know why, because there are improper widows and ferocious orphans. Yet it was enough for me to sniff the slightest scent of victim on a defendant for me to swing into action. And what action! A real tornado! My heart was on my sleeve. You would really have thought that justice slept with me every night. I am sure you would have admired the rightness of my tone, the appropriateness of my emotion, the persuasion and warmth, the restrained indignation of my speeches before the court. Nature favored me as to my physique, and the noble attitude comes effortlessly. Furthermore, I was buoyed up by two sincere feelings: the satisfaction of being on the right side of the bar and an instinctive scorn for judges in general. That scorn, after all, wasn't perhaps so instinctive. I know now that it had its reasons. But, seen from the outside, it looked rather like a passion. It can't be denied that, for the moment at least, we have to have judges, don't we? However, I could not understand how a man could offer himself to perform such a surprising function. I acccptcd the fact because I saw it, but rather as I accepted locusts. With this difference: that the invasions of those *Orthoptera* never brought me a sou, whereas I earned my living by carrying on a dialogue with people I scorned.

But, after all, I was on the right side; that was enough to satisfy my conscience. The feeling of the law, the satisfaction of being right, the joy of self-esteem, *cher monsieur,* are powerful incentives for keeping us upright or keeping us moving forward. On the other hand, if you deprive men of them, you transform them into dogs frothing with rage. How many crimes committed merely because their authors could not endure being wrong! I once knew a manufacturer who had a perfect wife, admired by all, and yet he deceived her. That man was literally furious to be in the wrong, to be blocked from receiving, or granting himself, a certificate of virtue. The more virtues his wife manifested, the more vexed he became. Eventually, living in the wrong became unbearable to him. What do you think he did then? He gave up deceiving her? Not at all. He killed her. That is how I entered into relations with him.

My situation was more enviable. Not only did I run no risk of joining the criminal camp (in particular I had no chance of killing my wife, being a bachelor), but I even took up their defense, on the sole condition that they should be noble murderers, as others are noble savages. The very manner in which I conducted that defense gave me great satisfactions. I was truly above reproach in my professional life. I never accepted a bribe, it goes without saying, and I never stooped either to any shady proceedings. And—this is even rarer—I never deigned to flatter any journalist to get him on my side, nor any civil servant whose friendship might be useful to me. I even had the luck of seeing the Legion of Honor offered to me two or three times and of being able to refuse it with a discreet dignity in which I found my true reward. Finally, I never charged the poor a fee and never boasted of it. Don't think for a moment, *cher monsieur,* that I am bragging. I take no credit for this. The avidity which in our society substitutes for ambition has always made me laugh. I was aiming higher; you will see that the expression is exact in my case.

But you can already imagine my satisfaction. I enjoyed my own nature to the fullest, and we all know there lies happiness, although, to soothe one another mutually, we occasionally pretend to condemn such joys as selfishness. At least I enjoyed that part of my nature which reacted so appropriately to the widow and orphan that eventually through exercise, it came to dominate my whole life.

The Ethical Paralegal: Principles and Practices

CHAPTER OVERVIEW

This chapter pulls together all the previous discussions of legal ethics, as applied to paralegals, to give you a complete sense of what it means to be an ethical paralegal. Being a truly ethical legal assistant means more than just ensuring that your conduct and communications follow ethical guidelines. Being ethical is not merely a way of acting: it is a way of being.

11.1 WHY BE ETHICAL?

Why should you choose to behave ethically? Other than the fact that it is the "right thing to do," there are several concrete and eminently practical reasons why you should follow the ethical course of conduct.

The first benefit of pursuing the ethical path concerns your career and professional development. Unlike several years ago, people in today's society change jobs frequently. Further, legal professionals are generally a rather close-knit group; establishing and maintaining a good reputation with peers, lawyers, the bench, and clients is essential to pursuing an outstanding career. Even though confidentiality is a fundamental ethic, reputations can spread quickly, for each legal professional deals with others daily. Thus, if one acquires a reputation for not being completely honest, being difficult to deal with, or possessing other negative characteristics, others in the profession are likely to know and discuss it. Additionally, if your conduct has been unethical and you are sanctioned, through a malpractice action, criminal allegations, or disciplinary actions, others in the profession will find out. Ensuring that your conduct never breaches ethical standards and that you maintain at least common courtesy in your relationship with others will help you develop an excellent professional reputation. This reputation will not only assist you in your current position, but also will make you very marketable to other firms in the future.

The fact that excellent work and ethical behavior go hand in hand is another positive result of ethical conduct. Although your task as a legal assistant is to do your job well, merely doing your job is not sufficient in a profession as competitive as the law. Getting the job done means getting it done ethically. For example, imagine that you were assigned the task of interviewing a witness and finding out what the witness knows that will benefit the case. You could meet with the witness and discuss the facts impartially, or you could suggest answers to the witness during the interview. Although suggesting answers might, in the short term, give the impression to your supervising attorney that you did a great job, think how embarrassing it would be later, during the deposition, if the witness said: "Well, I thought the light was green, but the defendant's paralegal convinced me it had to have been red." Everyone wants to be a superstar on the job, but being an excellent paralegal means not only doing the job effectively, but also performing your duties ethically.

Peace of mind is another benefit of being ethical. If you do something unethical, you may constantly fear the repercussions of your behavior. Will your supervising attorney find out? Will you lose your certification? Will you be fired? These doubts add unnecessary pressures to an already stressful career. Also, as previously discussed, being ethical is an essential element of doing excellent work; the satisfaction that comes from doing a job well is obviously a benefit of conforming to ethical standards.

Avoiding malpractice and criminal liability is another very good reason to be ethical. As you have seen in the cases excerpted in this textbook, malpractice actions and criminal liability can result from not following ethical guidelines when performing your duties as a legal professional. Simple things, such as telling your spouse or roommate about an especially interesting case in your firm, could result in either malpractice allegations or allegations of breaching ethical standards, if your story is relayed to others involved in the dispute. Further, entering the gray area of unauthorized practice could result in severe consequences. For example, if you have worked with a particular client for several years and are very friendly with that client, the client might very well feel that you are capable of answering questions usually directed to an attorney. In truth, you might *be* able to answer these questions, but in this situation your respect for the ethical guidelines concerning the unauthorized practice of law must overcome your temptation to use your knowledge. Don't fall into this trap. Not only could your advice be incorrect and result in liability against you and the firm, but the client could also suffer. Be aware that breaching ethical standards is more than a mistake, like a typo that can be erased; rather, it is a serious violation that can result in harsh and irreversible consequences.

Finally, as was mentioned in the discussion of maintaining your professional reputation, it surely seems that, in the long run, those who act ethically benefit from that choice in the things they have to face themselves. In the practice of law, as in most areas of life, what goes around truly does come around, both directly and indirectly. Even though you cannot control the behavior of others, your ethical treatment of others will increase the likelihood that others will treat you ethically and respectfully. Even if they do not, you always have the inner rewards of making the ethical choice. For example, it is common professional courtesy for lawyers to grant each other extensions of time to respond to motions, so long as this extension does not jeopardize the client's rights and remedies. Although an attorney might have a technical right not to grant the extension, that same attorney will probably need an extension herself in the future—what goes around, comes around. Remember that being zealous in your representation does not mean being nasty and overly aggressive; rather, zealous representation should be tempered with a regard for the common courtesies we all enjoy in everyday life. Knowing that unethical behavior is one of the aspects which defines your reputation in the legal community is another impetus for you to make ethical choices.

THE CASE OF THE DAILY DECISIONS

Paralegal Sherrie Lopez has just finished her daily meeting with her supervising attorney, Philip Michael. He has given her a list of things to do before the day is out. As she looks at the list, her throat becomes dry, as she realizes that, once again, she may not be able to perform some of the activities because they would violate ethical principles. First, attorney Philip asked Sherrie to watch and summarize videotapes of trials that were required for attorneys seeking advanced certification in litigation. Second, he wanted Sherrie to redo her time sheet to "find" an additional 10 hours of billable work, so that she would be within firm requirements. He asked her to call his wife and tell her he had to go out of town on a deposition, though Sherrie knew he had other plans. Finally, he offered her a half-day off if she would tell the women who attended her aerobics class, many of whom were wealthy, that he was a specialist in estate planning.

Sherrie has had it; each day attorney Philip requests that she perform unethical or questionable activities, and it makes her very uncomfortable. Sherrie decides to talk with Philip about her concerns. She enters his office and Philip says, "Oh, Sherrie, I'm glad you're here. Here's a $1,000 check for referring Thor Hesla as a client. Thanks a million; you're doing a great job." As Philip speaks, Sherrie is almost overwhelmed by the alcohol on his breath.

What ethical issues does Sherrie face, and how should she handle them?

11.2   PROFILE OF AN ETHICAL PARALEGAL

Like attorneys, every paralegal has a different style and personality. Individuals should of course use their uniqueness to their advantage in aspiring for excellence in the profession. However, styles and personalities must be tempered with general principles of ethical conduct. The following description of an ethical paralegal gives you a general profile of an ethical legal assistant. Of course, these guidelines are not to be followed robotically, but rather used to help you develop your identity as an ethical professional working in the legal system. These characteristics are:

1. Honesty and integrity
2. Respect for confidentiality
3. Excellent communication skills
4. Respect for clients
5. Respect for human diversity
6. Respect for the bench and bar
7. Respect for the paralegal profession
8. Competence.

"Another day in the quest for truth, justice, and the American way."

Honesty and integrity are probably the most fundamental and crucial traits of an ethical paralegal. Without basic honesty and integrity, it is doubtful that a legal assistant, by following the ethical standards, can truly be classified as an ethical paralegal. Honesty and integrity belong to an individual who has a commitment to hard work, societal rules, and ethical considerations. For example, nothing in the ethical rules specifically precludes a paralegal from reading a book while indicating on her timesheet that she summarized a deposition. Nothing precludes a legal assistant from taking a look in his supervising attorney's desk drawers when she is out of the office. However, most people, even those not in the legal profession, would agree that these two actions violate the very basic standards of integrity and honesty. It is important to make sure that you not only follow formalized ethical rules and guidelines, but also that you make honesty and integrity part of your professional life.

In chapter 3, on *confidentiality* and client secrets and confidences, you learned about the formal rules pertaining to confidentiality. However, the ability to "keep one's mouth shut" is absolutely critical to being an ethical paralegal. This point cannot be overemphasized. The ability to keep clients' secrets goes to the very heart of our legal system. Without this provision, our legal system would not be as protective and mindful of individual rights as it is now. Think of client confidences by analogy: Would you really trust a doctor and continue going to that doctor if you heard at a party that the doctor had told someone you had had an abortion? We are all entitled to our privacy, and as a legal professional your ability to keep these private matters private is absolutely critical to your success.

Excellent communication skills are another characteristic of the professional and ethical paralegal. Knowing what you can say and how to say it is essential to your success. Being clear and concise is important not only in your communications with clients, but also in your interactions with attorneys and legal secretaries. The principles of effective communication for a legal professional are no different from usual communication practices. However, ethical guidelines do apply to the content of a lawyer's or paralegal's communications. Ethical principles concerning confidentiality or the unauthorized practice of law, for example, circumscribe what a paralegal may communicate. Rules concerning advertising and solicitation also limit what may be communicated. Rules concerning zealous representation restrict what you may say to adverse parties or jurors. If you change jobs, you may be limited in communicating about cases you previously handled for an adverse party. Each of the ethical principles you have studied affects how a paralegal communicates with others.

Perhaps the most important characteristic of effective communication in legal work is meticulous attention to accurate and clear communication. Think of the ramifications of careless communication if you told a client that her case was dismissed with prejudice, when the dismissal you drafted and filed stated that the case was dismissed without prejudice. The client would think that the matter was over and no future cases could be filed against her with the same issues, when in fact the case could be subsequently revived. When communicating, either orally or in writing, paying attention to detail may make the difference between being ethical and being unethical.

Respecting clients is another trait of the ethical paralegal. Remember, clients are your profession's business, so for purely economic reasons it makes sense to nurture your clients. More importantly, when a client feels respected, that client will be helpful and cooperative. Most clients are frightened by the legal process; they are outsiders to the legal system and do not know how it works. Many clients also fear the consequences of their legal involvement. The ethical paralegal is not abusive or scornful of the client for having these concerns, but is instead sensitive to these fears and apprehensions. A respect for clients also involves a respect for that which belongs to them. Following good accounting procedures and ensuring that client funds are properly handled will help you show professional respect for those clients.

An ethical paralegal is also characterized by a *respect for human diversity*. In legal practice, as in most professions, you will interact with many different kinds of people, and you must put aside any personal bias or prejudice so that you can fulfill your responsibility as a professional to work productively with them. Because paralegals work with many individuals—jurors, witnesses, lawyers, clients, paralegals, secretaries, docket clerks, couriers, and legislators—each of whom has his or her own cultural identity, the effective professional cannot afford an inability to communicate with a certain kind of person. The ethical and effective paralegal communicates and interacts with all people; that implies an ability to handle and appreciate, rather than reject and fear, the cultural diversity of contemporary society.

Unfortunately, many are at a loss when dealing with persons who come from other cultures. In the following guest editorial, Professor Susan Chin gives some practical advice on how to succeed in managing cultural diversity in your work.

GUEST EDITORIAL

MANAGING CULTURAL DIVERSITY

By Susan Chin

Do you feel nervous, uncomfortable, or frightened when you walk into a room and almost everyone in the room is from a race or culture that is different from your own? What is your first thought: to leave or to stay? If your immediate reaction is to leave, then you are letting diversity manage you instead of *you* managing diversity.

DEMOGRAPHICS

America's population is changing dramatically. Because of higher birth rates and immigration, ethnic and racial minorities in the United States are growing approximately seven times faster than the white population. According to the U.S. Census, America's minorities could be in the majority by 2050. Diversity will be the norm. Your employer, colleague, client, or neighbor may well be from a cultural background different from your own. If you, as an individual and as a professional, are going to succeed in the 1990s and beyond, you must learn to communicate with people from other backgrounds or cultures and to manage diversity.

MANAGING DIVERSITY

Managing diversity, in this context, means being aware of cultural differences and how they affect interaction. Recognize that culture is more than that which is obvious—clothing and food. Culture is also values, attitudes, and behavior. Values create attitudes, and attitudes influence behavior.

Culture shapes views and behavior. Culture is something shared by members of a group and passed on by the older generation to the younger. Culture enables people to create a distinctive world around themselves, and it gives them their sense of identity.

The first step in managing diversity is recognizing your own cultural values. Realize that your values are not universal or common to all cultures. Arabs value the power of society over the individual, so individuals do not question those who are in positions of authority. Americans value individualism and play to win. In contrast, the Japanese believe in group effort or collectivism. They place a high value on harmony, so to the Japanese a perfect game is a tie game.

Next, learn about other cultures. Start by going to the library; read books about the cultures of your co-workers or neighbors. Cultural knowledge provides insight into people, and as you begin to understand people who are culturally different, you begin to understand your own culture and yourself. When you recognize that you are the product of your own culture and are culturally conditioned, you will find that the values, attitudes, and behavior of other cultures are more acceptable.

Make an effort to be friendly with people who are different. Compare similarities and differences. Similarities are easy to accept, and knowledge makes differences less threatening. Cultural awareness can help you establish good interpersonal relationships outside your own culture group.

Treat each person as an individual, so avoid stereotyping and generalizing. Be sensitive to people's feelings, and realize that every person is entitled to his cultural pride. Don't impose your own cultural standards on others. Above all, stop requiring that those who are different from you prove and reprove their worthiness. For example, it is often assumed that a man can get a job done, but a woman in a man's world has to prove over and over again that she can do the job.

Finally, when conflicts arise, try to figure out the basis for the problem. Five hundred years before Christ, Confucius commented that "By nature men are nearly alike; by practice . . . wide apart."

An example is eye contact. For one thing, Americans equate eye contact with honesty and openness. If an American is talking to a person who is always looking at the floor, the American might think that the other individual is hiding something. For Asians, however, lowered eyes are not an admission of guilt, but an indication of respect. Afro-Americans sometimes interpret the direct eye contact cultural style of whites as whites' attempting to dominate them. Secondly, Americans often consider it impolite when someone looks directly at them for an extended period of time. So they sometimes misinterpret the conduct of a Frenchman who is exhibiting his cultural tendency to hold prolonged eye contact.

In America, the owl is a symbol of wisdom, and "the wise old owl" is a common decoration in elementary school classrooms. Pity the newly arrived Asian immigrant children on their first day in an American school, for they see staring down on them a symbol of death.

CONCLUSION

Effective cross-cultural communication is not easy. Simply acknowledging that the population of this country is becoming more diverse does not generate understanding. You must move away from ethnocentrism, or the belief that your culture is the most important culture. You must free yourself of your preconception about culturally diverse people, your prejudices, and your stereotypes. If you don't begin now to value diversity, as we hurtle toward the next century, you will be left behind in a shrinking monocultural environment. For professional success and personal self-development, take the initiative and start learning to manage diversity.

■ Susan Chin is associate professor of general studies and chairperson of the Committee on Inter-Cultural Awareness at DeVry Institute of Technology. This essay was reprinted by permission of the author.

An ethical paralegal will show *respect for the bench and bar.* Properly addressing members of the judiciary is not only common courtesy, but is also required by most courts. Even if you know the judge personally, it would be irresponsible to address him in the hallway of the courthouse as "Bill" rather than "Judge" or "Your Honor." However, respect for the bench and bar includes more than ensuring that you address individuals properly. It also means that you respect the environment in which the law is practiced and the procedures that determine how that practice is to be carried out. As in sports, in which half the participants always lose, half the attorneys who try a case lose. By acting professionally whether your side wins or loses, you will be showing respect for the entire process and the profession.

Ethical paralegals will also show *respect for the paralegal profession.* They will work to improve the profession and the legal system. One of NFPA's ethical standards specifically requires that members of its organization work toward the betterment of the profession:

"Huh?"

I. Professional Responsibility

The paralegal is dedicated to the development of the paralegal profession and endeavors to expand the responsibilities and the scope of paralegal work.

Discussion: There is room for a great deal of growth in the paralegal profession and an opportunity to tap human resources to assist an overburdened legal system. This Affirmation of Responsibility aims to establish a positive attitude through which the paralegal may perceive the importance, responsibility and potential of the paralegal profession and work toward enhancing its professional status.

Canon 9 of NALA's Code of Ethics and Professional Responsibility provides that: "A legal assistant shall work continually to maintain integrity and a high degree of competency throughout the legal profession." Thus, both paralegal organizations recognize the importance of maintaining integrity and supporting the goals of the profession.

Like all professionals respecting and working to improve their own professions, legal assistants should bear in mind that their own actions reflect on all other legal assistants. Participating in paralegal associations at the state or national levels, working within your firm as a mentor to new paralegals, and working to develop ethical ways to better serve the poor and disenfranchised are ways to work for the improvement of the profession.

Ethical paralegals are concerned with *competence* and continually strive to improve their abilities. This quest to achieve and maintain competence is important in two respects. First, an ethical paralegal will continue her education, required or not, to maintain her knowledge and skills in her area of practice. Second, an ethical paralegal will not attempt to handle a case in which he is inexperienced without first advising his supervising attorney of his inabilities. Being ethical is almost synonymous with being competent, for a competent paralegal is always cognizant of ethical requirements and aspirations.

The characteristics that constitute this profile are not demands; they arc signposts. Each ethical legal professional will demonstrate these characteristics, but each will do it in his or her own way. We all recognize competence, but there are surely many ways of achieving it. This, then, is your task: to forge a professional identity in which you are your own person, integrating the ethical characteristics discussed here. For, as we have already pointed out, and you have doubtless realized on your own, being ethical is not just something you try to do—it is someone you try to be.

In the following guest editorial, Philip Lewin explores this notion of ethics as a matter of character.

BEING PROFESSIONAL IS A MATTER OF CHARACTER

by Philip Lewin

Aristotle makes a very interesting claim in his ethical theory. He argues that it is impossible for a person who is morally weak to be capable of correct reasoning and judgment in practical affairs. In effect, he is claiming that to be a professional, and to be capable of acting responsibly and with integrity and dignity, is a matter of character. It is not simply a matter of learning certain rules of law and applying them mechanically; it is not only a case of formally adhering to a code of professional ethics; rather, it is for the most part a matter of becoming the kind of person for whom the correct and responsible application of the law is as natural and automatic as breathing. Being a professional is not something one does during ordinary working hours, to be cast aside at the end of the workday with sweaty underwear; rather, it is something one is in the fabric of his being.

Aristotle's claim is somewhat surprising. It flies in the face of the popular wisdom of our highly individualistic culture that tells us to only be as moral as we need to be in order to avoid getting in trouble, that counsels us to be self-interested entrepreneurs pursuing our own gain, that cynically suggests the law has no integrity but simply formalizes the procedures various ruling elites have negotiated among themselves.

Instead, behaving as a professional is a matter of knowing how to apply the right rules at the right time in the right way. It is a question of knowing that our choices must be sensitive to context and nuance, to degree and circumstance. And it is also a question of how we come to make the kinds of choices we do, of how we learn to recognize context and circumstance in the first place. This is a question of how we come to inhabit our professional roles. Aristotle suggests that a responsible sensitivity can only be achieved insofar as it has been lived, insofar as one's own experience, rightly understood, has come to function as the tacit guide to one's professional behavior.

What can it mean to understand one's experience "rightly"? This is a difficult question not because we do not have an answer but because we have too many

answers and too few guidelines to constrain them. Should choices be made only with consideration of immediate needs and desires, or should they also consider family, or community, or country? Should the highest value be to gratify temptation, or should we instead honor "higher" values of restraint and sacrifice? Can we ever act with full recognition of and mastery over all the influences on our decisions, or must we recognize that rarely, if ever, do we fully understand the complexity of our motives?

Aristotle's answer to the question of rightly understanding experience was that to do so meant understanding how one's choices contributed to the formation and support of being in the kind of human community of which one would want to be a part. Indeed, if we look at some of the world's greatest literature—Shakespeare's *Hamlet,* for instance, or Sophocles'[s] *Oedipus Rex*— we see that such a concern deeply animates them. Oedipus chooses to discover the murderer of King Laios equally because the health of Thebes is at stake and because he simply is the kind of person who, as a matter of personal integrity, must know the truth even though this truth will destroy him. In a complementary way, Hamlet delays avenging his father's murder precisely because of his uncertainty that Denmark is morally worth such vengeance. Oedipus and Hamlet understand the necessity of action in terms of how their action contributes to the virtue of their community. The moral worthiness of Thebes fuels Oedipus's unrelenting inquiries, just as the moral corruption of Denmark leads Hamlet to despair of action. For both, the choice to act or not to act is indeed a choice to be or not to be; the decision emerges as second nature out of the kind of persons they have become, out of how they have been educated into the ethos of their cultures. Their actions arise out of what Aristotle means by character. And thinking more widely in Shakespeare for a moment, we see that the tragedies of Othello and Lear and Macbeth also arise from a breakdown, much like Hamlet's, in the congruity of an individual's sense of place in his community, whether that congruity is corrupted by others (as it is for Othello and Macbeth) or ruptured by the self (as it is for Lear). For Shakespeare as for Aristotle, a vision of the moral and social order provides the context against which one's sense of how to act takes form and is sustained.

Yet knowing that Shakespeare's vision was of an aristocratic society, or that the kind of community which Aristotle idealized was one in which women and slaves and foreigners and even manual laborers could never achieve full citizenship, might well lead us to feel that these are not the kinds of social orders with which *we* wish to be associated. We have chosen to replace an aristocratic order with a democratic one in which all people are fully empowered, to which all people may feel loyalty. Yet this choice has introduced a further set of problems. Indeed, if we look at more recent literature, we find that a prominent theme is the difficulty of knowing, as a person of character, what kind of community one ought to be loyal to. It is not a question of a clear standard that is not being realized, but of the lack of a clear standard altogether. Think of Meursault, in Camus's *The Stranger,* sleepwalking through life, pledging marriage, even committing murder, for want of a sense of place in an indifferent universe; or of Marlow, in Conrad's *Heart of Darkness,* finding solace that is no solace at all in having chosen loyalty to the savagery of Kurtz rather than to the hypocrisies of European imperialism. Having

rejected earlier visions of hierarchical order, we moderns often find that we have also relinquished a vision of moral community which could ground our individual development.

Earlier I suggested that only persons of character could truly be professionals because professionals are intimately concerned with the development of moral community. Within the framework of the law, participating in a moral community entails developing a sense of equity, a sensitivity to context and history, that offers guidance in how the law is practiced. But such a sense arises out of the kind of people we have become through the kinds of choices we have made over the course of our lives. And the possibilities of our self-formation as people of character arise out of the kind of community that supported our growth, and which we now, as adults, support in turn. We do not live in ancient Greece or Renaissance England; we have no guiding vision of a perfect society to which we piously adhere except the one that we imperfectly create through our practices in our daily creation of ourselves. To be a professional is a life task.

■ Philip Lewin is Associate Professor of Humanities at Clarkson University in Potsdam, New York. He is the author of the forthcoming *Epistemology and the Insane Soul* (SUNY Press, 1994). This essay is reprinted by permission of the author.

11.3 ETHICS: NOT JUST ONCE IN A BLUE MOON

When you first began your study of ethics, you may have thought that ethical dilemmas occurred only occasionally. However, after completing this textbook, you can see that not only is ethics a constantly evolving process, but also that ethical problems arise almost daily. Ethics, you now know, is no "once in a blue moon" kind of thing. The most ordinary situations can present ethical dilemmas to the legal professional, and, of course, unusual situations frequently present novel or challenging ethical issues. If you remember that every client and every case present ethical considerations, you will develop the sensitivity that will enable you to identify and handle the ethical dilemmas you will encounter.

You have also learned that being ethical is not a product you can buy—it is a process in which you are involved. The process is not separate from or alien to who you are. In fact, as Professor Lewin asserts, it is exactly who you are that is the key to whether you are an ethical professional. Perhaps you started this book thinking that you could just learn the rules about ethics and be done with it. Now you know that ethics is not only concerned with situations that may create ethical dilemmas, but that it is also concerned—perhaps primarily so—with helping you develop into the kind of person who is characterized by an ethical sensibility. Ethical rules and guidelines, whether they are disciplinary or aspirational, are useless if they fall on deaf ears. Learning about legal ethics and professional responsibility, therefore, really requires learning about and developing yourself. Just as legal practice offers ethical dilemmas regularly, not once in a blue moon, so is the part of you which makes ethical choices your constant companion, because that part of you is the whole you. And you are always there.

REVIEW QUESTIONS

1. What are the reasons for pursuing an ethical course of action?
2. What are the characteristics of the ethical paralegal?

CLOSING STATEMENT

LAW, LITERATURE, AND ETHICS

"Before the Law"
From **The Trial**
By Franz Kafka

Before the law stands a doorkeeper. To this doorkeeper there comes a man from the country and prays for admittance to the Law. But the doorkeeper says that he cannot grant admittance at the moment. The man thinks it over and then asks if he will be allowed in later. "It is possible," says the doorkeeper, "but not at the moment." Since the gate stands open, as usual, and the doorkeeper steps to one side, the man stoops to peer through the gateway into the interior. Observing that, the doorkeeper laughs and says: "If you are so drawn to it, just try to go in despite my veto. But take note: I am powerful. And I am only the least of the doorkeepers. From hall to hall there is one doorkeeper after another, each more powerful than the last. The third doorkeeper is already so terrible that even I cannot bear to look at him." These are difficulties the man from the country has not expected; the Law, he thinks, should surely be accessible at all times and to everyone, but as he now takes a closer look at the doorkeeper in his fur coat, with his big sharp nose and long, thin, black Tartar beard, he decides that it is better to wait until he gets permission to enter. The doorkeeper gives him a stool and lets him sit down at one side of the door. There he sits for days and years. He makes many attempts to be admitted, and wearies the doorkeeper by his importunity. The doorkeeper frequently has little interviews with him, asking him questions about his home and many other things, but the questions are put indifferently, as great lords put them, and always finish with the statement that he cannot be let in yet. The man, who has furnished himself with many things for his journey, sacrifices all he has, however valuable, to bribe the doorkeeper. The doorkeeper accepts everything, but always with the remark: "I am only taking it to keep you from thinking you have omitted anything." During these many years, the man fixes his attention almost continually on the doorkeeper. He forgets the other doorkeepers, and this first one seems to him the sole obstacle preventing access to the Law. He curses his bad luck, in his early years boldly and loudly; later, as he grows old, he only grumbles to himself. He becomes childish, and since in his yearlong contemplation of the doorkeeper he has come to know even the fleas in his fur collar, he begs the fleas as well to help him and to change the doorkeeper's mind. At length his eyesight begins to fail, and he does not know whether the world is really darker or whether his eyes are only deceiving him. Yet in his darkness he is now aware of a radiance that streams inextinguishably from the gateway of the Law. Now he has not very long to live. Before he dies, all his experiences in these long years gather themselves in his head to one point, a question he has not yet asked the doorkeeper. He waves him nearer, since he can no longer raise his stiffening body. The doorkeeper has to bend low toward him, for the difference in height has altered much to the man's disadvantage. "What do you want to know now?" asks the doorkeeper; "You are insatiable." "Everyone strives to reach the Law," says the man, "so how does it happen that for all these many years no one but myself has ever begged for admittance?" The doorkeeper recognizes that the man has reached his end, and, to let his failing senses catch the words, roars in his ear: "No one else could ever be admitted here since this gate was made only for you. I am now going to shut it."

APPENDIX A

ABA Model Guidelines for the Utilization of Legal Assistant Services

Preamble

State courts, bar associations, or bar committees in at least seventeen states have prepared recommendations for the utilization of legal assistant services. While their content varies, their purpose appears uniform: to provide lawyers with a reliable basis for delegating responsibility for performing a portion of the lawyer's tasks to legal assistants. The purpose of preparing model guidelines is not to contradict the guidelines already adopted or to suggest that other guidelines may be more appropriate in a particular jurisdiction. It is the view of the Standing Committee on Legal Assistants of the American Bar Association, however, that a model set of guidelines for the utilization of legal assistant services may assist many states in adopting or revising such guidelines. The Standing Committee is of the view that guidelines will encourage lawyers to utilize legal assistant services effectively and promote the growth of the legal assistant profession. In undertaking this project, the Standing Committee has attempted to state guidelines that conform with the American Bar Association's Model Rules of Professional Conduct, decided authority, and contemporary practice. Lawyers, of course, are to be first directed by Rule 5.3 of the Model Rules in the utilization of legal assistant services, and nothing contained in these guidelines is intended to be inconsistent with that rule. Specific ethical considerations in particular states, however, may require modification of these guidelines before their adoption. In the commentary after each guideline, we have attempted to identify the basis for the guideline and any issues of which we are aware that the guideline may present; those drafting such guidelines may wish to take them into account.

Guideline 1: **A lawyer is responsible for all of the professional actions of a legal assistant performing legal assistant services at the lawyer's direction and should take reasonable measures to ensure that the legal assistant's conduct is consistent with the lawyer's obligations under the ABA Model Rules of Professional Conduct.**

Comment to Guideline 1

An attorney who utilizes a legal assistant's services is responsible for determining that the legal assistant is competent to perform the tasks assigned, based on the legal assistant's education, training, and experience, and for ensuring that the legal assistant is familiar with the responsibilities of attorneys and legal assistants under the applicable rules governing professional conduct.

Under principles of agency law and rules governing the conduct of attorneys, lawyers are responsible for the actions and the work product of the non-lawyers they employ. Rule 5.3 of the Model Rules requires that partners and supervising attorneys ensure that the conduct of non-lawyer assistants is compatible with the lawyer's professional obligations. Several state guidelines have adopted this language. E.g., Commentary to Illinois Recommendation (A), Kansas Guideline III(a), New Hampshire Rule 35, Sub-Rule 9, and North Carolina Guideline 4. Ethical Consideration 3-6 of the Model Code encouraged lawyers to delegate tasks to legal assistants provided the lawyer maintained a direct relationship with the client, supervised appropriately, and had complete responsibility for the work product. The adoption of Rule 5.3, which incorporates these principles, implicitly reaffirms this encouragement.

Several states have addressed the issue of the lawyer's ultimate responsibility for work performed by subordinates. For example, Colorado Guideline 1.c, Kentucky Supreme Court Rule 3.700, Sub-Rule 2.C, and Michigan Guideline I provide: "The lawyer remains responsible for the actions of the legal assistant to the same extent as if such representation had been furnished entirely by the lawyer and such actions were those of the lawyer." New Mexico Guideline X states "[the] lawyer maintains ultimate responsibility for and has an ongoing duty to actively supervise the legal assistant's work performance, conduct and product." Connecticut Recommendation 2 and Rhode Island Guideline III state specifically that lawyers are liable for malpractice for the mistakes and omissions of their legal assistants.

Finally, the lawyer should ensure that legal assistants supervised by the lawyer are familiar with the rules governing attorney conduct and that they follow those rules. See Comment to Model Rule 5.3; Illinois Recommendation (A)(5), New Hampshire Supreme Court Rule 35, Sub-Rule 9, and New Mexico, Statement of Purpose; see also NALA's Model Standards and Guidelines for the Utilization of Legal Assistants, guidelines IV, V, and VIII (1985, revised 1990) (hereafter "NALA Guidelines").

The Standing Committee and several of those who have commented upon these Guidelines regard Guideline 1 as a comprehensive statement of general principle governing lawyers who utilize legal assistant services in the practice of law. As such it, in effect, is a part of each of the remaining Guidelines.

***Guideline 2:* Provided the lawyer maintains responsibility for the work product, a lawyer may delegate to a legal assistant any task normally performed by the lawyer except those tasks proscribed to one not licensed as a lawyer by statute, court rule, administrative rule or regulation, controlling authority, the ABA Model Rules of Professional Conduct, or these Guidelines.**

Comment to Guideline 2

The essence of the definition of the term legal assistant adopted by the ABA Board of Governors in 1986 is that, so long as appropriate supervision is maintained, many tasks normally performed by lawyers may be delegated to legal assistants. Of course, Rule 5.5 of the Model Rules, DR 3-101 of the Model Code, and most states specifically prohibit lawyers from assisting or aiding a non-lawyer in the unauthorized practice of law. Thus, while appropriate delegation of tasks to legal assistants is encouraged, the lawyer may not permit the legal assistant to engage in the "practice of law." Neither the Model Rules nor the Model Code define the "practice of law." EC 3-5 under the Model Code gave some

guidance by equating the practice of law to the application of the professional judgment of the lawyer in solving clients' legal problems. Further, ABA Opinion 316 (1967) states: "A lawyer can employ lay secretaries, lay investigators, lay detectives, lay researchers, accountants, lay scriveners, nonlawyer draftsmen or nonlawyer researchers. In fact, he may employ nonlawyers to do any task for him except counsel clients about law matters, engage directly in the practice of law, appear in court or appear in formal proceedings as part of the judicial process, so long as it is he who takes the work and vouches for it to the client and becomes responsible for it to the client."

Most state guidelines specify that legal assistants may not appear before courts, administrative tribunals, or other adjudicatory bodies unless their rules authorize such appearances; may not conduct depositions; and may not give legal advice to clients. E.g., Connecticut Recommendation 4; Florida EC 3-6 (327 So.2d at 16); and Michigan Guideline II. Also see NALA Guidelines IV and VI. But it is also important to note that, as some guidelines have recognized, pursuant to federal or state statute legal assistants are permitted to provide direct client representation in certain administrative proceedings. E.g., South Carolina Guideline II. While this does not obviate the attorney's responsibility for the legal assistant's work, it does change the nature of the attorney supervision of the legal assistant. The opportunity to use such legal assistant services has particular benefits to legal services programs and does not violate Guideline 2. See generally ABA Standards for Providers of Civil Legal Services to the Poor, Std. 6.3, at 6.17-6.18 (1986).

The Model Rules emphasize the importance of appropriate delegation. The key to appropriate delegation is proper supervision, which includes adequate instruction when assigning projects, monitoring of the project, and review of the completed project. The Supreme Court of Virginia upheld a malpractice verdict against a lawyer based in part on negligent actions of a legal assistant in performing tasks that evidently were properly delegable. *Musselman v. Willoughby Corp.*, 230 Va. 337, 337 S.E.2d 724 (1985). See also C. Wolfram, Modern Legal Ethics (1986), at 236, 896. All state guidelines refer to the requirement that the lawyer "supervise" legal assistants in the performance of their duties. Lawyers should also take care in hiring and choosing a legal assistant to work on a specific project to ensure that the legal assistant has the education, knowledge, and ability necessary to perform the delegated tasks competently. See Connecticut Recommendation 14, Kansas Standards I, II, and III, and New Mexico Guideline VIII. Finally, some states describe appropriate delegation and review in terms of the delegated work losing its identity and becoming "merged" into the work product of the attorney. See Florida EC 3-6 (327 So. 2d at 16).

Legal assistants often play an important role in improving communication between the attorney and the client. EC 3-6 under the Model Code mentioned three specific kinds of tasks that legal assistants may perform under appropriate lawyer supervision: factual investigation and research, legal research, and the preparation of legal documents. Some states delineate more specific tasks in their guidelines, such as attending client conferences, corresponding with and obtaining information from clients, handling witness execution of documents, preparing transmittal letters, maintaining estate/guardianship trust accounts, etc. See, e.g., Colorado (lists of specialized functions in several areas follow guidelines); Michigan, Comment to Definition of Legal Assistant; New York, Specialized Skills of Legal Assistants; Rhode Island Guideline II; and NALA Guideline IX. The two-volume Working with Legal Assistants, published by the Standing Committee in 1982, attempted to provide a general description of the types of tasks that may be delegated to legal assistants in various practice areas.

There are tasks that have been specifically prohibited in some states, but that may be delegated in others. For example, legal assistants may not supervise will executions or represent clients at real estate closings in some jurisdictions, but may in others. Compare Connecticut Recommendation 7 and Illinois State Bar Association Position Paper on Use of Attorney Assistants in Real Estate Transactions (May 16, 1984), which proscribe legal assistants conducting real estate closings, with Georgia "real estate job description," Florida Professional Ethics Committee Advisory Opinion 89-5 (1989), and Missouri, Comment to Guideline I, which permit legal assistants to conduct real estate closings. Also compare Connecticut Recommendation 8 (prohibiting attorneys from authorizing legal assistants to supervise will executions) with Colorado "estate planning job description," Georgia "estate, trusts, and wills job description," Missouri, Comment to Guideline I, and Rhode Island Guideline II (suggesting that legal assistants may supervise the execution of wills, trusts, and other documents).

Guideline 3: **A lawyer may not delegate to a legal assistant:**
    (a) Responsibility for establishing an attorney-client relationship.
    (b) Responsibility for establishing the amount of a fee to be charged for a legal service.
    (c) Responsibility for a legal opinion rendered to a client.

Comment to Guideline 3

The Model Rules and most state codes require that lawyers communicate with their clients in order

for clients to make well-informed decisions about their representation and resolution of legal issues. Model Rule 1.4. Ethical Consideration 3-6 under the Model Code emphasized that "delegation [of legal tasks to nonlawyers] is proper if the lawyer *maintains a direct relationship with his client,* supervises the delegated work and has complete professional responsibility for the work product." (Emphasis added.) Accordingly, most state guidelines also stress the importance of a direct attorney-client relationship. See Colorado Guideline 1, Florida EC 3-6, Illinois Recommendation (A)(1), Iowa EC 3-6(2), and New Mexico Guideline IV. The direct personal relationship between client and lawyer is necessary to the exercise of the lawyer's trained professional judgment.

An essential aspect of the lawyer-client relationship is the agreement to undertake representation and the related fee arrangement. The Model Rules and most states require that fee arrangements be agreed upon early on and be communicated to the client by the lawyer, in some circumstances in writing. Model Rule 1.5 and Comments. Many state guidelines prohibit legal assistants from "setting fees" or "accepting cases." See, e.g., Colorado Guideline 1 and NALA Guideline VI. Connecticut recommends that legal assistants be prohibited from accepting or rejecting cases or setting fees "if these tasks entail any discretion on the part of the paralegals." Connecticut Recommendation 9.

EC 3-5 states: "[T]he essence of the professional judgment of the lawyer is his educated ability to relate the general body and philosophy of law to a specific legal problem of a client; and thus, the public interest will be better served if only lawyers are permitted to act in matters involving professional judgment." Clients are entitled to their lawyers' professional judgment and opinion. Legal assistants may, however, be authorized to communicate legal advice so long as they do not interpret or expand on that advice. Typically, state guidelines phrase this prohibition in terms of legal assistants being forbidden from "giving legal advice" or "counseling clients about legal matters." See, e.g., Colorado Guideline 2, Connecticut Recommendation 6, Florida DR 3-104, Iowa EC 3-6(3), Kansas Guideline I, Kentucky Sub-Rule 2, New Hampshire Rule 35, Sub-Rule 1, Texas Guideline I, and NALA Guideline VI. Some states have more expansive wording that prohibits legal assistants from engaging in any activity that would require the exercise of independent legal judgment. Nevertheless, it is clear that all states, as well as the Model Rules, encourage direct communication between clients and a legal assistant insofar as the legal assistant is performing a task properly delegated by a lawyer. It should be noted that a lawyer who permits a legal assistant to assist in establishing the attorney-client relationship, communicating a fee, or preparing a legal opinion is not delegating responsibility for those matters and, therefore, may be complying with this guideline.

Guideline 4: It is the lawyer's responsibility to take reasonable measures to ensure that clients, courts, and other lawyers are aware that a legal assistant, whose services are utilized by the lawyer in performing legal services, is not licensed to practice law.

Comment to Guideline 4

Since, in most instances, a legal assistant is not licensed as a lawyer, it is important that those with whom the legal assistant deals are aware of that fact. Several state guidelines impose on the lawyer responsibility for instructing a legal assistant whose services are utilized by the lawyer to disclose the legal assistant's status in any dealings with a third party. See, e.g., Michigan Guideline III, part 5, New Hampshire Rule 35, Sub-Rule 8, and NALA Guideline V. While requiring the legal assistant to make such disclosure is one way in which the attorney's responsibility to third parties may be discharged, the Standing Committee is of the view that it is desirable to emphasize the lawyer's responsibility for the disclosure and leave to the lawyer the discretion to decide whether the lawyer will discharge that responsibility by direct communication wiih the client, by requiring the legal assistant to make the disclosure, by a written memorandum, or by some other means. Although in most initial engagements by a client it may be prudent for the attorney to discharge this responsibility with a writing, the guideline requires only that the lawyer recognize the responsibility and ensure that it is discharged. Clearly, when a client has been adequately informed of the lawyer's utilization of legal assistant services, it is unnecessary to make additional formalistic disclosures as the client retains the lawyer for other services.

Most state guidelines specifically endorse legal assistants signing correspondence so long as their status as a legal assistant is indicated by an appropriate title. E.g., Colorado Guideline 2; Kansas, Comment to Guideline IX; and North Carolina Guideline 9; also see ABA Informal Opinion 1367 (1976). The comment to New Mexico Guideline XI warns against the use of the title "associate" since it may be construed to mean associate-attorney.

Guideline 5: A lawyer may identify legal assistants by name and title on the lawyer's letterhead and on business cards identifying the lawyer's firm.

Comment to Guideline 5

Under Guideline 4, above, an attorney who employs a legal assistant has an obligation to ensure that the status of the legal assistant as a non-lawyer is fully disclosed. The primary purpose of this disclosure is to avoid confusion that might lead someone to believe that the legal assistant is a lawyer. The identification suggested by this guideline is consistent with that objective, while also affording the legal assistant recognition as an important part of the legal services team.

Recent ABA Informal Opinion 1527 (1989) provides that non-lawyer support personnel, including legal assistants, may be listed on a law firm's letterhead and reiterates previous opinions that approve of legal assistants having business cards. See also ABA Informal Opinion 1185 (1971). The listing must not be false or misleading and "must make it clear that the support personnel who are listed are not lawyers."

Nearly all state guidelines approve of business cards for legal assistants, but some prescribe the contents and format of the card. E.g., Iowa Guideline 4 and Texas Guideline VIII. All agree the legal assistant's status must be clearly indicated and the card may not be used in a deceptive way. New Hampshire Supreme Court Rule 7 approves the use of business cards so long as the card is not used for unethical solicitation.

Some states do not permit attorneys to list legal assistants on their letterhead. E.g., Kansas Guideline VIII, Michigan Guideline III, Sub-Rule 7, New Mexico Guideline XI, and North Carolina Guideline 9. Several of these states rely on earlier ABA Informal Opinions 619 (1962), 845 (1965), and 1000 (1977), all of which were expressly withdrawn by ABA Informal Opinion 1527. These earlier opinions interpreted the predecessor Model Code and DR 2-102(A), which, prior to *Bates v. State Bar of Arizona*, 433 U.S. 350 (1977), had strict limitations on the information that could be listed on letterheads. States which do permit attorneys to list names of legal assistants on their stationery, if the listing is not deceptive and the legal assistant's status is clearly identified, include: Arizona Committee on Rules of Professional Conduct Formal Opinion 3/90 (1990); Connecticut Recommendation 12; Florida Professional Ethics Committee Advisory Opinion 86-4 (1986); Hawaii, Formal Opinion 78-8-19 (1978, as revised 1984); Illinois State Bar Association Advisory Opinion 87-1 (1987); Kentucky Sub-Rule 6; Mississippi State Bar Ethics Committee Opinion No. 93 (1984); Missouri Guideline IV; New York State Bar Association Committee on Professional Ethics Opinion 500 (1978); Oregon, Ethical Opinion No. 349 (1977); and Texas, Ethics Committee Opinion 436 (1983). In light of the United States Supreme Court opinion in *Peel v. Attorney Registration and Disciplinary Commission of Illinois*, — U.S. — , 110 S. Ct. 2281 (1990), it may be that a restriction on letterhead identification of legal assistants that is not deceptive and clearly identifies the legal assistant's status violates the First Amendment rights of the lawyer.

Guideline 6: **It is the responsibility of a lawyer to take reasonable measures to ensure that all client confidences are preserved by a legal assistant.**

Comment to Guideline 6

A fundamental principle underlying the free exchange of information in a lawyer-client relationship is that the lawyer maintain the confidentiality of information relating to the representation. "It is a matter of common knowledge that the normal operation of a law office exposes confidential professional information to non-lawyer employees of the office. This obligates a lawyer to exercise care in selecting and training his employees so that the sanctity of all confidences and secrets of his clients may be preserved." EC 4-2, Model Code.

Rule 5.3 of the Model Rules requires "a lawyer who has direct supervisory authority over the non-lawyer [to] make reasonable efforts to ensure that the person's conduct is compatible with the professional obligations of the lawyer."The Comment to Rule 5.3 makes it clear that lawyers should give legal assistants "appropriate instruction and supervision concerning the ethical aspects of their employment, particularly regarding the obligation not to disclose information relating to the representation of the client." DR 4-101(D) under the Model Code provides that: "A lawyer shall exercise reasonable care to prevent his employees, associates and others whose services are utilized by him from discharging or using confidences or secrets of a client. . . ."

It is particularly important that the lawyer ensure that the legal assistant understands that *all* information concerning the client, even the mere fact that a person is a client of the firm, may be strictly confidential. Rule 1.6 of the Model Rules expanded the definition of confidential information ". . . not merely to matters communicated in confidence by the client but also to all information relating to the representation, whatever its source." It is therefore the lawyer's obligation to instruct clearly and to take reasonable steps to ensure the legal assistant's preservation of client confidences. Nearly all states that have guidelines for the utilization of legal assistants require the lawyer "to instruct legal assistants concerning client confidences" and "to exercise care to ensure that legal assistants comply" with the Code in this regard. Even if the client consents to divulging information, this information must not be used to the disadvantage of the client. See, e.g., Connecticut Recommendation 3: New Hampshire Rule 35, Sub-Rule 4; NALA Guideline V.

Guideline 7: **A lawyer should take reasonable measures to prevent conflicts of interest resulting from a legal assistant's other employment or interests insofar as such other employment or interests would present a conflict of interest if it were that of the lawyer.**

Comment to Guideline 7

A lawyer must make "reasonable efforts to ensure that [a] legal assistant's conduct is compatible with the professional obligations of the lawyer." Model Rule 5.3. These professional obligations include the duty to exercise independent professional judgment on behalf of a client, "free of compromising influences and loyalties." ABA Model Rules 1.7 through 1.13. Therefore, legal assistants should be instructed to inform the supervising attorney of any interest that could result in a conflict of interest or even give the appearance of a conflict. The guideline intentionally speaks to other employment rather than only past employment, since there are instances where legal assistants are employed by more than one law firm at the same time. The guideline's reference to "other interests" is intended to include personal relationships as well as instances where a legal assistant may have a financial interest (i.e., as stockholder, trust beneficiary or trustee, etc.) that would conflict with the client's in the matter in which the lawyer has been employed.

"Imputed Disqualification Arising from Change in Employment by Non-lawyer Employee," ABA Informal Opinion 1526 (1988), defines the duties of both the present and former employing lawyers and reasons that the restrictions on legal assistants' employment should be kept to "the minimum necessary to protect confidentiality" in order to prevent legal assistants from being forced to leave their careers, which "would disserve clients as well as the legal profession." The Opinion describes the attorney's obligations (1) to caution the legal assistant not to disclose any information and (2) to prevent the legal assistant from working on any matter on which the legal assistant worked for a prior employer or respecting which the employee has confidential information.

If a conflict is discovered, it may be possible to "wall" the legal assistant from the conflict area so that the entire firm need not be disqualified and the legal assistant is effectively screened from information concerning the matter. The American Bar Association has taken the position that what historically has been described as a "Chinese Wall" will allow non-lawyer personnel (including legal assistants) who are in possession of confidential client information to accept employment with a law firm opposing the former client so long as the wall is observed and effectively screens the non-lawyer from confidential information. ABA Informal Opinion 1526 (1988).

See also Tennessee Formal Ethics Opinion 89-F-118 (March 10, 1989). The implication of this Informal Opinion is that if a wall is not in place, the employer may be disqualified from representing either party to the controversy. One court has so held. *In re: Complex Asbestos Litigation,* No. 828684 (San Francisco Superior Court, September 19, 1989).

It is not clear that a wall will prevent disqualification in the case of a lawyer employed to work for a law firm representing a client with all adverse interest to a client of the lawyer's former employer. Under Model Rule 1.10, when a lawyer moves to a firm that represents an adverse party in a matter in which the lawyer's former firm was involved, absent a waiver by the client, the new firm's representation may continue only if the newly employed lawyer acquired no protected information and did not work directly on the matter in the former employment. The new Rules of Professional Conduct in Kentucky and Texas (both effective on January 1, 1990) specifically provide for disqualification. Rule 1.10(b) in the District of Columbia, which became effective January 1, 1991, does so as well. The Sixth Circuit, however, has held that the wall will effectively insulate the new firm from disqualification if it prevents the new lawyer-employee from access to information concerning the client with the adverse interest. *Manning v. Waring, Cox, James, Sklar & Allen,* 849 F.2d 222 (6th Cir. 1988). [As a result of the Sixth Circuit opinion, Tennessee revised its formal ethics opinion, which is cited above, and now applies the same rule to lawyers, legal assistants, law clerks, and legal secretaries.] See generally NFPA, "The Chinese Wall — Its Application to Paralegals" (1990).

The states that have guidelines that address the legal assistant conflict of interest refer to the lawyer's responsibility to ensure against personal, business or social interests of the legal assistant that would conflict with the representation of the client or impinge on the services rendered to the client. E.g., Kansas Guideline X, New Mexico Guideline V1, and North Carolina Guideline 7. Florida Professional Ethics Opinion 86-5 (1986) discusses a legal assistant's move from one firm to another and the obligations of each not to disclose confidences. See also Vermont Ethics Opinion 85-8 (1985) (a legal assistant is not bound by the Code of Professional Responsibility and, absent an absolute waiver by the client, the new firm should not represent client if legal assistant possessed confidential information from old firm).

Guideline 8: **A lawyer may include a charge for the work performed by a legal assistant in setting a charge for legal services.**

Comment to Guideline 8

The U.S. Supreme Court in *Missouri v. Jenkins,* 491 U.S. 274 (1989), held that in setting a reasonable attorney's fee under 28 U.S.C. § 1988, a legal fee may include a charge for legal assistant services at "market rates" rather than "actual cost" to the attorneys. This decision should resolve any question concerning the propriety of setting a charge for legal services based on work performed by a legal assistant. Its rationale favors setting a charge based on the "market" rate for such services, rather than their direct cost to the lawyer. This result was recognized by Connecticut Recommendation 11, Illinois Recommendation D, and Texas Guideline V prior to the Supreme Court decision. See also Fla. Stat. Ann. § 57.104 (1991 Supp.) (adopted in 1987 and permitting consideration of legal assistant services in computing attorney's fees) and Fla. Stat. Ann. § 744.108 (1991 Supp.) (adopted in 1989 and permitting recovery of "customary and reasonable charges for work performed by legal assistants" as fees for legal services in guardianship matters).

It is important to note, however, that *Missouri v. Jenkins* does not abrogate the attorney's responsibilities under Model Rule 1.5 to set a reasonable fee for legal services and it follows that those considerations apply to a fee that includes a fee for legal assistant services. Accordingly, the effect of combining a market rate charge for the services of lawyers and legal assistants should, in most instances, result in a lower total cost for the legal service than if the lawyer had performed the service alone.

Guideline 9: **A lawyer may not split legal fees with a legal assistant nor pay a legal assistant for the referral of legal business. A lawyer may compensate a legal assistant based on the quantity and quality of the legal assistant's work and the value of that work to a law practice, but the legal assistant's compensation may not be contingent, by advance agreement, upon the profitability of the lawyer's practice.**

Comment to Guideline 9

Model Rule 5.4 and DR 3-102(A) and 3-103(A) under the Model Code clearly prohibit fee "splitting" with legal assistants, whether characterized as splitting of contingent fees, "forwarding" fees, or other sharing of legal fees. Virtually all guidelines adopted by state bar associations have continued this prohibition in one form or another. It appears clear that a legal assistant may not be compensated on a contingent basis for a particular case or paid for "signing up" clients for a legal practice.

Having stated this prohibition, however, the guideline attempts to deal with the practical consideration of how a legal assistant properly may be compensated by an attorney or law firm. The linchpin of the prohibition seems to be the advance agreement of the lawyer to "split" a fee based on a pre-existing contingent arrangement. There is no general prohibition against a lawyer who enjoys a particularly profitable period recognizing the contribution of the legal assistant to that profitability with a discretionary bonus. Likewise, a lawyer engaged in a particularly profitable specialty of legal practice is not prohibited from compensating the legal assistant who aids materially in that practice more handsomely than the compensation generally awarded to legal assistants in that geographic area who work in law practices that are less lucrative. Indeed, any effort to fix a compensation level for legal assistants and prohibit greater compensation would appear to violate the federal antitrust laws. See, e.g., *Goldfarb v. Virginia State Bar,* 421 U.S. 773 (1975).

Guideline 10: **A lawyer who employs a legal assistant should facilitate the legal assistant's participation in appropriate continuing education and pro bono publico activities.**

Comment to Guideline 10

While Guideline 10 does not appear to have been adopted in the Guidelines of any state bar association, the Standing Committee on Legal Assistants believes that its adoption would be appropriate. For many years the Standing Committee on Legal Assistants has advocated that the improvement of formal legal assistant education will generally improve the legal services rendered by lawyers employing legal assistants and provide a more satisfying professional atmosphere in which legal assistants may work. See, e.g., ABA, Board of Governors, Policy on Legal Assistant Licensure and/or Certification, Statement 4 (February 6, 1986); ABA, Standing Committee on Legal Assistants, "Position Paper on the Question of Legal Assistant Licensure or Certification"

(December 10, 1985), at 6 and Conclusion 3. Recognition of the employing lawyer's obligation to facilitate the legal assistant's continuing professional education is, therefore, appropriate because of the benefits to both the law practice and the legal assistants and is consistent with the lawyer's own responsibility to maintain professional competence under Model Rule 1.1. See also EC 6-2 of the Model Code.

The Standing Committee is of the view that similar benefits will accrue to the lawyer and legal assistant if the legal assistant is included in the pro bono publico legal services that a lawyer has a clear obligation to provide under Model Rule 6.1 and, where appropriate, the legal assistant is encouraged to provide such services independently. The ability of a law firm to provide more pro bono publico services will be enhanced if legal assistants are included. Recognition of the legal assistant's role in such services is consistent with the role of the legal assistant in the contemporary delivery of legal services generally and is consistent with the lawyer's duty to the legal profession under Canon 2 of the Model Code.

THE STANDING COMMITTEE ON
LEGAL ASSISTANTS OF THE
AMERICAN BAR ASSOCIATION

May 1991

ADOPTED BY
ABA HOUSE OF DELEGATES

August 1991

APPENDIX B

NALA Code of Ethics and Professional Responsibility

Preamble

It is the responsibility of every legal assistant to adhere strictly to the accepted standards of legal ethics and to live by general principles of proper conduct. The performance of the duties of the legal assistant shall be governed by specific canons as defined herein in order that justice will be served and the goals of the profession attained.

The canons of ethics set forth hereafter are adopted by the National Association of Legal Assistants, Inc., as a general guide, and the enumeration of these rules does not mean there are not others of equal importance although not specifically mentioned.

Canon 1

A legal assistant shall not perform any of the duties that lawyers only may perform nor do things that lawyers themselves may not do.

Canon 2

A legal assistant may perform any task delegated and supervised by a lawyer so long as the lawyer is responsible to the client, maintains a direct relationship with the client, and assumes full professional responsibility for the work product.

Canon 3

A legal assistant shall not engage in the practice of law by accepting cases, setting fees, giving legal advice or appearing in court (unless otherwise authorized by court or agency rules).

Canon 4

A legal assistant shall not act in matters involving professional legal judgment as the services of a lawyer are essential in the public interest whenever the exercise of such judgment is required.

Canon 5

A legal assistant must act prudently in determining the extent to which a client may be assisted without the presence of a lawyer.

Canon 6

A legal assistant shall not engage in the unauthorized practice of law and shall assist in preventing the unauthorized practice of law.

Canon 7

A legal assistant must protect the confidences of a client, and it shall be unethical for a legal assistant to violate any statute now in effect or hereafter to be enacted controlling privileged communications.

Canon 8

It is the obligation of the legal assistant to avoid conduct which would cause the lawyer to be unethical or even appear to be unethical, and loyalty to the employer is incumbent upon the legal assistant.

Canon 9

A legal assistant shall work continually to maintain integrity and a high degree of competency throughout the legal profession.

Canon 10

A legal assistant shall strive for perfection through education in order to better assist the legal profession in fulfilling its duty of making legal services available to clients and the public.

Canon 11

A legal assistant shall do all other things incidental, necessary, or expedient for the attainment of the

379

ethics and responsibilities imposed by statute or rule of court.

Canon 12

A legal assistant is governed by the American Bar Association Model Code of Professional Responsibility and the American Bar Association Model Rules of Professional Conduct.

Adopted May, 1975
Revised November, 1979
Revised September, 1988

APPENDIX C

NFPA Affirmation of Responsibility

Preamble

The paralegal profession is committed to responsibility to the individual citizen and the public interest. In reexamining contemporary institutions and systems and in questioning the relationship of the individual to the law, members of the paralegal profession recognize that a redefinition of the traditional delivery of legal services is essential in order to meet the expressed needs of the general public.

This Affirmation of Responsibility asserts that the principles recognized by the National Federation of Paralegal Associations are essential to the continuing work of the paralegal.

Through this Affirmation of Responsibility, the National Federation of Paralegal Associations recognizes the responsibility placed upon each paralegal and encourages the dedication of the paralegal to the development of the profession.

I. Professional Responsibility

The paralegal is dedicated to the development of the paralegal profession and endeavors to expand the responsibilities and the scope of paralegal work.

Discussion: There is room for a great deal of growth in the paralegal profession and an opportunity to tap human resources to assist an overburdened legal system. This Affirmation of Responsibility aims to establish a positive attitude through which the paralegal may perceive the importance, responsibility and potential of the paralegal profession and work toward enhancing its professional status.

II. The Role of the Paralegal and the Unauthorized Practice of Law

The paralegal performs all functions permitted under law which are not in violation of the unauthorized practice of law statutes within the applicable jurisdiction.

Discussion: The increase in the number of paralegals has given rise to much discussion concerning what the paralegal may or may not do. This development has prompted new interpretations as to what constitutes the practice of law, and thus it is unwise to delineate exactly or to restrict the types of tasks which the paralegal may perform.

However, this Affirmation of Responsibility insists on compliance with regulations governing the practice of law as determined by the applicable jurisdiction. It is not within the scope of the Affirmation of Responsibility to change or challenge any of these statutes.

Whenever the paralegal performs tasks related to the delivery of legal services, it is the responsibility of the paralegal to insure that the applicable unauthorized practice of law statutes are not violated and that the best interests of the public are met. To this end, it is the responsibility of the paralegal to be aware of legislation affecting the paralegal profession and the legal welfare of the public.

III. Competence and Education

The paralegal maintains integrity and promotes competence through continuing education.

Discussion: The growth of a profession and the attainment and maintenance of individual competence require an ongoing incorporation of new concepts and techniques. Continuing education enables the paralegal to become aware of new developments in the field of law and provides the opportunity to improve skills used in the delivery of legal services.

The paralegal recognizes the importance of maintaining an interest in the development of continuing paralegal education. Professional competence is each

381

paralegal's responsibility. The exchange of ideas and skills benefits the profession, the legal community, and the general public.

IV.   Client Confidences

The paralegal is responsible for maintaining all client confidences.

Discussion: The paralegal is aware of the importance of preserving all client confidences. Such information is understood to be a vital part of the relationship between the paralegal and the client, facilitating the delivery of legal services. The confidentiality of this information is respected at all times.

V.   Protection of the Public Interest

The paralegal upholds the responsibility of protecting public interests by contributing to the delivery of quality legal services and by maintaining a sensitivity to public needs.

Discussion: The paralegal should make every effort to educate the public as to the services and tasks that paralegals may render. Such services may be performed within the setting of a law firm, public agency, governmental agency, business or within a defined program specifically addressing the needs of increased legal services to the public, including pro bono work.

The paralegal should inform the public of the scope of duties that the paralegal may perform and should encourage the public to examine issues and to explore innovative means by which an increased availability of moderate cost legal services may be obtained. It is also within the responsibility of the paralegal to maintain an interest in the development and continuation of paralegal education programs that address the public interest.

VI.   Support of Professional Association

The paralegal recognizes the necessity of membership and participation in the professional association.

Discussion: One of the hallmarks of any profession is its professional association, founded for the purpose, among many others, of determining standards and guidelines for the growth and development of the profession. The paralegal profession is in a dynamic stage of growth. The ability of individual paralegals to determine the direction and quality of that growth depends largely upon the success of the paralegal association in providing effective representation of and communication among members of the profession. Through the professional association, the paralegal is able to promote a cooperative effort with members of the legal community, paralegal educators and the general public to improve the quality of paralegal participation in the delivery of legal services.

The role which the paralegal occupies in the legal system is, to some extent, the result of the cumulative and cooperative efforts of paralegals working through the paralegal association. The continued and increased contribution of paralegals to the delivery of legal services is dependent upon a further delineation of their skills, qualifications and areas of responsibility. It is, therefore, incumbent upon each paralegal to promote the growth of the profession through support of and participation in the endeavors of the paralegal association.

GLOSSARY

abuse of discovery process Using unnecessary discovery not to obtain facts that are relevant and necessary for the case, but rather as a tactical tool to force the opposing party to settle or dismiss a claim.

abusive litigation Filing a lawsuit while knowing that no legal remedy exists, to coerce the opposing party to take a particular course of action.

advertising The marketing of legal services. Ethical legal advertising must be truthful and nondeceptive.

American Bar Association (ABA) The largest national organization for lawyers. Although membership is voluntary, almost half of the attorneys in the nation are members. Among other things, the ABA develops ethical codes for the legal profession.

appearance of impropriety Occurs when a legal professional does something that, although not technically unethical, may seem to be unethical to an observer.

attorney-client privilege The evidentiary principle that prohibits the disclosure of client communications concerning legal advice which have been given in confidence.

billable hours The amount of time a legal professional charges to specific clients for performing legal work for those clients. Attending firm meetings or continuing education seminars does not generate billable hours. Some firms establish minimum billable hours requirements and demand that legal professionals bill a certain amount to clients (e.g., 1,800 to 2,200 hours per year).

Canon The portion of the Model Code of Professional Responsibility stating the general guidelines for ethical conduct.

certification The process of assuring minimum competence. At present, NALA has the only certification program for paralegals. Disagreement exists as to whether certification of paralegals is a desirable development.

certified legal assistant (CLA) An individual who has successfully passed NALA's certification test.

Chinese walls Policies or procedures adopted by a firm to prevent one who may have a conflict of interest regarding a particular matter or case from having any contact or information about the matter or case, so that the entire firm will not be precluded from handling the case. Also called a *cone of silence.*

client security fund Fund created from the fees collected by bar associations or other legal organizations, through yearly assessments or voluntary contributions, to reimburse clients whose attorneys have absconded with client funds.

commingling A prohibited practice, which involves mixing an attorney's personal funds with funds belonging only to the client.

competence The minimum skill and experience a legal professional must possess to work on a case or matter in a particular area.

cone of silence *See* Chinese walls.

confidentiality The legal concept that communications between an attorney and client must not be revealed except under very limited exceptions.

383

conflict of interest Impairment of the legal professional's ability to represent the client effectively. This impairment can occur when personal interests, prior interests, or interests of former or current clients may divide the legal professional's loyalties.

contingency fee Legal fees, the amount of which depends on the outcome or settlement of a case. Under a contingency fee agreement, the attorney works not for a fixed or hourly fee but for a percentage of the client's settlement. Contingency fee agreements are not permitted in divorce or criminal matters.

continuing legal education (CLE) Specific courses that a legal professional must attend every year to maintain his or her license. In most states, CLE is mandatory for attorneys.

disbarment Losing one's license to practice law as a result of an ethical violation. In some cases, the disbarred lawyer may reapply for admission to practice after a specific period of time.

Disciplinary Rules (DR) The portion of the Model Code of Professional Responsibility that outlines the minimum standards of ethical behavior. Violation of DRs can result in prosecution for ethical violations.

disqualification The preclusion of a legal professional from working on a particular matter because that individual has a conflict of interest pertaining to the matter. This conflict of interest generally results from having worked on the opposing side of a case or having filed suit against the potential new client.

escrow account A bank account set up by an attorney or firm specifically for funds belonging to clients.

Ethical Considerations (EC) The portion of the Model Code of Professional Responsibility that is aspirational in nature.

fixed fee Legal fee set by agreeing to handle a legal matter for a certain amount, no matter how many hours are actually spent to complete the case. Also known as a *flat fee.*

flat fee Legal fee set by agreeing to handle a legal matter for a certain amount, no matter how many hours are actually spent to complete the case. Also known as a *fixed fee.*

freelance paralegal Paralegal who does not work for a single firm but for different lawyers, frequently on a case-by-case basis. Freelance paralegals are supervised by attorneys.

hourly fee Legal fee set by charging a client a certain amount per hour to work on a particular matter.

imputed disqualification The inability of an attorney or firm to handle a legal matter because one of the lawyers in the firm has a conflict of interest involving the matter, generally due to prior employment.

independent paralegal A paralegal whose work is not supervised by an attorney because the paralegal is working independently. Independent paralegals might violate the prohibition against the unauthorized practice of law.

ineffective assistance of counsel The Sixth Amendment to the United States Constitution guarantees criminal defendants competent legal representation. Ineffective assistance of counsel claims arise when there is a showing of deficient performance by counsel coupled with prejudice to the criminal defendant.

integrated bar A state bar association whose authority to discipline members has been delegated to it by the state's highest court. Membership in these bar associations is mandatory for attorneys in these states.

interest on lawyers' trust accounts (IOLTA) Interest earned on legal trust or escrow accounts is forwarded to the state bar or other bar organization for charitable purposes. There are three kinds of IOLTA accounts: voluntary, involuntary, and opt-out (those in which attorneys must participate unless they sign a form declaring that they do not want to participate).

issue conflict The conflict of interest that arises as a result of specializing in a particular class of client. Attorneys specializing in insurance defense might have a conflict of interest representing a plaintiff in an action against another insurance company, even if the attorney does not represent the company.

Lawyer Telecomputer Networking (LTN) A subscription-based service that enables legal professionals to tie their telecommunications systems into a powerful mainframe. This service includes electronic mail, bulletin boards, and group conferencing.

legal ethics The standard of conduct for legal professionals; rules delineating the proper behavior to be taken by legal professionals; the moral and professional duties of legal professionals toward each other, their clients, and the courts.

legal technician A paralegal who performs legal services without attorney supervision. Legal technicians are the subject of legislative attempts in various states, most notably California, to expand the range of activities nonlawyers are allowed to perform.

licensure The process of regulation by a state or a state-appointed board. There is presently no licensure of paralegals.

malpractice The tortious cause of action against a professional for failure to fulfill his or her duties to a client. Malpractice can result from unethical behavior or negligence. The four elements that must be proven for a successful malpractice action are: (1) proof of the attorney-client relationship; (2) acts that show breach of contract or negligence; (3) causation; and (4) ability to succeed on the merits, but for the lawyer's conduct.

mediation A method of alternative dispute resolution whereby the parties to a dispute negotiate a mutually agreeable settlement with the help of a trained, impartial third party.

Model Code of Professional Responsibility (Code) The first ethical guidelines adopted by the American Bar Association. The Code is broken down into Canons, Ethical Considerations, and Disciplinary Rules.

Model Guidelines for the Utilization of Legal Assistants (Model Guidelines) Guidelines adopted by the American Bar Association in 1991 to assist states in developing their own guidelines and to educate and encourage attorneys to use legal assistants properly.

Model Rules of Professional Conduct (Rules) The second set of ethical guidelines adopted by the American Bar Association, in 1982. Unlike the Model Code of Professional Responsibility, the Rules provide direct statements about ethical and unethical conduct. Most states used the Rules rather than the Code as the model for their state ethical guidelines.

Multistate Professional Responsibility Examination (MPRE) The test on professional responsibility and legal ethics that an attorney must pass, or have waived, prior to being admitted to a state bar.

National Association of Legal Assistants, Inc. (NALA) A voluntary association of professionals who are legal assistants. This organization has adopted a Code of Ethics and Professional Responsibility, similar to the ABA Code, as the ethical standards for its members. Unlike NFPA, NALA supports the certification of legal assistants.

National Federation of Paralegal Associations, Inc. (NFPA) The paralegal organization comprised of individual state organizations. The Affirmation of Responsibility is this organization's standard of ethical conduct. NFPA, unlike NALA, does not support the certification of paralegals.

nonintegrated bar A bar association that does not require mandatory membership for all attorneys licensed to practice in the state. In states with a nonintegrated bar, the state's highest appellate court maintains absolute authority over the attorneys licensed to practice in the state.

privileged documents Documents protected from disclosure under the principle of confidentiality, work product, or attorney-client privilege.

privileged network The concept that all nonattorney individuals working for a firm are bound by the duty of confidentiality.

pro bono "For the good of the public"; the provision of free legal services.

pro se The right to represent oneself without the benefit of legal counsel. Pro se representation is not considered the unauthorized practice of law.

reprimand The least severe form of punishment for an ethical violation. Also called a *reproval*. Reprimands can be given either publicly, in open court before other members of the bar, or privately, in the judge's or bar official's chambers. A reprimand essentially involves a discussion of why and how the subject conduct was unethical and what can be done to prevent further unethical actions.

retainer   A certain amount of money paid to an attorney, which assures the client that the lawyer will work for him and that the lawyer will get paid. Retainers are either refundable or nonrefundable. Refundable retainers provide that an attorney will bill her hours against the retainer at a certain rate and that any unused money will be returned to the client at the end of the representation. A nonrefundable retainer is directly payable to the attorney, without any accounting or billing of hours against the retainer, to guarantee the attorney's representation and availability.

Rule 11 violation   Occurs in a federal court proceeding when an attorney signs a pleading while knowing that there is no good faith basis for the remedy sought in the complaint or pleading.

sexual harassment   Unwelcome sexual advances, requests for sexual favors, and other verbal or physical conduct of a sexual nature which may create a hostile environment.

simultaneous representation   A conflict of interest that exists when the attorney represents opposing interests in the same case, such as plaintiff and defendant or buyer and seller.

solicitation   Actively seeking out new clients to gain legal business. Since it frequently results in undue influence, possible fraud, intimidation, or overreaching, solicitation is generally impermissible. Solicitation can be either direct (face-to-face) or indirect (through targeted mailings to individuals requiring specific legal assistance).

statutory fee   Fee that results from a provision in a statute which shifts the responsibility for paying legal fees to the offending party. Paralegal fees are included in statutory fees.

suspension   A punishment for an ethical violation, under which an attorney is not permitted to practice for a specific period of time. This form of punishment can last from a few days to several years, depending on the severity of the ethical violation and the lawyer's prior conduct.

unauthorized practice of law   Performing acts that require a legal license to perform, such as giving legal advice, representing clients in court, preparing legal documents without the supervision of a licensed attorney, and accepting or declining legal representation.

vicarious liability   Attorneys being held responsible for the unethical or negligent acts of their employees.

whistleblowing   Reporting unethical or illegal activity by management or co-workers.

work product doctrine   The evidentiary principle that precludes the disclosure of any work produced during the course of representation of a client, except under limited circumstances.

zealous representation   Fervently representing a client's interests within the bounds of legal ethics.

INDEX

NOTE: Italicized page numbers refer to non-text material.